Distributed Fusion Estimation for Sensor Networks with Communication Constraints

Wen-An Zhang • Bo Chen • Haiyu Song • Li Yu

Distributed Fusion Estimation for Sensor Networks with Communication Constraints

Science Press
Beijing

Springer

Wen-An Zhang
Department of Automation
Zhejiang University of Technology
Hangzhou, China

Bo Chen
Department of Automation
Zhejiang University of Technology
Hangzhou, China

Haiyu Song
Zhejiang Uni. of Finance & Economics
Hangzhou, China

Li Yu
Zhejiang University of Technology
Hangzhou, China

ISBN 978-981-10-0793-4 ISBN 978-981-10-0795-8 (eBook)
DOI 10.1007/978-981-10-0795-8

Jointly published with Science Press, Beijing
ISBN: 978-7-03-047505-3 Science Press, Beijing

Library of Congress Control Number: 2016935848

Printed on acid-free paper

This Springer imprint is published by Springer Nature
The registered company is Springer Science+Business Media Singapore Pte Ltd.

Preface

Advances in micro electromechanical systems and wireless technologies have allowed for the emergence of inexpensive micro-sensors with embedded processing and communication capabilities. A wireless sensor network (WSN) is a collection of these physically distributed micro-sensors communicating with one another over wireless links. In their various shapes and forms, the WSNs have greatly facilitated and enhanced the automated, remote, and intelligent monitoring of a large variety of physical systems and have found applications in various areas, such as industrial and building automation; environmental, traffic, wildlife, and health monitoring; and military surveillance. The purpose of a WSN is to provide users access to the information of interest from data gathered by spatially distributed sensors. In most applications, users are interested in a processed data that carries useful information of a physical plant rather than a measured data contaminated by noises. Therefore, it is not surprising that signal estimation, especially the multisensor fusion estimation, has been one of the most fundamental collaborative information processing problems in WSNs. The WSN, as a typical multisensor system, has greatly extended application areas of multisensor information fusion estimation, which was originally developed for military applications, such as target tracking and navigation. Although WSNs present attractive features, challenges associated with communication constraints, such as the scarcity of bandwidth and energy, as well as the delays and packet losses, in wireless communications have to be addressed in the WSN-based information fusion estimation and have attracted increasing research interest during the past decade.

This book provides the recent advances in distributed multisensor fusion estimation methods for WSNs with communication constraints, including the energy constraint, bandwidth constraint, communication delays, and packet losses. First, a review on the latest developments in the literature is presented in Chap. 1. Then, two energy-efficient fusion estimation methods, namely, the *transmission rate* method and the *packet size reduction* method, are introduced for sensor networks with energy constraints in Chaps. 2, 3, 4 and 5. Specifically, by slowing down the sampling and estimation rates, a multi-rate fusion estimation method is presented in Chap. 2 for sensor networks, where the sampling rate and the estimation rate are allowed to be different from each other and are parameters that can be designed to meet the energy constraints. In Chap. 3, a distributed state fusion estimation method is presented for sensor networks with nonuniform estimation rates, where the estimation rates among the various local estimators are allowed to be nonuniform and different from each other, that is, each local estimator is allowed to generate local estimates independently with an adjustable rate according to its power status. In Chap. 4, a distributed H_∞ fusion estimation method is introduced for sensor networks with nonuniform sampling rates, where the sampling rate of each sensor is allowed to be nonuniform and can be adjusted according to the sensor's power status. The energy-efficient fusion estimation method based on *packet size reduction* is introduced in Chap. 5, where a dimension reduction method is presented to reduce the size of packets containing the local estimates to be transmitted to the fusion estimator. The bandwidth constraint problem is considered in Chaps. 6 and 7. Specifically, a distributed H_∞ fusion estimation method is presented for sensor networks with quantized local estimates in Chap. 6. In Chap. 7, a hierarchical structure is presented for multisensor fusion estimation systems to reduce the communication burden of the fusion center. The communication uncertainties, including the delays and packet losses, are considered in Chaps. 8 and 9. Specifically, the fusion estimation for sensor networks with communication delays is introduced in Chap. 8, while the fusion estimation with both delays and packet losses is presented in Chap. 9.

The work was supported in part by the National Natural Science Foundation of China under Grant No. 61104063 and 61573319, the Research Fund for the Doctoral Program of Higher Education of China under Grant 20113317120001, the Fok Ying-Tong Education Foundation for Young Teachers in the Higher Education Institutions of China under Grant No.141064, and the Zhejiang Provincial Natural Science Foundation of China under Grant No. LR16F030005.

Hangzhou, China — Wen-An Zhang
Hangzhou, China — Bo Chen
Hangzhou, China — Haiyu Song
Hangzhou, China — Li Yu
October 2015

Contents

Symbols and Acronyms

$\Re$	Field of real numbers
$\Re^n$	n-Dimensional real Euclidean space
$\Re^{m\times n}$	Space of all $m \times n$ real matrices
I	Identity matrix
$\mathbf{0}$	Zero matrix
$A > 0$	Symmetric positive definite
$A \geqslant 0$	Symmetric positive semi-definite
$A < 0$	Symmetric negative definite
$A \leqslant 0$	Symmetric negative semi-definite
A^{T}	Transpose of matrix A
A^{-1}	Inverse of matrix A
$[a_{ij}]$	A matrix composed of elements a_{ij}, $i, j \in N$
$\mathrm{col}\{x_i\}_{i\in\phi}$	A column vector composed of elements x_i, $i \in \phi$
$\mathrm{Var}(x)$	Variance of the random vector x
$\mathrm{rank}(A)$	Rank of matrix A
$\rho(A)$	Spectral radius of matrix A
$\lambda_{\max}(A)$	Maximum eigenvalue of matrix A
$\lambda_{\min}(A)$	Minimum eigenvalue of matrix A
$\mathrm{Tr}(A)$	Trace of matrix A
$x \perp y$	Orthogonal vectors x and y
$\mathrm{proj}\{\cdot\}$	Projection operator
$\mathscr{L}(x_1, x_2, \ldots)$	Linear span of the vectors $x_1, x_2, \ldots$
$\mathrm{diag}\{\cdots\}$	Block-diagonal matrix
$\|\| \cdot \|\|$	Euclidean norm of a vector and its induced norm of a matrix
sup	Supremum
inf	Infimum
$\mathscr{L}_2[0, \infty)$	Space of square integrable functions on $[0, \infty)$
$l_2[0, \infty)$	Space of square summable infinite sequence on $[0, \infty)$
$\mathrm{Prob}\{x\}$	Probability of x
$\mathbf{E}\{x\}$	Expectation of x
$\mathrm{Var}(x)$	Variance of x, i.e., $\mathrm{Var}(x) = \mathbf{E}\{xx^{\mathrm{T}}\}$

WSN	Wireless sensor network
KF	Kalman filter
FC	Fusion center
MSE	Mean square error
LMI	Linear matrix inequality
BRL	Bounded real lemma
LTI	Linear time-invariant

Chapter 1
Introduction

1.1 Distributed Fusion Estimation for Sensor Networks

The multisensor fusion estimation has attracted considerable research interest during the past decades and has found applications in a variety of areas, such as target tracking and localization, guidance and navigation, and fault detection [1, 2, 5, 17]. Multisensor fusion is used because of potentially improved estimation accuracy [2, 71] and enhanced reliability and robustness against sensor failures. Many useful fusion estimation methods have been presented in the literature (see, e.g., [8, 12, 14, 20, 25, 36, 41, 46, 58, 69, 70, 75, 77, 80, 86] and the references therein). Recently, the rapid developments of wireless sensor networks (WSNs) have greatly widen applications of the multisensor fusion estimation theory, which in turn, helps the WSNs monitor the environment more accurately and efficiently. Therefore, the WSN-based multisensor fusion estimation and its applications have attracted considerable research interest during the past decade [22, 39, 57, 83].

It is known that the WSN consists of a group of sensor nodes which communicate with each other via wireless networks and the sensor nodes are usually powered by batteries. Therefore, the sensor nodes are usually constrained in energy, and developing energy-efficient algorithms for WSN-based estimation to reduce energy consumption and prolong network life is of great practical significance [9, 50, 54–56, 61, 82, 97]. Consider the situation where a WSN is deployed to observe and estimate states of a dynamically changing process, but the process is not changing too rapidly. Then it is wasteful from an energy perspective for sensors to transmit every measurement to an estimator to generate estimates, and this waste is amplified by packet losses which are usually unavoidable in WSNs [34, 64, 67, 68, 74, 78, 79, 85, 92]. Therefore, it is not surprising that many research works have been denoted to the design of energy-efficient estimation methods for sensor networks with energy constraints. There are mainly two approaches in the existing results, namely, the quantization method [3, 4, 18, 22–24, 26, 30, 37–40, 47, 50, 54, 56, 63, 65, 66, 73, 82, 89, 95] and dimension-reduction method

W.-A. Zhang et al., *Distributed Fusion Estimation for Sensor Networks with Communication Constraints*, DOI 10.1007/978-981-10-0795-8_1

[10, 22, 61, 96, 97]. In the quantization method, the measurements are quantized and represented by a finite number of bits before they are transmitted to the estimator for estimation. The coarser the quantization, the smaller the size of the packet packaging the measurements, and thus one is able to save energy consumptions in the packet transmissions. In the dimension-reduction method, the dimension of the measurement to be transmitted is reduced by applying some data compression methods [97]. Consequently, the size of the packet packaging the measurement to be transmitted is reduced, and the energy consumption in the packet transmission is thus reduced. The main idea in both the quantization method and the dimension-reduction method is to reduce the packet size and ultimately reduce the energy consumption in the packet transmissions. Therefore, they may be intuitively called as the *packet size approach*. Note that in the WSNs, data packets are transmitted through wireless communication channels, which are usually constrained in bandwidth, that is, the bit rate is constrained in communication. Thus, an advantage of the *packet size* approach is that it is able to save energy and meanwhile meet the bandwidth constraint. However, the quantization usually introduces nonlinear dynamics which adds difficulty to the estimator design; moreover, the design of quantizers involves additional computations. As investigated in [97], it is usually difficult to find a data compression operator analytically when one applies the dimension-reduction method. In this book, a novel dimension-reduction method will be introduced for energy-efficient fusion estimation without involving a data compression operator. The main idea of the proposed dimension-reduction method is that only partial components of each local estimate are selected to be transmitted to the fusion center to save communication energy, and the fusion center adopts compensation strategy to compensate the components of the local estimates that are not transmitted. Detailed results will be presented in Chap. 5. Actually, in addition to the *packet size approach*, a useful and straightforward approach to save energy is to slow down the information transmission rate in the sensors, for example, the sensors may measure and transmit measurements with an interval that is several times of the sampling period. Moreover, one may purposively close the sensor nodes to save power during certain time interval and wake them up when necessary. That is to say, in many situations, it is not necessary for sensors to transmit measurements and generate estimates at every sampling instants from the energy-efficient perspective, and the sensors may work and generate estimates with two rates, namely, a fast rate and a slow rate according to their power situations. The main idea in the aforementioned approach is to slow down the measurement transmission rate and ultimately slow down the estimation rate to save energies consumed in the communication, and then one is able to make a trade-off between energy efficiency and estimation performance by appropriately designing the information transmission rates. Therefore, the approach might be intuitively called as a *transmission rate approach* and will be introduced in detail in Chaps. 2, 3 and 4. Specifically, a multi-rate scheme by which the sensors exchange measurements with neighbors and generate local estimates at a slower time scale and generate fusion estimates at a faster time scale is proposed to reduce communication costs in Chap. 2, a state fusion method with nonuniform estimate rates is introduced in Chap. 3, and an H_∞ fusion estimation method with nonuniform sampling rates is presented in Chap. 4.

In WSNs, the multisensor fusion estimation could be done under the end-to-end information flow paradigm by communicating all the relevant measurements from various sensors to a central collector node, e.g., a sink node. Such a structure for fusion estimation is usually termed as a centralized one. The centralized structure is, however, a highly inefficient solution in WSNs, because it may cause long packet delay, consume large amounts of energies, and require a large bandwidth in the fusion center end and it has the potential for a critical failure point at the central collector node. An alternative solution is for the estimation to be performed *in-network* [19, 27, 33, 35], i.e., every sensor in the WSN with both sensing and computation capabilities performs not only as a sensor but also as an estimator, and it collects measurements only from its neighbors to generate estimates. Such a setup is usually called as the distributed structure and possesses several advantages, such as lower communication costs and bandwidth requirement in fusion center and higher reliability against sensor failures, as compared with the centralized structure. However, it is obvious that local estimates obtained at each sensor by the distributed structure are not optimal in the sense that not all the measurements in the WSN are used. Moreover, there exist disagreements among local estimates obtained at different sensors. In other words, local estimates at any two sensors may be different from each other. As pointed out in [51], such form of group disagreement regarding the signal estimates is highly undesirable for a peer-to-peer network of estimators. This gives rise to two issues that should be considered in designing a distributed estimation algorithm: (1) how could each sensor improve its local performance by taking full use of limited information from its neighbors? (2) how to reduce disagreements of local estimates among different sensors? Consensus strategy [4, 51, 52, 62, 84] and diffusion strategy [6, 7] have been presented in the literature to deal with the aforementioned two issues. The main idea of the consensus strategy is that all sensors should obtain the same estimate in steady state by using some consensus algorithms. In the diffusion strategy, both measurements and local estimates from neighboring sensors are used to generate estimates at each sensor. A hierarchical two-stage fusion estimation method will be introduced in Chaps. 2 and 7 for distributed fusion estimation.

Communication delays and packet losses are usually unavoidable in WSNs and are main sources deteriorating the estimation performance. Therefore, optimal estimation with delayed or missing measurements has attracted considerable research interest during the past decades. For example, the optimal estimation with delayed measurements has been investigated in [11, 16, 43, 45, 49, 53, 72, 81, 87, 90, 91, 93], and [13, 15, 21, 28, 31, 32, 42, 44, 48, 59, 60, 67, 88, 94] are devoted to the optimal estimation with missing measurements. However, most of the aforementioned results are concerned with single-sensor systems. For multisensor fusion estimation systems, the state estimation with uncertain observations was investigated in [76], while the robust minimum variance linear estimation for multiple sensors with different failure rates was presented in [29]. Based on the consensus strategy, a distributed H_∞ consensus filtering with multiple missing measurements was investigated in [64]. Subsequently, the optimal fusion estimation problems in the linear minimum variance sense have been investigated in [13] and [44] for multisensor systems with multiple packet dropouts. However, most of the existing results adopted the centralized fusion structure. For the multisensor fusion estimation with time delays, the information fusion problem was investigated in [72] and [43] for linear stochastic systems with delayed measurements, where the observation delays are assumed to be constant. Recently, based on the well-known federated filter, a practical architecture and some algorithms were discussed in [81] for the networked data fusion systems with time-varying delays, where the accurate time delay over each sampling period should be known for online computation of the estimators. Chapters 8 and 9 of this book are devoted to the design of multisensor fusion estimators for sensor networks with delays and packet losses. A novel model will be presented to describe the fusion system with delays and packet losses, and fusion estimators with matrix weights will be designed without resorting to the augmentation method as usually did in existing results. Moreover, some sufficient conditions for the boundness and convergence of the estimator will also be presented.

1.2 Book Organization

So far many important and interesting results have been presented for distributed multisensor fusion estimation for sensor networks. However, there lacks of a monograph to provide the up-to-date advances in the literature. Thus, the main purpose of this book is to fill such gap by providing some recent developments in the design of distributed fusion estimation for sensor networks with communication constraints. The materials adopted in the book are mainly based on research results of the authors.

Besides this short introduction, this book is organized as follows.

Chapter 1 provides a review on the background and latest developments of distributed fusion estimation for sensor networks with communication constraints in the literature.

Chapter 2 investigates the multi-rate distributed fusion estimation for sensor networks. A multi-rate scheme by which the sensors estimate states at a faster time scale and exchange information with neighbors at a slower time scale is proposed to reduce communication costs. The estimation is performed by taking into account the random packet losses in two stages. At the first stage, every sensor in the WSN collects measurements from its neighbors to generate a local estimate, then local estimates in the neighbors are further collected at the second stage to form a fused estimate to improve estimation performance and reduce disagreements among local estimates at different sensors. It is shown that the time scale of information exchange among sensors can be slower while still maintaining satisfactory estimation performance by using the developed estimation method.

Chapter 3 investigates the multisensor fusion estimation problem for sensor networks with nonuniform estimation rates. Firstly, each sensor generates local estimates with two rates, namely, a fast rate and a slow rate according to its power situation, where the estimation rates among the sensors are allowed to be different from each other. Secondly, a fusion rule with matrix weights is designed for each sensor to fuse available local estimates generated at different time scales. The fusion algorithm is applicable to both cases where the measurement noises are mutually correlated and are uncorrelated and is also applicable to the case where the sensors are not time synchronized. Two types of estimators are designed according to different considerations of design complexity and computation costs.

Chapter 4 is devoted to the problem of distributed sampled-data H_∞ filtering problem for sensor networks with nonuniform sampling periods. The measurements are sampled with nonuniform sampling periods, and each sensor in the network collects the sampled measurements only from its neighbors and runs a distributed H_∞ filtering algorithm to generate estimates. A sufficient existence condition for the distributed H_∞ filters is derived, and it is shown that the obtained condition critically depends on the sampling periods and the packet loss probabilities. The designed filters guarantee that the filtering system is mean square exponentially stable and all the filtering errors satisfy an average H_∞ noise attenuation level.

Chapter 5 addresses the distributed finite-horizon fusion Kalman filtering problem for a class of networked multisensor fusion systems with energy constraints. Only partial components of each local estimate are allowed to be transmitted to the fusion center over one sampling period. Then, a compensation strategy is used at the fusion center to compensate the untransmitted components of each local estimate, and a recursively distributed fusion Kalman filter is derived in the linear minimum variance sense. It is shown that the performance of the designed fusion filter is dependent on the selecting probability of each component of the local estimate; some criteria for the choice of the probabilities are derived such that the mean square errors of the fusion filter are bounded or convergent.

Chapter 6 focuses on the problem of the distributed H_∞ fusion filtering for a class of networked multisensor fusion systems with bandwidth constraints. Due to the limited bandwidth, only finite-level quantized local estimates are sent to the fusion center, and multiple finite-level logarithmic quantizers are adopted as the quantization strategy. The co-design of the fusion parameters and quantization parameters is converted into a convex optimization problem. It is shown that the performance of the fusion estimator provides better performance than each local estimator.

Chapter 7 is concerned with hierarchical fusion estimation problem for clustered sensor networks. The sensors within the same cluster are connected to a local estimator, and all the local estimators are linked with a fusion center. The fusion center and the local estimators are not required to be synchronous. A minimum variance estimation algorithm is presented for each cluster to aperiodically generate local estimates. A covariance intersection fusion strategy is presented for the fusion center to generate fused estimates by using asynchronous local estimates without knowing the cross-covariances among the local estimation errors.

Chapter 8 deals with the problem of robust fusion Kalman filtering for multisensor systems with randomly delayed measurements and parameter uncertainties. The stochastic parameter perturbations are considered, and the proposed fusion estimator is robust against the parameter uncertainties in the system model. Without resorting to the augmentation of system states and measurements, a robust optimal recursive filter for each subsystem is derived in the linear minimum variance sense by using the innovation analysis method. Based on the optimal fusion algorithm weighted by matrices, a robust distributed state fusion Kalman filter is derived, and the dimension of the designed filter is the same as the original system, which helps reduce computation costs as compared with the augmentation method.

Chapter 9 considers the problem of distributed Kalman filtering for a class of networked multisensor fusion systems with random delays and packet losses. A novel stochastic model is proposed to describe the estimation system with transmission delays and packet losses, and an optimal distributed fusion Kalman filter is designed based on the optimal fusion criterion weighted by matrices. Some sufficient conditions are derived such that the mean square error of the fusion filter is bounded or convergent.

References

1. Bar-Shalom Y, Li XR (1990) Multitarget-multisensor tracking: advanced applications, vol 1. Artech House, Norwood
2. Bar-Shalom Y, Li XR, Kirubarajan T (2001) Estimation with applications to tracking and navigation. Wilely, New York
3. Cabral FR, Brossier JM (2014) Scalar quantization for estimation: from an asymptotic design to a practical solution. IEEE Trans Signal Process 62(11):2860–2870
4. Carli R, Fagnani F, Frasca P, Zampieri S (2008) A probabilistic analysis of the average consensus algorithm with quantized communication. In: Proceedings of the 17th IFAC world congress, Seoul, pp 8062–8067
5. Carlson NA (1990) Federated square root filter for decentralized parallel processes. IEEE Trans Aerosp Electron Syst 26(3):517–529
6. Cattivelli FS, Sayed AH (2010) Diffusion strategies for distributed Kalman filtering and smoothing. IEEE Trans Autom Control 55(9):2069–2084
7. Cattivelli FS, Sayed AH (2010) Diffusion LMS strategies for distributed estimation. IEEE Trans Signal Process 58(3):1035–1048
8. Chang KC, Tian Z, Mori S (2004) Performance evaluation for MAP state estimate fusion. IEEE Trans Aerosp Electron Syst 40(2):706–714
9. Chang LY, Chen PY, Wang TY, Chen CS (2011) A low-cost VLSI architecture for robust distributed estimation in wireless sensor networks. IEEE Trans Circuit Syst-I Regul Pap 58(6):1277–1286
10. Chen HM, Zhang KS, Li XR (2004) Optimal data compression for multisensor target tracking with communication constraints. In: Proceedings of the 43th IEEE conference on decision and control, Atlantis, pp 8179–8184
11. Chen B, Yu L, Zhang WA (2011) Robust Kalman filtering for uncertain state delay systems with random observation delays and missing measurements. IET Control Theory Appl 5(17):1945–1954

12. Chen B, Yu L, Zhang WA, Liu AD (2013) Robust information fusion estimator for multiple delay-tolerant sensors with different failure rates. IEEE Trans Circuit Syst-I Regul Pap 60(2):401–414
13. Chiuso A, Schenato L (2011) Information fusion strategies and performance bounds in packet-drop networks. Automatica 47:1304–1316
14. Deng ZL, Gao Y, Mao L et al (2005) New approach to information fusion steady-state Kalman filtering. Automatica 41(10):1695–1707
15. Dong H, Wang Z, Ho DWC, Gao H (2010) Variance-constrainted H_∞ filtering for a class of nonlinear time-varying systems with multiple missing measurements: the finite-horizon case. IEEE Trans Signal Process 58(5):2534–2543
16. Dong H, Wang Z, Gao H (2010) Robust H_∞ filtering for a class of nonlinear networked systems with multiple stochastic communication delays and packet dropouts. IEEE Trans Signal Process 58(4):1957–1966
17. Dong HL, Wang ZD, Gao HJ (2012) Fault detection for Markovian jump systems with sensor saturations and randomly varying nonlinearities. IEEE Trans Circuit Syst-I Regul Pap 59(10):2354–2362
18. Dong H, Wang Z, Gao H (2012) Distributed filtering for a class of time-varying systems over sensor networks with quantization errors and successive packet dropouts. IEEE Trans Signal Process 60(6):3164–3173
19. Dimakis AG, Kar S, Moura JMF, Rabbat MG, Scaglione A (2010) Gossip algorithms for distributed signal processing. Proc IEEE 98(11):1847–1864
20. Duan Z, Li XR (2013) Lossless linear transformation of sensor data for distributed estimation fusion. IEEE Trans Signal Process 59(1):362–372
21. Epstein M, Shi L, Tiwari A, Murry R (2008) Probabilistic performance of state estimation across a lossy network. Automatica 44(12):3046–3053
22. Fang J, Li H (2008) Distributed adaptive quantization for wireless sensor networks: from delta modulation to maximum likelihood. IEEE Trans Signal Process 56(10):5246–5257
23. Fang J, Li H (2009) Hyperplane-based vector quantization for distributed estimation in wireless sensor networks. IEEE Trans Inf Theory 55:5682–5699
24. Fu MY, de Souza CE (2009) State estimation for linear discrete-time systems using quantized measurements. Automatica 45(12):2937–2945
25. Gan Q, Harris CJ (2001) Comparison of two measurement fusion methods for Kalman-filter-based multisensor data fusion. IEEE Trans Aerosp Electron Syst 37(1):273–280
26. Ghasemi N, Dey S (2008) Power-efficient dynamic quantization for multisensor HMM state estimation over fading channels. In: The 3rd international symposium on communications, control and signal processing, St Julians, pp 1553–1558
27. Giridhar A, Kumar PR (2006) Towards a theory of in-network computation in wireless sensor networks. IEEE Commun Mag 44(4):98–107
28. He LD, Han DF, Wang XF, Shi L (2013) Optimal linear state estimation over a packet-dropping network using linear temporal coding. Automatica 49(4):1075–1082
29. Hounkpevi FO, Yaz EE (2007) Robust minimum variance linear state estimators for multiple sensors with different failure rates. Automatica 43(7):1274–1280
30. Hu L, Wang Z, Liu X (2015) Dynamic state estimation of power systems with quantization effects: a recursive filter approach. IEEE Trans Neural Netw Learn Syst. doi:10.1109/TNNLS.2014.2381853
31. Huang M, Dey S (2007) Stability of Kalman filtering with Markovian packet losses. Automatica 43(4):598–607
32. Jin ZP, Gupta V, Murray RM (2006) State estimation over packet dropping networks using multiple description coding. Automatica 42(9):1441–1452
33. Kar S, Moura JMF (2011) Gossip and distributed Kalman filtering: weak consensus under weak detectability. IEEE Trans Signal Process 59(4):1766–1784
34. Kar S, Sinopoli B, Moura JMF (2012) Kalman filtering with intermittent observations: weak convergence to a stationary distribution. IEEE Trans Autom Control 57(2):405–420

35. Khan UA, Moura JMF (2008) Distributed the Kalamn filter for large-scale systems. IEEE Trans Signal Process 56(10):4919–4935
36. Kim KH (1994) Development of track to track fusion algorithm. In: Proceedings of the American control conference, Maryland, pp 1037–1041
37. Krishnamurthy V (1995) Estimation of quantized linear errors-in-variables models original research. Automatica 31(10):1459–1464
38. Lerdsuwanakij K, Chugg KM, Polydoros A (1999) Quantization-based estimation. In: Conference record of the thirty-third asilomar conference on signals, systems, and computers, Pacific Grove, pp 37–41
39. Li JL, AlRegib G (2009) Distributed estimation in energy-constrained wireless sensor networks. IEEE Trans Signal Process 57(10):3746–3758
40. Li HB, Fang J (2007) Distributed adaptive quantization and estimation for wireless sensor networks. IEEE Signal Process Lett 14(10):669–672
41. Li XR, Zhu YM, Wang J, Han CZ (2003) Optimal linear estimation fusion-part I: unified fusion rules. IEEE Trans Inf Theory 49(9):2192–2208
42. Liang Y, Chen TW, Pan Q (2010) Optimal linear state estimator with multiple packet dropouts. IEEE Trans Autom Control 55(6):1428–1433
43. Lv N, Sun SL (2009) Scalar-weighted fusion estimators for systems with multiple sensors and multiple delayed measurements. In: Proceedings of IEEE conference on decision and control, Shanghai, pp 7599–7602
44. Ma J, Sun S (2011) Information fusion estimators for systems with multiple sensors of different packet dropout rates. Inf Fusion 12(3):213–222
45. Ma L, Da F, Zhang KJ (2011) Exponential H_∞ filter design for discrete time-delay stochastic systems with markovian jump parameters and missing measurements. IEEE Trans Circuit Syst-I Regul Pap 58(5):994–1007
46. Manyika J, Durrant-Whyte H (1994) Data fusion and sensor management: a decentralized information-theoretic approach. Ellis Horwood, New York
47. Marano S, Matta V, Willett P (2005) Some approaches to quantization for distributed estimation with data association. IEEE Trans Signal Process 53(3):885–895
48. Matveev AS, Savkin AV (2003) The problem of state estimation via asynchronous communication channels with irregular transmission times. IEEE Trans Autom Control 48(4):670–676
49. Moayedi M, Foo YK, Soh YC (2010) Adaptive Kalman filtering in networked systems with random sensor delays, multiple packet dropouts and missing measurements. IEEE Trans Signal Process 58(3):1577–1588
50. Msechu EJ, Roumeliotis SI, Ribeiro A, Giannakis GB (2008) Decentralized quantized Kalman filtering with scalable communication cost. IEEE Trans Signal Process 56(8):3727–3741
51. Olfati-Saber R (2005) Distributed Kalman filter with embedded consensus filters. In: Proceedings of the 44th IEEE conference decision and control, Sevilla, pp 8179–8184
52. Olfati-Saber R (2007) Distributed Kalman filtering for sensor networks. In: Proceedings of the 46th IEEE conference on decision and control, New Orleans, pp 5492–5498
53. Penarrocha I, Sanchis R, Albertos P (2012) Estimation in multisensor networked systems with scarce measurements and time varying delays. Syst Control Lett 61:555–562
54. Ribeiro A, Giannakis GB (2006) Bandwidth-constrained distributed estimation for wireless sensor networks-part I: gaussian case. IEEE Trans Signal Process 54(3):1131–1143
55. Ribeiro A, Giannakis GB (2006) Bandwidth-constrained distributed estimation for wireless sensor networks-part II: unknown probability density function. IEEE Trans Signal Process 54(7):2784–2796
56. Ribeiro A, Giannakis GB, Roumeliotis SI (2006) SOI-KF: distributed Kalman filtering with low-cost communications using the sign of innovations. IEEE Trans Signal Process 54(12):4782–4795
57. Ribeiro A, Schizas ID, Roumeliotis SI, Giannakis GB (2010) Kalman filtering in wireless sensor networks. IEEE Control Syst Mag 30(2):66–86
58. Roecker JA, McGillem CD (1988) Comparison of two-sensor tracking methods based on state vector fusion and measurement fusion. IEEE Trans Aerosp Electron Syst 24(4):447–449

59. Sahebsara M, Chen TW, Shah SL (2007) Optimal H_2 filtering in networked control systems with multiple packet dropouts. IEEE Trans Autom Control 52(8):1508–1513
60. Schenato L (2008) Optimal estimation in networked control systems subject to random delay and packet drop. IEEE Trans Autom Control 53(5):1311–1317
61. Schizas ID, Giannakis GB, Luo ZQ (2007) Distributed estimation using reduced-dimensionality sensor observations. IEEE Trans Signal Process 55(8):4284–4299
62. Schizas I, Ribeiro A, Giannakis G (2007) Consensus in ad hoc WSNs with noisy links-part I: distributed estimation of deterministic signals. IEEE Trans Signal Process 56(1):350–364
63. Shen XJ, Varshney PK, Zhu YM (2007) Robust distributed maximum likelihood estimation with dependent quantized data. Automatica 43(6):1117–1123
64. Shen B, Wang ZD, Hung YS (2010) Distributed H_∞-consensus filtering in sensor networks with multiple missing measurements: the finite-horizon case. Automatica 46(10):1682–1688
65. Shen XJ, Zhu YM, You ZS (2010) A sensor quantization algorithm for best linear estimation fusion in bandwidth-constrained systems. In: The 2010 international conference on intelligent control and information processing, Dalian, pp 433–438
66. Shen X, Zhu Y, You Z (2011) An efficient sensor quantization algorithm for decentralized estimation fusion. Automatica 47:1053–1059
67. Silva EI, Solis MA (2013) An alternative look at the constant-gain Kalman filter for state estimation over erasure channels. IEEE Trans Autom Control 58(12):3259–3265
68. Sinopoli B, Schenato L, Franceschetti M, Poolla K, Jordan MI, Sastry SS (2004) Kalman filtering with intermittent observations. IEEE Trans Autom Control 49(9):1453–1464
69. Song EB, Zhu YM, Zhou J, You ZS (2007) Optimal Kalman filtering fusion with cross-correlated sensor noises. Automatica 43(8):1450–1456
70. Song E, Xu J, Zhu Y (2014) Optimal distributed Kalman filtering fusion with singular covariances of filtering errors and measurement noises. IEEE Trans Autom Control 59(5):1271–1282
71. Sun SL, Deng ZL (2004) Multi-sensor optimal information fusion Kalman filter. Automatica 40(6):1017–1023
72. Sun XJ, Deng ZL (2009) Information fusion wiener filter for the multisensor multichannel ARMA signals with time-delayed measurements. IET Signal Process 3(5):403–415
73. Sun SL, Lin JY, Xie LH, Xiao WD (2007) Quantized Kalman filtering. In: The 22nd IEEE international symposium on intelligent control, Singapore, pp 7–12
74. Sun SL, Xie LH, Xiao WD, Soh YC (2008) Optimal linear estimation for systems with multiple packet dropouts. Automatica 44(7):1333–1342
75. Tian X, Bar-Shalom Y (2009) Exact algorithm for four track-to-track fusion configurations: all you wanted to know but were afraid to ask. In: Proceedings of the 12th international conference on information fusion, Seattle, pp 537–544
76. Varshney RK, Varshney PK (1986) Recrusive estiamtion with uncertain observations in a multisensor environment. IEE Proc F Commun Radar Signal Process 133(6):527–523
77. Wang YM, Li XR (2012) Distributed estimation fusion with unavailable cross-correlation. IEEE Trans Aerosp Electron Syst 48(1):259–278
78. Wang ZD, Ho DWC, Liu XH (2003) Variance-constrained filtering for uncertain stochastic systems with missing measurements. IEEE Trans Autom Control 48(7):1254–1258
79. Wang ZD, Yang FW, Ho DWC, Liu XH (2005) Robust finite-horizon filtering for stochastic systems with missing measurements. IEEE Signal Process Lett 12(6):437–440
80. Willner D, Chang CB, Dunn KP (1976) Kalman filter algorithm for a multisensor system. In: Proceedings of the IEEE conference on decision and control, Clearwater, pp 570–574
81. Xia Y, Shang J, Chen J, Liu GP (2009) Networked data fusion with packet losses and variable delays. IEEE Trans Syst Man Cybern Part B Cybern 39(5):1107–1120
82. Xiao JJ, Cui SG, Luo ZQ, Goldsmith AJ (2006) Power scheduling of universal decentralized estimation in sensor networks. IEEE Trans Signal Process 54(2):413–422
83. Xiao JJ, Ribeiro A, Luo ZQ, Giannakis GB (2006) Distributed compression estimation using wireless sensor networks. IEEE Signal Process Mag 7:27–41
84. Xiao L, Boyd S, Kim SJ (2007) Distributed average consensus with least-mean-square deviation. J Parallel Distrib Comput 67(1):33–46

85. Xiao N, Xie LH, Fu MY (2009) Kalman filtering over unreliable communication networks with bounded Markovian packet dropouts. Int J Robust Nonlinear Control 19(16):1770–1786
86. Xu J, Song E, Luo Y, Zhu Y (2012) Optimal distributed Kalman filtering fusion algorithm without invertibility of estimation error and sensor noise covariances. IEEE Signal Process Lett 19(1):55–58
87. Yang F, Wang Z, Feng G, Liu X (2009) Robust filtering with randomly varying sensor delay: the finite-horizon case. IEEE Trans Circuit Syst-I Regul Pap 56(3):664–672
88. You KY, Fu MY, Xie LH (2011) Mean square stability for Kalman filtering with Markovian packet losses. Automatica 47(12):2647–2657
89. Zhang KS, Li XR (2004) Optimal sensor data quantization for best linear unbiased estimation fusion. In: The 43rd IEEE conference on decision and control, Nassau, pp 2656–2661
90. Zhang H, Xie L, Zhang D, Soh YC (2004) A reorganized innovation approach to linear estimation. IEEE Trans Autom Control 49(10):1810–1814
91. Zhang H, Feng G, Duan G, Lu X (2006) H_∞ filtering for multiple-time-delay measurements. IEEE Trans Signal Process 54(5):1681–1688
92. Zhang WA, Yu L, Song HB (2009) H_∞ filtering of networked discrete-time systems with random packet losses. Inf Sci 179(22):3944–3955
93. Zhang H, Feng G, Han C (2011) Linear estimation for random delay systems. Syst Control Lett 60(7):450–459
94. Zhang HS, Song X, Shi L (2012) Convergence and mean square stability of suboptimal estimator for systems with measurement packet dropping. IEEE Trans Autom Control 57(5):1248–1253
95. Zhou Y, Li JX (2009) Quantized measurement fusion for target tracking in wireless sensor networks. In: In the joint 48th IEEE conference on decision and control and the 28th Chinese control conference, Shanghai, pp 6835–6840
96. Zhu Y, Song E, Zhou J, You Z (2005) Optimal dimensionality reduction of sensor data in multisensor estimation fusion. IEEE Trans Signal Process 53(3):1631–1639
97. Zhu H, Schizas ID, Giannakis GB (2009) Power-efficient dimensionality reduction for distributed channel aware Kalman tracking using WSNs. IEEE Trans Signal Process 57(8):3193–3207

Chapter 2
Multi-rate Kalman Fusion Estimation for WSNs

2.1 Introduction

It is known that the WSNs are usually severely constrained in energy, and energy-efficient methods are thus important for WSN-based estimation to reduce energy consumption and to prolong network life. Several energy-efficient estimation methods have been available in the literature, such as the quantization method [1–6] and the data-compression method [1, 7–10]. The main idea in quantization and compression is to reduce the size of a data packet and thus to reduce energy consumption in transmitting and receiving packets, and they can be called as the packet size-based energy-efficient estimation methods. Actually, a useful and straightforward approach to saving energy is to slow down the information transmission rate in the sensors, for example, the sensors may measure and transmit measurements with a period that is several times of the sampling period. This is the *transmission rate method* to be presented in this chapter. Specifically, a multi-rate scheme by which the sensors estimate states at a faster time scale and exchange information with neighbors at a slower time scale is proposed to reduce communication cost. Packets exchanged among the sensors may be lost during the transmission, and several binary-valued white Bernoulli sequences are used to describe the random packet losses. Then, by applying a lifting technique as used in [11] and [12], the multi-rate estimation system is finally modeled as a single-rate discrete-time system with multiple stochastic parameters.

On the other hand, the distributed structure instead of the centralized structure will be adopted in this chapter to design the fusion estimation system. In the distributed structure, the WSN is considered to be a peer-to-peer network without a fusion center, and every sensor in the network collects information only from its neighbors to generate estimates. It is obvious that local estimates obtained at each sensor by such a distributed method are not optimal in the sense that not all the measurements in the WSN are used. Moreover, there exist disagreements among local estimates obtained at different sensors. In other words, local estimates at any

W.-A. Zhang et al., *Distributed Fusion Estimation for Sensor Networks with Communication Constraints*, DOI 10.1007/978-981-10-0795-8_2

two sensors may be different from each other. As pointed out in [13], such form of group disagreement regarding the signal estimates is highly undesirable for a peer-to-peer network of estimators. A two-stage hierarchical fusion estimation method will be presented in this chapter to help improve local estimation precision and reduce disagreement among local estimates. At the first stage, every sensor in the WSN collects measurements from neighboring sensors to generate a local estimate, and then local estimates from neighboring sensors are further collected to form a fused estimate at the second stage. By fusion of both measurements and local estimates, more information from different sensors are used to generate estimates in the two-stage method as compared with the one-stage one where only measurements are collected to generate estimates.

Then, by using the orthogonal projection principle and the innovation analysis approach, an estimation algorithm with a set of recursive Lyapunov and Riccati equations is presented to design the distributed estimators. The obtained estimation performances critically depend on the information transmission rate and the packet loss probabilities, and it is demonstrated by a simulation example of a maneuvering target tracking system that the time scale of information exchange among sensors can be slower while still maintaining satisfactory estimation performance by using the proposed estimation method.

2.2 Problem Statement

Consider a discrete-time stochastic linear system described by the following state-space model

$$x(k_{i+1}) = A_p x(k_i) + B_p \omega_p(k_i), \ i = 0, 1, 2, \dots \tag{2.1}$$

where $x(k_i) \in \Re^n$ is the system state, $\omega_p(k_i) \in \Re^p$ is a zero-mean white noise, $h_p = k_{i+1} - k_i$, and $\forall\, i = 0, 1, 2, \dots$ is the sampling period of system (2.1). A WSN consisting of N spatially distributed sensors is deployed to collect observations of system (2.1) according to the following observation models:

$$y_l(k_i) = C_{pl} x(k_i) + D_{pl} \upsilon_{pl}(k_i), l = 1, 2, \dots, N \tag{2.2}$$

where $y_l(k_i) \in \Re^{m_l}$ is the observation collected by sensor l at time instant k_i, $\upsilon_{pl}(k_i) \in \Re^{q_l}$ are white measurement noises with zero means, and A_p, B_p, C_{pl}, and D_{pl} are constant matrices with appropriate dimensions. $\omega_p(k_i)$ is uncorrelated with $\upsilon_{pl}(k_i)$, while $\upsilon_{pl}(k_i)$ are mutually correlated, and $\mathbf{E}\{\omega_p(k_i)\omega_p^{\mathrm{T}}(k_j)\} = Q_{\omega_p}\delta_{ij}$, $\mathbf{E}\{\upsilon_{pl}(k_i)\upsilon_{ps}^{\mathrm{T}}(k_j)\} = Q_{l,s}^{\upsilon_p}\delta_{ij}$, $l, s \in Z_0$, where $\delta_{ii} = 1$ and $\delta_{ij} = 0\ (i \neq j)$.

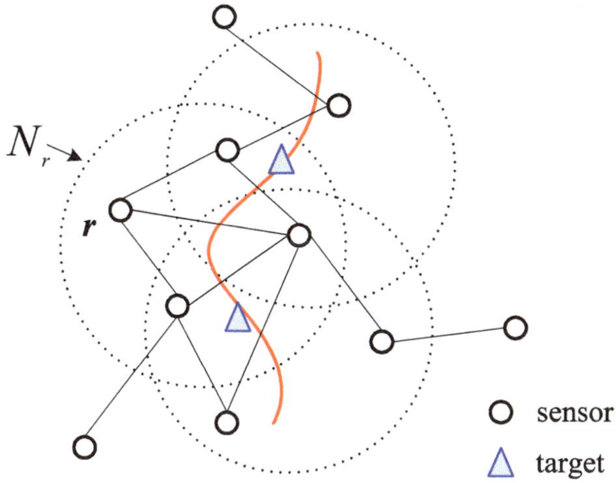

Fig. 2.1 A structure of the distributed estimation system

The WSN is considered to be a peer-to-peer network, there is no fusion center in the network, and every sensor in the network acts also as an estimator. A structure of the distributed fusion estimation system is schematically shown in Fig. 2.1. The observations are transmitted among the sensors in an ad hoc manner via unreliable wireless communication channels and may be subject to random packet losses. We say that two sensors are connected if they can communicate directly with each other, i.e., they can communicate with each other within one hop. For example, in Fig. 2.1, sensor 4 is connected to sensors 3, 5, and 6. Notice that a sensor is always connected to itself. The set of sensors connected to a certain sensor r is called the neighborhood of senor r and is denoted by $\mathcal{N}_r$, $r \in Z_0 \triangleq \{1, 2, \ldots, N\}$ (notice that $r \in \mathcal{N}_r$), and the number of neighbors of sensor r is given by the number of elements of $\mathcal{N}_r$, written as n_r. For example, in the neighborhood $\mathcal{N}_r$ in Fig. 2.1, one has $\mathcal{N}_r = \{3, 4, 5, 6\}$ and $n_r = 4$.

Denote by $L_{i,j}$, $i, j \in \mathcal{N}_r$ the link between sensor i and sensor j in a neighborhood. Then, the random packet loss in the link $L_{i,j}$ is described by a white binary distributed random process $\alpha_{i,j}(k_i)$, where $\alpha_{i,j}(k_i) = 1$ indicates that a packet transmitted from sensor i successfully arrives at sensor j at instant k_i, while $\alpha_{i,j}(k_i) = 0$ implies that a packet is lost during the transmission from sensor i to sensor j. $\theta_{i,j} \triangleq \mathbf{E}\{\alpha_{i,j}(k_i)\} = \text{Prob}\{\alpha_{i,j}(k_i) = 1\}$ is called the packet arriving probability (PAP), while $1 - \theta_{i,j} \triangleq 1 - \mathbf{E}\{\alpha_{i,j}(k_i)\} = \text{Prob}\{\alpha_{i,j}(k_i) = 0\}$ is called the packet loss probability (PLP). By definition, one has $\alpha_{i,j}(k_i) = \alpha_{j,i}(k_i)$, $\theta_{i,j} = \theta_{j,i}$, and $\theta_{i,i} = 1$. It is assumed that $\alpha_{l,r}(k_i)$, $\forall\ l \in \mathcal{N}_r$, $r \in Z_0$ are mutually independent and are also independent of $\omega_p(k_i)$, $\upsilon_{pl}(k_i)$, and the initial system state. All the sensors in the network are assumed to be time synchronized. Moreover, the sensors are time-driven, i.e., they calculate the state estimates periodically at certain time instants, and the sensors are not necessary to know the packet transmission status in the network.

Suppose that the dynamic of the stochastic process (2.1) is not changing too rapidly, then brutal force collection of every measurement at sampling instants k_i is a waste of energy, and this waste is amplified by packet losses. To reduce the energy waste, we suppose that every sensor r transmits measurements to its neighbors with a period h_m that is larger than the sampling period h_p. Denote t_i, $i = 0, 1, 2, \ldots$ as the measurement transmission instants, and then $h_m = t_{i+1} - t_i$, $i = 0, 1, 2, \ldots$. Thus, every sensor in the WSN collects measurements, runs a Kalman estimator, and calculates and outputs local estimates with a period h_m. In practice, one may expect to obtain estimates not only at the instances t_i but also at instances over the interval $(t_{i-1}, t_i]$; this is to say, one may expect to update the estimates at a rate that is higher than the estimate output rate. Suppose that estimates are updated at instances T_i and $\mathrm{T}_{i+1} - \mathrm{T}_i = h_e$, $i = 0, 1, 2, \ldots$. In this generic case, the estimation system runs with three rates, namely, the measurement sampling rate (also the system state updating rate), the measurement transmitting rate (also the estimate output rate), and the estimate updating rate. In what follows, the multi-rate estimation system model will be transformed into a single-rate system model for further development by using the lifting technique.

For simplicity but without loss of generality, it is assumed that both the measurement transmitting period h_m and the estimate updating period h_e are integer multiple of the measurement sampling period h_p and h_m is also integer multiple of h_e. Specifically, let $h_e = ah_p$ and $h_m = bh_e$, where a and b are positive integers and chosen as small as possible in practice under energy constraints of the sensor networks. Then, by applying the difference equation in (2.1) recursively, one obtains the following state equation with a state updating period of h_e

$$x(\mathrm{T}_{i+1}) = A_e x(\mathrm{T}_i) + B_e \omega_e(\mathrm{T}_i),\ i = 0, 1, 2, \ldots \tag{2.3}$$

where $A_e = A_p^a$ and

$$B_e = \begin{bmatrix} A_p^{a-1} B_p & \cdots & A_p B_p & B_p \end{bmatrix}$$

$$\omega_e(\mathrm{T}_i) = \begin{bmatrix} \omega_p^{\mathrm{T}}(\mathrm{T}_i) \ \omega_p^{\mathrm{T}}(\mathrm{T}_i + h_p) & \cdots & \omega_p^{\mathrm{T}}(\mathrm{T}_i + (a-1)h_p) \end{bmatrix}^{\mathrm{T}}$$

Similarly, applying the difference equation in (2.3) recursively leads to the following state equation with a state updating period of h_m

$$x(t_{i+1}) = A_m x(t_i) + B_m \omega_m(t_i),\ i = 0, 1, 2, \ldots \tag{2.4}$$

where $A_m = A_e^b$ and

$$B_m = \begin{bmatrix} A_e^{b-1} B_e & \cdots & A_e B_e & B_e \end{bmatrix}$$

$$\omega_m(t_i) = \begin{bmatrix} \omega_e^{\mathrm{T}}(t_i) \ \omega_e^{\mathrm{T}}(t_i + h_e) & \cdots & \omega_e^{\mathrm{T}}(t_i + (b-1)h_e) \end{bmatrix}^{\mathrm{T}}$$

The corresponding observation models are as follows:

$$y_l(t_i) = C_{pl}x(t_i) + D_{pl}\upsilon_{pl}(t_i), l = 1, 2, \ldots, N \tag{2.5}$$

By following the similar procedures for obtaining the equation (2.4), one has for $j = 1, 2, \ldots, b-1$ that

$$x(t_{i+1} - jh_e) = A_{mj}x(t_i) + B_{mj}\omega_m(t_i) \tag{2.6}$$

where $A_{mj} = A_e^{b-j}$ and

$$\begin{aligned} B_{m1} &= [A_e^{b-2}B_e \ \cdots \ A_eB_e \ B_e \ 0] \\ &\vdots \\ B_{m(b-1)} &= [B_e \ 0 \ \cdots \ 0] \end{aligned}$$

Define

$$\eta(t_i) = \left[x^{\mathrm{T}}(t_i) \ x^{\mathrm{T}}(t_i - h_e) \ \cdots \ x^{\mathrm{T}}(t_i - (b-1)h_e)\right]^{\mathrm{T}}$$

then one obtains the following augmented single-rate estimation system model from equations (2.4), (2.5) and (2.6):

$$\begin{cases} \eta(t_{i+1}) = A\eta(t_i) + B\omega_m(t_i) \\ y_l(t_i) = C_l\eta(t_i) + D_{pl}\upsilon_{pl}(t_i) \\ l = 1, 2, \ldots, N, \ i = 0, 1, 2, \ldots \end{cases} \tag{2.7}$$

where $C_l = [C_{pl} \ 0 \ \ldots \ 0]$ and

$$A = \begin{bmatrix} A_m & 0 \cdots 0 \\ A_{m1} & 0 \cdots 0 \\ \vdots & \vdots \ \vdots \ \vdots \\ A_{m(b-1)} & 0 \cdots 0 \end{bmatrix}, \ B = \begin{bmatrix} B_m \\ B_{m1} \\ \vdots \\ B_{m(b-1)} \end{bmatrix}$$

The initial states $x(t_0 - jh_e), j = 0, 1, \ldots, b-1$ are mutually uncorrelated and are also uncorrelated with $\omega_p(t_i)$ and $\upsilon_{pl}(t_i)$, $l = 1, 2, \ldots, N$ and satisfy

$$\mathbf{E}\{x(t_0 - jh_e)\} = \bar{x}_j, \ \mathbf{E}\left\{(x(t_0 - jh_e) - \bar{x}_j)(x(t_0 - jh_e) - \bar{x}_j)^{\mathrm{T}}\right\} = \bar{P}_j$$

where t_0 is the initial time.

At each instant t_i, every sensor collects measurements $y_l(t_i)$ from its neighbors to generate an unbiased state estimate $\hat{\eta}(t_{i+j}|t_i)$, where j is an integer, and thus the following estimates

$$\hat{x}(t_{i+j}|t_i), \hat{x}(t_{i+j} - h_e|t_i), \ldots, \hat{x}(t_{i+j} - (b-1)h_e|t_i)$$

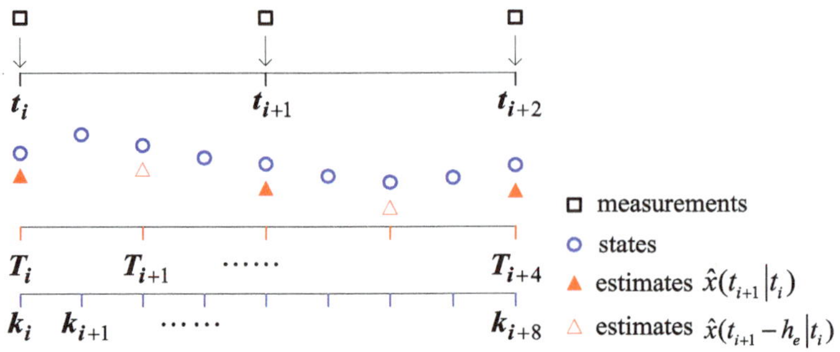

Fig. 2.2 An example of the multi-rate estimation

are obtained simultaneously in blocks. An example of the multi-rate state estimation is shown schematically in Fig. 2.2, where a one-step prediction is considered, and $h_m = 2h_e$, $h_e = 2h_p$, k_i are the measurement sampling instants (also the system state updating instants), T_i are the estimate updating instants, and t_i are the estimate output instants (also the measurement transmitting instants). At each instant t_i, every sensor collects measurements from its neighbors, and the predictions $\hat{x}(t_{i+1}|t_i)$ and $\hat{x}(t_{i+1} - h_e|t_i)$ are then generated simultaneously. In the system model (2.7), the state $x(t_i)$ is included in the augmented state $\eta(t_i)$. Notice that when filtering is considered, $\hat{x}(t_i - h_e|t_i)$, ..., $\hat{x}(t_i - (b-1)h_e|t_i)$ are all delayed estimates. So, one advantage of the proposed model is that it can provide at least one non-delayed estimate $\hat{x}(t_i|t_i)$, and this is important in many practical applications, such as real-time moving target tracking. Second, the lifted noise $\omega_m(t_i)$ is still uncorrelated with $\upsilon_{pl}(t_i)$, $l = 1, 2, \ldots, N$ provided that $\omega_p(k_i)$ and $\upsilon_{pl}(k_i)$ are uncorrelated.

In what follows, an estimation system model with random packet losses will be established based on the model (2.7). Denote by $z_l(t_i)$ the measurement that sensor r receives from sensor l, and then $z_l(t_i)$ might not equal $y_l(t_i)$ since $y_l(t_i)$ may be lost during the transmission. Suppose that the *hold input* mechanism [14] is adopted by all the sensors, i.e., sensor r will hold at its last available input when the current measurement is lost, and then one has in this scenario that

$$z_l(t_i) = \alpha_{l,r}(t_i)y_l(t_i) + (1 - \alpha_{l,r}(t_i))z_l(t_{i-1})$$

Stacking $z_l(t_i)$, $l \in \mathcal{N}_r$ into an augmented vector $Z_r(t_i) = \mathrm{col}\{z_l(t_i)\}_{l\in\mathcal{N}_r}$ which will be used to generate local estimates, one obtains

$$Z_r(t_i) = \mathrm{col}\{\alpha_{l,r}(t_i)y_l(t_i)\}_{l\in\mathcal{N}_r} + \mathrm{col}\{(1 - \alpha_{l,r}(t_i))z_l(t_{i-1})\}_{l\in\mathcal{N}_r} \tag{2.8}$$

It can be seen from (2.8) that the stochastic variables $\alpha_{l,r}(t_i)$ are incorporated into each element of the estimator input $Z_r(t_i)$, which makes the estimator design problem intractable. To remove the difficulty, the following auxiliary matrices

$$\Pi_{l,r} = \mathrm{diag}\left\{\underbrace{0,\ldots,0}_{l-1}, I_{l,r}, \underbrace{0,\ldots,0}_{n_r-l}\right\}, \ l \in \mathcal{N}_r$$

are introduced to rewrite $Z_r(t_i)$ in (2.8) as follows:

$$Z_r(t_i) = \left(\sum_{l\in\mathcal{N}_r} \alpha_{l,r}(t_i)\Pi_{l,r}\right) Y_r(t_i) + \left(I_r - \sum_{l\in\mathcal{N}_r} \alpha_{l,r}(t_i)\Pi_{l,r}\right) Z_r(t_{i-1}) \tag{2.9}$$

where $Y_r(t_i) = \mathrm{col}\{y_l(t_i)\}_{l\in\mathcal{N}_r}$, $I_{l,r} \in \Re^{m_l\times m_l}$, and $I_r \in \Re^{\bar{m}_r\times\bar{m}_r}$ are identity matrices and $\bar{m}_r = \sum_{l\in\mathcal{N}_r} m_l$. Denote

$$G_r = \mathrm{col}\{C_l\}_{l\in\mathcal{N}_r},\ H_r = \mathrm{diag}\{D_{pl}\}_{l\in\mathcal{N}_r},\ \upsilon_r(t_i) = \mathrm{col}\{\upsilon_{pl}(t_i)\}_{l\in\mathcal{N}_r}$$

and then $Y_r(t_i)$ is written as

$$Y_r(t_i) = G_r\eta(t_i) + H_r\upsilon_r(t_i) \tag{2.10}$$

Furthermore, denote

$$\xi_r(t_i) = \left[\eta^{\mathrm{T}}(t_i)\ Z_r^{\mathrm{T}}(t_{i-1})\right]^{\mathrm{T}},\ \nu_r(t_i) = \left[\omega_m^{\mathrm{T}}(t_i)\ \upsilon_r^{\mathrm{T}}(t_i)\right]^{\mathrm{T}}$$

and then one obtains the following augmented system model from (2.7), (2.9), and (2.10)

$$\begin{cases} \xi_r(t_{i+1}) = \tilde{A}_r(t_i)\xi_r(t_i) + \tilde{B}_r(t_i)\nu_r(t_i) \\ Z_r(t_i) = \tilde{C}_r(t_i)\xi_r(t_i) + \tilde{\upsilon}_r(t_i) \\ r \in Z_0,\ i = 0, 1, 2, \ldots \end{cases} \tag{2.11}$$

where $\tilde{\upsilon}_r(t_i) = \sum_{l\in\mathcal{N}_r} \alpha_{l,r}(t_i)\Pi_{l,r}H_r\upsilon_r(t_i)$, and

$$\tilde{A}_r(t_i) = \begin{bmatrix} A & 0 \\ \sum_{l\in\mathcal{N}_r} \alpha_{l,r}(t_i)\Pi_{l,r}G_r & I_r - \sum_{l\in\mathcal{N}_r} \alpha_{l,r}(t_i)\Pi_{l,r} \end{bmatrix}$$

$$\tilde{B}_r(t_i) = \mathrm{diag}\left\{B, \sum_{l\in\mathcal{N}_r} \alpha_{l,r}(t_i)\Pi_{l,r}H_r\right\}$$

$$\tilde{C}_r(t_i) = \begin{bmatrix} \sum_{l\in\mathcal{N}_r} \alpha_{l,r}(t_i)\Pi_{l,r}G_r & I_r - \sum_{l\in\mathcal{N}_r} \alpha_{l,r}(t_i)\Pi_{l,r} \end{bmatrix}$$

Let $Q_\omega = \mathbf{E}\left\{\omega_m(t_i)\omega_m^{\mathrm{T}}(t_i)\right\}$ and $Q_{\upsilon_r} = \mathbf{E}\left\{\upsilon_r(t_i)\upsilon_r^{\mathrm{T}}(t_i)\right\}$. Then

$$Q_\omega = \mathrm{diag}\{Q_{\omega_p}\}_{a\times b},\ Q_{\upsilon_r} = [Q_{l,s}^{\upsilon_p}],\ l,s \in \mathcal{N}_r$$

To reduce energy consumption, the *transmission rate method* is used, and it naturally results in a multi-rate estimation system. By using the lifting technique, the multi-rate estimation system with random packet losses is finally modeled as a single-rate system with multiple stochastic parameters as in equation (2.11). Note that, if $b = 1$, i.e., the estimate output rate equals the estimate updating rate ($h_m = h_e$), then $\eta(t_i)$ and $\omega_m(t_i)$ reduce to $x(\mathrm{T}_i)$ and $\omega_e(\mathrm{T}_i)$, respectively, while A, B, and C_l reduce to A_e, B_e, and C_{pl}, respectively, and thus the model (2.7) reduces to the model (2.3). Moreover, if $a = 1$ and $b = 1$, then $h_m = h_e = h_p$, $x(\mathrm{T}_i)$ becomes $x(k_i)$, $\omega_e(\mathrm{T}_i)$ reduces to $\omega_p(k_i)$, while A_e and B_e reduce to A_p and B_p, respectively, and thus the model (2.3) reduces to the model (2.1).

Based on the system model (2.11), a two-stage fusion estimation method will be proposed to help improve local estimation performance of each sensor and reduce disagreements among local estimates caused by the distributed structure of the estimation system. At each time step, every sensor collects measurements from its neighbors and runs a Kalman estimation algorithm to obtain a local estimate of the system state. At the second stage, the sensor further collects and fuses local estimates available at its neighbors to obtain a fused estimate. Thus, state estimation at each sensor based on local measurements and the further fused estimation based on the exchanged estimates among neighbors constitute the two-stage distributed fusion estimation at hand. Then, the objective of the chapter is described as follows.

Objective of the chapter: Design distributed Kalman estimators for system (2.11) with packet losses and establish relationships between the measurement transmission rate, PLPs, and estimation performances. The design is carried out in two stages. At the first stage, every sensor r, $r \in Z_0$ collects measurements from its neighborhood $\mathcal{N}_r$ and generates a local estimate $\hat{\eta}_r = g_r(y_l, \alpha_{l,r})_{l\in\mathcal{N}_r}$, where $g_r(\cdot)$ is a local Kalman estimation algorithm. At the second stage, sensor r collects local estimates from its neighborhood $\mathcal{N}_r$ and generates a fused estimate $\hat{\eta}_r^o = f_r(\hat{\eta}_l, \alpha_{l,r})_{l\in\mathcal{N}_r}$, where $f_r(\cdot)$ refers to a local fusion algorithm.

2.3 Two-Stage Distributed Estimation

2.3.1 Local Kalman Estimators

This subsection is devoted to the design of the local Kalman estimation algorithm $g_r(\cdot)$.

Taking expectations on $\tilde{A}_r(t_i)$, $\tilde{B}_r(t_i)$, and $\tilde{C}_r(t_i)$ yields, respectively:

$$\bar{A}_r \triangleq \mathbf{E}\left\{\tilde{A}_r(t_i)\right\} = \begin{bmatrix} A & 0 \\ \sum\limits_{l\in\mathcal{N}_r} \theta_{l,r}\Pi_{l,r}G_r & I_r - \sum\limits_{l\in\mathcal{N}_r} \theta_{l,r}\Pi_{l,r} \end{bmatrix}$$

$$\bar{B}_r \triangleq \mathbf{E}\left\{\tilde{B}_r(t_i)\right\} = \text{diag}\left\{B, \sum_{l\in\mathcal{N}_r} \theta_{l,r}\Pi_{l,r}H_r\right\}$$

$$\bar{C}_r \triangleq \mathbf{E}\left\{\tilde{C}_r(t_i)\right\} = \begin{bmatrix} \sum\limits_{l\in\mathcal{N}_r} \theta_{l,r}\Pi_{l,r}G_r & I_r - \sum\limits_{l\in\mathcal{N}_r} \theta_{l,r}\Pi_{l,r} \end{bmatrix}$$

Denoting

$$A_{0l,r} = \begin{bmatrix} 0 & 0 \\ \Pi_{l,r}G_r & -\Pi_{l,r} \end{bmatrix}, \quad C_{0l,r} = \begin{bmatrix} \Pi_{l,r}G_r & -\Pi_{l,r} \end{bmatrix}$$

one obtains

$$\begin{cases} \tilde{A}_r(t_i) - \bar{A}_r = \sum\limits_{l\in\mathcal{N}_r} (\alpha_{l,r}(t_i) - \theta_{l,r})A_{0l,r} \\ \tilde{C}_r(t_i) - \bar{C}_r = \sum\limits_{l\in\mathcal{N}_r} (\alpha_{l,r}(t_i) - \theta_{l,r})C_{0l,r} \end{cases} \tag{2.12}$$

Then, some lemmas which play important roles in the derivation of main results are first presented as follows:

Lemma 2.1 *From the distributions of $\alpha_{i,j}(t_i)$, it can be easily obtained for $\alpha_{i,j}(t_i) \neq \alpha_{r,s}(t_i)$, $i, j, r, s \in Z_0$ that*

$$\mathbf{E}\left\{\alpha_{i,j}^2(t_i)\right\} = \theta_{i,j}$$

$$\mathbf{E}\left\{\alpha_{i,j}(t_i)\alpha_{r,s}(t_i)\right\} = \theta_{i,j}\theta_{r,s}$$

$$\mathbf{E}\left\{(\alpha_{i,j}(t_i) - \theta_{i,j})^2\right\} = \theta_{i,j}(1 - \theta_{i,j})$$

$$\mathbf{E}\left\{(\alpha_{i,j}(t_i) - \theta_{i,j})(\alpha_{r,s}(t_i) - \theta_{r,s})\right\} = 0$$

Lemma 2.2 *For $r \in Z_0$, $\mathbf{E}\left\{\tilde{\upsilon}_r(t_i)\tilde{\upsilon}_r^{\mathrm{T}}(t_i)\right\}$ satisfies*

$$\mathbf{E}\left\{\tilde{\upsilon}_r(t_i)\tilde{\upsilon}_r^{\mathrm{T}}(t_i)\right\} \triangleq \Delta_{r,r} = \sum_{l\in\mathcal{N}_r} \theta_{l,r}\Pi_{l,r}H_r Q_{\upsilon_r} H_r^{\mathrm{T}} \Pi_{l,r}^{\mathrm{T}}$$
$$+\sum_{l\in\mathcal{N}_r}\sum_{j\in\mathcal{N}_r, j\neq l} \theta_{l,r}\theta_{j,r}\Pi_{l,r}H_r Q_{\upsilon_r} H_r^{\mathrm{T}} \Pi_{j,r}^{\mathrm{T}} \tag{2.13}$$

Proof Lemma 2.2 can be followed by Lemma 2.1.

Lemma 2.3 *Define the state covariance matrix as*

$$\Xi_{r,r}(t_i) \triangleq \mathbf{E}\left\{\xi_r(t_i)\xi_r^{\mathrm{T}}(t_i)\right\}$$

and then $\Xi_{r,r}(t_i)$ satisfies the following recursion:

$$\Xi_{r,r}(t_{i+1}) = \bar{A}_r \Xi_{r,r}(t_i)\bar{A}_r^{\mathrm{T}} + \mathrm{diag}\left\{BQ_\omega B^{\mathrm{T}},\ \Delta_{r,r}\right\}$$
$$+\sum_{l\in\mathcal{N}_r} \theta_{l,r}(1-\theta_{l,r})A_{0l,r}\Xi_{r,r}(t_i)A_{0l,r}^{\mathrm{T}} \tag{2.14}$$

where the initial value of $\Xi_{r,r}(t_i)$ at t_0 is given by

$$\Xi_{r,r}(t_0) = \begin{bmatrix} \Lambda_\eta & O_1 \\ O_1^{\mathrm{T}} & O_2 \end{bmatrix}$$

$$\Lambda_\eta \triangleq \mathbf{E}\left\{\eta(t_0)\eta^{\mathrm{T}}(t_0)\right\} = \mathrm{diag}\left\{\bar{P}_0 + \bar{x}_0\bar{x}_0^{\mathrm{T}}, \bar{P}_1 + \bar{x}_1\bar{x}_1^{\mathrm{T}}, \ldots, \bar{P}_{b-1} + \bar{x}_{b-1}\bar{x}_{b-1}^{\mathrm{T}}\right\}$$

and $O_1 \in \Re^{bn\times\bar{m}_r}$ and $O_2 \in \Re^{\bar{m}_r\times\bar{m}_r}$ are zero matrices.

Proof $\xi_r(t_{i+1})$ can be rewritten as

$$\xi_r(t_{i+1}) = \bar{A}_r\xi_r(t_i) + \left(\tilde{A}_r(t_i) - \bar{A}_r\right)\xi_r(t_i) + \tilde{B}_r(t_i)\nu_r(t_i) \tag{2.15}$$

Since $\mathbf{E}\{\tilde{A}_r(t_i) - \bar{A}_r\} = 0$ and $\xi_r(t_i)\bot\nu_r(t_i)$, one has by (2.15) that

$$\Xi_{r,r}(t_{i+1}) = \bar{A}_r\Xi_{r,r}(t_i)\bar{A}_r^{\mathrm{T}} + \mathbf{E}\left\{\left(\tilde{A}_r(t_i) - \bar{A}_r\right)\xi_r(t_i)\xi_r^{\mathrm{T}}(t_i)\left(\tilde{A}_r(t_i) - \bar{A}_r\right)^{\mathrm{T}}\right\}$$
$$+\mathbf{E}\left\{\tilde{B}_r(t_i)\nu_r(t_i)\nu_r^{\mathrm{T}}(t_i)\tilde{B}_r^{\mathrm{T}}(t_i)\right\} \tag{2.16}$$

It follows from (2.12) and Lemma 2.1 that

$$\begin{aligned}
&\mathbf{E}\left\{\left(\tilde{A}_r(t_i)-\bar{A}_r\right)\xi_r(t_i)\xi_r^{\mathrm{T}}(t_i)\left(\tilde{A}_r(t_i)-\bar{A}_r\right)^{\mathrm{T}}\right\}\\
&=\mathbf{E}\left\{\sum_{l\in\mathcal{N}_r}(\alpha_{l,r}(t_i)-\theta_{l,r})^2A_{0l,r}\xi_r(t_i)\xi_r^{\mathrm{T}}(t_i)A_{0l,r}^{\mathrm{T}}\right\}\\
&\quad+\mathbf{E}\left\{\sum_{l\in\mathcal{N}_r}\sum_{j\in\mathcal{N}_r,j\neq l}(\alpha_{l,r}(t_i)-\theta_{l,r})\left(\alpha_{j,r}(t_i)-\theta_{j,r}\right)\right.\\
&\quad\left.\times A_{0l,r}\xi_r(t_i)\xi_r^{\mathrm{T}}(t_i)A_{0j,r}^{\mathrm{T}}\right\}\\
&=\sum_{l\in\mathcal{N}_r}\theta_{l,r}(1-\theta_{l,r})A_{0l,r}\Xi_{r,r}(t_i)A_{0l,r}^{\mathrm{T}}
\end{aligned}\tag{2.17}$$

Since $\omega_m(t_i)$ and $\upsilon_r(t_i)$ are uncorrelated, one has by Lemma 2.2 that

$$\begin{aligned}
&\mathbf{E}\left\{\tilde{B}_r(t_i)\nu_r(t_i)\nu_r^{\mathrm{T}}(t_i)\tilde{B}_r^{\mathrm{T}}(t_i)\right\}\\
&=\mathbf{E}\left\{\mathrm{diag}\left\{B,\ \sum_{l\in\mathcal{N}_r}\alpha_{l,r}(t_i)\Pi_{l,r}H_r\right\}\begin{bmatrix}\omega_m(t_i)\\ \upsilon_r(t_i)\end{bmatrix}\right.\\
&\quad\left.\times\begin{bmatrix}\omega_m(t_i)\\ \upsilon_r(t_i)\end{bmatrix}^{\mathrm{T}}\mathrm{diag}\left\{B,\ \sum_{l\in\mathcal{N}_r}\alpha_{l,r}(t_i)\Pi_{l,r}H_r\right\}^{\mathrm{T}}\right\}\\
&=\mathrm{diag}\left\{BQ_\omega B^{\mathrm{T}},\ \Delta_{r,r}\right\}
\end{aligned}\tag{2.18}$$

Substituting (2.17) and (2.18) into (2.16) leads to (2.14). The proof is thus completed.

With Lemmas 2.1, 2.2 and 2.3 in hand, it is now ready to present design procedures for the finite-horizon local Kalman estimators. Let $\hat{\xi}_r(t_i|t_i)$ and $\hat{\xi}_r(t_{i+1}|t_i)$ denote, respectively, the unbiased linear minimum MSE filtered estimate and one-step predicted estimate of the state $\xi_r(t_i)$. Then, the recursive local Kalman filter for system (2.11) is given in the following theorem.

Theorem 2.1 *For system (2.11), the finite horizon local Kalman filter in the sensor r, $r\in Z_0$ is given by*

$$\varepsilon_r(t_i)=Z_r(t_i)-\bar{C}_r\hat{\xi}_r(t_i|t_{i-1})\tag{2.19}$$

$$\begin{aligned}
\Omega_r(t_i)&=\sum_{l\in\mathcal{N}_r}\theta_{l,r}(1-\theta_{l,r})C_{0l,r}\Xi_{r,r}(t_i)C_{0l,r}^{\mathrm{T}}\\
&\quad+\bar{C}_rP_{r,r}(t_i|t_{i-1})\bar{C}_r^{\mathrm{T}}+\Delta_{r,r}
\end{aligned}\tag{2.20}$$

$$K_r(t_i) = P_{r,r}(t_i|t_{i-1})\bar{C}_r^{\mathrm{T}}\Omega_r^{-1}(t_i) \tag{2.21}$$

$$\begin{aligned} F_r(t_i) = &\Bigg[\sum_{l\in\mathcal{N}_r}\theta_{l,r}(1-\theta_{l,r})A_{0l,r}\Xi_{r,r}(t_i)C_{0l,r}^{\mathrm{T}} \\ &+\bar{A}_rP_{r,r}(t_i|t_{i-1})\bar{C}_r^{\mathrm{T}} + \begin{bmatrix} 0 \\ \Delta_{r,r}\end{bmatrix}\Bigg]\Omega_r^{-1}(t_i) \end{aligned} \tag{2.22}$$

$$\hat{\xi}_r(t_i|t_i) = \hat{\xi}_r(t_i|t_{i-1}) + K_r(t_i)\varepsilon_r(t_i) \tag{2.23}$$

$$\hat{\xi}_r(t_{i+1}|t_i) = \bar{A}_r\hat{\xi}_r(t_i|t_{i-1}) + F_r(t_i)\varepsilon_r(t_i) \tag{2.24}$$

$$P_{r,r}(t_i|t_i) = P_{r,r}(t_i|t_{i-1}) - K_r(t_i)\Omega_r(t_i)K_r^{\mathrm{T}}(t_i) \tag{2.25}$$

$$\begin{aligned} P_{r,r}(t_{i+1}|t_i) = &\sum_{l\in\mathcal{N}_r}\theta_{l,r}(1-\theta_{l,r})(A_{0l,r}-F_r(t_i)C_{0l,r}) \\ &\times\Xi_{r,r}(t_i)(A_{0l,r}-F_r(t_i)C_{0l,r})^{\mathrm{T}} \\ &+\mathrm{diag}\left\{BQ_\omega B^{\mathrm{T}},\ \Delta_{r,r}\right\} \\ &+\left(\bar{A}_r - F_r(t_i)\bar{C}_r\right)P_{r,r}(t_i|t_{i-1})\left(\bar{A}_r - F_r(t_i)\bar{C}_r\right)^{\mathrm{T}} \\ &-\left[0\ \ \varphi_{r,r}^{\mathrm{T}}(t_i)\right] - \left[0\ \ \varphi_{r,r}^{\mathrm{T}}(t_i)\right]^{\mathrm{T}} + \varrho_{r,r}(t_i) \end{aligned} \tag{2.26}$$

where $\varepsilon_r(t_i)$ is the innovation sequence with covariance

$$\Omega_r(t_i) \triangleq \mathbf{E}\left\{\varepsilon_r(t_i)\varepsilon_r^{\mathrm{T}}(t_i)\right\}$$

$K_r(t_i)$ and $F_r(t_i)$ are gain matrices of the filter and the one-step predictor, respectively; $P_{r,r}(t_i|t_i)$ and $P_{r,r}(t_i|t_{i-1})$ are the covariance matrices of the filtering error and the prediction error, respectively; and the initial values of $\hat{\xi}_r(t_i|t_{i-1})$ and $P_{r,r}(t_i|t_{i-1})$ at t_0 are given, respectively, by

$$\hat{\xi}_r(t_0|t_{-1}) = \begin{bmatrix}\eta_0 \\ 0\end{bmatrix}$$

$$P_{r,r}(t_0|t_{-1}) = \begin{bmatrix}\Lambda_P & O_1 \\ O_1^{\mathrm{T}} & O_2\end{bmatrix}$$

$$\Lambda_P = \mathrm{diag}\left\{\bar{P}_0, \bar{P}_1, \ldots, \bar{P}_{b-1}\right\}$$

$$\eta_0 \triangleq \mathbf{E}\{\eta(t_0)\} = \left[\bar{x}_0^{\mathrm{T}}\ \bar{x}_1^{\mathrm{T}}\ \ldots\ \bar{x}_{b-1}^{\mathrm{T}}\right]^{\mathrm{T}}$$

and

$$\begin{aligned}\varphi_{r,r}(t_i) &= \sum_{l\in\mathcal{N}_r} \theta_{l,r}\Pi_{l,r}H_r Q_{\upsilon_r} H_r^{\mathrm{T}} \Pi_{l,r}^{\mathrm{T}} F_r^{\mathrm{T}}(t_i) \\ &\quad + \sum_{l\in\mathcal{N}_r}\sum_{j\in\mathcal{N}_r, j\neq l} \theta_{l,r}\theta_{j,r}\Pi_{l,r}H_r Q_{\upsilon_r} H_r^{\mathrm{T}} \Pi_{j,r}^{\mathrm{T}} F_r^{\mathrm{T}}(t_i) \\ \varrho_{r,r}(t_i) &= \sum_{l\in\mathcal{N}_r} \theta_{l,r} F_r(t_i)\Pi_{l,r}H_r Q_{\upsilon_r} H_r^{\mathrm{T}} \Pi_{l,r}^{\mathrm{T}} F_r^{\mathrm{T}}(t_i) \\ &\quad + \sum_{l\in\mathcal{N}_r}\sum_{j\in\mathcal{N}_r, j\neq l} \theta_{l,r}\theta_{j,r} F_r(t_i)\Pi_{l,r}H_r Q_{\upsilon_r} H_r^{\mathrm{T}} \Pi_{j,r}^{\mathrm{T}} F_r^{\mathrm{T}}(t_i)\end{aligned}$$

Proof The innovation $\varepsilon_r(t_i)$ is defined as

$$\varepsilon_r(t_i) \triangleq Z_r(t_i) - \hat{Z}_r(t_i|t_{i-1}) \tag{2.27}$$

Taking projection of both sides of the output equation in (2.11) onto the linear space $L(Z_r(t_0), Z_r(t_1)\ , \ldots, Z_r(t_{i-1}))$ yields

$$\begin{aligned}\hat{Z}_r(t_i|t_{i-1}) &= \bar{C}_r\hat{\xi}_r(t_i|t_{i-1}) + \left(\sum_{l\in\mathcal{N}_r}\theta_{l,r}\Pi_{l,r}H_r\right) \\ &\quad \times \mathrm{proj}\{\upsilon_r(t_i)|Z_r(t_0), Z_r(t_1), \ldots, Z_r(t_{i-1})\}\end{aligned} \tag{2.28}$$

Define a set $\vartheta_r(t_i) \triangleq \bigcup_{l\in\mathcal{N}_r}\beta_{l,r}(t_i)$, where

$$\beta_{l,r}(t_i) = \{\alpha_{l,r}(t_0), \alpha_{l,r}(t_1), \ldots, \alpha_{l,r}(t_i)\}$$

Then, one has by (2.11) that

$$Z_r(t_i) \in L(\upsilon_r(t_i), \nu_r(t_{i-1}), \ldots, \nu_r(t_0), \xi_r(t_0))_{\vartheta_r(t_i)} \tag{2.29}$$

where $L(\cdot)_{\vartheta_r(t_i)}$ denotes that the linear space $L(\cdot)$ is dependent on the stochastic parameters in the set $\vartheta_r(t_i)$. It follows from (2.29) that

$$\begin{aligned}L(Z_r(t_0), Z_r(t_1), \ldots, Z_r(t_{i-1})) &\subset L(\upsilon_r(t_{i-1}), \ldots, \\ &\quad \upsilon_r(t_0), \nu_r(t_{i-2}), \ldots, \nu_r(t_0), \xi_r(t_0))_{\vartheta_r(t_{i-1})}\end{aligned} \tag{2.30}$$

Since $\upsilon_r(t_i)\perp L(\upsilon_r(t_{i-1}), \ldots, \upsilon_r(t_0), \nu_r(t_{i-2}), \ldots, \nu_r(t_0),\ \xi_r(t_0))_{\vartheta_r(t_{i-1})}$, it follows from (2.30) that

$$\upsilon_r(t_i)\perp L(Z_r(t_0), Z_r(t_1), \ldots, Z_r(t_{i-1})) \tag{2.31}$$

Since $\mathbf{E}\{\upsilon_r(t_i)\} = 0$, (2.31) implies that

$$\text{proj}\{\upsilon_r(t_i)|Z_r(t_0), Z_r(t_1), \ldots, Z_r(t_{i-1})\} = 0$$

which together with (2.28) and (2.27) yields (2.19).

By projection [15], one has the following equations for determining the filtered estimate $\hat{\xi}_r(t_i|t_i)$:

$$\hat{\xi}_r(t_i|t_i) = \hat{\xi}_r(t_i|t_{i-1}) + K_r(t_i)\varepsilon_r(t_i) \tag{2.32}$$

$$K_r(t_i) = \mathbf{E}\left\{\xi_r(t_i)\varepsilon_r^{\mathrm{T}}(t_i)\right\}\Omega_r^{-1}(t_i) \tag{2.33}$$

Notice that (2.32) is just the equation in (2.23). Define the prediction error as $\tilde{\xi}_r(t_i|t_{i-1}) = \xi_r(t_i) - \hat{\xi}_r(t_i|t_{i-1})$ and then substituting $Z_r(t_i)$ in (2.11) into (2.19) leads to

$$\varepsilon_r(t_i) = \left(\tilde{C}_r(t_i) - \bar{C}_r\right)\xi_r(t_i) + \bar{C}_r\tilde{\xi}_r(t_i|t_{i-1}) + \tilde{\upsilon}_r(t_i) \tag{2.34}$$

Since $\xi_r(t_i)\perp\upsilon_r(t_i)$, $\tilde{\xi}_r(t_i|t_{i-1})\perp\upsilon_r(t_i)$ and $\mathbf{E}\{\tilde{C}_r(t_i) - \bar{C}_r\} = 0$, one has by (2.34) that

$$\begin{aligned}\Omega_r(t_i) = {} & \mathbf{E}\left\{\left(\tilde{C}_r(t_i) - \bar{C}_r\right)\xi_r(t_i)\xi_r^{\mathrm{T}}(t_i)\left(\tilde{C}_r(t_i) - \bar{C}_r\right)^{\mathrm{T}}\right\} \\ & +\mathbf{E}\left\{\bar{C}_r\tilde{\xi}_r(t_i|t_{i-1})\tilde{\xi}_r^{\mathrm{T}}(t_i|t_{i-1})\bar{C}_r^{\mathrm{T}}\right\} \\ & +\mathbf{E}\left\{\tilde{\upsilon}_r(t_i)\tilde{\upsilon}_r^{\mathrm{T}}(t_i)\right\}\end{aligned} \tag{2.35}$$

By (2.12) and Lemma 2.1, and following the similar derivation procedures as in (2.17), one obtains

$$\begin{aligned}& \mathbf{E}\left\{\left(\tilde{C}_r(t_i) - \bar{C}_r\right)\xi_r(t_i)\xi_r^{\mathrm{T}}(t_i)\left(\tilde{C}_r(t_i) - \bar{C}_r\right)^{\mathrm{T}}\right\} \\ & \quad = \sum_{l\in\mathcal{N}_r}\theta_{l,r}(1-\theta_{l,r})C_{0l,r}\Xi_{r,r}(t_i)C_{0l,r}^{\mathrm{T}}\end{aligned} \tag{2.36}$$

Then, (2.20) follows from (2.35), (2.36) and Lemma 2.2. Substituting (2.34) into (2.33) and taking the facts

$$\mathbf{E}\left\{\tilde{C}_r(t_i) - \bar{C}_r\right\} = 0,\ \xi_r(t_i)\perp\upsilon_r(t_i),\ \hat{\xi}_r(t_i|t_{i-1})\perp\tilde{\xi}_r(t_i|t_{i-1})$$

into account yield

$$
\begin{aligned}
K_r(t_i) &= \mathbf{E}\left\{\xi_r(t_i)\tilde{\xi}_r(t_i|t_{i-1})\bar{C}_r^{\mathrm{T}}\right\}\Omega_r^{-1}(t_i) \\
&= \mathbf{E}\left\{\left(\hat{\xi}_r(t_i|t_{i-1})+\tilde{\xi}_r(t_i|t_{i-1})\right)\tilde{\xi}_r(t_i|t_{i-1})\bar{C}_r^{\mathrm{T}}\right\}\Omega_r^{-1}(t_i) \\
&= P_{r,r}(t_i|t_{i-1})\bar{C}_r^{\mathrm{T}}\Omega_r^{-1}(t_i)
\end{aligned} \tag{2.37}
$$

By projection [15], one has the following equations for determining the one-step predicted estimate $\hat{\xi}_r(t_{i+1}|t_i)$:

$$
\hat{\xi}_r(t_{i+1}|t_i) = \hat{\xi}_r(t_{i+1}|t_{i-1}) + F_r(t_i)\varepsilon_r(t_i) \tag{2.38}
$$

$$
F_r(t_i) = \mathbf{E}\left\{\xi_r(t_{i+1})\varepsilon_r^{\mathrm{T}}(t_i)\right\}\Omega_r^{-1}(t_i) \tag{2.39}
$$

Taking both sides of the state equation in (2.11) onto the space $L(Z_r(t_0), Z_r(t_1), \ldots, Z_r(t_{i-1}))$ yields

$$
\begin{aligned}
\hat{\xi}_r(t_{i+1}|t_{i-1}) = \bar{A}_r\hat{\xi}_r(t_i|t_{i-1}) + \bar{B}_r \\
\times \mathrm{proj}\{\nu_r(t_i)|Z_r(t_0), Z_r(t_1), \ldots, Z_r(t_{i-1})\}
\end{aligned} \tag{2.40}
$$

It follows from (2.30) that $\nu_r(t_i) \perp L(Z_r(t_0), Z_r(t_1), \ldots, Z_r(t_{i-1}))$, which together with the fact $\mathbf{E}\{\nu_r(t_i)\} = 0$ leads to

$$
\mathrm{proj}\{\nu_r(t_i)|Z_r(t_0), Z_r(t_1), \ldots, Z_r(t_{i-1})\} = 0 \tag{2.41}
$$

Combining (2.38), (2.40), and (2.41) yields (2.24). Substituting the state equation in (2.11) into (2.39) yields

$$
\begin{aligned}
F_r(t_i) = &\ \mathbf{E}\left\{\tilde{A}_r(t_i)\xi_r(t_i)\varepsilon_r^{\mathrm{T}}(t_i)\right\}\Omega_r^{-1}(t_i) \\
&+ \mathbf{E}\left\{\tilde{B}_r(t_i)\nu_r(t_i)\varepsilon_r^{\mathrm{T}}(t_i)\right\}\Omega_r^{-1}(t_i)
\end{aligned} \tag{2.42}
$$

Substitute (2.34) into (2.42), and then one obtains by (2.12), Lemma 2.1, and $\xi_r(t_i) \perp \nu_r(t_i)$, $\hat{\xi}_r(t_i|t_{i-1}) \perp \tilde{\xi}_r(t_i|t_{i-1})$ and $\mathbf{E}\{\alpha_{l,r}(t_i) - \theta_{l,r}\} = 0$ that

$$
\begin{aligned}
&\mathbf{E}\left\{\tilde{A}_r(t_i)\xi_r(t_i)\varepsilon_r^{\mathrm{T}}(t_i)\right\} \\
&= \mathbf{E}\left\{\tilde{A}_r(t_i)\xi_r(t_i)\xi_r^{\mathrm{T}}(t_i)\left(\tilde{C}_r(t_i)-\bar{C}_r\right)^{\mathrm{T}} + \tilde{A}_r(t_i)\xi_r(t_i)\tilde{\xi}_r^{\mathrm{T}}(t_i|t_{i-1})\bar{C}_r^{\mathrm{T}}\right\} \\
&= \mathbf{E}\left\{\left[\bar{A}_r + \sum_{l\in\mathcal{N}_r}(\alpha_{l,r}(t_i)-\theta_{l,r})A_{0l,r}\right]\xi_r(t_i)\xi_r^{\mathrm{T}}(t_i)\right.
\end{aligned}
$$

$$
\begin{aligned}
&\times\left.\left(\sum_{l\in\mathcal{N}_r}(\alpha_{l,r}(t_i)-\theta_{l,r})C_{0l,r}\right)^{\mathrm{T}}\right\}\\
&+\mathbf{E}\left\{\tilde{A}_r(t_i)(\hat{\xi}_r^{\mathrm{T}}(t_i|t_{i-1})+\tilde{\xi}_r^{\mathrm{T}}(t_i|t_{i-1}))\tilde{\xi}_r^{\mathrm{T}}(t_i|t_{i-1})\bar{C}_r^{\mathrm{T}}\right\}\\
&=\sum_{l\in\mathcal{N}_r}\theta_{l,r}(1-\theta_{l,r})A_{0l,r}\Xi_{r,r}(t_i)C_{0l,r}^{\mathrm{T}}+\bar{A}_rP_{r,r}(t_i|t_{i-1})\bar{C}_r^{\mathrm{T}}
\end{aligned}\tag{2.43}
$$

Since $\xi_r(t_i)\perp\nu_r(t_i)$, $\tilde{\xi}_r(t_i|t_{i-1})\perp\nu_r(t_i)$, and $\omega_m(t_i)\perp\upsilon_r(t_i)$, one has by Lemma 2.2 that

$$
\mathbf{E}\left\{\tilde{B}_r(t_i)\nu_r(t_i)\varepsilon_r^{\mathrm{T}}(t_i)\right\}=\begin{bmatrix}0 & \Delta_{r,r}^{\mathrm{T}}\end{bmatrix}^{\mathrm{T}}\tag{2.44}
$$

Combining (2.42), (2.43) and (2.44) leads to (2.22).

Derivation procedures for the covariance matrices $P_{r,r}(t_{i+1}|t_i)$ and $P_{r,r}(t_i|t_i)$ are presented as follows. Substituting (2.24) and the state equation in (2.11) into the right-hand side of the equation $\tilde{\xi}_r(t_{i+1}|t_i)=\xi_r(t_{i+1})-\hat{\xi}_r(t_{i+1}|t_i)$, one has by (2.12) and (2.34) that

$$
\begin{aligned}
\tilde{\xi}_r(t_{i+1}|t_i)&=\left[\bar{A}_r+\sum_{l\in\mathcal{N}_r}(\alpha_{l,r}(t_i)-\theta_{l,r})A_{0l,r}\right]\xi_r(t_i)\\
&\quad-\bar{A}_r\hat{\xi}_r(t_i|t_{i-1})+\tilde{B}_r(t_i)\nu_r(t_i)-F_r(t_i)\varepsilon_r(t_i)\\
&=\bar{A}_r\tilde{\xi}_r(t_i|t_{i-1})+\left[\sum_{l\in\mathcal{N}_r}(\alpha_{l,r}(t_i)-\theta_{l,r})A_{0l,r}\right.\\
&\quad\left.-F_r(t_i)\sum_{l\in\mathcal{N}_r}(\alpha_{l,r}(t_i)-\theta_{l,r})C_{0l,r}\right]\xi_r(t_i)\\
&\quad+\tilde{B}_r(t_i)\nu_r(t_i)-F_r(t_i)\bar{C}_r\tilde{\xi}_r(t_i|t_{i-1})\\
&\quad-F_r(t_i)\sum_{l\in\mathcal{N}_r}\alpha_{l,r}(t_i)\Pi_{l,r}H_r\upsilon_r(t_i)\\
&=\sum_{l\in\mathcal{N}_r}(\alpha_{l,r}(t_i)-\theta_{l,r})(A_{0l,r}-F_r(t_i)C_{0l,r})\xi_r(t_i)\\
&\quad+\left(\bar{A}_r-F_r(t_i)\bar{C}_r\right)\tilde{\xi}_r(t_i|t_{i-1})+\tilde{B}_r(t_i)\nu_r(t_i)\\
&\quad-\sum_{l\in\mathcal{N}_r}\alpha_{l,r}(t_i)F_r(t_i)\Pi_{l,r}H_r\upsilon_r(t_i)
\end{aligned}\tag{2.45}
$$

Since $\xi_r(t_i)\perp\nu_r(t_i)$, $\xi_r(t_i)\perp\upsilon_r(t_i)$, $\tilde{\xi}_r(t_i|t_{i-1})\perp\nu_r(t_i)$, $\tilde{\xi}_r(t_i|t_{i-1})\perp\upsilon_r(t_i)$, and $\mathbf{E}\{\alpha_{l,r}(t_i)-\theta_{l,r}\}=0$, one has by Lemma 2.1 and (2.18) and following the similar derivation procedures as in (2.17) that

$$
\begin{aligned}
&P_{r,r}(t_{i+1}|t_i)\\
&=\mathbf{E}\left\{\tilde{\xi}_r(t_{i+1}|t_i)\tilde{\xi}_r^{\mathrm{T}}(t_{i+1}|t_i)\right\}\\
&=\sum_{l\in\mathcal{N}_r}\theta_{l,r}(1-\theta_{l,r})(A_{0l,r}-F_r(t_i)C_{0l,r})\Xi_{r,r}(t_i)(A_{0l,r}-F_r(t_i)C_{0l,r})^{\mathrm{T}}\\
&\quad+\left(\bar{A}_r-F_r(t_i)\bar{C}_r\right)P_{r,r}(t_i|t_{i-1})\left(\bar{A}_r-F_r(t_i)\bar{C}_r\right)^{\mathrm{T}}\\
&\quad-\mathbf{E}\left\{\tilde{B}_r(t_i)\nu_r(t_i)\sigma_r^{\mathrm{T}}(t_i)\right\}\\
&\quad-\mathbf{E}\left\{\sigma_r(t_i)\left(\tilde{B}_r(t_i)\nu_r(t_i)\right)^{\mathrm{T}}\right\}\\
&\quad+\mathrm{diag}\left\{BQ_\omega B^{\mathrm{T}},\ \Delta_{r,r}\right\}\\
&\quad+\mathbf{E}\left\{\sigma_r(t_i)\sigma_r^{\mathrm{T}}(t_i)\right\}
\end{aligned}
\tag{2.46}
$$

where $\sigma_r(t_i)=\sum_{l\in\mathcal{N}_r}\alpha_{l,r}(t_i)F_r(t_i)\Pi_{l,r}H_r\upsilon_r(t_i)$. By following the similar derivation procedures as in (2.44), one obtains

$$
\mathbf{E}\left\{\tilde{B}_r(t_i)\nu_r(t_i)\sigma_r^{\mathrm{T}}(t_i)\right\}=\left[0\ \ \varphi_{r,r}^{\mathrm{T}}(t_i)\right]^{\mathrm{T}} \tag{2.47}
$$

Moreover, it follows from Lemma 2.1 that

$$
\mathbf{E}\left\{\sigma_r(t_i)\sigma_r^{\mathrm{T}}(t_i)\right\}=\varrho_{r,r}(t_i) \tag{2.48}
$$

Combining (2.46), (2.47), and (2.48) leads to (2.26).

Substituting (2.23) into the right-hand side of the equation $\tilde{\xi}_r(t_i|t_i)\triangleq\xi_r(t_i)-\hat{\xi}_r(t_i|t_i)$ yields

$$
\tilde{\xi}_r(t_i|t_i)=\tilde{\xi}_r(t_i|t_{i-1})-K_r(t_i)\varepsilon_r(t_i) \tag{2.49}
$$

Let $\Phi(t_i)=\mathbf{E}\{\tilde{\xi}_r(t_i|t_{i-1})\varepsilon_r^{\mathrm{T}}(t_i)\}$, and then it follows from (2.49) that

$$
\begin{aligned}
P_{r,r}(t_i|t_i)&=\mathbf{E}\left\{\tilde{\xi}_r(t_i|t_i)\tilde{\xi}_r^{\mathrm{T}}(t_i|t_i)\right\}\\
&=P_{r,r}(t_i|t_{i-1})-K_r(t_i)\Phi^{\mathrm{T}}(t_i)-\Phi(t_i)K_r^{\mathrm{T}}(t_i)\\
&\quad+K_r(t_i)\Omega_r(t_i)K_r^{\mathrm{T}}(t_i)
\end{aligned}
\tag{2.50}
$$

Since $\hat{\xi}_r(t_i|t_{i-1}) \perp \varepsilon_r(t_i)$, one has by (2.33) that

$$\begin{aligned}\Phi(t_i) &= \mathbf{E}\left\{\left(\xi_r(t_i) - \hat{\xi}_r(t_i|t_{i-1})\right)\varepsilon_r^{\mathrm{T}}(t_i)\right\} \\ &= \mathbf{E}\left\{\xi_r(t_i)\varepsilon_r^{\mathrm{T}}(t_i)\right\} \\ &= K_r(t_i)\Omega_r(t_i)\end{aligned} \tag{2.51}$$

Substituting (2.51) into (2.50) leads to (2.25). The proof is thus completed.

Theorem 2.1 provides a set of recursive equations for designing the finite-horizon local Kalman filters as a by-product; the local one-step predictor is also given. Denote $\hat{\eta}_r(t_{i+k}|t_i)$ and $P^{\eta}_{r,r}(t_{i+k}|t_i)$ $(k = 0, 1)$, respectively, the estimate of the system state $\eta(t_i)$ and the corresponding error covariance generated at sensor r. Then, $\hat{\eta}_r(t_{i+k}|t_i)$ and $P^{\eta}_{r,r}(t_{i+k}|t_i)$ are given by

$$\begin{aligned}\hat{\eta}_r(t_{i+k}|t_i) &= [I_{bn} \ \ O_1]\hat{\xi}_r(t_{i+k}|t_i) \\ P^{\eta}_{r,r}(t_{i+k}|t_i) &= [I_{bn} \ \ O_1]P_{r,r}(t_{i+k}|t_i)[I_{bn} \ \ O_1]^{\mathrm{T}}\end{aligned}$$

where $I_{bn} \in \Re^{bn \times bn}$ is an identity matrix.

In Theorem 2.1, every sensor r in the WSN generates local estimates by using measurements only from its neighbors. Each local estimate thus obtained is suboptimal in the sense that not all the measurements in the WSN are used. Moreover, there may exist disagreements among local estimates at different sensors. Similar to [13], one may define some *disagreement potentials* as follows to characterize the disagreement of local estimates in the neighborhood $\mathcal{N}_r$ $(r \in Z_0)$:

$$\kappa_r(t_i) = \frac{1}{2n_r}\sum_{u,s\in\mathcal{N}_r} \|\hat{\eta}_u(t_{i+k}|t_i) - \hat{\eta}_s(t_{i+k}|t_i)\|^2 \tag{2.52}$$

$$\psi_r(t_i) = \frac{1}{2n_r}\sum_{u,s\in\mathcal{N}_r} \left[\mathrm{Tr}(P^{\eta}_{u,u}(t_{i+k}|t_i)) - \mathrm{Tr}(P^{\eta}_{s,s}(t_{i+k}|t_i))\right]^2 \tag{2.53}$$

where $k = 0, 1$, and $\kappa_r(t_i)$ and $\psi_r(t_i)$ are the *disagreement potential* of estimates and the *disagreement potential* of estimation performances, respectively. Notice that at each time step, not only a measurement but also a local estimate is available at each sensor. Therefore, one efficient way to improve each local estimation performance and reduce the disagreement is to further collect local estimates available at neighboring sensors and then generate a fused estimate at every sensor in the WSN. This gives rise to the two-stage estimation strategy. Different from the approach in [16] where a fusion rule with scalar weights is used, a fusion criterion weighted by matrices in the linear minimum variance sense will be used in this chapter to generate fused estimates, and the main results will be presented in the following subsection.

2.3.2 Distributed Fusion Estimation

In this subsection, a fusion criterion weighted by matrices in the linear minimum variance sense is applied to generate fusion estimates for every sensor r, $r \in Z_0$, and the criterion is first given in the following lemma.

Lemma 2.4 ([17]) *Let $\hat{x}_i$, $i \in \bar{Z} \triangleq \{1, 2, \ldots, m\}$ be unbiased estimates of a stochastic state vector $x \in \Re^n$. Let the estimation errors be $\tilde{x}_i = x_i - \hat{x}_i$. Assume that $\tilde{x}_i$ and $\tilde{x}_j$, $i \neq j$ are correlated, and define the covariance and cross-covariance matrices as $P_{ii} = \mathbf{E}\{\tilde{x}_i\tilde{x}_i^{\mathrm{T}}\}$ and $P_{ij} = \mathbf{E}\{\tilde{x}_i\tilde{x}_j^{\mathrm{T}}\}$ $(i \neq j)$, respectively. Then, the optimal fusion estimate of x with matrix weights is given by*

$$\hat{x}_o = \sum_{i=1}^{m} A_{oi}\hat{x}_i \tag{2.54}$$

where the optimal matrix weights A_{oi}, $i \in \bar{Z}$ are computed by

$$\mathrm{col}\left\{A_{oi}^{\mathrm{T}}\right\}_{i\in\bar{Z}} = \Psi^{-1}e\left(e^{\mathrm{T}}\Psi^{-1}e\right)^{-1}$$

$\Psi = [P_{ij}]$, $i, j \in \bar{Z}$ is an $nm \times nm$ symmetric positive-definite matrix, and $e = [\underbrace{I_n, \ldots, I_n}_{m}]^{\mathrm{T}}$, $I_n \in \Re^{n\times n}$ is an identity matrix. The corresponding covariance matrix of the fused estimation error is computed by $P_o = (e^{\mathrm{T}}\Psi^{-1}e)^{-1}$, and one has that $P_o \leq P_{ii}$, $i \in \bar{Z}$.

When local estimates calculated by the estimators in Theorem 2.1 are available at the sensors in the WSN, every sensor r, $r \in Z_0$ then collects them from its neighborhood $\mathcal{N}_r$ to generate a fused estimate according to the fusion rule in Lemma 2.4. Note that the links in the WSN are subject to packet losses, local estimates $\hat{\xi}_l$, $l \in \mathcal{N}_r$ may be lost during the transmission, and thus only the estimates that successfully arrive at the sensor r are used to generate the fused estimate $\hat{\eta}_{or}$ of the system state η. Let $\bar{\mathcal{N}}_r(t_i)$ denote the index set of the estimates $\hat{\xi}_l$ that are successfully received by sensor r at instant t_i and $\bar{n}_r(t_i)$ denote the number of elements in $\bar{\mathcal{N}}_r(t_i)$. Then, by Lemma 2.4, one has the following theorem that determines the fused estimates and the corresponding covariance matrix of the estimation error at sensor r, $r \in Z_0$:

Theorem 2.2 *For system (2.11), the fusion estimator in the sensor r, $r \in Z_0$ is given by*

$$\hat{\eta}_{or}(t_{i+k}|t_i) = \sum_{u\in\bar{\mathcal{N}}_r(t_i)} \bar{A}_{ou,k}(t_i)\hat{\eta}_u(t_{i+k}|t_i),\ k = 0, 1 \tag{2.55}$$

where

$$\hat{\eta}_u(t_{i+k}|t_i) = [I_{bn} \;\; O_1]\hat{\xi}_u(t_{i+k}|t_i)$$

and the optimal matrix weights $\bar{A}_{ou,k}(t_i)$, $u \in \bar{\mathcal{N}}_r(t_i)$ *are computed by*

$$\begin{aligned}&\text{col}\left\{\bar{A}^{\mathrm{T}}_{ou,k}(t_i)\right\}_{u\in\bar{\mathcal{N}}_r(t_i)}\\&= \Upsilon^{-1}_{r,k}(t_i)e_r(t_i)\left(e^{\mathrm{T}}_r(t_i)\Upsilon^{-1}_{r,k}(t_i)e_r(t_i)\right)^{-1},\; k=0,1\end{aligned} \tag{2.56}$$

where $\Upsilon_{r,k}(t_i) = [P^{\eta}_{u,s}(t_{i+k}|t_i)]$, $u, s \in \bar{\mathcal{N}}_r(t_i)$ *is an* $bn\bar{n}_r(t_i) \times bn\bar{n}_r(t_i)$ *symmetric positive-definite matrix, and*

$$\begin{aligned}P^{\eta}_{u,s}(t_{i+k}|t_i) &= [I_{bn} \;\; O_1]P_{u,s}(t_{i+k}|t_i)[I_{bn} \;\; O_1]^{\mathrm{T}}\\ e_r(t_i) &= [\underbrace{I_{bn}, \ldots, I_{bn}}_{\bar{n}_r(t_i)}]^{\mathrm{T}}\end{aligned}$$

The corresponding covariance matrix of the fusion estimation error is computed by $P^{\eta}_{or}(t_{i+k}|t_i) = (e^{\mathrm{T}}_r(t_i)\Upsilon^{-1}_{r,k}(t_i)e_r(t_i))^{-1}$, *and one has that* $P^{\eta}_{or}(t_{i+k}|t_i) \le P^{\eta}_{u,u}(t_{i+k}|t_i)$, $u \in \bar{\mathcal{N}}_r(t_i)$. *The estimates* $\hat{\xi}_u(t_{i+k}|t_i)$ *and the covariance matrices* $P_{u,u}(t_{i+k}|t_i)$ *are computed by the recursive equations in Theorem 2.1.*

Proof Theorem 2.2 follows directly from Lemma 2.4.

It can be seen from (2.56) that computation of the cross-covariance matrices $P_{u,s}(t_{i+k}|t_i)$, $k = 0, 1$, $u, s \in \bar{\mathcal{N}}_r(t_i)$, $u \ne s$ is one of the key issues in applying the fusion estimator in Theorem 2.2. In what follows, computation procedures for the cross-covariances $P_{u,s}(t_{i+k}|t_i)$ will be presented, but before which, some useful lemmas are first given as follows:

Lemma 2.5 *For any two augmented measurement noise vectors* $\upsilon_u(t_i)$ *and* $\upsilon_s(t_i)$, $u, s \in \mathcal{N}_r$, $u \ne s$, *define* $Q_{\upsilon_u\upsilon_s} = \mathbf{E}\{\upsilon_u(t_i)\upsilon^{\mathrm{T}}_s(t_i)\}$. *Then, one has*

$$Q_{\upsilon_u\upsilon_s} = [\zeta_{l,j}], l \in \mathcal{N}_u, j \in \mathcal{N}_s \tag{2.57}$$

where $\zeta_{l,j} = \begin{cases} Q^{\upsilon_p}_{l,l}, & l, j \in \mathcal{N}_{u,s},\; l = j \\ Q^{\upsilon_p}_{l,j}, & \textit{otherwise}\end{cases}$ *and* $\mathcal{N}_{u,s} = \mathcal{N}_u \cap \mathcal{N}_s$.

Lemma 2.6 *For* $u, s \in \mathcal{N}_r$ *and* $u \ne s$, $\mathbf{E}\left\{\tilde{\upsilon}_u(t_i)\tilde{\upsilon}^{\mathrm{T}}_s(t_i)\right\}$ *satisfies*

$$\begin{aligned}\mathbf{E}\left\{\tilde{\upsilon}_u(t_i)\tilde{\upsilon}^{\mathrm{T}}_s(t_i)\right\} &\triangleq \Delta_{u,s}\\ &= \theta_{s,u}(1-\theta_{s,u})\Pi_{s,u}H_uQ_{\upsilon_u\upsilon_s}H^{\mathrm{T}}_s\Pi^{\mathrm{T}}_{u,s}\\ &\quad + \sum_{l\in\mathcal{N}_u}\sum_{j\in\mathcal{N}_s}\theta_{l,u}\theta_{j,s}\Pi_{l,u}H_uQ_{\upsilon_u\upsilon_s}H^{\mathrm{T}}_s\Pi^{\mathrm{T}}_{j,s}\end{aligned} \tag{2.58}$$

Proof Since $u \in \mathcal{N}_r$ and $s \in \mathcal{N}_r$, i.e., sensor u and sensor s are neighbors, one has $u \in \mathcal{N}_s$ and $s \in \mathcal{N}_u$. Moreover, by the facts $\alpha_{s,u}(t_i) = \alpha_{u,s}(t_i)$ and $\theta_{s,u} = \theta_{u,s}$, one has by Lemma 2.1 that

$$
\begin{aligned}
\mathbf{E}\left\{\tilde{\upsilon}_u(t_i)\tilde{\upsilon}_s^{\mathrm{T}}(t_i)\right\} &= \mathbf{E}\left\{\left(\sum_{l\in\mathcal{N}_u}\alpha_{l,u}(t_i)\Pi_{l,u}H_u\upsilon_u(t_i)\right)\right.\\
&\qquad\left.\times\left(\sum_{j\in\mathcal{N}_s}\alpha_{j,s}(t_i)\Pi_{j,s}H_s\upsilon_s(t_i)\right)^{\mathrm{T}}\right\}\\
&= \mathbf{E}\left\{\left(\sum_{l\in\mathcal{N}_u}\alpha_{l,u}(t_i)\Pi_{l,u}H_u\upsilon_u(t_i)\right)\right.\\
&\qquad\left.\times\left(\alpha_{u,s}(t_i)\Pi_{u,s}H_s\upsilon_s(t_i)\right)^{\mathrm{T}}\right\}\\
&\quad+\mathbf{E}\left\{\sum_{l\in\mathcal{N}_u}\sum_{j\in\mathcal{N}_s,j\neq u}\alpha_{l,u}(t_i)\alpha_{j,s}(t_i)\Pi_{l,u}H_u\upsilon_u(t_i)\upsilon_s^{\mathrm{T}}(t_i)H_s^{\mathrm{T}}\Pi_{j,s}^{\mathrm{T}}\right\}\\
&= \sum_{l\in\mathcal{N}_u,l\neq s}\theta_{l,u}\theta_{u,s}\Pi_{l,u}H_uQ_{\upsilon_u\upsilon_s}H_s^{\mathrm{T}}\Pi_{u,s}^{\mathrm{T}}\\
&\quad+\theta_{s,u}\Pi_{s,u}H_uQ_{\upsilon_u\upsilon_s}H_s^{\mathrm{T}}\Pi_{u,s}^{\mathrm{T}}\\
&\quad+\sum_{l\in\mathcal{N}_u}\sum_{j\in\mathcal{N}_s,j\neq u}\theta_{l,u}\theta_{j,s}\Pi_{l,u}H_uQ_{\upsilon_u\upsilon_s}H_s^{\mathrm{T}}\Pi_{j,s}^{\mathrm{T}}\\
&= \theta_{s,u}(1-\theta_{s,u})\Pi_{s,u}H_uQ_{\upsilon_u\upsilon_s}H_s^{\mathrm{T}}\Pi_{u,s}^{\mathrm{T}}\\
&\quad+\sum_{l\in\mathcal{N}_u}\theta_{l,u}\theta_{u,s}\Pi_{l,u}H_uQ_{\upsilon_u\upsilon_s}H_s^{\mathrm{T}}\Pi_{u,s}^{\mathrm{T}}\\
&\quad+\sum_{l\in\mathcal{N}_u}\sum_{j\in\mathcal{N}_s,j\neq u}\theta_{l,u}\theta_{j,s}\Pi_{l,u}H_uQ_{\upsilon_u\upsilon_s}H_s^{\mathrm{T}}\Pi_{j,s}^{\mathrm{T}}\\
&= \Delta_{u,s}
\end{aligned}
\tag{2.59}
$$

The proof is thus completed.

Lemma 2.7 *Define the state cross-covariance matrix as*

$$
\Xi_{u,s}(t_i) \triangleq \mathbf{E}\left\{\xi_u(t_i)\xi_s^{\mathrm{T}}(t_i)\right\}
$$

where $u, s \in \mathcal{N}_r$ and $u \neq s$. Then $\Xi_{u,s}(t_i)$ satisfies the following recursion:

$$\begin{aligned}\Xi_{u,s}(t_{i+1}) &= \theta_{s,u}(1-\theta_{s,u})A_{0s,u}\Xi_{u,s}(t_i)A_{0u,s}^{\mathrm{T}} \\ &\quad +\bar{A}_u\Xi_{u,s}(t_i)\bar{A}_s^{\mathrm{T}} + \mathrm{diag}\{BQ_\omega B^{\mathrm{T}},\ \Delta_{u,s}\}\end{aligned} \tag{2.60}$$

where the initial value of $\Xi_{u,s}(t_i)$ at t_0 is given by $\Xi_{u,s}(t_0) = \Xi_{u,u}(t_0)$.

Proof It follows from (2.15) that

$$\Xi_{u,s}(t_{i+1}) = \mathbf{E}\left\{\xi_u(t_{i+1})\xi_s^{\mathrm{T}}(t_{i+1})\right\} = \bar{A}_u\Xi_{u,s}(t_i)\bar{A}_s^{\mathrm{T}} + \chi_1 + \chi_2 \tag{2.61}$$

where

$$\begin{aligned}\chi_1 &= \mathbf{E}\left\{\left(\tilde{A}_u(t_i) - \bar{A}_u\right)\xi_u(t_i)\xi_s^{\mathrm{T}}(t_i)\left(\tilde{A}_s(t_i) - \bar{A}_s\right)^{\mathrm{T}}\right\} \\ \chi_2 &= \mathbf{E}\left\{\tilde{B}_u(t_i)v_u(t_i)v_s^{\mathrm{T}}(t_i)\tilde{B}_s^{\mathrm{T}}(t_i)\right\}\end{aligned}$$

Noting $u \in \mathcal{N}_s$, $s \in \mathcal{N}_u$, and $u \neq s$, and by (2.12), Lemma 2.1, and the facts $\alpha_{s,u}(t_i) - \alpha_{u,s}(t_i)$ and $\theta_{s,u} = \theta_{u,s}$, onc obtains that

$$\begin{aligned}\chi_1 &= \mathbf{E}\left\{\left[\sum_{l\in\mathcal{N}_u}(\alpha_{l,u}(t_i) - \theta_{l,u})A_{0l,u}\right]\xi_u(t_i)\xi_s^{\mathrm{T}}(t_i)\right. \\ &\qquad \left.\times\left[\sum_{j\in\mathcal{N}_s}(\alpha_{j,s}(t_i) - \theta_{j,s})A_{0j,s}\right]^{\mathrm{T}}\right\} \\ &= \theta_{s,u}\left(1-\theta_{s,u}\right)A_{0s,u}\Xi_{u,s}(t_i)A_{0u,s}^{\mathrm{T}}\end{aligned} \tag{2.62}$$

Since $\omega_m(t_i)$ and $v_l(t_i)$, $l \in \mathcal{N}_r$ are uncorrelated, one has by Lemma 2.6 that

$$\begin{aligned}\chi_2 &= \mathbf{E}\left\{\mathrm{diag}\left\{B,\ \sum_{l\in\mathcal{N}_u}\alpha_{l,u}(t_i)\Pi_{l,u}H_u\right\}\begin{bmatrix}\omega_m(t_i)\\ v_u(t_i)\end{bmatrix}\right. \\ &\qquad \left.\times\begin{bmatrix}\omega_m(t_i)\\ v_s(t_i)\end{bmatrix}^{\mathrm{T}}\mathrm{diag}\left\{B,\ \sum_{j\in\mathcal{N}_s}\alpha_{j,s}(t_i)\Pi_{j,s}H_s\right\}^{\mathrm{T}}\right\} \\ &= \mathrm{diag}\left\{BQ_\omega B^{\mathrm{T}},\ \Delta_{u,s}\right\}\end{aligned} \tag{2.63}$$

Substituting (2.62) and (2.63) into (2.61) leads to (2.60). The proof is thus completed.

A set of equations for calculating the cross-covariances $P_{u,s}(t_{i+k}|t_i)$, $k = 0, 1$, $u, s \in \mathcal{N}_r$, $u \neq s$ are now presented in the following theorem based on Lemmas 2.5, 2.6 and 2.7.

Theorem 2.3 *For system (2.11), the cross-covariance of local Kalman estimation errors between the sensors u and s in the neighborhood $\mathcal{N}_r$, $r \in Z_0$ satisfies the following recursive equations:*

$$P_{u,s}(t_i|t_i) = \Gamma_1 + \Gamma_2 + \Gamma_3 \tag{2.64}$$

$$\begin{aligned} P_{u,s}(t_{i+1}|t_i) = {} & \Gamma_4 + \Gamma_5 + \Gamma_6 + \operatorname{diag}\left\{BQ_\omega B^{\mathrm{T}},\ \Delta_{u,s}\right\} \\ & - \left[0\ \ \varphi_{u,s}^{\mathrm{T}}(t_i)\right]^{\mathrm{T}} - [0\ \ \pi_{u,s}(t_i)] \end{aligned} \tag{2.65}$$

where

$$\begin{aligned}
\Gamma_1 &= \left(\bar{I}_u - K_u(t_i)\bar{C}_u\right) P_{u,s}(t_i|t_{i-1}) \left(\bar{I}_s - K_s(t_i)\bar{C}_s\right)^{\mathrm{T}} \\
\Gamma_2 &= \theta_{s,u}(1-\theta_{s,u})K_u(t_i)C_{0s,u}\Xi_{u,s}(t_i)C_{0u,s}^{\mathrm{T}}K_s^{\mathrm{T}}(t_i) \\
\Gamma_3 &= \theta_{s,u}(1-\theta_{s,u})K_u(t_i)\Pi_{s,u}H_uQ_{\upsilon_u\upsilon_s}H_s^{\mathrm{T}}\Pi_{u,s}^{\mathrm{T}}K_s^{\mathrm{T}}(t_i) \\
&\quad + \sum_{l\in\mathcal{N}_u}\sum_{j\in\mathcal{N}_s}\theta_{l,u}\theta_{j,s}K_u(t_i)\Pi_{l,u}H_uQ_{\upsilon_u\upsilon_s}H_s^{\mathrm{T}}\Pi_{j,s}^{\mathrm{T}}K_s^{\mathrm{T}}(t_i) \\
\Gamma_4 &= \theta_{s,u}(1-\theta_{s,u})(A_{0s,u} - F_u(t_i)C_{0s,u})\Xi_{u,s}(t_i) \\
&\quad \times (A_{0u,s} - F_s(t_i)C_{0u,s})^{\mathrm{T}} \\
\Gamma_5 &= (\bar{A}_u - F_u(t_i)\bar{C}_u)P_{u,s}(t_i|t_{i-1})(\bar{A}_s - F_s(t_i)\bar{C}_s)^{\mathrm{T}} \\
\Gamma_6 &= \theta_{s,u}(1-\theta_{s,u})F_u(t_i)\Pi_{s,u}H_uQ_{\upsilon_u\upsilon_s}H_s^{\mathrm{T}}\Pi_{u,s}^{\mathrm{T}}F_s^{\mathrm{T}}(t_i) \\
&\quad + \sum_{l\in\mathcal{N}_u}\sum_{j\in\mathcal{N}_s}\theta_{l,u}\theta_{j,s}F_u(t_i)\Pi_{l,u}H_uQ_{\upsilon_u\upsilon_s}H_s^{\mathrm{T}}\Pi_{j,s}^{\mathrm{T}}F_s^{\mathrm{T}}(t_i) \\
\varphi_{u,s}(t_i) &= \theta_{s,u}(1-\theta_{s,u})\Pi_{s,u}H_uQ_{\upsilon_u\upsilon_s}H_s^{\mathrm{T}}\Pi_{u,s}^{\mathrm{T}}F_s^{\mathrm{T}}(t_i) \\
&\quad + \sum_{l\in\mathcal{N}_u}\sum_{j\in\mathcal{N}_s}\theta_{l,u}\theta_{j,s}\Pi_{l,u}H_uQ_{\upsilon_u\upsilon_s}H_s^{\mathrm{T}}\Pi_{j,s}^{\mathrm{T}}F_s^{\mathrm{T}}(t_i) \\
\pi_{u,s}(t_i) &= \theta_{s,u}(1-\theta_{s,u})F_u(t_i)\Pi_{s,u}H_uQ_{\upsilon_u\upsilon_s}H_s^{\mathrm{T}}\Pi_{u,s}^{\mathrm{T}} \\
&\quad + \sum_{l\in\mathcal{N}_u}\sum_{j\in\mathcal{N}_s}\theta_{l,u}\theta_{j,s}F_u(t_i)\Pi_{l,u}H_uQ_{\upsilon_u\upsilon_s}H_s^{\mathrm{T}}\Pi_{j,s}^{\mathrm{T}}
\end{aligned}$$

and $\bar{I}_u \in \Re^{bn+\bar{m}_u}$ and $\bar{I}_s \in \Re^{bn+\bar{m}_s}$ are identity matrices; $Q_{\upsilon_u\upsilon_s}$ and $\Delta_{u,s}$ are given by (2.57) and (2.58), respectively; and $\Xi_{u,s}(t_i)$ is computed by (2.60), the initial value of $P_{u,s}(t_i|t_{i-1})$ at t_0 is given by $P_{u,s}(t_0|t_{-1}) = P_{u,u}(t_0|t_{-1})$.

Proof Substituting (2.19) into (2.23) yields

$$\hat{\xi}_u(t_i|t_i) = \left(\bar{I}_u - K_u(t_i)\bar{C}_u\right)\hat{\xi}_u(t_i|t_{i-1}) + K_u(t_i)Z_u(t_i),\ u \in \mathcal{N}_r \tag{2.66}$$

Substituting the output equation in (2.11) into (2.66) leads to

$$\begin{aligned}
\hat{\xi}_u(t_i|t_i) &= \left(\bar{I}_u - K_u(t_i)\bar{C}_u\right)\hat{\xi}_u(t_i|t_{i-1}) \\
&\quad + K_u(t_i)\tilde{C}_u(t_i)\xi_u(t_i) \\
&\quad + \sum_{l\in\mathcal{N}_u}\alpha_{l,u}(t_i)K_u(t_i)\Pi_{l,u}H_u\upsilon_u(t_i) \\
&= \left(\bar{I}_u - K_u(t_i)\bar{C}_u\right)\hat{\xi}_u(t_i|t_{i-1}) + K_u(t_i)\bar{C}_u\xi_u(t_i) \\
&\quad + K_u(t_i)\left(\tilde{C}_u(t_i) - \bar{C}_u\right)\xi_u(t_i) \\
&\quad + \sum_{l\in\mathcal{N}_u}\alpha_{l,u}(t_i)K_u(t_i)\Pi_{l,u}H_u\upsilon_u(t_i) \\
&= \hat{\xi}_u(t_i|t_{i-1}) + K_u(t_i)\bar{C}_u\tilde{\xi}_u(t_i|t_{i-1}) \\
&\quad + K_u(t_i)\left(\tilde{C}_u(t_i) - \bar{C}_u\right)\xi_u(t_i) \\
&\quad + \sum_{l\in\mathcal{N}_u}\alpha_{l,u}(t_i)K_u(t_i)\Pi_{l,u}H_u\upsilon_u(t_i)
\end{aligned} \tag{2.67}$$

Subtracting $\xi_u(t_i)$ from both sides of (2.67) and taking (2.12) into account yield

$$\begin{aligned}
\tilde{\xi}_u(t_i|t_i) &= \left(\bar{I}_u - K_u(t_i)\bar{C}_u\right)\tilde{\xi}_u(t_i|t_{i-1}) \\
&\quad - \sum_{l\in\mathcal{N}_u}\left(\alpha_{l,u}(t_i) - \theta_{l,u}\right)K_u(t_i)C_{0l,u}\xi_u(t_i) \\
&\quad - \sum_{l\in\mathcal{N}_u}\alpha_{l,u}(t_i)K_u(t_i)\Pi_{l,u}H_u\upsilon_u(t_i)
\end{aligned} \tag{2.68}$$

Since $\tilde{\xi}_u(t_i|t_{i-1})$ consists of the linear combination of $\{\omega_m(t_{i-2}), \ldots, \omega_m(t_0), \upsilon_u(t_{i-1}), \ldots, \upsilon_u(t_1), \xi_u(t_0)\}$, applying the projection property [15] and following the similar derivation procedures as in (2.29), (2.30) and (2.31), one has

$$\tilde{\xi}_u(t_i|t_{i-1}) \perp \upsilon_s(t_i)$$

Moreover, since $\xi_u(t_i) \perp \upsilon_s(t_i)$, $\mathbf{E}\{\alpha_{l,u}(t_i) - \theta_{l,u}\} = 0$, and $\mathbf{E}\{\alpha_{j,s}(t_i) - \theta_{j,s}\} = 0$, $l \in \mathcal{N}_u, j \in \mathcal{N}_s$, one has by (2.68) that

$$\begin{aligned} P_{u,s}(t_i|t_i) &= \mathbf{E}\left\{\tilde{\xi}_u(t_i|t_i)\tilde{\xi}_s^{\mathrm{T}}(t_i|t_i)\right\} \\ &= \left(\bar{I}_u - K_u(t_i)\bar{C}_u\right) P_{u,s}(t_i|t_{i-1}) \left(\bar{I}_s - K_s(t_i)\bar{C}_s\right)^{\mathrm{T}} \\ &\quad + \chi_3 + \chi_4 \end{aligned} \tag{2.69}$$

where

$$\begin{aligned} \chi_3 = \mathbf{E}&\left\{\left[\sum_{l\in\mathcal{N}_u}(\alpha_{l,u}(t_i) - \theta_{l,u})K_u(t_i)C_{0l,u}\right]\xi_u(t_i)\right. \\ &\left.\times\xi_s^{\mathrm{T}}(t_i)\left[\sum_{j\in\mathcal{N}_s}(\alpha_{j,s}(t_i) - \theta_{j,s})K_s(t_i)C_{0j,s}\right]^{\mathrm{T}}\right\} \\ \chi_4 = \mathbf{E}&\left\{\left(\sum_{l\in\mathcal{N}_u}\alpha_{l,u}(t_i)K_u(t_i)\Pi_{l,u}H_u\right)\upsilon_u(t_i)\upsilon_s^{\mathrm{T}}(t_i)\right. \\ &\left.\times\left(\sum_{j\in\mathcal{N}_s}\alpha_{j,s}(t_i)K_s(t_i)\Pi_{j,s}H_s\right)^{\mathrm{T}}\right\} \end{aligned}$$

Since $u \in \mathcal{N}_s$, $s \in \mathcal{N}_u$, and $u \neq s$, one obtains by Lemma 2.1 and $\alpha_{s,u}(t_i) = \alpha_{u,s}(t_i)$ and $\theta_{s,u} = \theta_{u,s}$ that

$$\chi_3 = \Gamma_2 \tag{2.70}$$

By following the similar derivation procedures as in the proof of Lemma 2.6, one has that

$$\chi_4 = \Gamma_3 \tag{2.71}$$

Combining (2.69), (2.70) and (2.71) leads to (2.64). Notice that one has to calculate $P_{u,s}(t_i|t_{i-1})$ in computing $P_{u,s}(t_i|t_i)$. Since the following facts hold

$$\begin{aligned} &\xi_u(t_i) \perp \nu_s(t_i) \\ &\xi_u(t_i) \perp \upsilon_s(t_i) \\ &\tilde{\xi}_u(t_i|t_{i-1}) \perp \nu_s(t_i) \\ &\tilde{\xi}_u(t_i|t_{i-1}) \perp \upsilon_s(t_i) \end{aligned}$$

$$\mathbf{E}\{\alpha_{l,u}(t_i) - \theta_{l,u}\} = 0$$
$$\mathbf{E}\{\alpha_{j,s}(t_i) - \theta_{j,s}\} = 0$$
$$l \in \mathcal{N}_u,\ j \in \mathcal{N}_s$$

one has by (2.45), (2.63), Lemma 2.1, and following the similar derivation procedures as in (2.62) that

$$\begin{aligned} P_{u,s}(t_{i+1}|t_i) = {} & \Gamma_4 + \Gamma_5 + \operatorname{diag}\left\{BQ_\omega B^{\mathrm{T}},\ \Delta_{u,s}\right\} \\ & + \mathbf{E}\left\{\rho_u(t_i)\rho_s^{\mathrm{T}}(t_i)\right\} - \mathbf{E}\left\{\tilde{B}_u(t_i)\nu_u(t_i)\rho_s^{\mathrm{T}}(t_i)\right\} \\ & - \mathbf{E}\left\{\rho_u(t_i)(\tilde{B}_s(t_i)\nu_s(t_i))^{\mathrm{T}}\right\} \end{aligned} \tag{2.72}$$

where

$$\rho_u(t_i) = \sum_{l \in \mathcal{N}_u} \alpha_{l,u}(t_i) F_u(t_i) \Pi_{l,u} H_u \upsilon_u(t_i)$$

$$\rho_s(t_i) - \sum_{j \in \mathcal{N}_s} \alpha_{j,s}(t_l) F_s(t_l) \Pi_{j,s} H_s \upsilon_s(t_\iota)$$

By following the similar derivation procedures as in the proof of Lemma 2.6, one obtains

$$\mathbf{E}\left\{\rho_u(t_i)\rho_s^{\mathrm{T}}(t_i)\right\} = \Gamma_6 \tag{2.73}$$

By following the similar derivation procedures as in (2.63) and Lemma 2.6, one has

$$\mathbf{E}\left\{\tilde{B}_u(t_i)\nu_u(t_i)\rho_s^{\mathrm{T}}(t_i)\right\} = \left[0\ \ \varphi_{u,s}^{\mathrm{T}}(t_i)\right]^{\mathrm{T}} \tag{2.74}$$

$$\mathbf{E}\left\{\rho_u(t_i)(\tilde{B}_s(t_i)\nu_s(t_i))^{\mathrm{T}}\right\} = \left[0\ \ \pi_{u,s}(t_i)\right] \tag{2.75}$$

Combining (2.72), (2.73), (2.74) and (2.75) yields (2.65). The proof is thus completed.

By fusing local estimates, more measurements from different sensors are used to generate fused estimates at every sensor, which helps improve local estimation performance and reduce the disagreement of local estimates. Similar to (2.52) and (2.53), one may define some *disagreement potentials* as follows to characterize the performance of the distributed estimation algorithm in Theorems 2.2 and 2.3:

$$\kappa_r^o(t_i) = \frac{1}{2n_r} \sum_{u,s \in \mathcal{N}_r} \|\hat{\eta}_{ou}(t_{i+k}|t_i) - \hat{\eta}_{os}(t_{i+k}|t_i)\|^2 \tag{2.76}$$

$$\psi_r^o(t_i) = \frac{1}{2n_r} \sum_{u,s \in \mathcal{N}_r} \left[\mathrm{Tr}(P_{ou}^{\eta}(t_{i+k}|t_i)) - \mathrm{Tr}(P_{os}^{\eta}(t_{i+k}|t_i))\right]^2 \tag{2.77}$$

where $k = 0, 1$, $\kappa_r^o(t_i)$, and $\psi_r^o(t_i)$ are, respectively, the *disagreement potential* of the fused estimates and the *disagreement potential* of the fused estimation performances in the neighborhood $\mathcal{N}_r$, and some smaller κ_r^o and ψ_r^o imply a better performance of the estimation algorithm in Theorems 2.2 and 2.3.

It can be seen from Theorems 2.1, 2.2 and 2.3 that the estimation performance assessed by the error covariances critically depend on the parameter b that determines the measurement transmission rate, and thus one may see how the measurement transmission rate can affect the estimation performance by applying the algorithms in Theorems 2.1, 2.2, and 2.3. On the other hand, the proposed two-stage fusion estimation needs more computation and communication costs as compared with the one-stage one. Nevertheless, the multi-rate scheme helps reduce communication costs significantly since the transmission rate of the measurements and local estimates is slowed down, and it is well known that computation consumes much less energy than communication in WSNs. Energy saved from the multi-rate scheme can be used to implement the second-stage fusion estimation which helps improve estimation performance. Thus, the two-stage estimation may achieve a better performance without consuming more energy than the one-stage estimation.

2.4 Simulations

In this section, simulations of a maneuvering target tracking system are presented to demonstrate the effectiveness of the proposed estimator design method, where the target's position and velocity evolve according to the state-space model in (2.1) with

$$A_p = \begin{bmatrix} 1 & h_p \\ 0 & 1 \end{bmatrix}, B_p = \sqrt{10} \begin{bmatrix} h_p^2/2 \\ h_p \end{bmatrix} \tag{2.78}$$

where h_p is the sampling period. The state is $x(k_i) = [x_p^{\mathrm{T}}(k_i) \quad x_v^{\mathrm{T}}(k_i)]^{\mathrm{T}}$, where $x_p(k_i)$ and $x_v(k_i)$ are the position and velocity of the maneuvering target at time k_i, respectively. Suppose that the target is not moving too fast, and we take $h_p = 0.5\,\mathrm{s}$ in the simulation.

A wireless sensor network with 12 sensor nodes is deployed to monitor the target, and the topology of the WSN is shown in Fig. 2.3. The wireless links in the WSN may be subject to random packet losses. Suppose that only the position of the target is measurable, and the observation equations of the sensors are given by (2.2), where $\upsilon_{pl}(k_i) = c_l\omega_0(k_i) + \upsilon_{0l}(k_i)$, $\omega_0(k_i)$ is a zero-mean white noise with variance Q_{ω_0}, $\upsilon_{0l}(k_i)$ are zero-mean white noises with variances $Q_{\upsilon_{0l}}$, $\upsilon_{0l}(k_i)$ are mutually uncorrelated and are independent of $\omega_0(k_i)$, $\omega_0(k_i)$ and $\upsilon_{0l}(k_i)$ are uncorrelated with $\omega_p(k_i)$, and

$$C_{p1} = [1 \quad 0],\ C_{p2} = [0.8 \quad 0]$$

$$C_{p3} = [0.7 \quad 0],\ C_{p4} = [0.6 \quad 0],\ C_{p5} = [0.5 \quad 0]$$

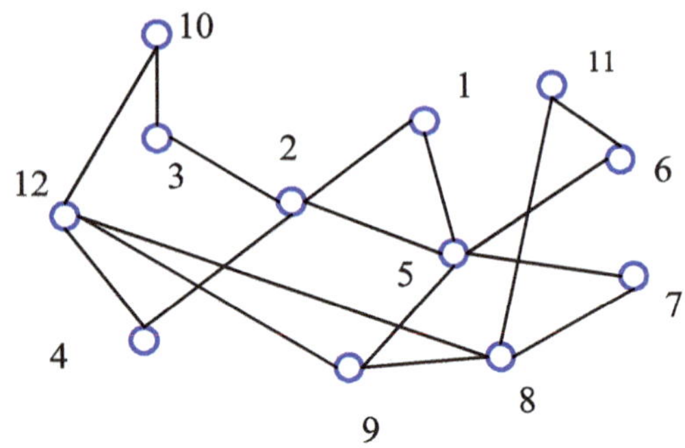

Fig. 2.3 Network topology with $N = 12$ sensor nodes

$$C_{p6} = [0.4\ \ 0],\ C_{p7} = [0.3\ \ 0],\ C_{p8} = [0.2\ \ 0]$$
$$C_{p9} = [1\ \ 0],\ C_{p10} = [0.8\ \ 0],\ C_{p11} = [0.6\ \ 0]$$
$$C_{p12} = [0.7\ \ 0],\ D_{pl} = 1,\ l = 1, 2, \ldots, 12$$

It can be easily calculated that

$$Q_{l,l}^{\upsilon_p} = c_l^2 Q_{\omega 0} + Q_{\upsilon 0 l},\ Q_{l,s}^{\upsilon_p} = c_l c_s Q_{\omega 0},\ l \neq s,\ l, s = 1, 2, \ldots, 12$$

In the simulation, we take $c_l = 0.1l$ and

$$Q_{\omega_p} = 0.1,\ Q_{\omega 0} = 1$$
$$Q_{\upsilon 01} = 0.4,\ Q_{\upsilon 02} = 0.7$$
$$Q_{\upsilon 03} = 0.4,\ Q_{\upsilon 04} = 0.4$$
$$Q_{\upsilon 05} = 0.3,\ Q_{\upsilon 06} = 0.2$$
$$Q_{\upsilon 07} = 0.3,\ Q_{\upsilon 08} = 0.3$$
$$Q_{\upsilon 09} = 0.5,\ Q_{\upsilon 010} = 0.4$$
$$Q_{\upsilon 011} = 0.3,\ Q_{\upsilon 012} = 0.1$$

It can be seen from the topology of the WSN that sensors 2 and 5 are directly connected to sensor 1, and thus they are neighbors of the sensor 1, and the neighborhood $\mathcal{N}_1$ consists of three sensors, and they are sensors 1, 2, 5. In what follows, estimation at the sensors in neighborhood $\mathcal{N}_1$ will be considered to show the effectiveness of the proposed estimator design. At each instant t_i, sensor 1 collects measurements from itself and sensors 2 and 5 to generate local estimates, and then at the second stage, sensor 1 collects local estimates from itself and sensors 2 and 5 to form fused estimates.

We first consider the situation where $a = b = 2$, i.e., the sensors in $\mathcal{N}_1$ collect measurements from their neighborhoods and generate estimates with period $h_m = 2\,\text{s}$ which is 4 times of the sampling period, and the estimates are updated with period $h_e = 1$ s which is 2 times of the sampling period. By slowing down the measurement transmission rate and the estimate updating rate, one may expect to save energies consumed in communications and computations. The PLPs in the links $L_{2,1}$ and $L_{5,1}$ are supposed to be $1-\theta_{2,1} = 1-\theta_{5,1} = 0.2$. The initial time is $t_0 = 0$, and the initial state is given by $x(0) = x(-1) = [1\ \ 0.5]^{\mathrm{T}}$, and $\bar{x}_0 = \bar{x}_1 = [1.5\ \ 1.0]^{\mathrm{T}}$, $\bar{P}_0 = \bar{P}_1 = \mathrm{diag}\{0.25, 0.25\}$. By applying Theorems 2.1, 2.2 and 2.3, the true values and the filtered fusion estimates of the target positions obtained at sensor 1 are depicted in Fig. 2.4a, while Fig. 2.4b depicts the true values and the filtered fusion estimates of the target velocities. It can be seen that the sensor 1 is able to track the maneuvering target well in the presence of random packet losses and with slow measurement transmission rate. Figure 2.5 shows the individual estimation performance (assessed by the trace of estimation error covariance) of every sensor in the neighborhood $\mathcal{N}_1$. It can be seen from Fig. 2.5 that the estimation performance at sensor 1 is improved by using the two-stage fusion strategy and the fusion estimator outperforms each of its local estimators.

The advantage of the two-stage fusion estimation strategy is further shown in Figs. 2.6 and 2.7. In Fig. 2.6. It can be seen that the estimation performance may be improved by using more measurements from different sensors, and the estimation performance can be further improved by fusing local estimates from its neighborhood. The disagreement of estimates and disagreement of estimation performances obtained by two estimation strategies (one-stage estimation and two-stage estimation) are shown, respectively, in Fig. 2.7a, b. It is clearly shown by Fig. 2.7 that both the disagreement of estimate and the disagreement of estimation performance are significantly reduced by using the two-stage estimation strategy.

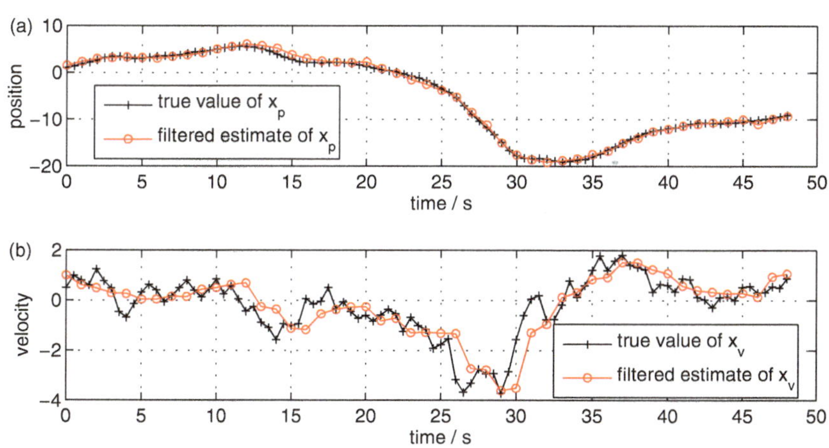

Fig. 2.4 True values and fused estimates (obtained at sensor 1) of the target positions and velocities with $a = 2$, $b = 2$, $\theta_{2,1} = \theta_{5,1} = 0.5$

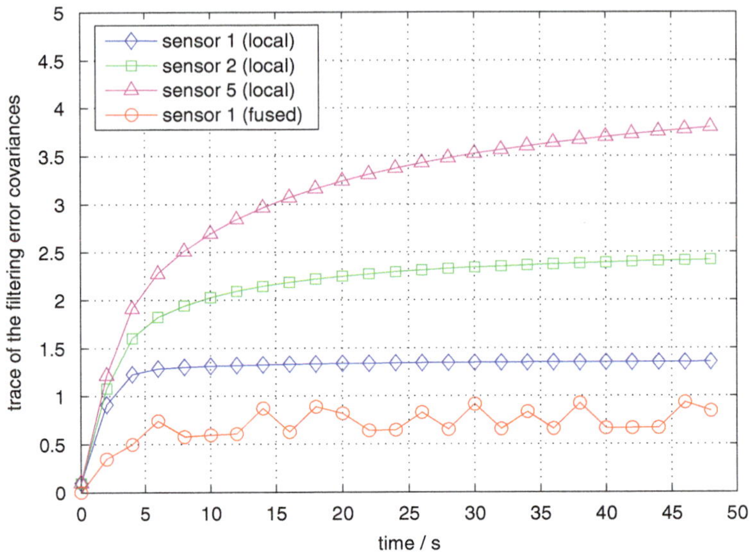

Fig. 2.5 Estimation performances obtained at the sensors in the neighborhood $\mathcal{N}_1$ with $a = 2$, $b = 2$, $\theta_{2,1} = \theta_{5,1} = 0.8$

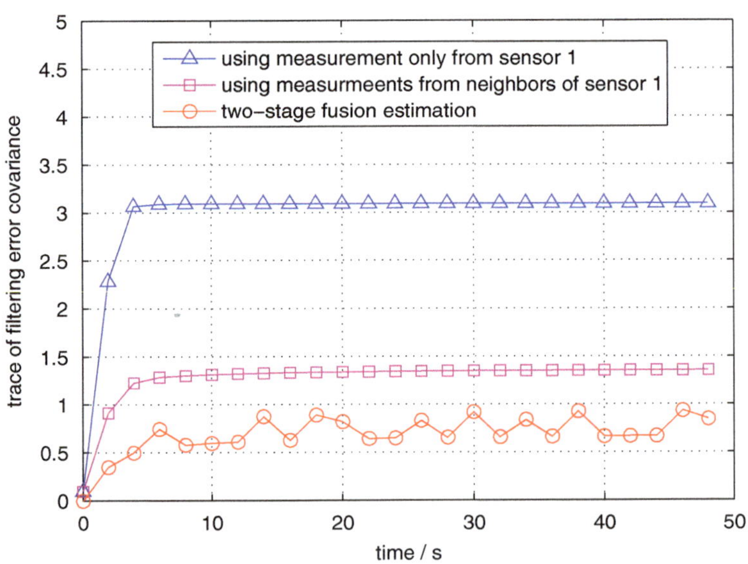

Fig. 2.6 Estimation performances of sensors 1 with different estimation strategies, $a = 2$, $b = 2$, $\theta_{2,1} = \theta_{5,1} = 0.8$

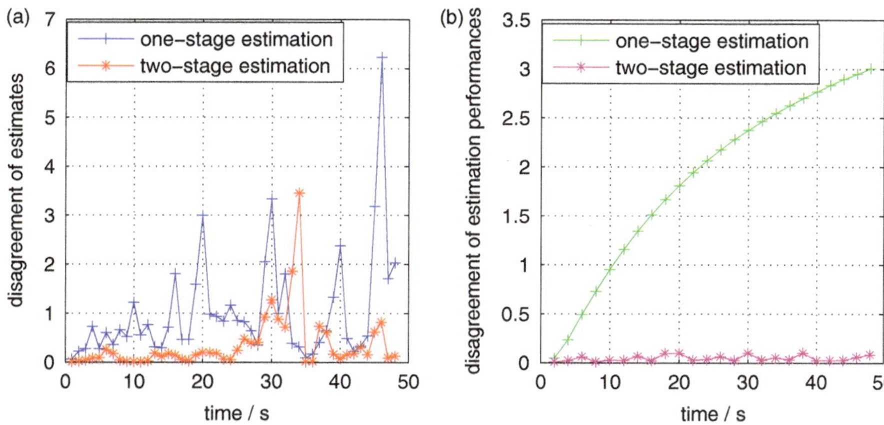

Fig. 2.7 Comparison of disagreement potentials in two estimation strategies, $a = 2$, $b = 2$, $\theta_{2,1} = \theta_{5,1} = 0.8$

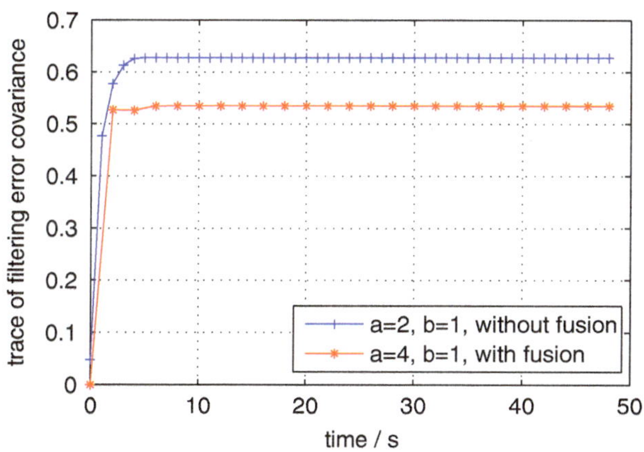

Fig. 2.8 Comparison of estimation performance and energy consumption in two estimation strategies, $\theta_{2,1} = \theta_{5,1} = 0.9$

Notice that the two-stage estimation usually causes more communication costs as compared with the normal one-stage estimation, because, besides of measurements, local estimates in the neighborhood should also be transmitted among sensors in the group to generate a fused estimate. Fortunately, by slowing down the measurement transmission and estimate updating rates, energies can be saved to implement the two-stage estimation. In this way, the two-stage strategy may be realized to improve each local estimation performance and reduce the disagreement of estimates among different sensors without consuming more energies than the normal one-stage strategy. An example is shown in Fig. 2.8 which depicts filtering performances obtained at sensor 1 with $\theta_{2,1} = \theta_{5,1} = 0.9$. The curve with plus symbol in Fig. 2.8 shows the filtering performance obtained by using the one-stage estimation strategy with $a = 2$ and $b = 1$, i.e., sensor 1 collects measurements from sensors 2 and 5 and generates estimates with a period of 1 s, and thus totally 4 times of measurement transmissions and 2 times of estimate computations are involved over every 2 s by using the one-stage estimation. The curve with star in Fig. 2.8 shows the filtering performance obtained by using the two-stage estimation strategy with $a = 4$ and $b = 1$, i.e., sensor 1 collects not only measurements but also local estimates from sensors 2 and 5 and generates fused estimates with a period of 2 s, and therefore totally 4 times of measurement transmissions and 2 times of estimate computations are involved over every 2 s by using the two-stage estimation. It thus can be observed from Fig. 2.8 that, though the two strategies consume the same communication and computation costs, the two-stage estimation is able to provide a better performance than the one-stage estimation, confirming that the two-stage strategy may outperform the one-stage one without increasing energy consumption due to the benefits from slowing down the measurement transmission rate.

In what follows, we will show how the packet loss and the measurement transmission period may affect the estimation performances. Figure 2.9 shows the filtering performances of the sensors in $\mathcal{N}_1$ with different PLPs, and Fig. 2.10 shows filtering performances of the sensors in $\mathcal{N}_1$ with different measurement transmission periods. It can be seen from Figs. 2.9 and 2.10 that packet loss degrades estimation

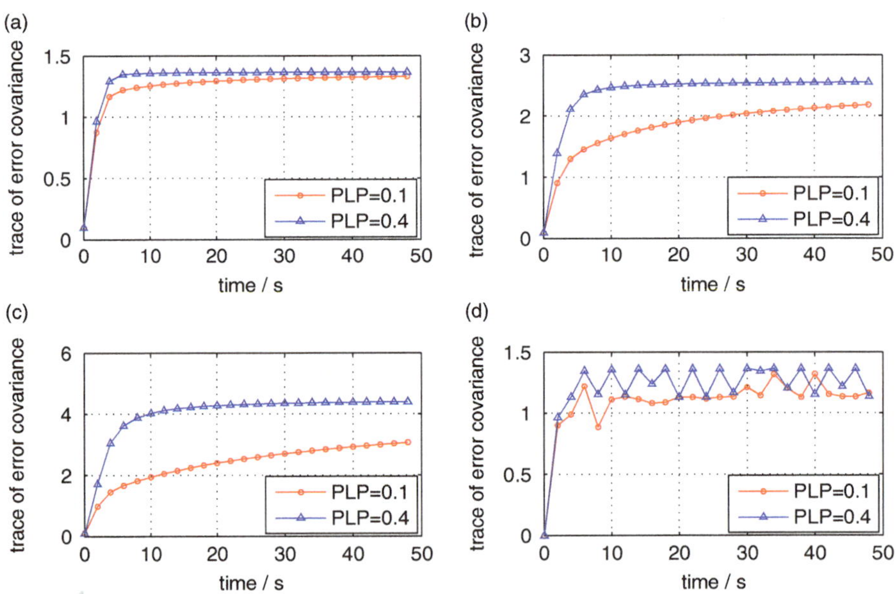

Fig. 2.9 Estimation performances of sensors in $\mathcal{N}_1$ with different PLPs, $a = 2$, $b = 2$. (**a**) Local estimation performances of sensor 1. (**b**) Local estimation performances of sensor 2. (**c**) Local estimation performances of sensor 5. (**d**) Fusion estimation performances of sensor 1

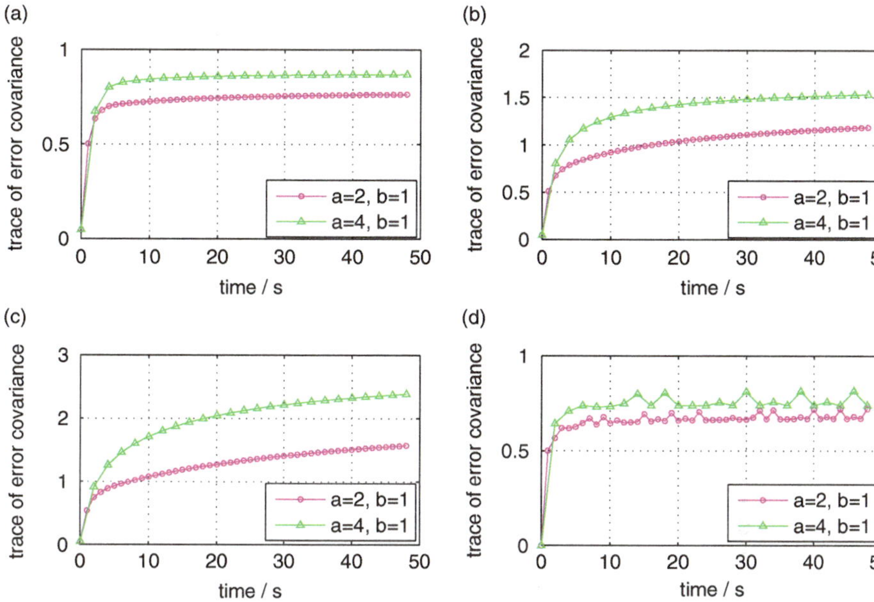

Fig. 2.10 Estimation performances of sensors in $\mathcal{N}_1$ with different measurement transmission periods, $\theta_{2,1} = \theta_{5,1} = 0.8$. (**a**) Local estimation performances of sensor 1. (**b**) Local estimation performances of sensor 2. (**c**) Local estimation performances of sensor 5. (**d**) Fusion estimation performances of sensor 1

performance and a smaller measurement transmission period leads to a better estimation performance, which are as expected and demonstrate the effectiveness of the proposed estimator design method.

2.5 Conclusions

An energy-efficient distributed fusion estimation algorithm has been developed in this chapter for estimating states of discrete-time linear stochastic systems with slowly changing dynamics and random packet losses in WSN environment. A *transmission rate method* was proposed to reduce energy consumption in exchanging information among sensors, and a two-stage fusion estimation method has been proposed to improve each local estimate and reduce disagreements of local estimates. It is shown that the obtained estimation performance critically depends on the measurement transmission rate and the packet loss probabilities and that the time scale of information exchange among sensors can be slower while still maintaining satisfactory estimation performance. However, it is assumed in this chapter that the estimator generates estimates periodically with a uniform rate. In the next chapter, this restriction will be removed, and a novel fusion estimation method with nonuniform estimation rates will be developed.

References

1. Fang J, Li HB (2008) Distributed adaptive quantization for wireless sensor networks: from delta modulation to maximum likelihood. IEEE Trans Signal Process 56(10):5246–5257
2. Fang J, Li H (2009) Hyperplane-based vector quantization for distributed estimation in wireless sensor networks. IEEE Trans Inf Theory 55:5682–5699
3. Sun SL, Lin JY, Xie LH, Xiao WD (2007) Quantized Kalman filtering. In: The 22nd IEEE international symposium on intelligent control, Singapore, pp 7–12
4. Zhou Y, Li JX (2009) Quantized measurement fusion for target tracking in wireless sensor networks. In: In the joint 48th IEEE conference on decision and control and the 28th Chinese control conference, Shanghai, pp 6835–6840
5. Ghasemi N, Dey S (2008) Power-efficient dynamic quantization for multisensor HMM state estimation over fading channels. In: The 3rd international symposium on communications, control and signal processing, St Julians, pp 1553–1558
6. Ribeiro A, Giannakis GB, Roumeliotis SI (2006) SOI-KF: distributed Kalman filtering with low-cost communications using the sign of innovations. IEEE Trans Signal Process 54(12):4782–4795
7. Schizas ID, Giannakis GB, Luo ZQ (2007) Distributed estimation using reduced-dimensionality sensor observations. IEEE Trans Signal Process 55(8):4284–4299
8. Zhu H, Schizas ID, Giannakis GB (2009) Power-efficient dimensionality reduction for distributed channel aware Kalman tracking using WSNs. IEEE Trans Signal Process 57(8):3193–3207
9. Zhu Y, Song E, Zhou J, You Z (2005) Optimal dimensionality reduction of sensor data in multisensor estimation fusion. IEEE Trans Signal Process 53(3):1631–1639
10. Chen HM, Zhang KS, Li XR (2004) Optimal data compression for multisensor target tracking with communication constraints. In: Proceedings of the 43th IEEE conference on decision and control, Atlantis, pp 8179–8184
11. Liang Y, Chen TW, Pan Q (2009) Multi-rate optimal state estimation. Int J Control 82(11):2059–2076
12. Liang Y, Chen TW, Pan Q (2010) Multi-rate stochastic H_∞ filtering for networked multi-sensor fusion. Automatica 46(2):437–444
13. Olfati-Saber R (2005) Distributed Kalman filter with embedded consensus filters. In: Proceedings of the 44th IEEE conference decision and control, Sevilla, pp 8179–8184
14. Zhang WA, Yu L, Song HB (2009) H_∞ filtering of networked discrete-time systems with random packet losses. Inf Sci 179(22):3944–3955
15. Anderson BDO, Moore JB (1979) Optimal filtering. Prentice-Hall, Englewood Cliffs
16. Cattivelli FS, Sayed AH (2010) Diffusion strategies for distributed Kalman filtering and smoothing. IEEE Trans Autom Control 55(9):2069–2084
17. Sun SL, Deng ZL (2004) Multi-sensor optimal information fusion Kalman filter. Automatica 40(6):1017–1023

Chapter 3
Kalman Fusion Estimation for WSNs with Nonuniform Estimation Rates

3.1 Introduction

As mentioned in Chap. 2, developing energy-efficient algorithms for WSN-based estimation is of great practical significance since the sensor nodes are usually constrained in energy. As usually did in WSNs, one may purposively close the sensor nodes to save power during certain time interval and wake them up when necessary. That is to say, in many situations, it is not necessary for sensors to transmit measurements and generate estimates at every sampling instant from the energy-efficiency perspective, and the sensors may work and generate estimates with two rates, namely, a fast rate and a slow rate according to their power situations. Therefore, adopting a nonuniform estimation rate is a more preferable strategy for sensor network-based estimation system with energy constraints.

An example of multisensor track-to-track fusion estimation with nonuniform estimation rates is shown in Fig. 3.1, where each sensor i broadcasts its local estimates to the other sensors and meanwhile collects local estimates from itself and the other sensors to generate fused estimates at instants $t_{i,k}$, $k = 0, 1, 2, \ldots$. It can be seen from Fig. 3.1 that the number of local estimates for fusing at each sensor is time varying, and local estimates available for fusing at a particular sensor may be generated in various different time scales. These problems caused by the asynchronism add much difficulty to the design of fusion rules, especially, the computation of cross-covariances of estimation errors across different sensors. Hence, there are two issues that should be considered in designing fusion estimators with nonuniform estimation rates. The first issue is how to design an optimal local estimator for each sensor with a nonuniform estimation rate, and the second issue is how to design an optimal fusion rule for each estimator to fuse local estimates generated at different time scales.

W.-A. Zhang et al., *Distributed Fusion Estimation for Sensor Networks with Communication Constraints*, DOI 10.1007/978-981-10-0795-8_3

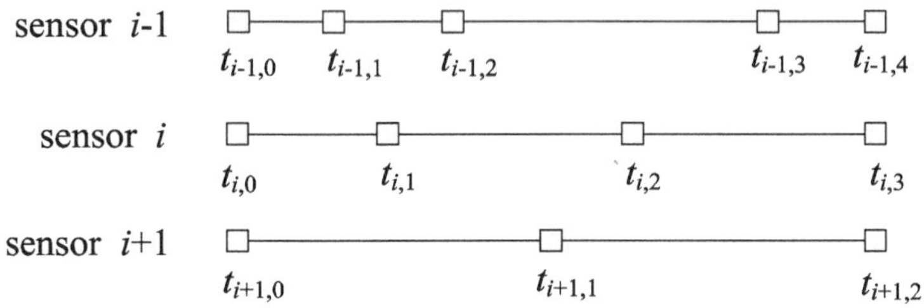

Fig. 3.1 An example of multisensor fusion with nonuniform estimation rates

For the first issue, some relevant results have been presented in the literature on networked estimation with packet losses [1–4] or estimation with sensor failures [5]. In these results, it is usually assumed that the estimator input keeps the last available value or is set to zero if the current measurement is lost, and the estimates are then generated with a uniform rate at every sampling instant. Therefore, the aforementioned results are essentially not applicable to the nonuniform estimation problem. Recently, a stochastic sampling method was presented in [6] to design sampled-data H_∞ filters with a filtering rate taking two values according to a known probability distribution law. For the single-sensor scenario, the method in [6] is useful for the nonuniform estimation problem. If each local estimation is performed periodically with a single rate, then the problem in the aforementioned second issue can be immediately solved by applying some distributed fusion methods as presented in [7–12] (where estimation rates at different sensors are required to be the same) or by using the multi-scale state fusion method as presented in [13–15] (where estimation rates at different sensors are allowed to be different). When considering the problems in both the aforementioned two issues, few result is available in the literature except for [16–18]. In [16], the ratio between the sampling rates of different sensors is allowed to be any positive integer, and some of the estimators are allowed to generate local estimates with nonuniform rates. Thus, the result in [16] extends those as given in [13–15]. However, it is required in the algorithm in [16] that at least one estimator should generate its local estimates uniformly with a single rate, and all the other estimation rates are integer multiple of this single rate. In [17] and [18], some very general asynchronous fusion estimation methods were presented for multisensor systems, which allow for out of sequence data and latent data. However, the results in [17] and [18] were concerned with the sampled-data fusion estimation, where the estimators estimate states at some discrete instants for a continuous-time process. In the sampled-data fusion estimation, it is required that all the local estimates are time stamped so that each estimator is able to calculate exact state-transition matrices and some corresponding integration terms at every estimation instant. These state-transition matrices and integration terms are then used to lift the states at sampling instants to those at the fusion estimation instants. In this way, some well-developed fusion rules were then applied to design the fusion estimators. For discrete-time systems, the approaches in [17] and [18] are not applicable to solve the problem in the aforementioned issue two since one is unable to lift the states at sampling instants to those at estimation instants by using state-transition matrices.

This chapter presents a design method for multisensor track-to-track fusion estimators with nonuniform estimation rates, and the aforementioned two issues will be addressed. In the estimation system, a WSN with a group of sensors is deployed to monitor the outputs of a discrete-time stochastic dynamic process, and each sensor acts also as an estimator. At the first stage, each sensor generates local estimates with a nonuniform rate by using its own measurements, and it is assumed that the estimation rate switches between a fast one and a slow one according to a white Bernoulli random process, and each local estimation system is modeled as a discrete-time system with a stochastic parameter. Then, the optimal local estimators are designed by using innovation analysis and projection principle. At the second stage, each sensor collects and fuses local estimates from itself and the other sensors to generate fused estimates. The fusion algorithm is designed by using the lifting technique and a distributed fusion rule with matrix weights in the linear minimum variance sense, and a set of recursive equations are presented to compute the estimation error cross-covariances. Since the estimation rates at different sensors are allowed to be different from each other, the proposed fusion algorithm is able to fuse local estimates generated at different time scales. Then, each sensor generates fused estimates according to the fusion rule, if local estimates from the other sensors are available, and keeps its own estimates as the fused ones otherwise. Two types of fusion estimators are designed according to different considerations of design complexity and computation costs, and the convergence of the type II estimators is also discussed.

3.2 Problem Statement

Consider a linear discrete stochastic system described by the following state-space model

$$x(\mathrm{T}_{k+1}) = Ax(\mathrm{T}_k) + B\omega(\mathrm{T}_k),\ k = 0, 1, 2, \ldots \tag{3.1}$$

where $x(\mathrm{T}_k) \in \Re^n$ is the system state and $\omega(\mathrm{T}_k) \in \Re^{q_\omega}$ is a zero-mean white noise with variance Q_ω, i.e., $\mathbf{E}\{\omega(\mathrm{T}_k)\omega^{\mathrm{T}}(\mathrm{T}_t)\} = Q_\omega\delta(k-t)$, where $\delta(k)$ is the Dirac Delta function. The sampling period is denoted by h and $h = \mathrm{T}_{k+1} - \mathrm{T}_k$, $k = 0, 1, 2, \ldots$. A group of N sensors are deployed to monitor the outputs of system (3.1), and the output equations are given by

$$y_i(\mathrm{T}_k) = C_i x(\mathrm{T}_k) + D_i\upsilon_i(\mathrm{T}_k),\ i \in Z_0 \triangleq \{1, 2, \ldots, N\} \tag{3.2}$$

where $y_i(\mathrm{T}_k) \in \Re^{p_i}$ and $\upsilon_i(\mathrm{T}_k) \in \Re^{q_i}$ are zero-mean white measurement noises with variances $Q^{\upsilon}_{i,i}$, i.e., $\mathbf{E}\{\upsilon_i(\mathrm{T}_k)\upsilon_i^{\mathrm{T}}(\mathrm{T}_t)\} = Q^{\upsilon}_{i,i}\delta(k-t)$. The noises υ_i are mutually correlated, and the covariance of υ_i and υ_j is given by $\mathbf{E}\{\upsilon_i(\mathrm{T}_k)\upsilon_j^{\mathrm{T}}(\mathrm{T}_t)\} = Q_{i,j}^{\upsilon}\delta(k-t)$, $i,j \in Z_0$ and $i \neq j$. Each sensor i generates estimates with two rates, namely, a fast rate and a slow rate denoted by $h_{i1} = a_{i1}h$ and $h_{i2} = a_{i2}h$, respectively, where a_{i1} and a_{i2} are positive integers and $a_{i1} < a_{i2}$. The sensor may switch between the two rates according to its power situation, requirements of estimation performance, and dynamic changes of the process under monitoring. Denote by $t_{i,k}$, $k = 0, 1, 2, \ldots$ the instants at which the estimates are generated at sensor i, $i \in Z_0$. Then, the estimation rate is denoted by $h_i(t_{i,k}) = t_{i,k+1} - t_{i,k}$ and $h_i(t_{i,k}) \in \{h_{i1}, h_{i2}\}$. Then, the output equation at time scale $t_{i,k}$ is represented by

$$y_i(t_{i,k}) = C_i x_i(t_{i,k}) + D_i \upsilon_i(t_{i,k}),\ i \in Z_0 \tag{3.3}$$

where $x_i(t_{i,k})$ denotes the system state at time scale $t_{i,k}$.

There is no fusion center in the estimation system, each sensor acts also as an estimator. Each sensor i first generates local estimates $\hat{x}_i = f_i(y_i)$ by using measurements from itself and then generates fused estimates $\hat{x}_{oi} = g_i(\hat{x}_1, \ldots, \hat{x}_N)$ by using available local estimates from itself and the other sensors, where $f_i(.)$ and $g_i(.)$ are the local estimation algorithm and the fusion rule to be designed at sensor i, respectively. Since $t_{i,k}$ is generally not equal to $t_{j,k}$ for any $i,j \in Z_0$ and $i \neq j$, $k = 0, 1, 2, \ldots$, the fusion rule $g_i(.)$ should be able to fuse local estimates generated at different time scales. Denote by $P_{i,i}$ and P_{oi} the local estimation error covariance and the fused estimation error covariance of sensor i, respectively. Then, the objective of this chapter is as follows.

Objective of the chapter: For system (3.1) and (3.3) with nonuniform estimation rates, design an optimal local estimator $f_i(.)$ and an optimal fusion rule $g_i(.)$ with matrix weights for each sensor such that the fused estimates $\hat{x}_{oi}(t_{i,k}|t_{i,k})$ are unbiased optimal estimates of the system state $x_i(t_{i,k})$, i.e., $\mathbf{E}\{\hat{x}_{oi}(t_{i,k}|t_{i,k})\} = \mathbf{E}\{x_i(t_{i,k})\}$, and $P_{oi}(t_{i,k}|t_{i,k}) = \min\{P(t_{i,k}|t_{i,k})\}$, $P_{oi}(t_{i,k}|t_{i,k}) \leq P_{i,i}(t_{i,k}|t_{i,k})$, where $P(t_{i,k}|t_{i,k})$ denotes the estimation error covariance of an arbitrary fusion estimator with matrix weights, $i \in Z_0$.

3.3 Modeling of the Estimation System

It can be seen from (3.1) and (3.3) that the system state in (3.1) evolves with a constant period h, while the estimates $\hat{x}_i$ are generated with a time-varying period $h_i(t_{i,k})$. Therefore, (3.1) and (3.3) are essentially a multi-rate estimation system model which cannot be directly used for designing fusion estimators, and a single-rate estimation system model is necessary and will be established in this section. By applying the state equation (3.1) recursively, one obtains a new state equation with time scale $t_{i,k}$ as follows:

$$x_i(t_{i,k+1}) = A_i(t_{i,k}) x_i(t_{i,k}) + \omega_i(t_{i,k}),\ i \in Z_0 \tag{3.4}$$

where $A_i(t_{i,k}) = A^{a_i(t_{i,k})}$, $a_i(t_{i,k}) \in \{a_{i1}, a_{i2}\}$, and

$$\omega_i(t_{i,k}) = \sum_{j=0}^{a_i(t_{i,k})-1} A^{a_i(t_{i,k})-j-1} B\omega(t_{i,k} + jh)$$

From the expression of $\omega_i(t_{i,k})$, it can be seen that $\omega_i(t_{i,k})$ is zero mean. Besides, since $t_{i,k} + jh < t_{i,k} + a_i(t_{i,k})h = t_{i,k+1}$, $\forall\, j = 0, 1, \ldots, a_i(t_{i,k}) - 1$, one has $\mathbf{E}\{\omega_i(t_{i,k})\omega_i^{\mathrm{T}}(t_{i,l})\} = 0$, $\forall\, l \neq k$. Moreover, let $Q_{\omega_i}(t_{i,k}) = \mathrm{Var}(\omega_i(t_{i,k}))$, one has

$$Q_{\omega_i}(t_{i,k}) = \sum_{j=0}^{a_i(t_{i,k})-1} A^{a_i(t_{i,k})-j-1} B Q_\omega B^{\mathrm{T}} \left(A^{a_i(t_{i,k})-j-1}\right)^{\mathrm{T}}$$

Thus, $\omega_i(t_{i,k})$ is a zero-mean white noise with a time-varying variance.

It is assumed that the sensors do not know a priori the exact values of the estimation rate, but instead, the sensors only know that $h_i(t_{i,k})$ switches between $a_{i1}h$ and $a_{i2}h$ randomly with known probabilities. Specifically, it is assumed that $h_i(t_{i,k})$ takes $a_{i1}h$ and $a_{i2}h$ according to a white binary-valued Bernoulli sequence $\rho_i(t_{i,k}) \in \{0, 1\}$, and $h_i(t_{i,k})$ takes $a_{i1}h$ if $\rho_i(t_{i,k}) = 1$ and takes value $a_{i2}h$ if $\rho_i(t_{i,k}) = 0$, i.e.,

$$\begin{aligned}
\mathrm{Prob}\{h_i(t_{i,k}) = a_{i1}h\} &= \mathrm{Prob}\{\rho_i(t_{i,k}) = 1\} \\
\mathrm{Prob}\{h_i(t_{i,k}) = a_{i2}h\} &= \mathrm{Prob}\{\rho_i(t_{i,k}) = 0\}
\end{aligned} \tag{3.5}$$

Then, $a_i(t_{i,k})$ and $A_i(t_{i,k})$ can be written as

$$a_i(t_{i,k}) = \rho_i(t_{i,k})a_{i1} + (1 - \rho_i(t_{i,k}))a_{i2} \tag{3.6}$$

$$A_i(t_{i,k}) = \rho_i(t_{i,k})A_{i1} + (1 - \rho_i(t_{i,k}))A_{i2} \tag{3.7}$$

where $A_{il} = A^{a_{il}}$, $l = 1, 2$. By (3.6), $\omega_i(t_{i,k})$ can be rewritten as

$$\begin{aligned}
\omega_i(t_{i,k}) = {} & \rho_i(t_{i,k}) \sum_{j=0}^{a_{i1}-1} A^{a_{i1}-j-1} B\omega(t_{i,k} + jh) \\
& + (1 - \rho_i(t_{i,k})) \sum_{j=0}^{a_{i2}-1} A^{a_{i2}-j-1} B\omega(t_{i,k} + jh),\ i \in Z_0
\end{aligned} \tag{3.8}$$

Suppose that $h_i(t_{i,k})$ takes value $a_{i1}h$ with probability $\bar{\rho}_i$, then it follows from the distribution of $\rho_i(t_{i,k})$ that $\mathbf{E}\{\rho_i(t_{i,k})\} = \bar{\rho}_i$ and

$$\begin{cases}
\mathbf{E}\left\{\rho_i(t_{i,k})^2\right\} = \bar{\rho}_i,\ \mathbf{E}\left\{(1 - \rho_i(t_{i,k}))^2\right\} = 1 - \bar{\rho}_i \\
\mathbf{E}\{\rho_i(t_{i,k})(1 - \rho_i(t_{i,k}))\} = 0 \\
\mathrm{Cov}(\rho_i(t_{i,k})) = \mathrm{Cov}(1 - \rho_i(t_{i,k})) = \bar{\rho}_i(1 - \bar{\rho}_i)
\end{cases} \tag{3.9}$$

For notational convenience, in what follows we will denote

$$\begin{aligned} \theta_{i1}(t_{i,k}) &= \rho_i(t_{i,k}),\ \theta_{i2}(t_{i,k}) = 1 - \rho_i(t_{i,k}) \\ \bar{\theta}_{i1} &= \bar{\rho}_i,\ \bar{\theta}_{i2} = 1 - \bar{\rho}_i,\ i \in Z_0 \end{aligned} \tag{3.10}$$

Then, by (3.8) and (3.9), the variance of the noise $\omega_i(t_{i,k})$ is

$$Q_{\omega_i} = \sum_{l=1}^{2} \bar{\theta}_{il} \sum_{j=0}^{a_{il}-1} A^{a_{il}-j-1} B Q_{\omega} B^{\mathrm{T}} \left(A^{a_{il}-j-1}\right)^{\mathrm{T}} \tag{3.11}$$

The probabilities $\bar{\rho}_i$, $i \in Z_0$ are parameters that are assigned a priori according to facts such as power situations of the sensors and requirements of estimation performance. For example, for the sensor with full power, one may set a relatively large probability of working at the fast estimation rate. In this way, one is able to make a trade-off between estimation performance and energy consumptions of the sensors.

In what follows, two types of fusion estimators will be designed based on the system model (3.3), (3.4), (3.7), and (3.8). The following assumptions are needed in the derivation of the main results.

Assumption 3.1 $\forall\ i \in Z_0$, the initial states $x_i(t_{i,0}) = x(\mathrm{T}_0)$ are uncorrelated to $\omega(\mathrm{T}_k)$ and $\upsilon_i(\mathrm{T}_k)$, and $\mathbf{E}\{x(\mathrm{T}_0)\} = x_0$, $\mathrm{Var}(x(\mathrm{T}_0) - x_0) = P_0$, $\omega(\mathrm{T}_k)$ is uncorrelated to $\upsilon_i(\mathrm{T}_k)$.

Assumption 3.2 $\forall\ i \in Z_0$, $\rho_i(t_{i,k})$ are mutually independent and are independent of $x_i(t_{i,0})$, $\omega(\mathrm{T}_k)$ and $\upsilon_i(\mathrm{T}_k)$.

3.4 Design of the Fusion Estimators (Type I)

3.4.1 Design of Local Estimators

Lemma 3.1 *Denote by $\Theta_i(t_{i,k})$ the variance of the state in (3.4), i.e., $\Theta_i(t_{i,k}) = \mathrm{Var}(x_i(t_{i,k}))$, then $\Theta_i(t_{i,k})$ satisfies the following recursive equation*

$$\Theta_i(t_{i,k+1}) = \sum_{l=1}^{2} \bar{\theta}_{il} A_{il} \Theta_i(t_{i,k}) A_{il}^{\mathrm{T}} + Q_{\omega_i},\ i \in Z_0 \tag{3.12}$$

Proof Equation (3.12) can be followed by (3.4), (3.9) and the fact $x_i(t_{i,k}) \perp \omega_i(t_{i,k})$.

Lemma 3.2 *Let* $\bar{A}_i = \mathrm{E}\{A_i(t_{i,k})\} = \sum_{l=1}^{2} \bar{\theta}_{il} A_{il}$ *and* $X_i(t_{i,k}) = \sum_{l=1}^{2} (\theta_{il}(t_{i,k}) - \bar{\theta}_{il}) A_{il} x_i(t_{i,k})$, *then* $\tilde{\Theta}_i(t_{i,k}) = \mathrm{Var}(X_i(t_{i,k}))$ *satisfies*

$$\tilde{\Theta}_i(t_{i,k}) = \sum_{l=1}^{2} \bar{\theta}_{il} A_{il} \Theta_i(t_{i,k}) A_{il}^{\mathrm{T}} - \bar{A}_i \Theta_i(t_{i,k}) \bar{A}_i^{\mathrm{T}} \tag{3.13}$$

Proof Equation (3.13) can be followed by (3.9) and some similar procedures as in (2.15), (2.16), (2.17) and (2.18) in Chap. 2.

For sensor i, $i \in Z_0$, denote by $P_{i,i}(t_{i,k}|t_{i,k})$ and $P_{i,i}(t_{i,k}|t_{i,k-1})$ the filtering error covariance matrix and the one-step prediction error covariance matrix, respectively. Then, the optimal local estimator for sensor i is given in the following theorem.

Theorem 3.1 *For sensor i with a nonuniform estimation rate* $h_i(t_{i,k})$ *satisfying (3.5), the local recursive optimal linear estimator is given by*

$$\hat{x}_i(t_{i,k+1}|t_{i,k}) = \bar{A}_i \hat{x}_i(t_{i,k}|t_{i,k}) \tag{3.14}$$

$$\hat{x}_i(t_{i,k+1}|t_{i,k+1}) = \hat{x}_i(t_{i,k+1}|t_{i,k}) + K_i(t_{i,k+1}) \varepsilon_i(t_{i,k+1}) \tag{3.15}$$

$$\varepsilon_i(t_{i,k+1}) = y_i(t_{i,k+1}) - C_i \hat{x}_i(t_{i,k+1}|t_{i,k}) \tag{3.16}$$

$$K_i(t_{i,k+1}) = P_{i,i}(t_{i,k+1}|t_{i,k}) C_i^{\mathrm{T}} \Omega_i^{-1}(t_{i,k+1}) \tag{3.17}$$

$$\Omega_i(t_{i,k+1}) = C_i P_{i,i}(t_{i,k+1}|t_{i,k}) C_i^{\mathrm{T}} + D_i Q_{i,i}^{\upsilon} D_i^{\mathrm{T}} \tag{3.18}$$

$$P_{i,i}(t_{i,k+1}|t_{i,k}) = \bar{A}_i P_{i,i}(t_{i,k}|t_{i,k}) \bar{A}_i^{\mathrm{T}} + \tilde{\Theta}_i(t_{i,k}) + Q_{\omega_i} \tag{3.19}$$

$$\begin{aligned} P_{i,i}(t_{i,k+1}|t_{i,k+1}) = {} & (I - K_i(t_{i,k+1}) C_i) P_{i,i}(t_{i,k+1}|t_{i,k}) \\ & \times (I - K_i(t_{i,k+1}) C_i)^{\mathrm{T}} \\ & + K_i(t_{i,k+1}) D_i Q_{i,i}^{\upsilon} D_i^{\mathrm{T}} K_i^{\mathrm{T}}(t_{i,k+1}) \end{aligned} \tag{3.20}$$

where $\varepsilon_i(t_{i,k}) = y_i(t_{i,k}) - \hat{y}_i(t_{i,k}|t_{i,k-1})$ *is the innovation,* $\Omega_i(t_{i,k}) = \mathrm{Var}(\varepsilon_i(t_{i,k}))$, $\hat{x}_i(t_{i,0}|t_{i,0}) = x_0$, $P_{i,i}(t_{i,0}|t_{i,0}) = P_0$.

Proof Theorem 3.1 can be followed by Lemmas 3.1 and 3.2 and some similar approaches in Theorem 2.1.

3.4.2 Design of the Fusion Rule

At the fusion stage, each sensor collects available local estimates from itself and the other sensors to generate fused estimates. Since the measurement noises are mutually correlated, the estimation errors at the various sensors are also mutually correlated, and one has to compute the cross-covariances of the estimation errors in the fusion estimation. Moreover, since the local estimates from different sensors

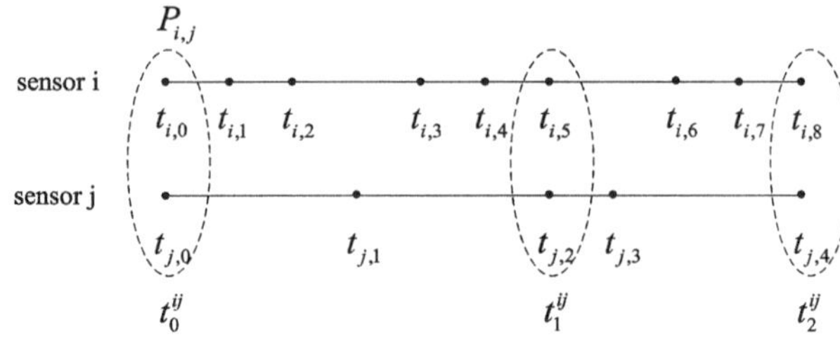

Fig. 3.2 Illustration for asynchronous fusion estimation

are generated at different time scales, the updating rates of the cross-covariances are nonuniform and the number of local estimates for fusion at a particular sensor is time varying. For any two sensors i and j, denote by t_k^{ij}, $k = 0, 1, 2, \dots$ the time instants when $\hat{x}_i$ and $\hat{x}_j$ are available for fusion. An example of fusion estimation with two sensors is shown in Fig. 3.2 to illustrate the above statements and the notation t_k^{ij}. In Fig. 3.2, sensor i generates local estimates with rate $h_i(t_{i,k}) \in \{h, 2h\}$, while the local estimates are calculated in sensor j with rate $h_j(t_{j,k}) \in \{h, 3h\}$. $P_{i,j}$ denotes the cross-covariance of the estimation errors at sensors i and j. At instants $t_{i,0}$, $t_{i,5}$, and $t_{i,8}$, sensor i fuses local estimates from itself and sensor j to generate fused estimates. At instants $t_{i,1}$, $t_{i,2}$, $t_{i,3}$, $t_{i,4}$, $t_{i,6}$, and $t_{i,7}$, local estimates from sensor j are not available, and sensor i thus keeps its own local estimates as the fused ones. The cross-covariance $P_{i,j}$ is computed only at the instants t_0^{ij}, t_1^{ij} and t_2^{ij}, where $t_0^{ij} = t_{i,0} = t_{j,0}$, $t_1^{ij} = t_{i,5} = t_{j,2}$, and $t_2^{ij} = t_{i,8} = t_{j,4}$, and it can be seen that $P_{i,j}$ is updated with a nonuniform rate.

From the above analysis, an optimal fusion rule, which is able to treat the variation of the number of local estimates, is needed in developing the asynchronous fusion algorithm. Let $\mathcal{N}_i(t_{i,k})$ denotes the index set of local estimates $\hat{x}_l$, $l \in Z_0$ that are available for fusion at sensor i, and $m_i(t_{i,k})$ denotes the number of elements in $\mathcal{N}_i(t_{i,k})$. It is clear that $m_i(t_{i,k}) \leq N$ and $\mathcal{N}_i(t_{i,k}) \subseteq Z_0$. Then, by Lemma 3.3 one has the following theorem that determines the fused estimates and the corresponding covariances of the estimation errors at sensor i, $i \in Z_0$.

Theorem 3.2 *For the system (3.3) and (3.4) with nonuniform estimation rates, the fusion estimator at sensor i, $i \in Z_0$ is given by*

$$\hat{x}_{oi}(t_{i,k}|t_{i,k}) = \sum_{l \in \mathcal{N}_i(t_{i,k})} \bar{A}_{i,l}(t_{i,k}) \hat{x}_l(t_{i,k}|t_{i,k}) \tag{3.21}$$

where the optimal matrix weights $\bar{A}_{i,l}(t_{i,k})$, $l \in \mathcal{N}_i(t_{i,k})$ are computed by

$$\text{col}\left\{\bar{A}_{i,l}^{\mathrm{T}}(t_i)\right\}_{l \in \mathcal{N}_i(t_{i,k})} = \Upsilon_i^{-1}(t_{i,k}) e_i(t_{i,k}) \left(e_i^{\mathrm{T}}(t_{i,k}) \Upsilon_i^{-1}(t_{i,k}) e_i(t_{i,k})\right)^{-1} \tag{3.22}$$

$\Upsilon_i(t_{i,k}) = [P_{l,j}(t_{i,k}|t_{i,k})]$, $l, j \in \mathcal{N}_i(t_{i,k})$ is an $nm_i(t_{i,k}) \times nm_i(t_{i,k})$ symmetric positive-definite matrix and $e_i(t_{i,k}) = \underbrace{[I, \dots, I]}_{m_i(t_{i,k})}^{\mathrm{T}}$. The corresponding covariance matrix of

the fusion estimation error is computed by $P_{oi}(t_{i,k}|t_{i,k}) = (e_i^{\mathrm{T}}(t_{i,k})\Upsilon_i^{-1}(t_{i,k})e_i(t_{i,k}))^{-1}$, *and one has that* $P_{oi}(t_{i,k}|t_{i,k}) \le P_{l,l}(t_{i,k}|t_{i,k})$, $l \in \mathcal{N}_i(t_{i,k})$, *i.e., the fusion estimation is more accurate than each local one. The local estimates* $\hat{x}_l(t_{i,k}|t_{i,k})$ *and the covariance matrices* $P_{l,l}(t_{i,k}|t_{i,k})$ *are computed by the recursive equations in Theorem 3.1.*

Proof Theorem 3.2 follows directly from Lemma 2.4.

Since the number of local estimates for fusion at sensor i is time varying, the dimension of the matrix $\Upsilon_i(t_{i,k})$ is also time varying. If there is no local estimate from the other sensors, then $\Upsilon_i(t_{i,k})$ reduces to $P_{i,i}(t_{i,k}|t_{i,k})$, and $\hat{x}_{oi}(t_{i,k}|t_{i,k})$ reduces to $\hat{x}_i(t_{i,k}|t_{i,k})$, i.e., sensor i keeps its own estimate as the fused one.

If the measurement noises are uncorrelated, then $P_{l,j}(t_{i,k}|t_{i,k}) = 0$, $l \neq j$, and $\Upsilon_i(t_{i,k})$ and $P_{oi}(t_{i,k}|t_{i,k})$ reduces to

$$\Upsilon_i(t_{i,k}) = \mathrm{diag}\{P_{l,l}(t_{i,k}|t_{i,k})\}_{l \in \mathcal{N}_i(t_{i,k})}$$

$$P_{oi}(t_{i,k}|t_{i,k}) = \left(\sum_{l \in \mathcal{N}_i(t_{i,k})} P_{l,l}(t_{i,k}|t_{i,k})\right)^{-1}$$

In this case, it is not necessary to calculate the cross-covariances of estimation errors from different sensors, and each sensor just collects local estimates and their corresponding error covariances from itself and the other sensors to generate fused estimates. Otherwise, it can be seen from (3.22) that the computation of the cross-covariances $P_{i,j}$ is one of the key issues in applying the fusion estimators in Theorem 3.2. In what follows, a procedure for the computation of the cross-covariances will be presented.

Consider any two sensors i and j in the estimation system, $i, j \in Z_0$, $i \neq j$. Let

$$t_{i,i_k} = \{t_{i,l}|t_{i,l} = t_k^{ij},\ l = 0, 1, 2, \ldots;\ k = 0, 1, 2, \ldots\} \tag{3.23}$$

$$t_{j,j_k} = \{t_{j,l}|t_{j,l} = t_k^{ij},\ l = 0, 1, 2, \ldots;\ k = 0, 1, 2, \ldots\} \tag{3.24}$$

Taking the situation in Fig. 3.2 for example, one has

$$i_k:\ i_0 = 0,\ i_1 = 5,\ i_2 = 8$$

$$j_k:\ j_0 = 0,\ j_1 = 2,\ j_2 = 4$$

Let $n_s(t_k^{ij})$ denote the number of sampling periods over the interval $[t_k^{ij}, t_{k+1}^{ij}]$ at sensor s, where $s = i, j$. Considering the interval $[t_0^{ij}, t_1^{ij}]$ in Fig. 3.2 for example, one has $n_i(t_0^{ij}) = 5$ and $n_j(t_0^{ij}) = 2$, and

$$t_1^{ij} - t_0^{ij} = h_i(t_{i,0}) + h_i(t_{i,1}) + h_i(t_{i,2}) + h_i(t_{i,3}) + h_i(t_{i,4})$$

$$t_1^{ij} - t_0^{ij} = h_j(t_{j,0}) + h_j(t_{j,1})$$

For $l \in Z_i \triangleq \{0, 1, \ldots, n_i(t_k^{ij})\}$ and $q \in Z_j \triangleq \{0, 1, \ldots, n_j(t_k^{ij})\}$, let

$$\tau_{i,l}\left(t_k^{ij}\right) = \sum_{s=1}^{l} h_i(t_{i,i_k+s-1}) \tag{3.25}$$

$$\tau_{j,q}\left(t_k^{ij}\right) = \sum_{s=1}^{q} h_j(t_{j,j_k+s-1}) \tag{3.26}$$

where the summation in (3.25) equals zero if $l < s$ and that in (3.26) equals to zero if $q < s$. Denote by $\psi_{i,l}(t_k^{ij})$, $l \in \{0, 1, \ldots, n_i(t_k^{ij}) - 1\}$ and $\psi_{j,q}(t_k^{ij})$, $q \in \{0, 1, \ldots, n_j(t_k^{ij}) - 1\}$, respectively, the sampling intervals of sensors i and j over the period $[t_k^{ij}, t_{k+1}^{ij}]$. Then, one has

$$\begin{aligned}\psi_{i,l}\left(t_k^{ij}\right) = \left[t_k^{ij} + \tau_{i,l}\left(t_k^{ij}\right),\ t_k^{ij} + \tau_{i,l+1}\left(t_k^{ij}\right)\right], \\ l \in \bar{Z}_i \triangleq \left\{0, 1, \ldots, n_i\left(t_k^{ij}\right) - 1\right\}\end{aligned} \tag{3.27}$$

$$\begin{aligned}\psi_{j,q}\left(t_k^{ij}\right) = \left[t_k^{ij} + \tau_{j,q}\left(t_k^{ij}\right),\ t_k^{ij} + \tau_{j,q+1}\left(t_k^{ij}\right)\right], \\ q \in \bar{Z}_j \triangleq \left\{0, 1, \ldots, n_j\left(t_k^{ij}\right) - 1\right\}\end{aligned} \tag{3.28}$$

If $\psi_{i,l}(t_k^{ij}) \cap \psi_{j,q}(t_k^{ij}) \neq \phi$, then let

$$\begin{aligned}&\psi_{i,l}\left(t_k^{ij}\right) \cap \psi_{j,q}\left(t_k^{ij}\right) \\ &= \left[t_k^{ij} + \tau_{i,l}\left(t_k^{ij}\right) + u_{i,l}\left(t_k^{ij}\right)h,\right. \\ &\qquad \left. t_k^{ij} + \tau_{i,l}\left(t_k^{ij}\right) + \left(u_{i,l}\left(t_k^{ij}\right) + \pi_{l,q}\left(t_k^{ij}\right)\right)h\right] \\ &= \left[t_k^{ij} + \tau_{j,q}\left(t_k^{ij}\right) + u_{j,q}\left(t_k^{ij}\right)h,\right. \\ &\qquad \left. t_k^{ij} + \tau_{j,q}\left(t_k^{ij}\right) + \left(u_{j,q}\left(t_k^{ij}\right) + \pi_{l,q}\left(t_k^{ij}\right)\right)h\right]\end{aligned} \tag{3.29}$$

where $\pi_{l,q}(t_k^{ij})h$ is the overlap of the two time intervals $\psi_{i,l}(t_k^{ij})$ and $\psi_{j,q}(t_k^{ij})$, while $t_k^{ij} + \tau_{i,l}(t_k^{ij}) + u_{i,l}(t_k^{ij})h$ and $t_k^{ij} + \tau_{j,q}(t_k^{ij}) + u_{j,q}(t_k^{ij})h$ are the instants when the overlap begins to happen at sensors i and j, respectively. Taking the interval $[t_0^{ij}, t_1^{ij}]$ in Fig. 3.2 for example, it can be seen that

$$\psi_{i,2}\left(t_0^{ij}\right) = \left[t_0^{ij} + \tau_{i,2}\left(t_0^{ij}\right),\ t_0^{ij} + \tau_{i,3}\left(t_0^{ij}\right)\right] = [t_{i,2},\ t_{i,3}]$$

$$\psi_{j,1}\left(t_0^{ij}\right) = \left[t_0^{ij} + \tau_{j,1}\left(t_0^{ij}\right),\ t_0^{ij} + \tau_{j,2}\left(t_0^{ij}\right)\right] = [t_{j,1},\ t_{j,2}]$$

and

$$\begin{aligned}&\psi_{i,2}\left(t_0^{ij}\right)\cap\psi_{j,1}\left(t_0^{ij}\right)\\&=\left[t_0^{ij}+\tau_{i,2}\left(t_0^{ij}\right)+h,\ t_0^{ij}+\tau_{i,2}\left(t_0^{ij}\right)+2h\right]\\&=\left[t_0^{ij}+\tau_{j,1}\left(t_0^{ij}\right),\ t_0^{ij}+\tau_{j,1}\left(t_0^{ij}\right)+h\right]\end{aligned}$$

and one has $u_{i,2}(t_0^{ij})=1$, $u_{j,1}(t_0^{ij})=0$, and $\pi_{2,1}(t_0^{ij})=1$.

A recursive equation for computing the cross-covariances $P_{i,j}(t_k^{ij}|t_k^{ij})$, $i,\ j\in Z_0$, $i\neq j$ is now presented in the following theorem.

Theorem 3.3 *For the system (3.3) and (3.4) with nonuniform estimation rates, the cross-covariance of local estimation errors at sensors i and j, $i,j\in Z_0$, $i\neq j$ satisfies the following recursive equation*

$$P_{i,j}\left(t_{k+1}^{ij}|t_{k+1}^{ij}\right)=\sum_{l=1}^{3}\chi_l \tag{3.30}$$

where

$$\begin{aligned}\chi_1=&\prod_{l=1}^{n_i\left(t_k^{ij}\right)}\left(\bar{A}_i-K_i\left(t_k^{ij}+\tau_{i,l}\left(t_k^{ij}\right)\right)C_i\bar{A}_i\right)P_{i,j}\left(t_k^{ij}|t_k^{ij}\right)\\&\times\left[\prod_{q=1}^{n_j\left(t_k^{ij}\right)}\left(\bar{A}_j-K_j\left(t_k^{ij}+\tau_{j,q}\left(t_k^{ij}\right)\right)C_j\bar{A}_j\right)\right]^{\mathrm{T}}\end{aligned} \tag{3.31}$$

$$\begin{aligned}\chi_2=&\sum_{l=0}^{n_i\left(t_k^{ij}\right)-1}\sum_{q=0}^{n_j\left(t_k^{ij}\right)-1}\prod_{s=l+2}^{n_i\left(t_k^{ij}\right)}\left(\bar{A}_i-K_i\left(t_k^{ij}+\tau_{i,s}\left(t_k^{ij}\right)\right)\right.\\&\left.\times C_i\bar{A}_i\right)\left(I-K_i\left(t_k^{ij}+\tau_{i,l+1}\left(t_k^{ij}\right)\right)C_i\right)\\&\times\Upsilon_{l,q}\left(t_k^{ij}\right)\left(I-K_j\left(t_k^{ij}+\tau_{j,q+1}\left(t_k^{ij}\right)\right)C_j\right)^{\mathrm{T}}\\&\times\left[\prod_{s=q+2}^{n_j\left(t_k^{ij}\right)}\left(\bar{A}_j-K_j\left(t_k^{ij}+\tau_{j,s}\left(t_k^{ij}\right)\right)C_j\bar{A}_j\right)\right]^{\mathrm{T}}\end{aligned} \tag{3.32}$$

$$\Upsilon_{l,q}\left(t_k^{ij}\right) = \begin{cases} 0, & \psi_{i,l}\left(t_k^{ij}\right) \cap \psi_{j,q}\left(t_k^{ij}\right) = \phi \\ \bar{\Upsilon}_{l,q}\left(t_k^{ij}\right), & \psi_{i,l}\left(t_k^{ij}\right) \cap \psi_{j,q}\left(t_k^{ij}\right) \neq \phi \end{cases}, l \in \bar{Z}_i,\ q \in \bar{Z}_j \tag{3.33}$$

$$\bar{\Upsilon}_{l,q}\left(t_k^{ij}\right) = \sum_{r=1}^{2}\sum_{s=1}^{2}\bar{\theta}_{ir}\bar{\theta}_{js}\sum_{\beta=1}^{\pi_{l,q}\left(t_k^{ij}\right)+1} A^{a_{ir}-u_{i,l}\left(t_k^{ij}\right)-\beta}$$
$$\times BQ_{\omega}B^{\mathrm{T}}\left(A^{a_{js}-u_{j,q}\left(t_k^{ij}\right)-\beta}\right)^{\mathrm{T}} \tag{3.34}$$

$$\chi_3 = K_i\left(t_{k+1}^{ij}\right) D_i Q_{i,j}^{\upsilon} D_j^{\mathrm{T}} K_j^{\mathrm{T}}\left(t_{k+1}^{ij}\right) \tag{3.35}$$

and the initial value of $P_{i,j}(t_{k+1}^{ij}|t_{k+1}^{ij})$ *is given by* $P_{i,j}(t_0^{ij}|t_0^{ij}) = P_{i,i}(t_0^{ij}|t_0^{ij})$.

Proof Subtracting $x_i(t_{i,k+1})$ from both sides of (3.14) and taking (3.4) into consideration, one obtains

$$\tilde{x}_i(t_{i,k+1}|t_{i,k}) = \bar{A}_i\tilde{x}_i(t_{i,k}|t_{i,k}) + X_i(t_{i,k}) + \omega_i(t_{i,k}) \tag{3.36}$$

Subtracting $x_i(t_{i,k+1})$ from both sides of (3.15) and taking (3.16) and (3.3) into account, one obtains

$$\begin{aligned}\tilde{x}_i(t_{i,k+1}|t_{i,k+1}) &= (I - K_i(t_{i,k+1})C_i)\tilde{x}_i(t_{i,k+1}|t_{i,k}) \\ &\quad - K_i(t_{i,k+1})D_i\upsilon_i(t_{i,k+1})\end{aligned} \tag{3.37}$$

Substituting (3.36) into (3.37) yields

$$\begin{aligned}\tilde{x}_i(t_{i,k+1}|t_{i,k+1}) &= \left(\bar{A}_i - K_i(t_{i,k+1})C_i\bar{A}_i\right)\tilde{x}_i(t_{i,k}|t_{i,k}) \\ &\quad + \sum_{l=1}^{2}\left(\theta_{il}(t_{i,k}) - \bar{\theta}_{il}\right)(I - K_i(t_{i,k+1})C_i)A_{il}x_i(t_{i,k}) \\ &\quad + (I - K_i(t_{i,k+1})C_i)\omega_i(t_{i,k}) - K_i(t_{i,k+1})D_i\upsilon_i(t_{i,k+1})\end{aligned} \tag{3.38}$$

Applying (3.38) recursively, yields the following state equation of the estimation error at the time scale t_k^{ij}

$$\tilde{x}_i\left(t_{k+1}^{ij}|t_{k+1}^{ij}\right) = \sum_{l=1}^{3}\xi_{il}\left(t_k^{ij}\right) - \xi_{i4}\left(t_k^{ij}\right) \tag{3.39}$$

where

$$\xi_{i1}\left(t_k^{ij}\right) = \prod_{l=1}^{n_i\left(t_k^{ij}\right)} \left(\bar{A}_i - K_i\left(t_k^{ij} + \tau_{i,l}\left(t_k^{ij}\right)\right) C_i\bar{A}_i\right) \tilde{x}_i\left(t_k^{ij}|t_k^{ij}\right) \tag{3.40}$$

$$\begin{aligned}\xi_{i2}\left(t_k^{ij}\right) = & \sum_{l=0}^{n_i\left(t_k^{ij}\right)-1} \prod_{s=l+2}^{n_i\left(t_k^{ij}\right)} \left(\bar{A}_i - K_i\left(t_k^{ij} + \tau_{i,s}\left(t_k^{ij}\right)\right) C_i\bar{A}_i\right) \\ & \times\left(I - K_i\left(t_k^{ij} + \tau_{i,l+1}\left(t_k^{ij}\right)\right) C_i\right) \\ & \times \sum_{r=1}^{2}\left(\theta_{ir}\left(t_k^{ij} + \tau_{i,l}\left(t_k^{ij}\right)\right) - \bar{\theta}_{ir}\right) A_{ir} x_i\left(t_k^{ij} + \tau_{i,l}\left(t_k^{ij}\right)\right)\end{aligned} \tag{3.41}$$

$$\begin{aligned}\xi_{i3}\left(t_k^{ij}\right) = & \sum_{l=0}^{n_i\left(t_k^{ij}\right)-1} \prod_{s=l+2}^{n_i\left(t_k^{ij}\right)} \left(\bar{A}_i - K_i\left(t_k^{ij} + \tau_{i,s}\left(t_k^{ij}\right)\right) C_i\bar{A}_i\right) \\ & \times\left(I - K_i\left(t_k^{ij} + \tau_{i,l+1}\left(t_k^{ij}\right)\right) C_i\right) \omega_i\left(t_k^{ij} + \tau_{i,l}\left(t_k^{ij}\right)\right)\end{aligned} \tag{3.42}$$

$$\begin{aligned}\xi_{i4}\left(t_k^{ij}\right) = & \sum_{l=1}^{n_i\left(t_k^{ij}\right)} \prod_{s=l+1}^{n_i\left(t_k^{ij}\right)} \left(\bar{A}_i - K_i\left(t_k^{ij} + \tau_{i,s}\left(t_k^{ij}\right)\right) C_i\bar{A}_i\right) \\ & \times K_i\left(t_k^{ij} + \tau_{i,l}\left(t_k^{ij}\right)\right) D_i \upsilon_i\left(t_k^{ij} + \tau_{i,l}\left(t_k^{ij}\right)\right)\end{aligned} \tag{3.43}$$

and we define that $\prod_{j=a}^{b} f(j) = I$ if $b < a$ in (3.40), (3.41), (3.42) and (3.43).

For $i, j \in Z_0$ and $i \neq j$, define the cross-covariance of estimation errors in sensors i and j as $P_{i,j}(t_k^{ij}|t_k^{ij}) = \mathbf{E}\{\tilde{x}_i(t_k^{ij}|t_k^{ij})\tilde{x}_j^{\mathrm{T}}(t_k^{ij}|t_k^{ij})\}$. Then, since $\mathbf{E}\{\theta_{ir}(t_k^{ij}+\tau_{i,l}(t_k^{ij}))-\bar{\theta}_{ir}\} = 0$, $r = 1, 2$, $l = 0, 1, \ldots, n_i(t_k^{ij})$, $\tilde{x}_i(t_k^{ij}|t_k^{ij}) \perp \omega_j(t_k^{ij} + \tau_{j,q}(t_k^{ij}))$, $\tilde{x}_i(t_k^{ij}|t_k^{ij}) \perp \upsilon_j(t_k^{ij} + \tau_{j,q}(t_k^{ij}))$, $q = 0, 1, \ldots, n_j(t_k^{ij})$, one has by (3.39), (3.40), (3.41), (3.42) and (3.43) that

$$P_{i,j}\left(t_{k+1}^{ij}|t_{k+1}^{ij}\right) = \sum_{l=1}^{4} \mathbf{E}\left\{\xi_{il}\left(t_k^{ij}\right) \xi_{jl}^{\mathrm{T}}\left(t_k^{ij}\right)\right\} \tag{3.44}$$

By following some routine computations, one has

$$\mathbf{E}\left\{\xi_{i1}\left(t_k^{ij}\right) \xi_{j1}^{\mathrm{T}}\left(t_k^{ij}\right)\right\} = \chi_1 \tag{3.45}$$

For all $l = 1, 2$ and $s = 1, 2$, one has by Assumption 3.2 that

$$\mathbf{E}\left\{(\theta_{il}(t_{i,k}) - \theta_{il})(\theta_{js}(t_{j,k}) - \theta_{js})\right\} = 0,\ i, j \in Z_0,\ i \neq j \tag{3.46}$$

It follows from (3.46) that

$$\mathbf{E}\left\{\xi_{i2}\left(t_k^{ij}\right)\xi_{j2}^{\mathrm{T}}\left(t_k^{ij}\right)\right\} = 0 \tag{3.47}$$

For $l \in \bar{Z}_i,\ q \in \bar{Z}_j$, let

$$\Upsilon_{l,q}\left(t_k^{ij}\right) = \mathbf{E}\left\{\omega_i\left(t_k^{ij} + \tau_{i,l}\left(t_k^{ij}\right)\right)\omega_j^{\mathrm{T}}\left(t_k^{ij} + \tau_{j,q}\left(t_k^{ij}\right)\right)\right\} \tag{3.48}$$

If $\psi_{i,l}(t_k^{ij}) \cap \psi_{j,q}(t_k^{ij}) = \phi$, then since $\omega(t_{i,k})$ is a white noise, one has by (3.8) that $\Upsilon_{l,q}(t_k^{ij}) = 0$. If $\psi_{i,l}(t_k^{ij}) \cap \psi_{j,q}(t_k^{ij}) \neq \phi$, then one has by (3.8) and (3.9) that

$$\begin{aligned}
\Upsilon_{l,q}\left(t_k^{ij}\right) &= \mathbf{E}\left\{\sum_{r=1}^{2}\theta_{ir}\left(t_k^{ij} + \tau_{i,l}\left(t_k^{ij}\right)\right)\sum_{\beta=0}^{a_{ir}-1}A^{a_{ir}-\beta-1}\right.\\
&\quad \times B\omega\left(t_k^{ij} + \tau_{i,l}\left(t_k^{ij}\right) + \beta h\right)\left[\sum_{r=1}^{2}\theta_{js}\left(t_k^{ij} + \tau_{j,q}\left(t_k^{ij}\right)\right)\right.\\
&\quad \left.\left.\times\sum_{\beta=0}^{a_{js}-1}A^{a_{js}-\beta-1}B\omega\left(t_k^{ij} + \tau_{j,q}\left(t_k^{ij}\right) + \beta h\right)\right]^{\mathrm{T}}\right\}\\
&= \mathbf{E}\left\{\sum_{r=1}^{2}\theta_{ir}\left(t_k^{ij} + \tau_{i,l}\left(t_k^{ij}\right)\right)\sum_{\beta=u_{i,l}\left(t_k^{ij}\right)}^{u_{i,l}\left(t_k^{ij}\right)+\pi_{l,q}\left(t_k^{ij}\right)}A^{a_{ir}-\beta-1}\right.\\
&\quad \times B\omega\left(t_k^{ij} + \tau_{i,l}\left(t_k^{ij}\right) + \beta h\right)\left[\sum_{r=1}^{2}\theta_{js}\left(t_k^{ij} + \tau_{j,q}\left(t_k^{ij}\right)\right)\right.\\
&\quad \left.\left.\times\sum_{\beta=u_{j,q}\left(t_k^{ij}\right)}^{u_{j,q}\left(t_k^{ij}\right)+\pi_{l,q}\left(t_k^{ij}\right)}A^{a_{js}-\beta-1}B\omega\left(t_k^{ij} + \tau_{j,q}\left(t_k^{ij}\right) + \beta h\right)\right]^{\mathrm{T}}\right\}\\
&= \bar{\Upsilon}_{l,q}\left(t_k^{ij}\right)
\end{aligned} \tag{3.49}$$

Thus, one obtains (3.33). It follows from (3.42) and (3.48) that

$$\mathbf{E}\left\{\xi_{i3}\left(t_k^{ij}\right)\xi_{j3}^{\mathrm{T}}\left(t_k^{ij}\right)\right\} = \chi_2 \tag{3.50}$$

Since $t_k^{ij} + \tau_{i,l} \neq t_k^{ij} + \tau_{j,q}$, $\forall\ l \in \{1, 2, \ldots, n_i(t_k^{ij}) - 1\}$, $q \in \{1, 2, \ldots, n_j(t_k^{ij}) - 1\}$, and $t_k^{ij} + \tau_{i,n_i(t_k^{ij})} = t_k^{ij} + \tau_{j,n_j(t_k^{ij})}$, one obtains

$$\mathbf{E}\left\{\xi_{i4}\left(t_k^{ij}\right)\xi_{j4}^{\mathrm{T}}\left(t_k^{ij}\right)\right\} = \chi_3 \tag{3.51}$$

Then, (3.30) follows from (3.44), (3.45), (3.47), (3.50), and (3.51). The proof is thus completed.

Based on Theorems 3.1, 3.2 and 3.3, the track-to-track fusion estimation algorithm with two rates in sensor i, $i \in Z_0$ is given as follows.

Algorithm 3.1

Step 1: Sensor i generates its local estimates $\hat{x}_i$ by applying the recursive equations in Theorem 3.1.

Step 2: Sensor i collects available local estimates, error covariances and estimator gain matrices from itself and the other sensors.

Step 3: If there is no local estimates from the other sensors, then sensor i keeps its own local estimate as the fused one. Otherwise, it determines the parameters $u_{i,l}$, $u_{j,q}$ and $\pi_{l,q}$, $i, j \in Z_0$, $i \neq j$, $l \in \bar{Z}_i$, $q \in \bar{Z}_j$ according to the time stamps in the local estimates and then generates fused estimates according to the recursive equations and the fusion rule in Theorems 3.2 and 3.3.

If the estimation rate $h_i(t_{i,k})$, $i \in Z_0$ are known exactly by the sensors a priori at every estimation instant, then standard Kalman estimators can be designed for each local estimation system, and the corresponding fusion algorithm can be designed by following the similar lines as presented in this section.

3.5 Design of the Fusion Estimators (Type II)

In the type I fusion estimator, it can be seen from Algorithm 3.1 that one has to determine the parameters $u_{i,l}$, $u_{j,q}$, and $\pi_{l,q}$ in computing the cross-covariances. This section will present another design method for the fusion estimators, and the parameter determination procedures as in the type I fusion estimators will be removed.

3.5.1 Estimator Design

We will first present a new model for each local estimation system. It follows from (3.7) and $\theta_{i1}(t_{i,k}) + \theta_{i2}(t_{i,k}) = 1$ that

$$\begin{aligned} A_i(t_{i,k}) &= \theta_{i1}(t_{i,k})A_{i1} + (1-\theta_{i1}(t_{i,k}))A_{i2} \\ &= A_{i2} + \theta_{i1}(t_{i,k})(A_{i1} - A_{i2}) \end{aligned} \tag{3.52}$$

Substituting (3.52) into (3.4) leads to

$$x_i(t_{i,k+1}) = A_{i2}x_i(t_{i,k}) + \tilde{\omega}_i(t_{i,k}), \; i \in Z_0 \tag{3.53}$$

where

$$\tilde{\omega}_i(t_{i,k}) = \theta_{i1}(t_{i,k})(A_{i1} - A_{i2})x_i(t_{i,k}) + \omega_i(t_{i,k}) \tag{3.54}$$

By (3.9), Assumption 3.2 and the fact $x_i(t_{i,k}) \perp \omega_i(t_{i,k})$, one has

$$\mathrm{Var}(\tilde{\omega}_i(t_{i,k})) = B_i(t_{i,k})B_i^{\mathrm{T}}(t_{i,k}) \tag{3.55}$$

where

$$\begin{aligned} B_i(t_{i,k}) &= [\vartheta_i(t_{i,k}) \; \kappa_1 \; \kappa_2] \\ \vartheta_i(t_{i,k}) &= \bar{\theta}_{i1}^{1/2}(A_{i1} - A_{i2})\Theta_i^{1/2}(t_{i,k}) \\ \kappa_l &= \left[\bar{\theta}_{il}^{1/2}A^{a_{il}-1}BQ_\omega^{1/2} \; \ldots \; \bar{\theta}_{il}^{1/2}ABQ_\omega^{1/2} \; \bar{\theta}_{il}^{1/2}BQ_\omega^{1/2}\right], \; l = 1, 2 \end{aligned}$$

Moreover, one has by Assumptions 3.1 and 3.2 that $\tilde{\omega}_i(t_{i,k})$ is a zero-mean white random process. Therefore, random processes $\tilde{\omega}_i(t_{i,k})$ and $B_i(t_{i,k})\nu(t_{i,k})$ have the same (first- and second-order) statistics, where $\nu(t_{i,k})$ is a zero-mean unit-variance white random process that is uncorrelated to $\upsilon_i(t_{i,k})$, $i \in Z_0$. Thus, the system model in (3.4) can be rewritten as

$$x_i(t_{i,k+1}) = A_{i2}x_i(t_{i,k}) + B_i(t_{i,k})\nu(t_{i,k}), \; i \in Z_0 \tag{3.56}$$

It can be seen from (3.56) that each local estimation system is described as a linear time-varying stochastic system. Then, a standard Kalman estimator can be designed to estimate the state $x_i(t_{i,k})$ based on the system model (3.56), and the estimator is given in the following lemma.

Lemma 3.3 *For sensor i with a nonuniform estimation rate $h_i(t_{i,k})$ satisfying (3.5), the local recursive Kalman estimator for system (3.56) is given by*

$$\begin{aligned}\hat{x}_i(t_{i,k+1}|t_{i,k+1}) &= (I - K_i(t_{i,k+1})C_i)A_{i2}\hat{x}_i(t_{i,k}|t_{i,k})\\ &\quad + K_i(t_{i,k+1})y_i(t_{i,k+1}) \end{aligned} \tag{3.57}$$

$$\begin{aligned}K_i(t_{i,k+1}) &= P_{i,i}(t_{i,k+1}|t_{i,k})C_i^{\mathrm{T}}(C_iP_{i,i}(t_{i,k+1}|t_{i,k})C_i^{\mathrm{T}}\\ &\quad + D_iQ_{i,i}^{\upsilon}D_i^{\mathrm{T}})^{-1}\end{aligned} \tag{3.58}$$

$$P_{i,i}(t_{i,k+1}|t_{i,k}) = A_{i2}P_{i,i}(t_{i,k}|t_{i,k})A_{i2}^{\mathrm{T}} + B_i(t_{i,k})B_i^{\mathrm{T}}(t_{i,k}) \tag{3.59}$$

$$\begin{aligned}P_{i,i}(t_{i,k+1}|t_{i,k+1}) &= (I - K_i(t_{i,k+1})C_i)\\ &\quad \times P_{i,i}(t_{i,k+1}|t_{i,k})(I - K_i(t_{i,k+1})C_i)^{\mathrm{T}}\\ &\quad + K_i(t_{i,k+1})D_iQ_{i,i}^{\upsilon}D_i^{\mathrm{T}}K_i^{\mathrm{T}}(t_{i,k+1})\end{aligned} \tag{3.60}$$

where $\hat{x}_i(t_{i,0}|t_{i,0}) = x_0$, $P_{i,i}(t_{i,0}|t_{i,0}) = P_0$, and the state variance $\Theta_i(t_{i,k})$ in $B_i(t_{i,k})$ is computed by the recursive equation in (3.12).

When the local estimates computed by the recursive equations in Lemma 3.3 are available, each sensor then collects local estimates, error covariances, and Kalman gain matrices from itself and the other sensors to generate fused estimates according to the fusion rule given in Theorem 3.2. Similar to the design of the type I fusion estimator, one has to calculate the estimation error cross-covariances in the second-stage fusion estimation, and a recursive equation for computing the cross-covariances $P_{i,j}(t_k^{ij}|t_k^{ij})$ for the type II fusion estimators is presented in the following theorem.

Theorem 3.4 *For the system (3.3) and (3.56) with nonuniform estimation rates, the cross-covariance of local estimation errors at sensors i and j, $i, j \in Z_0$, $i \neq j$ satisfies the following recursive equation*

$$P_{i,j}\left(t_{k+1}^{ij}|t_{k+1}^{ij}\right) = \sum_{l=1}^{3}\Gamma_l \tag{3.61}$$

where

$$\begin{aligned}\Gamma_1 &= \prod_{l=1}^{n_i\left(t_k^{ij}\right)}\left(A_{i2} - K_i\left(t_k^{ij} + \tau_{i,l}\left(t_k^{ij}\right)\right)C_iA_{i2}\right)P_{i,j}\left(t_k^{ij}|t_k^{ij}\right)\\ &\quad \times \left[\prod_{q=1}^{n_j\left(t_k^{ij}\right)}\left(A_{j2} - K_j\left(t_k^{ij} + \tau_{j,q}\left(t_k^{ij}\right)\right)C_jA_{j2}\right)\right]^{\mathrm{T}}\end{aligned} \tag{3.62}$$

$$
\begin{aligned}
\Gamma_2 = & \prod_{s=2}^{n_i\left(t_k^{ij}\right)} \left(A_{i2} - K_i\left(t_k^{ij} + \tau_{i,s}\left(t_k^{ij}\right)\right) C_i A_{i2}\right) \\
& \times \left(I - K_i\left(t_k^{ij} + \tau_{i,1}\left(t_k^{ij}\right)\right) C_i\right) \\
& \times B_i\left(t_k^{ij}\right) B_j^{\mathrm{T}}\left(t_k^{ij}\right)\left(I - K_j\left(t_k^{ij} + \tau_{j,1}\left(t_k^{ij}\right)\right) C_j\right)^{\mathrm{T}} \\
& \times \left[\prod_{s=2}^{n_j\left(t_k^{ij}\right)} \left(A_{j2} - K_j\left(t_k^{ij} + \tau_{j,s}\left(t_k^{ij}\right)\right) C_j A_{j2}\right)\right]^{\mathrm{T}}
\end{aligned} \tag{3.63}
$$

$$
\Gamma_3 = K_i\left(t_{k+1}^{ij}\right) D_i Q_{i,j}^{\upsilon} D_j^{\mathrm{T}} K_j^{\mathrm{T}}\left(t_{k+1}^{ij}\right) \tag{3.64}
$$

and the state variance $\Theta_i(t_k^{ij})$ in $B_i(t_k^{ij})$ is computed by the recursive equation in (3.12); the initial value of $P_{i,j}(t_{k+1}^{ij}|t_{k+1}^{ij})$ is given by $P_{i,j}(t_0^{ij}|t_0^{ij}) = P_{i,i}(t_0^{ij}|t_0^{ij})$.

Proof It follows from (3.56), (3.57) and (3.3) that

$$
\begin{aligned}
\tilde{x}_i(t_{i,k+1}|t_{i,k+1}) = & (I - K_i(t_{i,k+1})C_i)A_{i2}\tilde{x}_i(t_{i,k}|t_{i,k}) \\
& + (I - K_i(t_{i,k+1})C_i)B_i(t_{i,k})\nu(t_{i,k}) \\
& - K_i(t_{i,k+1})D_i\upsilon_i(t_{i,k+1})
\end{aligned} \tag{3.65}
$$

Applying (3.65) recursively, yields the following state equation of the estimation error at the time scale t_k^{ij}

$$
\tilde{x}_i\left(t_{k+1}^{ij}|t_{k+1}^{ij}\right) = \eta_{i1}\left(t_k^{ij}\right) + \eta_{i2}\left(t_k^{ij}\right) - \eta_{i3}\left(t_k^{ij}\right) \tag{3.66}
$$

where

$$
\begin{aligned}
\eta_{i1}\left(t_k^{ij}\right) = & \prod_{l=1}^{n_i\left(t_k^{ij}\right)} \left(A_{i2} - K_i\left(t_k^{ij} + \tau_{i,l}\left(t_k^{ij}\right)\right)\right. \\
& \left. \times C_i A_{i2}\right) \tilde{x}_i\left(t_k^{ij}|t_k^{ij}\right)
\end{aligned} \tag{3.67}
$$

$$
\begin{aligned}
\eta_{i2}\left(t_k^{ij}\right) = & \sum_{l=0}^{n_i\left(t_k^{ij}\right)-1} \prod_{s=l+2}^{n_i\left(t_k^{ij}\right)} \left(A_{i2} - K_i\left(t_k^{ij} + \tau_{i,s}\left(t_k^{ij}\right)\right)\right. \\
& \left. \times C_i A_{i2}\right)\left(I - K_i\left(t_k^{ij} + \tau_{i,l+1}\left(t_k^{ij}\right)\right) C_i\right)
\end{aligned}
$$

$$\times B_i\left(t_k^{ij}+\tau_{i,l}\left(t_k^{ij}\right)\right)\nu\left(t_k^{ij}+\tau_{i,l}\left(t_k^{ij}\right)\right) \tag{3.68}$$

$$\eta_{i3}\left(t_k^{ij}\right)=\sum_{l=1}^{n_i\left(t_k^{ij}\right)}\prod_{s=l+1}^{n_i\left(t_k^{ij}\right)}\left(A_{i2}-K_i\left(t_k^{ij}+\tau_{i,s}\left(t_k^{ij}\right)\right)C_iA_{i2}\right)$$
$$\times K_i\left(t_k^{ij}+\tau_{i,l}\left(t_k^{ij}\right)\right)D_i\upsilon_i\left(t_k^{ij}+\tau_{i,l}\left(t_k^{ij}\right)\right) \tag{3.69}$$

and we define that $\prod_{j=a}^{b} f(j)=I$ if $b<a$ in (3.67), (3.68) and (3.69). Since

$$\tilde{x}_i\left(t_k^{ij}|t_k^{ij}\right)\perp\nu\left(t_k^{ij}+\tau_{j,q}\left(t_k^{ij}\right)\right)$$
$$\tilde{x}_i\left(t_k^{ij}|t_k^{ij}\right)\perp\upsilon_j\left(t_k^{ij}+\tau_{j,q}\left(t_k^{ij}\right)\right),\ q=0,1,\ldots,n_j\left(t_k^{ij}\right)$$

one has by (3.66), (3.67), (3.68) and (3.69) that

$$P_{i,j}\left(t_{k+1}^{ij}|t_{k+1}^{ij}\right)=\sum_{l=1}^{3}\mathbf{E}\left\{\eta_{il}\left(t_k^{ij}\right)\eta_{jl}^{\mathrm{T}}\left(t_k^{ij}\right)\right\} \tag{3.70}$$

Direct computation yields

$$\mathbf{E}\left\{\eta_{i1}\left(t_k^{ij}\right)\eta_{j1}^{\mathrm{T}}\left(t_k^{ij}\right)\right\}=\Gamma_1 \tag{3.71}$$

Let

$$\Upsilon_{l,q}^{\nu}\left(t_k^{ij}\right)=\mathbf{E}\left\{\nu\left(t_k^{ij}+\tau_{i,l}\left(t_k^{ij}\right)\right)\nu^{\mathrm{T}}\left(t_k^{ij}+\tau_{j,q}\left(t_k^{ij}\right)\right)\right\},\ l\in\bar{Z}_i,\ q\in\bar{Z}_j \tag{3.72}$$

Then, direct computation gives

$$\mathbf{E}\left\{\eta_{i2}\left(t_k^{ij}\right)\eta_{j2}^{\mathrm{T}}\left(t_k^{ij}\right)\right\}$$
$$=\sum_{l=0}^{n_i\left(t_k^{ij}\right)-1}\sum_{q=0}^{n_j\left(t_k^{ij}\right)-1}\prod_{s=l+2}^{n_i\left(t_k^{ij}\right)}\left(A_{i2}-K_i\left(t_k^{ij}+\tau_{i,s}\left(t_k^{ij}\right)\right)\right.$$
$$\left.\times C_iA_{i2}\right)\left(I-K_i\left(t_k^{ij}+\tau_{i,l+1}\left(t_k^{ij}\right)\right)C_i\right)$$
$$\times B_i\left(t_k^{ij}+\tau_{i,l}\left(t_k^{ij}\right)\right)B_j^{\mathrm{T}}\left(t_k^{ij}+\tau_{j,q}\left(t_k^{ij}\right)\right)\Upsilon_{l,q}^{\nu}\left(t_k^{ij}\right)$$

$$
\times \left(I - K_j\left(t_k^{ij} + \tau_{j,q+1}\left(t_k^{ij}\right)\right) C_j\right)^{\mathrm{T}}
$$

$$
\times \left[\prod_{s=q+2}^{n_j\left(t_k^{ij}\right)} \left(A_{j2} - K_j\left(t_k^{ij} + \tau_{j,s}\left(t_k^{ij}\right)\right) C_j A_{j2}\right)\right]^{\mathrm{T}} \tag{3.73}
$$

Note that

$$
\begin{cases} t_k^{ij} + \tau_{i,l} \neq t_k^{ij} + \tau_{j,q} \\ \forall\, l \in \left\{1, \ldots, n_i\left(t_k^{ij}\right) - 1\right\},\ q \in \left\{1, \ldots, n_j\left(t_k^{ij}\right) - 1\right\} \\ t_k^{ij} + \tau_{i,l} = t_k^{ij} + \tau_{j,q},\ l = 0,\ q = 0 \end{cases} \tag{3.74}
$$

Then, since ν is a white noise, one has by (3.72) and (3.74) that

$$
\Upsilon_{l,q}^{\nu}\left(t_k^{ij}\right) = \begin{cases} 0,\ l \neq 0,\ q \neq 0 \\ 1,\ l = 0,\ q = 0 \end{cases} \tag{3.75}
$$

Substituting (3.75) into (3.73) leads to

$$
\mathbf{E}\left\{\eta_{i2}\left(t_k^{ij}\right) \eta_{j2}^{\mathrm{T}}\left(t_k^{ij}\right)\right\} = \Gamma_2 \tag{3.76}
$$

By following some similar derivations for (3.51), one obtains

$$
\mathbf{E}\left\{\eta_{i3}\left(t_k^{ij}\right) \eta_{j3}^{\mathrm{T}}\left(t_k^{ij}\right)\right\} = \Gamma_3 \tag{3.77}
$$

Then, (3.61) follows from (3.70), (3.71), (3.76), and (3.77). The proof is thus completed.

By lifting the stochastic parts in the system matrix $A_i(t_{i,k})$ into the noise, we obtain a reformulated system model with a constant system matrix and a unit-variance noise as shown in (3.56), and this reformulated system model helps derive the type II estimator with a simpler structure as compared with the type I estimator. It can be seen from Theorem 3.4 that in designing the type II estimators, it is not necessary to know the parameters $u_{i,l}$, $u_{j,q}$ and $\pi_{l,q}$ as required in the type I estimators. However, the disadvantage of the type II estimator is that the matrix $B_i(t_{i,k})$, $i \in Z_0$ is an augmented one, which increases computation costs.

In the state equation (3.56), A_{i2} is a constant matrix, while $B_i(t_{i,k})$ is a time-varying one depending on the state variance $\Theta_i(t_{i,k})$, and $B_i(t_{i,k})$ converges to a constant value if $\Theta_i(t_{i,k})$ is convergent. Then, it is well known from the standard Kalman filtering that the local estimators designed in Theorem 3.4 may converge to steady-state estimators. The convergence analysis for the type II fusion estimators will be presented in the next subsection.

3.5.2 Convergence of the Estimator

We have the following lemma about the convergence of the state variance $\Theta_i(t_{i,k})$, $i \in Z_0$.

Lemma 3.4 *If there exists a matrix* $Q_i > 0$ *and a scalar* $0 < \lambda_i < 1$ *such that the following inequality*

$$\Omega_i \triangleq \sum_{l=1}^{2} \bar{\theta}_{il} A_{il}^{\mathrm{T}} Q_i A_{il} - \lambda_i^2 Q_i < 0, \; i \in Z_0 \tag{3.78}$$

holds, then the state variance $\Theta_i(t_{i,k})$ *converges exponentially fast to a steady-state value, and the steady-state value denoted by* $\bar{\Theta}_i$ *is independent of the initial value* $\Theta_i(t_{i,0})$.

Proof Consider the following dynamic system

$$\check{x}_i(t_{i,k+1}) = A_i(t_{i,k})\check{x}_i(t_{i,k}), \; i \in Z_0 \tag{3.79}$$

Let $\check{\Theta}_i(t_{i,k}) = \mathrm{Var}(\check{x}_i(t_{i,k}))$, then by (3.9), $\check{\Theta}_i(t_{i,k})$ satisfies the following recursive equation

$$\check{\Theta}_i(t_{i,k+1}) = \sum_{l=1}^{2} \bar{\theta}_{il} A_{il} \check{\Theta}_i(t_{i,k}) A_{il}^{\mathrm{T}} \tag{3.80}$$

Choose the following Lyapunov function for system (3.79)

$$V_i(t_{i,k}) = \check{x}_i^{\mathrm{T}}(t_{i,k}) Q_i \check{x}_i(t_{i,k}) \tag{3.81}$$

Then, one has by (3.9), (3.78), (3.79), and (3.81) that

$$\mathbf{E}\{V_i(t_{i,k+1})|\check{x}_i(t_{i,k})\} - \lambda_i^2 V_i(t_{i,k}) = \check{x}_i^{\mathrm{T}}(t_{i,k}) \Omega_i \check{x}_i(t_{i,k}) < 0 \tag{3.82}$$

Applying (3.82) recursively, yields

$$\mathbf{E}\{V_i(t_{i,k})|\check{x}_i(t_{i,0})\} < \lambda_i^{2(t_{i,k}-t_{i,0})} V_i(t_{i,0}) \tag{3.83}$$

Thus, if the inequality (3.78) holds, then it can be seen from (3.83) that the Lyapunov function $V_i(t_{i,k})$ converges to zero exponentially fast. Moreover, it follows from (3.83) that

$$\begin{aligned} &\lambda_{\min}(Q_i)\mathbf{E}\{\|\check{x}_i(t_{i,k})\|^2|\check{x}_i(t_{i,0})\} \\ &\leq \mathbf{E}\{V_i(t_{i,k})|\check{x}_i(t_{i,0})\} \\ &< \lambda_i^{2(t_{i,k}-t_{i,0})} \lambda_{\max}(Q_i)\|\check{x}_i(t_{i,0})\|^2 \end{aligned} \tag{3.84}$$

which leads to

$$\mathbf{E}\{\|\check{x}_i(t_{i,k})\|^2|\check{x}_i(t_{i,0})\} < \epsilon\lambda_i^{2(t_{i,k}-t_{i,0})}\|\check{x}_i(t_{i,0})\|^2$$

where $\epsilon = \lambda_{\max}(Q_i)/\lambda_{\min}(Q_i)$. The above inequality implies that the system (3.79) is mean square exponentially stable. Thus, the inequality (3.78) guarantees that the state variance $\check{\Theta}_i(t_{i,k})$ converges exponentially fast to zero. Furthermore, by following some similar derivation procedures as in Proposition A.3 in [19], one has that the convergence of $\check{\Theta}_i(t_{i,k})$ guarantees the convergence of $\Theta_i(t_{i,k})$, and the limit of $\Theta_i(t_{i,k})$ is independent of the initial value $\Theta_i(t_{i,0})$. The proof is thus completed.

Since $B_i(t_{i,k})$ depends on $\Theta_i(t_{i,k})$, the convergence of $\Theta_i(t_{i,k})$ implies the convergence of $B_i(t_{i,k})$. Denoted by $\bar{B}_i$ the steady-state value of $B_i(t_{i,k})$, then $\bar{B}_i$ is given by

$$\bar{B}_i = \begin{bmatrix}\bar{\vartheta}_i \ \kappa_1 \ \kappa_2\end{bmatrix} \tag{3.85}$$

where $\bar{\vartheta}_i = \bar{\theta}_{i1}^{1/2}(A_{i1} - A_{i2})\bar{\Theta}_i^{1/2}$. Since $\Theta_i(t_{i,k})$ converges exponentially fast to its steady-state value, $B_i(t_{i,k})$ also converges exponentially fast to $\bar{B}_i$, i.e., there exist a constant T* such that $B_i(t_{i,k}) = \bar{B}_i$ when $t_{i,k} > \mathrm{T}^*$. Then, it is well known from the standard Kalman filtering that the recursive estimators designed by Lemma 3.3 may converge to steady-state Kalman estimators, and the Kalman gain matrices $K_i(t_{i,k})$ and the estimation error covariances $P_{i,i}(t_{i,k})$ may converge to steady-state values. Moreover, since Theorem 3.2 indicates that the fused estimation error covariance is always smaller or equal to each of the local estimation error covariances, the convergence of local estimation error covariances implies that the fused estimation error covariance is bounded. Then, the convergence of the type II fusion estimators is presented in the following theorem.

Theorem 3.5 *For the estimation system in sensor i with a estimation rate $h_i(t_{i,k})$ satisfying (3.5), if*

(1) there exists a matrix $Q_i > 0$ and a scalar $0 < \lambda_i < 1$ such that the following linear matrix inequality

$$\begin{bmatrix} -\lambda_i^2 Q_i & \Xi_{1i} \\ \Xi_{1i}^{\mathrm{T}} & -\Xi_{2i} \end{bmatrix} < 0, \ i \in Z_0 \tag{3.86}$$

holds, where $\Xi_{1i} = [\bar{\theta}_{i1}^{1/2} A_{i1}^{\mathrm{T}} Q_i \ \bar{\theta}_{i2}^{1/2} A_{i2}^{\mathrm{T}} Q_i]$ and $\Xi_{2i} = \mathrm{diag}\{Q_i, Q_i\}$.

(2) (A_{i2}, C_i) is observable and $(A_{i2}, \bar{B}_i)$ is controllable, $i \in Z_0$.

then, the local Kalman estimator given in Theorem 3.4 converges to a steady-state linear time-invariant estimator, i.e.,

$$\lim_{k\to\infty} K_i(t_{i,k}) = K_i^*, \ \lim_{k\to\infty} P_{i,i}(t_{i,k}|t_{i,k}) = P_{i,i}^*$$

and the fused estimation error covariance $P_{oi}(t_{i,k}|t_{i,k})$ is bounded.

Proof By Schur complement lemma, the inequality (3.86) is equivalent to $\Omega_i < 0$; thus, one has by Lemma 3.3 that the condition (1) guarantees that $B_i(t_{i,k})$ converges exponentially fast to $\bar{B}_i$. Moreover, the condition (2) is well known for the existence of a steady-state estimator. More details about the condition (2) can be found in the literature, such as [20]. On the other hand, it follows from Theorem 3.2 that $P_{oi}(t_{i,k}|t_{i,k}) \leq P_{l,l}(t_{i,k}|t_{i,k})$, $l \in \mathcal{N}_i(t_{i,k})$. Therefore, the convergence of $P_{i,i}(t_{i,k}|t_{i,k})$, $i \in Z_0$ implies that $P_{oi}(t_{i,k}|t_{i,k})$ is bounded. The proof is thus completed.

Remark 3.1 In the design of the type II fusion estimators, after the local estimators converge, one may apply the steady-state ones for the remaining time, and then it is not necessary for each sensor to calculate the estimator gain and transmit the gain and the estimation error covariance to the other sensors for fusion. In this way, one may expect to save both computation and communication costs by using the steady-state type II estimators. However, it should be noted that additional conditions as given in (3.86) may require to be satisfied to guarantee the convergence of the type II estimators, which restricts applications of the steady-state estimators.

Remark 3.2 By the results in Theorems 3.3 and 3.4, the fusion estimators of both type I and type II are able to calculate the estimation error cross-covariances with a nonuniform rate, and thus the fusion algorithms are adaptive to the variation of the number of local estimates for fusion, that is, each sensor just picks up the available local estimates to generate fused ones and keeps its own estimate as the fused one if there is no local estimate from the other sensors. Therefore, the proposed fusion algorithms are easy for implementation and are also applicable to situations where the sensors are not time synchronized. Moreover, by simply setting $P_{i,j} = 0, i \neq j$ in Theorem 3.2, the estimators are also applicable to the case where the measurement noises are uncorrelated.

Remark 3.3 For the general case where each estimator works at multiple rates, the estimator design method can be similarly obtained by Theorems 3.1, 3.2, 3.3, 3.4 and 3.5 and Lemma 3.3.

3.6 Simulations

In this section, simulations of two examples are presented to demonstrate the effectiveness of the proposed design method.

Example 3.1 Consider a maneuvering target tracking system where the target's position and velocity evolve according to the following state-space model [21]

$$\begin{bmatrix} x_p(\mathrm{T}_{k+1}) \\ x_v(\mathrm{T}_{k+1}) \end{bmatrix} = \begin{bmatrix} 1 & h \\ 0 & 1 \end{bmatrix} \begin{bmatrix} x_p(\mathrm{T}_k) \\ x_v(\mathrm{T}_k) \end{bmatrix} + \sqrt{10} \begin{bmatrix} h^2/2 \\ h \end{bmatrix} \omega(\mathrm{T}_k) \tag{3.87}$$

where $x_p(\mathrm{T}_k)$ and $x_v(\mathrm{T}_k)$ are the position and velocity of the target at time T_k, respectively, h is the sampling period, and $\omega(\mathrm{T}_k)$ is a zero-mean white noise with variance Q_ω. Let $x(\mathrm{T}_k) = [x_p(\mathrm{T}_k) \;\; x_v(\mathrm{T}_k)]^{\mathrm{T}}$, then we take $h = 0.5$ s, $Q_\omega = 1$ and $x(\mathrm{T}_0) = x(0) = [1 \;\; 0.5]^{\mathrm{T}}$ in the simulation.

The target is monitored by three sensors, and suppose that only the position of the target is measurable. There is no fusion center in the estimation system, and each sensor acts also as an estimator. Each sensor measures the position of the maneuvering target and generates local estimates of the position and velocity by using the measurements from itself and then collects available local estimates from itself and the other sensors to generate fused estimates of the position and velocity of the target according to the designed fusion algorithms. Each sensor i, $i \in \{1, 2, 3\}$ generates estimates with a nonuniform rate $h_i(t_{i,k}) = t_{i,k+1} - t_{i,k}$, where $t_{i,k}$, $k = 0, 1, 2, \ldots$ are instants when the measurements are collected and estimates are generated. Then, the measurement equations of the three sensors at time scale $t_{i,k}$ are given by (3.3) with

$$C_1 = [0.8 \;\; 0],\; C_2 = [0.7 \;\; 0],\; C_3 = [1 \;\; 0]$$

$$D_1 = 0.6,\; D_2 = 0.7,\; D_3 = 0.5$$

and the measurement noises are given by

$$\upsilon_i(\mathrm{T}_k) = c_i\omega_0(\mathrm{T}_k) + \upsilon_{0i}(\mathrm{T}_k),\; i = 1, 2, 3 \tag{3.88}$$

where $\omega_0(\mathrm{T}_k)$ is a zero-mean white noise with variance Q_{ω_0}, $\upsilon_{0i}(\mathrm{T}_k)$ are zero-mean white noises with variances $Q_{\upsilon_{0i}}$, $\upsilon_{0i}(\mathrm{T}_k)$ are mutually uncorrelated and are independent of $\omega_0(\mathrm{T}_k)$, and $\omega_0(\mathrm{T}_k)$ and $\upsilon_{0i}(\mathrm{T}_k)$ are uncorrelated with the process noise $\omega(\mathrm{T}_k)$. It is clear that the noises given by (3.88) are mutually correlated, and it can be calculated that $Q^{\upsilon}_{i,i} = c_i^2 Q_{\omega_0} + Q_{\upsilon_{0i}}$ and $Q^{\upsilon}_{i,j} = c_i c_j Q_{\omega_0}$, $i \neq j$, $i, j = 1, 2, 3$. In the simulation, we take $c_i = 0.5i$, $Q_{\omega_0} = 1$, $Q_{\upsilon_{01}} = 1.75$, $Q_{\upsilon_{02}} = 0.5$, and $Q_{\upsilon_{03}} = 0$.

Each sensor generates estimates with two rates, a fast one and a slow one, specifically, suppose that

$$h_1(t_{1,k}) \in \{h,\; 2h\},\; h_2(t_{2,k}) \in \{2h,\; 3h\},\; h_3(t_{3,k}) \in \{h,\; 3h\} \tag{3.89}$$

Then, $a_{11} = 1$, $a_{12} = 2$, $a_{21} = 2$, $a_{22} = 3$, $a_{31} = 1$, $a_{32} = 3$. For $i = 1, 2, 3$, assume that $h_i(t_{i,k})$ takes $a_{il}h$, $l = 1, 2$ according to a white binary-valued Bernoulli sequence $\rho_i(t_{i,k}) \in \{0, 1\}$. Specifically, $h_i(t_{i,k})$ takes $a_{i1}h$ if $\rho_i(t_{i,k}) = 1$ and takes $a_{i2}h$ if $\rho_i(t_{i,k}) = 0$. Then, $h_i(t_{i,k})$ takes $a_{i1}h$ with probability $\bar{\rho}_i = \mathbf{E}\{\rho_i(t_{i,k})\}$ and takes $a_{i2}h$ with probability $1 - \bar{\rho}_i$, $i = 1, 2, 3$. In the simulation, we take $\bar{\rho}_1 = \bar{\rho}_2 = \bar{\rho}_3 = 0.5$.

In this example, we consider the type I fusion estimator. Suppose that the initial local estimates are $\hat{x}_i(t_{i,0}|t_{i,0}) = \hat{x}_i(0|0) = x_0 = [1.2 \;\; 0.8]^{\mathrm{T}}$. Then, by applying the estimator design method in Theorems 3.1, 3.2 and 3.3, the true values and the fused estimates of the target positions and velocities obtained at sensor 1 are depicted in Fig. 3.3. It can be seen that the sensor is able to track the maneuvering target well

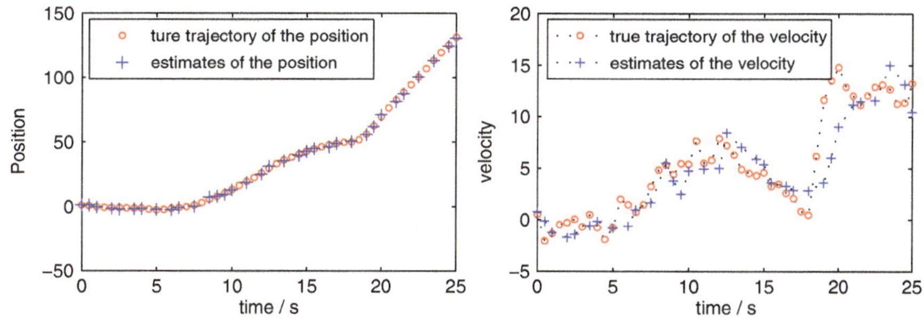

Fig. 3.3 Target tracking results (obtained at sensor 1)

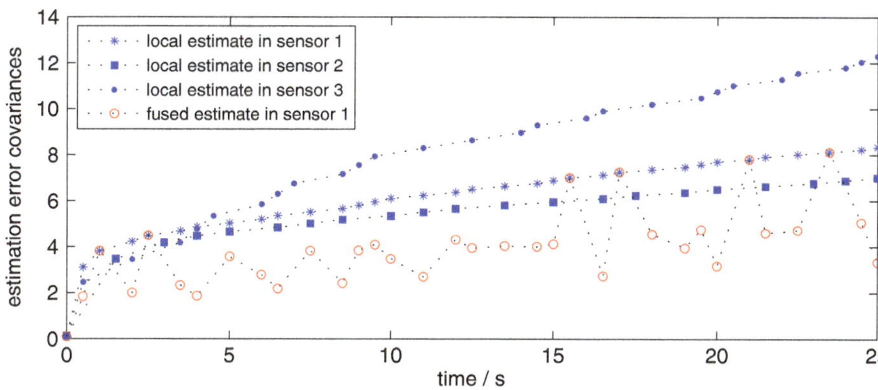

Fig. 3.4 Local estimation error covariances in sensors 1–3 and the fused estimation error covariance in sensor 1

with a nonuniform estimation rate. Figures 3.4, 3.5 and 3.6 shows the individual estimation performance (assessed by the trace of estimation error covariance) of the three sensors, where the curves with circle depict the fused estimation performance, while the other curves show the local estimation performance. At the first stage, each sensor generates local estimates with a nonuniform rate by using measurements from itself. At the second stage, each sensor keeps its own local estimates as the fused ones if there is no local estimates from the other sensors. Otherwise, it just collects the available local estimates to generate fused ones according to the fusion rule given in Theorem 3.2. It can be seen from Figs. 3.4, 3.5 and 3.6 that the estimation performance in each sensor is improved by fusing local estimates, showing the effectiveness of the designed estimators.

Example 3.2 Consider system (3.1) with

$$A = \begin{bmatrix} 0.3 & 0.4 \\ 0.2 & 0.3 \end{bmatrix},\ B = \begin{bmatrix} 1 \\ 0.5 \end{bmatrix} \tag{3.90}$$

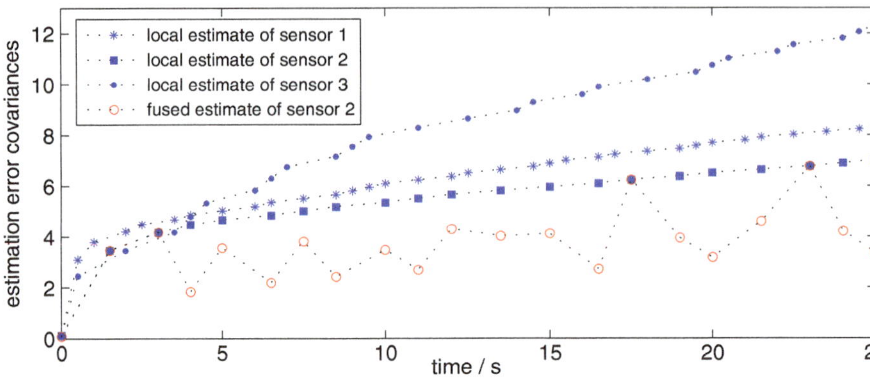

Fig. 3.5 Local estimation error covariances in sensors 1–3 and the fused estimation error covariance in sensor 2

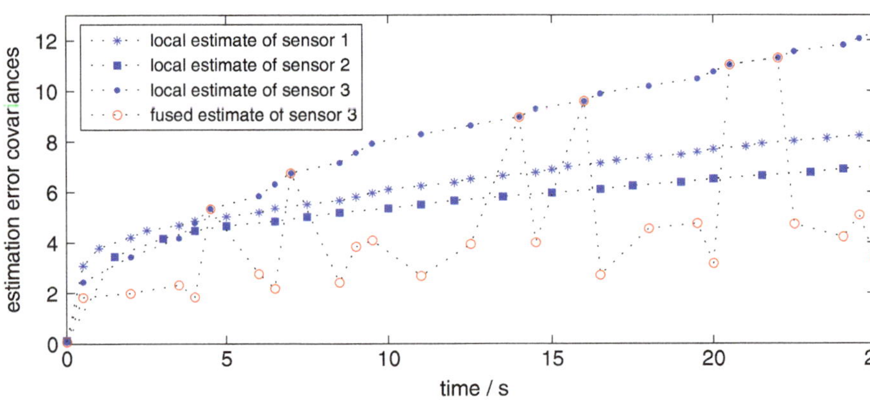

Fig. 3.6 Local estimation error covariances in sensors 1–3 and the fused estimation error covariance in sensor 3

and $\omega(\mathrm{T}_k)$ is a zero-mean white noise with variance Q_ω. In the simulation, we take the sampling period $h = 0.5$ s, the variance $Q_\omega = 1$, and the initial state $x(\mathrm{T}_0) = x(0) = [0.9\ \ 0.6]^{\mathrm{T}}$.

Similar to the setup in Example 3.1, the process in (3.90) is monitored by three sensors. Each sensor generates estimates with a nonuniform rate $h_i(t_{i,k})$, $i = 1, 2, 3$, and it is assumed that $h_i(t_{i,k})$ take values according to (3.89). Then, the measurement equations of the three sensors at time scale $t_{i,k}$ are given by (3.3) with

$$C_1 = [0.6\ 0],\ C_2 = [0.8\ 0],\ C_3 = [0.2\ 0],\ D_1 = 0.6,\ D_2 = 0.7,\ D_3 = 0.5$$

and the measurement noises are given by (3.88) with $c_i = 0.5i$, $Q_{\omega_0} = 1$, $Q_{\upsilon_{01}} = 1.5$, $Q_{\upsilon_{02}} = 0.2$, and $Q_{\upsilon_{03}} = 0$. For $i = 1, 2, 3$, assume that $h_i(t_{i,k})$ takes $a_{il}h$,

$l = 1, 2$ according to a white binary-valued Bernoulli sequence $\rho_i(t_{i,k}) \in \{0, 1\}$. Let $\bar{\rho}_i = \mathbf{E}\{\rho_i(t_{i,k})\}$, then $h_i(t_{i,k})$ takes $a_{i1}h$ with probability $\bar{\rho}_i$ and takes $a_{i2}h$ with probability $1 - \bar{\rho}_i$. In the simulation, we take $\bar{\rho}_1 = \bar{\rho}_2 = \bar{\rho}_3 = 0.5$.

In this example, we consider the type II fusion estimator. By using the LMI control toolbox, it is found that the linear matrix inequalities in (3.86) are feasible for $0.48 \le \lambda_1 < 1$, $0.28 \le \lambda_2 < 1$, and $0.50 \le \lambda_3 < 1$. Thus, $\Theta_i(t_{i,k})$, $i = 1, 2, 3$ are convergent, and the steady-state values of $\Theta_i(t_{i,k})$ are

$$\bar{\Theta}_1 = \bar{\Theta}_2 = \bar{\Theta}_3 = \begin{bmatrix} 1.3774 & 0.7650 \\ 0.7650 & 0.4362 \end{bmatrix}$$

Substituting $\bar{\Theta}_i$ into $\bar{B}_i$, it can be verified that $(A_{i2}, \bar{B}_i)$, $i = 1, 2, 3$ are controllable. On the other hand, it can be checked that (A_{i2}, C_i), $i = 1, 2, 3$ are observable. Therefore, one has by Theorem 3.5 that the three local Kalman estimators designed by applying Lemma 3.3 are convergent, and the fusion estimation error covariances obtained by applying Theorems 3.2 and 3.4 are bounded. Suppose that the initial local estimates are $\hat{x}_i(t_{i,0}|t_{i,0}) = \hat{x}_i(0|0) = x_0 = [0.8 \;\; 0.8]^{\mathrm{T}}$. Then, the simulations are shown in Figs. 3.7, 3.8 and 3.9, where the black curves show the local estimation performance and the red curves depict the fused estimation performance. It can be seen that the local estimation error covariances in the three sensors converge. Moreover, the three local estimator gains also converge to steady-state values after three steps of iterations, and the steady-state estimator gains are

$$K_1^* = [0.6002 \;\; 0.3236]^{\mathrm{T}}, \; K_2^* = [0.6133 \;\; 0.3392]^{\mathrm{T}}, \; K_3^* = [0.8683 \;\; 0.4783]^{\mathrm{T}}$$

Therefore, we implement the steady-state estimators from the fourth step to save computation and communication costs. It can be seen from Figs. 3.7, 3.8 and 3.9

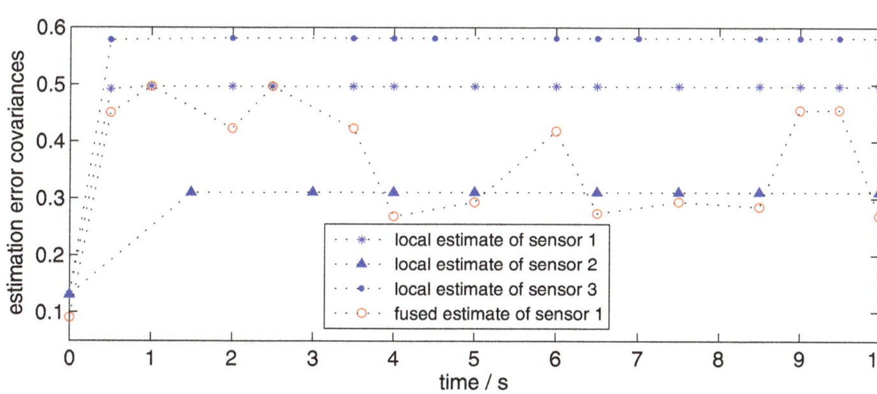

Fig. 3.7 Local estimation error covariances in sensors 1–3 and the fused estimation error covariance in sensor 1

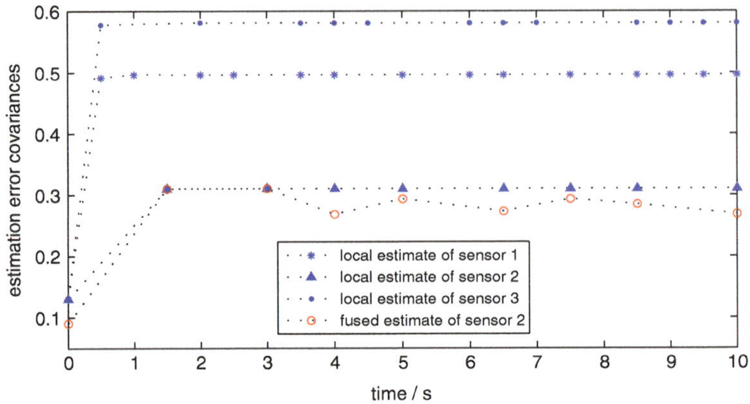

Fig. 3.8 Local estimation error covariances in sensors 1–3 and the fused estimation error covariance in sensor 2

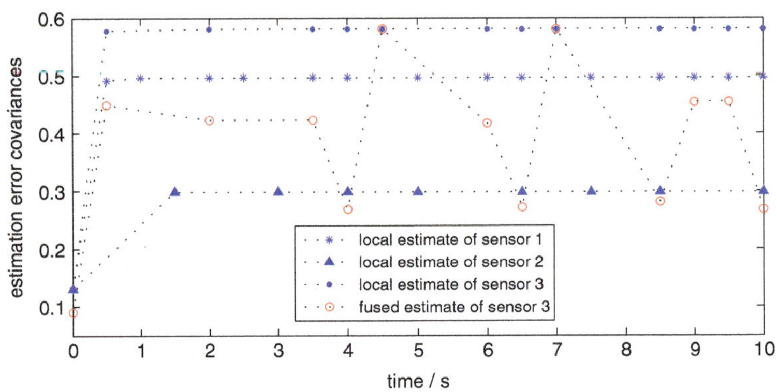

Fig. 3.9 Local estimation error covariances in sensors 1–3 and the fused estimation error covariance in sensor 3

that the estimators provides satisfactory performance. Moreover, the estimation performance in each sensor is improved by fusing local estimates from the other sensors, showing the effectiveness of the proposed fusion estimator.

3.7 Conclusions

A track-to-track fusion estimation algorithm has been presented in this chapter for multisensor discrete-time stochastic systems with nonuniform estimation rates. A fusion algorithm was designed for each sensor to fuse available local estimates generated at different time scales, where the estimation rates at different sensors are allowed to be different from each other. The algorithm is applicable to both cases where the sensor noises are mutually correlated and are uncorrelated and can be further extended for fusion estimation where the sensors are not strictly time synchronized. The proposed algorithm is useful for energy-efficient fusion in sensor networks with power constraints, and the sensors may adjust their estimation rates according to their power situations and make a satisfactory trade-off between energy consumption and estimation performance.

References

1. Sinopoli B, Schenato L, Franceschetti M, Poolla K, Jordan MI, Sastry SS (2001) Kalman filtering with intermittent observations. IEEE Trans Autom Control 49(9):1453–1464
2. Huang M, Dey S (2007) Stability of Kalman filtering with Markovian packet losses. Automatica 43(4):598–607
3. Zhang WA, Feng G, Yu L (2011) Optimal linear estimation for networked systems with communication constraints. Automatica 47(9):1992–2000
4. Dong H, Wang Z, Gao H (2012) Distributed filtering for a class of time-varying systems over sensor networks with quantization errors and successive packet dropouts. IEEE Trans Signal Process 60(6):3164–3173
5. Hounkpevi FO, Yaz EE (2007) Robust minimum variance linear state estimators for multiple sensors with different failure rates. Automatica 43(7):1274–1280
6. Shen B, Wang ZD, Liu XH (2011) A stochastic sampled-data approach to distributed H_∞ filtering in sensor networks. IEEE Trans Circuit Syst-I Regul Pap 58(9):2237–2246
7. Carlson NA (1990) Federated square root filter for decentralized parallel processes. IEEE Trans Aerosp Electron Syst 26(3):517–529
8. Kim KH (1994) Development of track to track fusion algorithm. In: Proceedings of the American control conference, Baltimore, pp 1037–1041
9. Sun SL, Deng ZL (2004) Multi-sensor optimal information fusion Kalman filter. Automatica 40(6):1017–1023
10. Bar-Shalom Y, Li XR (1990) Multitarget-multisensor tracking: advanced applications, vol 1. Artech House, Norwood
11. Chong CY, Chang KC, Mori S (1986) Distributed tracking in distributed sensor networks. In: Proceedings of the 1986 American control conference, Seattle, pp 1863–1868
12. Chong CY, Mori S, Chang KC (1990) Distributed multitarget multisensor tracking. In: Bar-Shalom Y (ed) Multitarget-multisensor tracking: advanced applications, vol 1. Artech House, Norwood
13. Cristi R, Tummala M (2000) Multirate, multiresolution, recursive Kalman filter. Signal Process 80(9):1945–1958
14. Fabrizio A, Luciano A (2000) Filterbanks design for multisensor data fusion. IEEE Signal Process Lett 7(5):100–103
15. Hong L (1992) Distributed filtering using set models. IEEE Trans Aerosp Electron Syst 27(4):715–724
16. Yan LP, Liu BS, Zhou DH (2007) Asynchronous multirate multisensor information fusion algorithm. IEEE Trans Aerosp Electron Syst 43(3):1135–1146
17. Alouani AT, Gray JE, McCabe DH (2005) Theory of distributed estimation using multiple asynchroous sensors. IEEE Trans Aerosp Electron Syst 41(2):717–722
18. Hu YY, Duan ZS, Zhou DH (2010) Estimation fusion with general asynchronous multi-rate sensors. IEEE Trans Aerosp Electron Syst 46(4):2090–2102

19. Wang F, Balakrishnan V (2002) Robust Kalman filters for linear time-varying systems with stochastic parametric uncertainties. IEEE Trans Signal Process 50(4):803–813
20. Anderson BDO, Moore JB (1979) Optimal filtering. Prentice-Hall, Englewood Cliffs
21. Liang Y, Chen TW, Pan Q (2009) Multi-rate optimal state estimation. Int J Control 82(11):2059–2076

Chapter 4
H_∞ Fusion Estimation for WSNs with Nonuniform Sampling Rates

4.1 Introduction

In Chap. 3, Kalman fusion filters are designed for sensor networks with nonuniform estimation rates. Though the celebrated Kalman filtering is commonly regarded as one of the most popular and useful approaches to filtering problem, it usually assumes that the system model is precise and that the external noises are white Gaussian. Such assumptions may not hold in many practical applications. In this case, one may resort to other useful filtering algorithms. The H_∞ filtering is among these useful algorithms, it provides a guaranteed noise attenuation level and does not have to know exact statistical information of external noises.

In this chapter, an H_∞ fusion filter will be designed for sensor networks with nonuniform sampling periods. Although there have been a lot of results on sampled-data estimation (see, e.g., [1–7] and the references therein), few of them are concerned with the nonuniform sampling except for [8–11]. In [8], finite-horizon H_∞ filters were designed for continuous time-varying systems with nonuniform sampling periods. In [9], Kalman filters were designed for a nonuniformly sampled multi-rate system. In [10], an input-delay approach was used to design sampled-data H_∞ filters with a time-varying sampling period which is assumed to take values over a continuous interval. In many practical applications, the sampling period may not necessarily take infinitely many values over a continuous interval but take only a finite number of values. For example, in some target tracking systems, target states are sampled with a small period to improve tracking performance when the target is moving fast and are sampled with a large period to save power when the target is moving slowly, and thus the sampling period takes only two values and switches between them. In this scenario, the input-delay approach may no longer be applicable. Recently, a stochastic sampling method was presented in [11] to design sampled-data H_∞ filters with a time-varying sampling period taking only two values according to a known probability distribution law. Note that the distributed estimation is not considered in all the aforementioned results. Until very recently,

W.-A. Zhang et al., *Distributed Fusion Estimation for Sensor Networks with Communication Constraints*, DOI 10.1007/978-981-10-0795-8_4

the stochastic sampling method is used in [12] to study the distributed sampled-data H_∞ filtering problem, and it was also assumed in [12] that the sampling period takes only two values according to a known probability distribution law.

In this chapter, a continuous-time LTI system is considered, and the measurements of the system are sampled by each sensor in the network with a time-varying period taking a finite number of values. An innovation-like quantity is defined for each filter based on the sampled measurement and the state of the filter. Then, at each time step, each sensor in the network collects both innovation-like quantities and filter states to generate estimates. Random packet losses, which are usually unavoidable in sensor networks and may degrade estimation performance [13–16], are further considered, and the filtering error system is described as a discrete-time switched system with multiple stochastic parameters and a finite number of subsystems. By using the average dwell time method for switched systems, a sufficient condition is derived for the existence of the distributed sampled-data H_∞ fusion filters. It is shown that the obtained condition depends on both the values and variation rate of the sampling periods and the packet loss probabilities. It is also shown that the design of the filters can be accomplished by solving a convex optimization problem subject to linear matrix inequality constraints, and the resulting filtering system is mean square exponentially stable, and all the filtering errors in the sensor network satisfy an average H_∞ noise attenuation level.

4.2 Problem Statement

Consider a continuous-time LTI system described by the following state-space model:

$$\begin{cases} \dot{x}(t) = A_p x(t) + B_p w_p(t) \\ z(t) = L_p x(t) \end{cases} \tag{4.1}$$

where $x(t) \in \Re^{n_x}$ is the system state, $z(t) \in \Re^{n_z}$ is the signal to be estimated, and $w_p(t)$ is the disturbance input belonging to $\mathscr{L}_2[0, +\infty)$. A sensor network consisting of m sensors is deployed to collect observations of system (4.1) according to the following observation models:

$$\begin{cases} y_{(l)}(t_k) = C_{p(l)} x(t_k) + D_{p(l)} v_{p(l)}(t_k) \\ l \in Z_y \triangleq \{1, 2, \ldots, m\} \end{cases} \tag{4.2}$$

where $y_{(l)}(t_k) \in \Re^{n_{yl}}$ is the observation collected by sensor l at discrete instants t_k, $k = 0, 1, 2, \ldots$, and $0 = t_0 < t_1 < \cdots < t_k < \cdots$, $v_{p(l)}(t_k) \in \Re^{n_{vl}}$, $l = 1, 2, \ldots, m$ are measurement noises belonging to $l_2[0, +\infty)$, A_p, B_p, L_p, $C_{p(l)}$ and $D_{p(l)}$ are constant matrices with appropriate dimensions. At time instants t_k, $k = 0, 1, 2, \ldots$ each sensor collects measurements from its neighbors and gives an estimate of $z(t_k)$.

Define the measurement sampling period as $h_k \triangleq t_{k+1} - t_k$, then h_k is not necessarily constant but may vary with k. Suppose that h_k takes only a finite number of values. Specifically, let $h_k = n_k \mathrm{T}_0$, where $n_k \in \{i_1, i_2, \ldots, i_n\}$, $i_1 < i_2 < \cdots < i_n$, T_0 is a constant, and $i_j, j = 1, 2, \ldots, n$ are positive integers. Then, h_k takes n values and

$$h_k \in \bar{Z} \triangleq \{i_1 \mathrm{T}_0, \ldots, i_n \mathrm{T}_0\} \tag{4.3}$$

A switched system model of the discrete-time version of system (4.1), (4.2) and (4.3) is first given as follows. Discretizing system (4.1) with period h_k and applying a zero-order hold, one obtains

$$\begin{cases} x(t_{k+1}) &= A(h_k)x(t_k) + B(h_k)w_p(t_k) \\ z(t_k) &= L_p x(t_k),\ k = 0, 1, 2, \ldots \end{cases} \tag{4.4}$$

where

$$A(h_k) = \mathrm{e}^{A_p h_k},\ B(h_k) = \int_0^{h_k} \mathrm{e}^{A_p \tau} \mathrm{d}\tau B_p$$

Denote

$$A_0 = \mathrm{e}^{A_p \mathrm{T}_0},\ B_0 = \int_0^{\mathrm{T}_0} \mathrm{e}^{A_p \tau} \mathrm{d}\tau B_p$$

then one has

$$A(h_k) = \mathrm{e}^{A_p n_k \mathrm{T}_0} = \left(\mathrm{e}^{A_p \mathrm{T}_0}\right)^{n_k} = A_0^{n_k} \tag{4.5}$$

$$\begin{aligned} B(h_k) &= \int_0^{n_k \mathrm{T}_0} \mathrm{e}^{A_p \tau} \mathrm{d}\tau B_p \\ &= \left(\sum_{i=0}^{n_k - 1} \int_{i\mathrm{T}_0}^{(i+1)\mathrm{T}_0} \mathrm{e}^{A_p \tau} \mathrm{d}\tau \right) B_p \\ &= \left(\sum_{i=0}^{n_k - 1} \mathrm{e}^{A_p i \mathrm{T}_0} \int_0^{\mathrm{T}_0} \mathrm{e}^{A_p \tau} \mathrm{d}\tau \right) B_p \\ &= \sum_{i=0}^{n_k - 1} A_0^i B_0 \end{aligned} \tag{4.6}$$

It can be seen from (4.5) and (4.6) that $A(h_k)$ and $B(h_k)$ explicitly depend on n_k which is varying over different sampling intervals and takes n distinct values. Thus, the discrete-time version of the aperiodic sampled-data system (4.1), (4.2) and (4.3) is essentially a switched system with a finite number of subsystems. Moreover, define a piecewise constant switching signal $\sigma(t) \in Z_\sigma \triangleq \{1, 2, \ldots, n\}$ and let $A_{\sigma(t_k)} = A_0^{i_{\sigma(t_k)}}$ and $B_{\sigma(t_k)} = \sum_{j=1}^{i_{\sigma(t_k)}} A_0^{j-1} B_0$, then it follows from (4.5) and (4.6) that the system (4.2), (4.3) and (4.4) can be rewritten as the following discrete-time switched system:

$$S_{\sigma(t_k)} : \begin{cases} x(t_{k+1}) = A_{\sigma(t_k)} x(t_k) + B_{\sigma(t_k)} w_p(t_k) \\ y_{(l)}(t_k) = C_{p(l)} x(t_k) + D_{p(l)} v_{p(l)}(t_k) \\ z(t_k) = L_p x(t_k), \ l \in Z_y, \ k = 0, 1, 2, \ldots \end{cases} \tag{4.7}$$

Some modeling methods for sampled-data systems with nonuniform sampling periods have been presented in the literature, such as the input-delay method [17] and the uncertain system method [18, 19]. However, the aforementioned methods are not applicable to model the considered filtering system since they assume that the sampling period take infinitely many values over a continuous interval. In this chapter, a switched system approach is proposed to model the sampled-data filtering system with nonuniform sampling periods, and the filtering system is finally described as a discrete-time switched system with a finite number of subsystems as shown in (4.7). Each subsystem of (4.7) describes the sampled-data filtering system (4.1), (4.2) and (4.3) with a constant sampling period taking a value in $\bar{Z}$. Moreover, $A_{\sigma(t_k)}$ and $B_{\sigma(t_k)}$ depend critically on the sampling periods, which enables us to establish relations between the sampling periods and filtering performance.

The sensor network deployed to monitor the plant is considered to be a peer-to-peer network, there is no estimation center in the network, and every sensor in the network acts also as an estimator. The measurements are transmitted among the sensors in an ad hoc manner via unreliable wireless communication channels and may be subject to random packet losses. We say that two sensors are connected if they can communicate directly with each other, i.e., they can communicate with each other within one hop. Notice that a sensor is always connected to itself. The set of sensors connected to a certain sensor r is called the neighborhood of sensor r and is denoted by $\mathcal{N}_r$ (notice that $r \in \mathcal{N}_r$). A structure of such a distributed estimation system for sensor networks has been shown in Fig. 2.1. Denote by $L_{(ij)}$, $i, j \in \mathcal{N}_r$ the link between sensor i and sensor j in a neighborhood. Then, the random packet loss in the link $L_{(ij)}$ is described by a binary-valued Bernoulli random process $\alpha_{(ij)}(t_k) \in \{0, 1\}$, where $\alpha_{(ij)}(t_k) = 1$ indicates that a packet transmitted from sensor i successfully arrives at sensor j at instant t_k, while $\alpha_{(ij)}(t_k) = 0$ implies that a packet is lost during the transmission from sensor i to sensor j. $\theta_{(ij)} \triangleq \mathbf{E}\{\alpha_{(ij)}(t_k)\} = \text{Prob}\{\alpha_{(ij)}(t_k) = 1\}$ is called the packet arriving probability (PAP), while $1 - \theta_{(ij)} \triangleq 1 - \mathbf{E}\{\alpha_{(ij)}(t_k)\} = \text{Prob}\{\alpha_{(ij)}(t_k) = 0\}$ is called the packet loss probability (PLP). Since a packet transmitted from sensor i to sensor j and from sensor j to sensor i goes through the same link $L_{(ij)}$, it is natural to see that $\alpha_{(ij)}(t_k) = \alpha_{(ji)}(t_k)$ and $\theta_{(ij)} = \theta_{(ji)}$. Besides, since the measurement $y_{(l)}(t_k)$ is always available for sensor l itself, one has $\alpha_{(ii)}(t_k) = 1$ and $\theta_{(ii)} = 1$. It is assumed that $\alpha_{(rl)}(t_k)$, $l \in \mathcal{N}_r$, $r \in Z_y$ are mutually independent.

At each time step, every sensor collects information from its neighbors and runs an H_∞ filtering algorithm to generate an estimate of $z(t_k)$. Consider the following switching-mode-dependent linear filter for sensor r, $r \in Z_y$.

$$f_{(r)\sigma(t_k)}: \begin{cases} \hat{x}_{(r)}(t_{k+1}) = F_{(rr)\sigma(t_k)}\hat{x}_{(r)}(t_k) \\ \qquad + G_{(rr)\sigma(t_k)}\varepsilon_{(r)}(t_k) + u_{(r)}(t_k) \\ u_{(r)}(t_k) = \sum\limits_{l\in\mathcal{N}_r/\{r\}} F_{(rl)\sigma(t_k)}\hat{x}^o_{(l)}(t_k) \\ \qquad + \sum\limits_{l\in\mathcal{N}_r/\{r\}} G_{(rl)\sigma(t_k)}\varepsilon^o_{(l)}(t_k) \\ \hat{z}_{(r)}(t_k) = L_{(r)\sigma(t_k)}\hat{x}_r(t_k) \end{cases} \tag{4.8}$$

where $\hat{x}_{(r)}(t_k)$ is the state of the filter $f_{(r)\sigma(t_k)}$ and is also an estimate of the plant's state $x(t_k)$, $\hat{z}_{(r)}(t_k)$ is the estimate of $z(t_k)$ in sensor r, $\hat{x}^o_{(l)}(t_k) = \alpha_{(rl)}(t_k)\hat{x}_{(l)}(t_k)$, $\varepsilon^o_{(l)}(t_k) = \alpha_{(rl)}(t_k)\varepsilon_{(l)}(t_k)$, $l \in \mathcal{N}_r/\{r\}$, $\varepsilon_{(l)}(t_k) \triangleq y_{(l)}(t_k) - C_{p(l)}\hat{x}_{(l)}(t_k)$ is an innovation-like quantity in sensor l, $l \in \mathcal{N}_r$, and $\hat{x}^o_{(l)}(t_k)$ and $\varepsilon^o_{(l)}(t_k)$ are, respectively, the filter state and the innovation-like quantity received by sensor r from sensor l, $l \in \mathcal{N}_r/\{r\}$, $F_{(rl)\sigma(t_k)}$, $G_{(rl)\sigma(t_k)}$ and $L_{(r)\sigma(t_k)}$, $l \in \mathcal{N}_r$, $r \in Z_y$ are the switching-mode-dependent filter gain matrices to be designed. At each time step, the sensor r collects both the filter states and innovation-like quantities from its neighbors to generate the estimate $\hat{z}_{(r)}(t_k)$, and the quantity $u_{(r)}(t_k)$ represents the information received from its neighbors.

It is implicitly assumed in (4.8) that all the sensors in the network are time synchronized and have the same sampling period h_k, $\forall\ k = 0, 1, 2, \ldots$. Besides, the *zero input* mechanism [14] is applied in (4.8), i.e., $\hat{x}^o_{(l)}(t_k)$ and $\varepsilon^o_{(l)}(t_k)$ are, respectively, set to zero when $\hat{x}_{(l)}(t_k)$ and $\varepsilon_{(l)}(t_k)$ are lost during the transmissions. A similar structure of the distributed filter in (4.8) has been used in [20] to investigate distributed H_∞-consensus filtering for sensor networks, and the structure is actually motivated by the standard Kalman filter which uses innovations and filtered estimates at past time steps to generate filtered estimates at current time step.

A filtering error system model is established as follows based on (4.7) and (4.8). Substituting (4.2) into (4.8) and taking into account the facts $\alpha_{(rr)}(t_k) = 1$ and $\theta_{(rr)} = 1$, one obtains

$$\begin{aligned} \hat{x}_{(r)}(t_{k+1}) = &\sum_{l\in\mathcal{N}_r} \alpha_{(rl)}(t_k)(F_{(rl)\sigma(t_k)} - G_{(rl)\sigma(t_k)}C_{p(l)}) \\ &\times\hat{x}_{(l)}(t_k) + \sum_{l\in\mathcal{N}_r} \alpha_{(rl)}(t_k)G_{(rl)\sigma(t_k)}C_{p(l)}x(t_k) \\ &+ \sum_{l\in\mathcal{N}_r} \alpha_{(rl)}(t_k)G_{(rl)\sigma(t_k)}D_{p(l)}v_{p(l)}(t_k) \end{aligned} \tag{4.9}$$

For $j \in Z_y$, denote

$$
\begin{aligned}
\hat{x}(t_k) &= \mathrm{col}\left\{\hat{x}_{(l)}(t_k)\right\}_{l \in Z_y} \\
v(t_k) &= \mathrm{col}\{v_{p(l)}(t_k)\}_{l \in Z_y} \\
x_m(t_k) &= \mathrm{col}\{x(t_k)\}_m \\
F_{(r)\sigma(t_k)} &= \mathrm{col}^{\mathrm{T}}\left\{F^{\mathrm{T}}_{(rl)\sigma(t_k)}\right\}_{l \in Z_y} \\
G_{(r)\sigma(t_k)} &= \mathrm{col}^{\mathrm{T}}\left\{G^{\mathrm{T}}_{(rl)\sigma(t_k)}\right\}_{l \in Z_y} \\
F_{\sigma(t_k)} &= \mathrm{col}\{F_{(r)\sigma(t_k)}\}_{r \in Z_y} \\
G_{\sigma(t_k)} &= \mathrm{col}\{G_{(r)\sigma(t_k)}\}_{r \in Z_y} \\
C_{(j)} &= \mathrm{diag}\{\delta(j-1)C_{p(1)}, \ldots, \delta(j-m)C_{p(m)}\} \\
D_{(j)} &= \mathrm{diag}\{\delta(j-1)D_{p(1)}, \ldots, \delta(j-m)D_{p(m)}\} \\
\Pi_{(j)} &= \mathrm{diag}\{\delta(j-1)I_n, \ldots, \delta(j-m)I_n\} \\
\Delta_{(j)}(t_k) &= \mathrm{diag}\{\alpha_{(1j)}(t_k)I_n, \ldots, \alpha_{(mj)}(t_k)I_n\}
\end{aligned}
\tag{4.10}
$$

where $\forall\ l \notin \mathcal{N}_r$, $F_{(rl)\sigma(t_k)} = \mathbf{0}$ and $G_{(rl)\sigma(t_k)} = \mathbf{0}$, and $\delta \in \{0, 1\}$ is the Kronecker delta function. Then, one obtains from (4.9) and (4.10) that

$$
\begin{aligned}
\hat{x}(t_{k+1}) = &\sum_{j=1}^{m} \Delta_{(j)}(t_k)(F_{\sigma(t_k)}\Pi_{(j)} - G_{\sigma(t_k)}C_{(j)})\hat{x}(t_k) \\
&+ \sum_{j=1}^{m} \Delta_{(j)}(t_k)G_{\sigma(t_k)}C_{(j)}x_m(t_k) \\
&+ \sum_{j=1}^{m} \Delta_{(j)}(t_k)G_{\sigma(t_k)}D_{(j)}v(t_k)
\end{aligned}
\tag{4.11}
$$

Moreover, denote

$$
\begin{aligned}
A_{m\sigma(t_k)} &= \mathrm{diag}\{A_{\sigma(t_k)}\}_m \\
B_{m\sigma(t_k)} &= \mathrm{diag}\{B_{\sigma(t_k)}\}_m \\
w_{mp}(t_k) &= \mathrm{col}\{w_p(t_k)\}_m
\end{aligned}
$$

then one obtains from the state equation in (4.7) that

$$
x_m(t_{k+1}) = A_{m\sigma(t_k)}x_m(t_k) + B_{m\sigma(t_k)}w_{mp}(t_k) \tag{4.12}
$$

Define the estimation errors as

$$e_{(r)}(t_k) \triangleq z(t_k) - \hat{z}_{(r)}(t_k), r \in Z_y$$

and denote

$$\begin{aligned} e(t_k) &= \mathrm{col}\{e_{(r)}(t_k)\}_{r\in Z_y} \\ \xi(t_k) &= \left[x_m^{\mathrm{T}}(t_k)\ \hat{x}^{\mathrm{T}}(t_k)\right]^{\mathrm{T}} \\ \nu(t_k) &= \left[w_{mp}^{\mathrm{T}}(t_k)\ v^{\mathrm{T}}(t_k)\right]^{\mathrm{T}} \\ \bar{L}_p &= \mathrm{diag}\{L_p\}_m \\ L_{\sigma(t_k)} &= \mathrm{diag}\{L_{(r)\sigma(t_k)}\}_{r\in Z_y} \end{aligned}$$

Then, one obtains the following filtering error system from (4.7), (4.8), (4.11), and (4.12).

$$\Im_{\sigma(t_k)}: \begin{cases} \xi(t_{k+1}) = \tilde{A}_{\sigma(t_k)}\xi(t_k) + \tilde{B}_{\sigma(t_k)}\nu(t_k) \\ e(t_k) = \bar{C}_{\sigma(t_k)}\xi(t_k),\ k = 0, 1, 2, \ldots \end{cases} \tag{4.13}$$

where

$$\begin{aligned} \tilde{A}_{\sigma(t_k)} &= \begin{bmatrix} A_{m\sigma(t_k)} & \mathbf{0} \\ \sum_{j=1}^{m} \Delta_{(j)}(t_k)G_{\sigma(t_k)}C_{(j)} & \chi_1 \end{bmatrix} \\ \chi_1 &= \sum_{j=1}^{m} \Delta_{(j)}(t_k)(F_{\sigma(t_k)}\Pi_{(j)} - G_{\sigma(t_k)}C_{(j)}) \\ \tilde{B}_{\sigma(t_k)} &= \mathrm{diag}\left\{B_{m\sigma(t_k)}, \sum_{j=1}^{m} \Delta_{(j)}(t_k)G_{\sigma(t_k)}D_{(j)}\right\} \\ \bar{C}_{\sigma(t_k)} &= \left[\bar{L}_p\ \ -L_{\sigma(t_k)}\right] \end{aligned}$$

In the considered filtering system, each sensor collects both measurements and estimates from its neighbors to generate its own estimates. Since the measurements and estimates may be lost during the transmission, several stochastic variables used to describe the random packet loss processes are incorporated into the proposed filtering error system model (4.13), which adds new difficulties to the design of the filters. In what follows, an average dwell time approach will be proposed to design the distributed H_∞ filters. Suppose that the average activation rate of the subsystem $\Im_i$, $i \in Z_\sigma$ over the interval $[t_0, t_k)$ is ρ_i. Then, the subsystem $\Im_i$ appears $\tau_i(t_k) = \rho_i k$ times over the interval $[t_0, t_k)$, and one has $\sum_{i=1}^{n} \rho_i = 1$. Let $t_{k(1)}, \ldots, t_{k(s)}$, $s \geq 1$ denote the switching instants of $\sigma(t)$ over the interval $[t_0, t_k)$, where $t_{k(j)} \in \{t_1, \dots, t_{k-1}\}, j = 1, 2, \dots, s$, and $t_0 < t_{k(1)} < \dots < t_{k(s)} < t_k$. Denote $t^-_{k(j)}, j \in \{1, 2, \dots, s\}$ the instant that is immediately before $t_{k(j)}$. Then, the following useful definitions are first given before proceeding further.

Definition 4.1 ([21]) For $k \geq 1$, let $N_\sigma(t_0, t_k)$, denote the number of switchings of the switching signal $\sigma(t)$ over the interval $[t_0, t_k)$. If $N_\sigma(t_0, t_k) \leq N_0 + k/\tau_a$ holds for $N_0 \geq 0$ and $\tau_a > 0$, then τ_a is called the average dwell time and N_0 the chatter bound.

The idea of the average dwell time in Definition 4.1 is that there may exist consecutive switchings separated by less than τ_a sampling periods, but the average time interval between consecutive switchings is not less than τ_a sampling periods. For simplicity, but without loss of generality, N_0 is set to 0 in the subsequent development, and one has in this case that $\tau_a \geq 1$ since $N_\sigma(t_0, t_k) \leq k$. The switching signal $\sigma(t_k)$ is determined by the variation of the sampling periods. Specifically, $\Im_{\sigma(t_k)}$ switches from one subsystem to another when the sampling period h_k varies from one value to another. Thus, it can be seen from the definition of τ_a that the parameter $\frac{1}{\tau_a}$ shows the variation rate of the sampling period, and this is one of the main motivations of using the average dwell time method for the filtering analysis and design, which will hclp cstablish rclations between filtering performance and the variation rate of the sampling period.

Definition 4.2 For any given initial conditions $\varphi(t_0) \triangleq (\xi(t_0), \alpha_{(rl)}(t_0), l \in \mathcal{N}_r, r \in Z_y)$, the system $\Im_{\sigma(t_k)}$ with $v(t_k) = 0$ is mean square exponentially stable if its solutions satisfy

$$\mathbf{E}\left\{\|\xi(t_k)\|^2 | \varphi(t_0)\right\} \leq c\lambda^k \|\xi(t_0)\|^2, \forall\, k \geq 0$$

where $c > 0$ is a constant and $\lambda < 1$ is the decay rate.

Definition 4.3 The filtering errors $e_{(r)}(t_k)$, $r = 1, 2, \dots, m$ are said to satisfy a prescribed average H_∞ noise attenuation level γ if, under zero initial condition, the inequality

$$\sum_{r=1}^{m} \|e_{(r)}\|^2_{\mathbf{E}_2} \leq \gamma^2 \sum_{r=1}^{m} \|\vartheta_{(r)}\|^2_2$$

holds for all nonzero $w_p(t_k) \in l_2[0, +\infty)$ and $v_{p(r)}(t_k) \in l_2[0, +\infty)$, where

$$\|e_{(r)}\|_{\mathbf{E}_2} = \mathbf{E}\left\{\sum_{k=0}^{\infty} \|e_{(r)}(t_k)\|^2\right\}^{1/2}$$

$$\vartheta_{(r)}(t_k) = \left[w_p^{\mathrm{T}}(t_k) \;\; v_{p(r)}^{\mathrm{T}}(t_k)\right]^{\mathrm{T}}, \; r \in Z_y$$

The H_∞ filtering is concerned with the design of filters which ensure a bound on the $\mathcal{L}_2$-induced gain from noises to filtering errors, and Definition 4.3 gives a definition on the filtering performance of the H_∞ filter to be designed in the following sections.

The distributed sampled-data H_∞ fusion filtering problem addressed in this paper is expressed as follows: Consider the distributed sampled-data filtering problem, and given a system in (4.1), (4.2) and (4.3), determine the filter gain matrices $F_{(rl)\sigma(t_k)}$, $G_{(rl)\sigma(t_k)}$, and $L_{(r)\sigma(t_k)}$, $l \in \mathcal{N}_r$, $r \in Z_y$ of the filter in (4.8) such that the filtering error system (4.13) with nonuniform sampling periods is mean square exponentially stable satisfies a prescribed average H_∞ noise attenuation level for all admissible random packet losses.

4.3 H_∞ Performance Analysis

Let

$$\Theta_{(j)} \triangleq \mathbf{E}\{\Delta_{(j)}(t_k)\} = \mathrm{diag}\{\theta_{(1j)}I_n, \ldots, \theta_{(mj)}I_n\},\ j \in Z_y$$

$$\bar{A}_{\sigma(t_k)} \triangleq \mathbf{E}\left\{\tilde{A}_{\sigma(t_k)}\right\} = \begin{bmatrix} A_{m\sigma(t_k)} & \mathbf{0} \\ \sum_{j=1}^{m} \Theta_{(j)} G_{\sigma(t_k)} C_{(j)} & \chi_2 \end{bmatrix}$$

$$\chi_2 = \sum_{j=1}^{m} \Theta_{(j)} (F_{\sigma(t_k)} \Pi_{(j)} - G_{\sigma(t_k)} C_{(j)})$$

$$\bar{B}_{\sigma(t_k)} \triangleq \mathbf{E}\left\{\tilde{B}_{\sigma(t_k)}\right\} = \mathrm{diag}\left\{B_{m\sigma(t_k)}, \sum_{j=1}^{m} \Theta_{(j)} G_{\sigma(t_k)} D_{(j)}\right\}$$

Then, the following theorem gives a sufficient condition for the filtering error system $\Im_{\sigma(t_k)}$ to be mean square exponentially stable and all the filtering errors satisfying a prescribed average H_∞ noise attenuation level.

Theorem 4.1 *Consider the filtering error system (4.13). For given positive scalars* γ, $\mu > 1$, $\lambda_i < 1$, *and* $\lambda < 1$, *if there exist matrices* $P_i > 0$, $i = 1, 2, \ldots, n$ *such that* $\tau_a > \tau_a^* \triangleq \ln \mu / \ln \lambda^{-1}$, $\lambda > \bar{\lambda}$, *and the following matrix inequalities*

$$\begin{cases} \Omega_i \triangleq \Lambda_i^{\mathrm{T}} \bar{P}_i \Lambda_i + \mathrm{diag}\left\{\bar{C}_i^{\mathrm{T}} \bar{C}_i - \lambda_i P_i, -\gamma^2 I\right\} < 0 \\ P_i \le \mu P_s, \forall\, i, s \in Z_\sigma \end{cases} \tag{4.14}$$

hold, then the filtering error system (4.13) is mean square exponentially stable with decay rate $\varepsilon = \mu^{1/\tau_a}\bar{\lambda}$ *and all the filtering errors satisfy an average* H_∞ *noise attenuation level* $\bar{\gamma} = \gamma\sqrt{\frac{1-\underline{\lambda}}{1-\bar{\lambda}/\underline{\lambda}}}$, *where* $\bar{\lambda} = \max_{i\in Z_\sigma} \lambda_i$, $\underline{\lambda} = \min_{i\in Z_\sigma} \lambda_i$, *and*

$$
\begin{aligned}
\Lambda_i^{\mathrm{T}} &= \begin{bmatrix} \bar{A}_i^{\mathrm{T}} & \bar{\Theta}_{c(1)} A_{(1)i}^{\mathrm{T}} & \cdots & \bar{\Theta}_{c(m)} A_{(m)i}^{\mathrm{T}} \\ \bar{B}_i^{\mathrm{T}} & \bar{\Theta}_{c(1)} B_{(1)i}^{\mathrm{T}} & \cdots & \bar{\Theta}_{c(m)} B_{(m)i}^{\mathrm{T}} \end{bmatrix} \\
A_{(j)i} &= \begin{bmatrix} \mathbf{0} & \mathbf{0} \\ G_i C_{(j)} & F_i \Pi_{(j)} - G_i C_{(j)} \end{bmatrix} \\
B_{(j)i} &= \mathrm{diag}\left\{\mathbf{0}, G_i D_{(j)}\right\} \\
\bar{P}_i &= \mathrm{diag}\{P_i\}_{m+1}, \bar{\Theta}_{c(j)} = \mathrm{diag}\{\mathbf{0}, \Theta_{c(j)}\} \\
\Theta_{c(j)} &= \mathrm{diag}\left\{ \sqrt{\theta_{(1j)}(1-\theta_{(1j)})} I_n, \ldots, \sqrt{\theta_{(mj)}(1-\theta_{(mj)})} I_n \right\}, \ j \in Z_y
\end{aligned}
$$

Proof Denote $\bar{\Delta}_{(j)}(t_k) = \mathrm{diag}\{0, \Delta_{(j)}(t_k)\}$ and $\bar{\Theta}_{(j)} = \mathrm{diag}\{0, \Theta_{(j)}\}$, $\forall\, j \in Z_y$, then the filtering error system in (4.13) can be rewritten as

$$
\begin{cases}
\xi(t_{k+1}) = \bar{A}_{\sigma(t_k)}\xi(t_k) + \bar{B}_{\sigma(t_k)}\nu(t_k) \\
\qquad + \sum_{j=1}^{m}\left(\bar{\Delta}_{(j)}(t_k) - \bar{\Theta}_{(j)}\right) A_{(j)\sigma(t_k)}\xi(t_k) \\
\qquad + \sum_{j=1}^{m}\left(\bar{\Delta}_{(j)}(t_k) - \bar{\Theta}_{(j)}\right) B_{(j)\sigma(t_k)}\nu(t_k) \\
e(t_k) = \bar{C}_{\sigma(t_k)}\xi(t_k), \ k = 0, 1, 2, \ldots
\end{cases} \tag{4.15}
$$

Since $\alpha_{(rl)}(t_k)$, $l \in \mathcal{N}_r$, $r \in Z_y$ are mutually independent, one has

$$
\mathbf{E}\left\{\left(\bar{\Delta}_{(j)}(t_k) - \bar{\Theta}_{(j)}\right)\left(\bar{\Delta}_{(i)}(t_k) - \bar{\Theta}_{(i)}\right)\right\} = \begin{cases} \bar{\Theta}_{c(j)}, & i = j \\ \mathbf{0}, & i \neq j \end{cases} \tag{4.16}
$$

Let

$$
\begin{aligned}
&\Upsilon(t_k) \triangleq \|e(t_k)\|^2 - \gamma^2\|\nu(t_k)\|^2, \\
&\varphi(t_k) \triangleq (\xi(t_k), \alpha_{(rl)}(t_k), l \in \mathcal{N}_r, r \in Z_y), \ \forall\, k = 0, 1, 2, \ldots
\end{aligned}
$$

and choose the Lyapunov function $V_{\sigma(t_k)}(t_k) = \xi^{\mathrm{T}}(t_k)P_{\sigma(t_k)}\xi(t_k)$ for system (4.15). Then, $\forall\, i \in Z_\sigma$, one has by (4.14), (4.15) and (4.16) and the fact $\mathbf{E}\{(\bar{\Delta}_{(j)}(t_k) - \bar{\Theta}_{(j)})\} = \mathbf{0}$ that

$$
\begin{aligned}
&\mathbf{E}\{V_i(t_{k+1})|\varphi(t_k)\} \\
&= \mathbf{E}\left\{\xi^{\mathrm{T}}(t_{k+1})P_i\xi(t_{k+1})|\varphi(t_k)\right\} - \lambda_i\xi^{\mathrm{T}}(t_k)P_i\xi(t_k) \\
&\quad + \Upsilon(t_k) + \lambda_i V_i(t_k) - \Upsilon(t_k) \\
&= \eta^{\mathrm{T}}(t_k)\Omega_i\eta(t_k) + \lambda_i V_i(t_k) - \Upsilon(t_k) \\
&< \lambda_i V_i(t_k) - \Upsilon(t_k)
\end{aligned} \tag{4.17}
$$

where $\eta(t_k) = [\xi^{\mathrm{T}}(t_k)\ \ \nu^{\mathrm{T}}(t_k)]^{\mathrm{T}}$. Setting $t_k = t_{k^{(s)}}$ and $t_k = t_{k^{(s)}+1}$ in the inequality in (4.17), one obtains, respectively,

$$\mathbf{E}\left\{V_{\sigma\left(t_{k^{(s)}}\right)}(t_{k^{(s)}+1})|\varphi(t_{k^{(s)}})\right\} < \lambda_{\sigma\left(t_{k^{(s)}}\right)} V_{\sigma\left(t_{k^{(s)}}\right)}(t_{k^{(s)}}) - \Upsilon(t_{k^{(s)}}) \tag{4.18}$$

$$\mathbf{E}\left\{V_{\sigma\left(t_{k^{(s)}}\right)}(t_{k^{(s)}+2})|\varphi(t_{k^{(s)}+1})\right\} < \lambda_{\sigma\left(t_{k^{(s)}}\right)} V_{\sigma\left(t_{k^{(s)}}\right)}(t_{k^{(s)}+1}) - \Upsilon(t_{k^{(s)}+1}) \tag{4.19}$$

Taking expectation $\mathbf{E}\{\cdot|\varphi(t_{k^{(s)}})\}$ on both sides of the inequality in (4.19) and taking into account (4.18) yield

$$\mathbf{E}\left\{V_{\sigma\left(t_{k^{(s)}}\right)}(t_{k^{(s)}+2})|\varphi(t_{k^{(s)}})\right\} < \lambda^2_{\sigma\left(t_{k^{(s)}}\right)} V_{\sigma\left(t_{k^{(s)}}\right)}(t_{k^{(s)}}) - \lambda_{\sigma\left(t_{k^{(s)}}\right)} \Upsilon(t_{k^{(s)}}) - \mathbf{E}\{\Upsilon(t_{k^{(s)}+1})|\varphi(t_{k^{(s)}})\} \tag{4.20}$$

Applying the procedures in (4.18), (4.19) and (4.20) recursively for $t = t_{k^{(s)}}$, $t_{k^{(s)}+1}, \ldots, t_k$, one obtains

$$\begin{aligned}\mathbf{E}\{V_{\sigma(t_k)}(t_k)|\varphi(t_{k^{(s)}})\} &= \mathbf{E}\left\{V_{\sigma\left(t_{k^{(s)}}\right)}(t_k)|\varphi(t_{k^{(s)}})\right\}\\ &< \lambda^{k-k^{(s)}}_{\sigma\left(t_{k^{(s)}}\right)} V_{\sigma\left(t_{k^{(s)}}\right)}(t_{k^{(s)}})\\ &\quad - \sum_{j=k^{(s)}}^{k-1} \lambda^{k-1-j}_{\sigma\left(t_{k^{(s)}}\right)} \mathbf{E}\{\Upsilon(t_j)|\varphi(t_{k^{(s)}})\}\end{aligned} \tag{4.21}$$

Similarly, one has for $a = 1, 2, \ldots, s$ that

$$\begin{aligned}\mathbf{E}\left\{V_{\sigma\left(t^-_{k^{(a)}}\right)}(t_{k^{(a)}})|\varphi(t_{k^{(a-1)}})\right\} &= \mathbf{E}\left\{V_{\sigma\left(t_{k^{(a-1)}}\right)}(t_{k^{(a)}})|\varphi(t_{k^{(a-1)}})\right\}\\ &< \lambda^{k^{(a)}-k^{(a-1)}}_{\sigma\left(t_{k^{(a-1)}}\right)} V_{\sigma\left(t_{k^{(a-1)}}\right)}(t_{k^{(a-1)}})\\ &\quad - \sum_{j=k^{(a-1)}}^{k^{(a)}-1} \lambda^{k^{(a)}-1-j}_{\sigma\left(t_{k^{(a-1)}}\right)} \mathbf{E}\{\Upsilon(t_j)|\varphi(t_{k^{(a-1)}})\}\end{aligned} \tag{4.22}$$

where $t_{k^0} = t_0$. It follows from the inequality $P_i \le \mu P_s$ that

$$V_{\sigma\left(t_{k^{(a)}}\right)}(t_{k^{(a)}}) \le \mu V_{\sigma\left(t^{-}_{k^{(a)}}\right)}(t_{k^{(a)}}),\ a = 1, 2, \ldots, s \tag{4.23}$$

Thus, one has by (4.21) and (4.23) that

$$\begin{aligned}\mathbf{E}\left\{V_{\sigma(t_k)}(t_k)|\varphi(t_{k^{(s)}})\right\} &< \mu\lambda^{k-k^{(s)}}_{\sigma\left(t_{k^{(s)}}\right)} V_{\sigma\left(t^{-}_{k^{(s)}}\right)}(t_{k^{(s)}}) \\ &\quad - \sum_{j=k^{(s)}}^{k-1} \lambda^{k-1-j}_{\sigma\left(t_{k^{(s)}}\right)} \mathbf{E}\{\Upsilon(t_j)|\varphi(t_{k^{(s)}})\}\end{aligned} \tag{4.24}$$

Taking expectation $\mathbf{E}\{\cdot|\varphi(t_{k^{(s-1)}})\}$ on both sides of the inequality in (4.24) and considering (4.22) yield

$$\begin{aligned}&\mathbf{E}\{V_{\sigma(t_k)}(t_k)|\varphi(t_{k^{(s-1)}})\} \\ &< \mu\lambda^{k-k^{(s)}}_{\sigma\left(t_{k^{(s)}}\right)} \lambda^{k^{(s)}-k^{(s-1)}}_{\sigma\left(t_{k^{(s-1)}}\right)} V_{\sigma\left(t_{k^{(s-1)}}\right)}(t_{k^{(s-1)}}) \\ &\quad - \sum_{j=k^{(s)}}^{k-1} \lambda^{k-1-j}_{\sigma\left(t_{k^{(s)}}\right)} \mathbf{E}\{\Upsilon(t_j)|\varphi(t_{k^{(s-1)}})\} \\ &\quad - \mu\lambda^{k-k^{(s)}}_{\sigma\left(t_{k^{(s)}}\right)} \sum_{j=k^{(s-1)}}^{k^{(s)}-1} \lambda^{k^{(s)}-1-j}_{\sigma\left(t_{k^{(s-1)}}\right)} \mathbf{E}\{\Upsilon(t_j)|\varphi(t_{k^{(s-1)}})\}\end{aligned} \tag{4.25}$$

Applying (4.25) recursively, one obtains

$$\begin{aligned}\mathbf{E}\{V_{\sigma(t_k)}(t_k)|\varphi(t_0)\} &< \mu^{N_\sigma(t_0,t_k)} \lambda^{k-k^{(s)}}_{\sigma\left(t_{k^{(s)}}\right)} \\ &\quad \times \lambda^{k^{(s)}-k^{(s-1)}}_{\sigma\left(t_{k^{(s-1)}}\right)} \cdots \lambda^{k^{(1)}}_{\sigma(t_0)} V_{\sigma(t_0)}(t_0) - \Psi(\Upsilon)\end{aligned} \tag{4.26}$$

where

$$\begin{aligned}\Psi(\Upsilon) = {}& \mu^{N_\sigma(t_0,t_{k-1})} \lambda^{k-k^{(s)}}_{\sigma\left(t_{k^{(s)}}\right)} \prod_{j=1}^{s-1} \lambda^{k^{(j+1)}-k^{(j)}}_{\sigma\left(t_{k^{(j)}}\right)} \\ & \times \sum_{j=0}^{k^{(1)}-1} \lambda^{k^{(1)}-1-j}_{\sigma(t_0)} \mathbf{E}\{\Upsilon(t_j)|\varphi(t_0) + \mu^{N_\sigma(t_0,t_{k-1})-1}\end{aligned}$$

$$\times\lambda^{k-k^{(s)}}_{\sigma\left(t_{k^{(s)}}\right)}\prod_{j=2}^{s-1}\lambda^{k^{(j+1)}-k^{(j)}}_{\sigma\left(t_{k^{(j)}}\right)}\sum_{j=k^{(1)}}^{k^{(2)}-1}\lambda^{k^{(2)}-1-j}_{\sigma\left(t_{k^{(1)}}\right)}$$

$$\times\mathbf{E}\{\Upsilon(t_j)|\varphi(t_0)\}+\cdots+\mu^0\sum_{j=k^{(s)}}^{k-1}\lambda^{k-1-j}_{\sigma\left(t_{k^{(s)}}\right)}\mathbf{E}\{\Upsilon(t_j)|\varphi(t_0)\}$$

Now, we consider the exponential stability of the filtering error system (4.13) for $\nu(t_k)=0$. One has by (4.26) and Definition 4.1 that

$$\begin{aligned}
&\mathbf{E}\{V_{\sigma(t_k)}(t_k)|\varphi(t_0)\}\\
&<\mu^{N_\sigma(t_0,t_k)}\lambda^{k-k^{(s)}}_{\sigma\left(t_{k^{(s)}}\right)}\lambda^{k^{(s)}-k^{(s-1)}}_{\sigma\left(t_{k^{(s-1)}}\right)}\cdots\lambda^{k^{(1)}}_{\sigma(t_0)}V_{\sigma(t_0)}(t_0)\\
&<\mu^{N_\sigma(t_0,t_k)}\bar{\lambda}^kV_{\sigma(t_0)}(t_0)\\
&<\left(\mu^{1/\tau_a}\bar{\lambda}\right)^kV_{\sigma(t_0)}(t_0)\\
&=\varepsilon^kV_{\sigma(t_0)}(t_0)
\end{aligned}\tag{4.27}$$

Let $\beta_1=\min_{i\in Z_\sigma}\lambda_{\min}(P_i)$ and $\beta_2=\max_{i\in Z_\sigma}\lambda_{\max}(P_i)$, then it follows from (4.27) that

$$\beta_1\mathbf{E}\left\{\|\xi(t_k)\|^2|\varphi(t_0)\right\}\leq\mathbf{E}\{V_{\sigma(t_k)}(t_k)|\varphi(t_0)\}<\varepsilon^kV_{\sigma(t_0)}(t_0)\leq\beta_2\varepsilon^k\|\xi(t_0)\|^2$$

which yields

$$\mathbf{E}\left\{\|\xi(t_k)\|^2|\varphi(t_0)\right\}<\sqrt{\frac{\beta_2}{\beta_1}\varepsilon^k\|\xi(t_0)\|^2}$$

Moreover, $\tau_a>\tau_a^*$ and $\lambda>\bar{\lambda}$ guarantee that $\varepsilon<1$. Thus, it is concluded from Definition 4.2 that the filtering error system (4.13) with $\nu(t_k)=0$ is mean square exponentially stable with decay rate ε.

To prove the H_∞ noise attenuation performance, we consider $\nu(t_k)\neq0$. Replace $\mathbf{E}\{\Upsilon(t_j)|\varphi(t_0)\}$ in $\Psi(\Upsilon)$ by $\mathbf{E}\{\|e(t_j)\|^2|\varphi(t_0)\}$ and $\|\nu(t_j)\|^2$ and denote the resulting terms by $\Psi(e)$ and $\Psi(\nu)$, respectively, then $\Psi(\Upsilon)$ can be written as $\Psi(\Upsilon)=\Psi(e)-\gamma^2\Psi(\nu)$. Then, under zero initial condition, one has by (4.26) that $\Psi(\Upsilon)<0$, and thus

$$\begin{aligned}
&\sum_{j=0}^{k-1}\mu^{N_\sigma(t_j,t_{k-1})}\underline{\lambda}^{k-1-j}\mathbf{E}\left\{\|e(t_j)\|^2|\varphi(t_0)\right\}\leq\Psi(e)\\
&<\gamma^2\Psi(\nu)\leq\gamma^2\sum_{j=0}^{k-1}\mu^{N_\sigma(t_j,t_{k-1})}\bar{\lambda}^{k-1-j}\|\nu(t_j)\|^2
\end{aligned}\tag{4.28}$$

It follows from $N_\sigma(t_j, t_{k-1}) \le \dfrac{k-1-j}{\tau_a}$ and $\tau_a > \ln\mu/\ln\lambda^{-1}$ that $N_\sigma(t_j, t_{k-1}) \le \dfrac{\ln\lambda^{-(k-1-j)}}{\ln\mu}$, which together with the facts $\mu > 1$ and $N_\sigma(t_j, t_{k-1}) \ge 0$ yield

$$1 \le \mu^{N_\sigma(t_j,t_{k-1})} \le \lambda^{-(k-1-j)} \tag{4.29}$$

Thus, one has by (4.28) and (4.29) that

$$\sum_{j=0}^{k-1} \underline{\lambda}^{k-1-j}\mathbf{E}\left\{\|e(t_j)\|^2|\varphi(t_0)\right\} < \gamma^2 \sum_{j=0}^{k-1}(\bar{\lambda}/\lambda)^{k-1-j}\|\nu(t_j)\|^2 \tag{4.30}$$

Summing both sides of the inequality in (4.30) from $k = 1$ to $+\infty$ and changing the order of the summation lead to

$$\begin{aligned}
&(1-\underline{\lambda})^{-1}\sum_{j=0}^{+\infty}\mathbf{E}\left\{\|e(t_j)\|^2|\varphi(t_0)\right\}\\
&=\sum_{k=1}^{+\infty}\sum_{j=0}^{k-1}\underline{\lambda}^{k-1-j}\mathbf{E}\left\{\|e(t_j)\|^2|\varphi(t_0)\right\}\\
&<\gamma^2\sum_{k=1}^{+\infty}\sum_{j=0}^{k-1}\left(\bar{\lambda}/\lambda\right)^{k-1-j}\|\nu(t_j)\|^2\\
&=\gamma^2\left(1-\bar{\lambda}/\lambda\right)^{-1}\sum_{j=0}^{+\infty}\|\nu(t_j)\|^2
\end{aligned} \tag{4.31}$$

which implies that

$$\begin{aligned}
\sum_{r=1}^{m}\|e_{(r)}\|_{\mathbf{E}_2}^2 &= \|e\|_{\mathbf{E}_2}^2\\
&< \gamma^2\frac{1-\underline{\lambda}}{1-\bar{\lambda}/\lambda}\|\nu\|_2^2\\
&= \gamma^2\frac{1-\underline{\lambda}}{1-\bar{\lambda}/\lambda}\left(n\|w_p\|_2^2+\sum_{r=1}^{m}\|v_{p(r)}\|_2^2\right)\\
&= \gamma^2\frac{1-\underline{\lambda}}{1-\bar{\lambda}/\lambda}\sum_{r=1}^{m}\|\vartheta_{(r)}\|_2^2
\end{aligned}$$

Therefore, it can be concluded from Definition 4.3 that the m filtering errors satisfy an average H_∞ noise attenuation level $\bar{\gamma} = \gamma\sqrt{\dfrac{1-\underline{\lambda}}{1-\bar{\lambda}/\lambda}}$. The proof is thus completed.

4.4 H_∞ Filter Design

An existence condition for the distributed H_∞ filters of form (4.8) is given in the following theorem based on Theorem 4.1.

Theorem 4.2 *For given positive scalars γ, $\mu > 1$, $\lambda_i < 1$, and $\lambda < 1$, if there exist matrices $P_{i1} > 0$, P_{i2}, $P_{i3} > 0$, R_i, S_i, Q_{ij}, $\bar{F}_{(rl)i}$, $\bar{G}_{(rl)i}$, $L_{(r)i}$, $i = 1, 2, \ldots, n$, $j = 1, 2, \ldots, m$, $l \in \mathcal{N}_r$, $r = 1, 2, \ldots, m$ such that $\tau_a > \tau_a^*$, $\lambda > \bar{\lambda}$, and the following linear matrix inequalities (LMIs)*

$$\begin{cases} \bar{\Omega}_i \triangleq \begin{bmatrix} \operatorname{diag}\{\lambda_i P_i, \gamma^2 I\} & \begin{bmatrix} \Phi_a & \Phi_c & \Phi_e \\ \Phi_b & \Phi_d & \mathbf{0} \end{bmatrix} \\ * & \operatorname{diag}\{\Xi_{0i}, \Xi_i, I\} \end{bmatrix} > 0 \\ P_i \le \mu P_s, \forall\, i, s \in Z_\sigma \end{cases} \tag{4.32}$$

hold, then the filters in (4.8) guarantee that the filtering error system (4.13) is mean square exponentially stable with decay rate ε and all the filtering errors satisfy an average H_∞ noise attenuation level $\bar{\gamma}$, and the filter gain matrices are given by $F_i = Q_i^{-\mathrm{T}} \bar{F}_i$, $G_i = Q_i^{-\mathrm{T}} \bar{G}_i$ and L_i, where

$$\Phi_a^{\mathrm{T}} = \begin{bmatrix} \chi_3 & \chi_4 \\ \chi_5 & \chi_6 \end{bmatrix}$$

$$\Phi_b^{\mathrm{T}} = \begin{bmatrix} B_{mi}^{\mathrm{T}} R_i & B_{mi}^{\mathrm{T}} S_i \\ \sum_{j=1}^m D_{(j)}^{\mathrm{T}} \bar{G}_i^{\mathrm{T}} \Theta_{(j)} & \sum_{j=1}^m D_{(j)}^{\mathrm{T}} \bar{G}_i^{\mathrm{T}} \Theta_{(j)} \end{bmatrix}$$

$$\Phi_{c(j)}^{\mathrm{T}} = \begin{bmatrix} C_{(j)}^{\mathrm{T}} \bar{G}_i^{\mathrm{T}} \Theta_{c(j)} & C_{(j)}^{\mathrm{T}} \bar{G}_i^{\mathrm{T}} \Theta_{c(j)} \\ \chi_7 & \chi_8 \end{bmatrix}, \quad j = 1, 2, \ldots, m$$

$$\Phi_{d(j)}^{\mathrm{T}} = \begin{bmatrix} \mathbf{0} & \mathbf{0} \\ D_{(j)}^{\mathrm{T}} \bar{G}_i^{\mathrm{T}} \Theta_{c(j)} & D_{(j)}^{\mathrm{T}} \bar{G}_i^{\mathrm{T}} \Theta_{c(j)} \end{bmatrix}, \quad j = 1, 2, \ldots, m$$

$$\Phi_c^{\mathrm{T}} = \begin{bmatrix} \Phi_{c(1)}^{\mathrm{T}} & \cdots & \Phi_{c(m)}^{\mathrm{T}} \end{bmatrix}, \quad \Phi_d^{\mathrm{T}} = \begin{bmatrix} \Phi_{d(1)}^{\mathrm{T}} & \cdots & \Phi_{d(m)}^{\mathrm{T}} \end{bmatrix}$$

$$\Phi_e^{\mathrm{T}} = \begin{bmatrix} \bar{L}_p & -L_i \end{bmatrix}^{\mathrm{T}}$$

$$\Xi_{0i} = \begin{bmatrix} R_i + R_i^{\mathrm{T}} - P_{i1} & Q_i^{\mathrm{T}} + S_i - P_{i2} \\ * & Q_i + Q_i^{\mathrm{T}} - P_{i3} \end{bmatrix}$$

$$\Xi_i = \operatorname{diag}\{\Xi_{0i}\}_m, \quad P_i = \begin{bmatrix} P_{i1} & P_{i2} \\ * & P_{i3} \end{bmatrix}$$

$$Q_i = \operatorname{diag}\{Q_{i1}, \ldots, Q_{im}\}$$

$$\bar{F}_{(r)i} = \operatorname{col}^{\mathrm{T}} \left\{ \bar{F}_{(rl)i}^{\mathrm{T}} \right\}_{l \in Z_y}, \quad \text{where } \bar{F}_{(rl)i} = \mathbf{0}, \ \forall\, l \notin \mathcal{N}_r$$

$$\bar{G}_{(r)i} = \text{col}^{\mathrm{T}}\left\{\bar{G}^{\mathrm{T}}_{(rl)i}\right\}_{l\in Z_y}, \quad \bar{G}_{(rl)i} = \mathbf{0}, \forall\, l \notin \mathcal{N}_r$$

$$\bar{F}_i = \text{col}\left\{\bar{F}_{(r)i}\right\}_{r\in Z_y}, \quad \bar{G}_i = \text{col}\left\{\bar{G}_{(r)i}\right\}_{r\in Z_y}$$

$$L_i = \text{diag}\{L_{(r)i}\}_{r\in Z_y}$$

$$\chi_3 = A^{\mathrm{T}}_{mi}R_i + \sum_{j=1}^{m} C^{\mathrm{T}}_{(j)}\bar{G}^{\mathrm{T}}_i\Theta_{(j)}$$

$$\chi_4 = A^{\mathrm{T}}_{mi}S_i + \sum_{j=1}^{m} C^{\mathrm{T}}_{(j)}\bar{G}^{\mathrm{T}}_i\Theta_{(j)}$$

$$\chi_5 = \sum_{j=1}^{m} \Pi^{\mathrm{T}}_{(j)}\bar{F}^{\mathrm{T}}_i\Theta_{(j)} - \sum_{j=1}^{m} C^{\mathrm{T}}_{(j)}\bar{G}^{\mathrm{T}}_i\Theta_{(j)}$$

$$\chi_6 = \sum_{j=1}^{m} \Pi^{\mathrm{T}}_{(j)}\bar{F}^{\mathrm{T}}_i\Theta_{(j)} - \sum_{j=1}^{m} C^{\mathrm{T}}_{(j)}\bar{G}^{\mathrm{T}}_i\Theta_{(j)}$$

$$\chi_7 = \Pi^{\mathrm{T}}_{(j)}\bar{F}^{\mathrm{T}}_i\Theta_{c(j)} - C^{\mathrm{T}}_{(j)}\bar{G}^{\mathrm{T}}_i\Theta_{c(j)}$$

$$\chi_8 = \Pi^{\mathrm{T}}_{(j)}\bar{F}^{\mathrm{T}}_i\Theta_{c(j)} - C^{\mathrm{T}}_{(j)}\bar{G}^{\mathrm{T}}_i\Theta_{c(j)}$$

Proof By Theorem 4.1 in [22], $\Omega_i < 0$ is equivalent to that there exists a matrix V_i such that the matrix inequality

$$\tilde{\Omega}_i \triangleq \begin{bmatrix} \text{diag}\left\{\lambda_i P_i - \bar{C}^{\mathrm{T}}_i\bar{C}_i, \gamma^2 I\right\} & \Lambda^{\mathrm{T}}_i V_i \\ * & V_i + V^{\mathrm{T}}_i - \bar{P}_i \end{bmatrix} > 0$$

holds. Let V_i be a block-diagonal matrix: $V_i = \text{diag}\{V_{0i}\}_{m+1}$, where $V_{0i} = \begin{bmatrix} R_i & S_i \\ Q_i & Q_i \end{bmatrix}$. Denote $\bar{F}_i = Q^{\mathrm{T}}_i F_i$ and $\bar{G}_i = Q^{\mathrm{T}}_i G_i$. Then, one can directly obtain the LMIs $\bar{\Omega}_i > 0$ in (4.32) from the inequality $\tilde{\Omega}_i > 0$ by following some routine matrix manipulations, Schur complement lemma, and the relations $\Theta_{(j)}Q_i = Q_i\Theta_{(j)}$ and $\Theta_{c(j)}Q_i = Q_i\Theta_{c(j)}$. The rest of the proof is similar to that for Theorem 4.1 and is omitted. The proof is thus completed.

In Theorem 4.2, the existence condition for the filters is given in terms of LMIs which is convex in the scalar γ^2. Therefore, one may solve the following optimization problem to obtain the filter gain matrices that minimize the H_∞ noise attenuation level for given λ_i and λ, $i = 1, 2, \ldots, n$.

$$\min \kappa \quad \text{s.t. (4.32) with } \kappa = \gamma^2 \tag{4.33}$$

If κ^* is the optimal value of the objective function in the above minimization problem, then the designed filters guarantee that all the filtering errors satisfy an average H_∞ noise attenuation level $\bar{\gamma}^* = \sqrt{\dfrac{\kappa^*(1-\lambda)}{1-\bar{\lambda}/\lambda}}$.

The condition $\tau_a > \tau_a^*$ in Theorems 4.1 and 4.2 indicates that the variation rate of the sampling periods should be small enough to guarantee an existence of the H_∞ filters. Thus, Theorems 4.1 and 4.2 implicitly establish a relationship between the variation rate of the sampling period and the filtering performance. Since $\tau_a \geq 1$, $\mu\lambda < 1$ guarantees that $\tau_a > \tau_a^*$. Therefore, in case that τ_a is not known exactly in practice, one may use the condition $\mu\lambda < 1$ instead of $\tau_a > \tau_a^*$ in Theorems 4.1 and 4.2. Then, the exponential decay rate ε is bounded by $\varepsilon \leq \varepsilon^* \triangleq \mu\bar{\lambda}$.

Since switching-mode-dependent filters are designed, it is implicitly assumed that the sampling periods are known a priori by each sensor in the network, and each of the filters switches its gains according to the variation of the sampling periods. In case that the sampling periods are not known a priori, one may design switching-mode-independent filters by following the similar procedures as given in Theorems 4.1 and 4.2.

Based on Theorem 4.2, the design of the distributed H_∞ filters is summarized in the following algorithm.

Algorithm 4.1

Step 1: Solve the optimization problem (4.33) off-line to get the filter gain matrices F_i, G_i and L_i, $i = 1, 2, \ldots, n$.
Step 2: At each sampling instant t_k, each sensor r broadcasts its measurement $y_r(t_k)$ and local estimate $\hat{x}_r(t_k)$ to its neighbors and meanwhile collects measurements $y_l(t_k)$ and local estimates $\hat{x}_l(t_k)$, $l \in \mathcal{N}_r/\{r\}$ from its neighbors.
Step 3: Each sensor calculates the estimate $\hat{x}_r(t_{k+1})$ according to (4.8).

4.5 Simulations

Consider a continuous stirred tank reactor (CSTR) shown schematically in Fig. 4.1, where A and B are the educt and the desired product, respectively, C_{A0} is the low concentration of educt A, C_B is the concentration of the product B, and ϑ denotes the reactor temperature. The balance equations of the CSTR are given by [23]

$$\frac{\mathrm{d}C_A}{\mathrm{d}t} = \frac{F}{V}(C_{A0} - C_A) - k_1 C_A \tag{4.34}$$

$$\frac{\mathrm{d}C_B}{\mathrm{d}t} = -\frac{F}{V}C_B + k_1 C_A - k_2 C_B \tag{4.35}$$

$$\begin{aligned}\frac{\mathrm{d}\vartheta}{\mathrm{d}t} &= \frac{F}{V}(\vartheta_0 - \vartheta) + \frac{k_w A_R}{\rho C_P V}(\vartheta_k - \vartheta) \\ &\quad - \frac{k_1 C_A \Delta H_R^{AB} + k_2 C_B \Delta H_R^{BC}}{\rho C_P}\end{aligned} \tag{4.36}$$

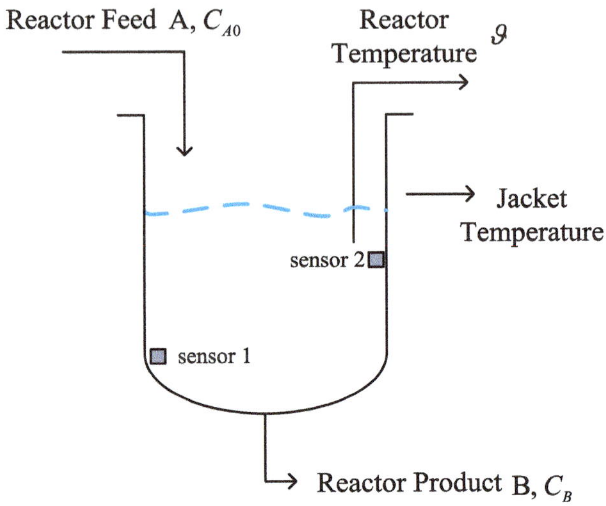

Fig. 4.1 Continuous stirred tank reactor

Table 4.1 Model parameters and main operating point

$k_0 = 1.2467 \times 10^{12}\,\mathrm{h}^{-1}$	$E_{A1,2}/R = 9867.5\,\mathrm{K}$
$\Delta H_R^{AB} = 4.2\,\mathrm{kJ/mol}$	$\Delta H_R^{BC} = -11\,\mathrm{kJ/mol}$
$\rho = 0.9342\,\mathrm{kg/l}$	$C_P = 3.01\,\mathrm{kJ/kg\,K}$
$A_R = 0.215\,\mathrm{m}^2$	$V = 10.01$
$\vartheta_0 = 403.15\,\mathrm{K}$	$k_w = 4032\,\mathrm{kJ/h\,m^2K}$
$C_{As} = 1.235\,\mathrm{mol/l}$	$C_{A0} = 5.1\,\mathrm{mol/l}$
$C_{Bs} = 0.9\,\mathrm{mol/l}$	$\vartheta_s = 407.29\,\mathrm{K}$
$F/V = 0.3138$	

where F is the normalized process stream inflow, V is the volume flow, ρ is the density, C_P is the heat capacity, ΔH_R is the reaction enthalpy, k_1 and k_2 are the rate coefficients which depend exponentially on the reactor temperature. The model parameters and main operating point of the CSTR (4.34), (4.35) and (4.36) are given in Table 4.1.

Based on (4.34), (4.35) and (4.36), the linearized state-space model of the CSTR near the operating point is given by

$$\dot{x}(t) = A_p x(t) + B_p \omega_p(t) \tag{4.37}$$

where $x(t) = [x_1(t)\ x_2(t)\ x_3(t)]^{\mathrm{T}}$, $x_1(t)$, and $x_2(t)$ are, respectively, the concentration of the educt A and the product B at time instant t, $x_3(t)$ is the temperature of the reactor at instant t, $\omega_p(t)$ is the noise belonging to $\mathscr{L}_2[0, +\infty)$, $B_p = [0\ \ 1\ \ 0]^{\mathrm{T}}$, and

A_p is the linearized system matrix given by

$$A_p = \begin{bmatrix} -\frac{F}{V} - k_1 & 0 & \frac{E_{A1}}{R\vartheta_s^2} k_1 C_{As} \\ k_1 & -\frac{F}{V} - k_2 & a_{23} \\ -\frac{k_1 \Delta H_R^{AB}}{\rho C_P} & -\frac{k_2 \Delta H_R^{BC}}{\rho C_P} & a_{33} \end{bmatrix}$$

$$= \begin{bmatrix} -0.9388 & 0 & 0.0459 \\ 0.625 & -0.9388 & -0.0125 \\ -0.9335 & 2.4449 & -0.8894 \end{bmatrix}$$

where

$$a_{23} = -\frac{E_{A1}}{R\vartheta_s^2} k_1 C_{As} + \frac{E_{A2}}{R\vartheta_s^2} k_2 C_{Bs}$$

$$a_{33} = -\frac{F}{V} - \frac{k_w A_R}{\rho C_P V} + \frac{E_{A1} k_1 C_{As} \Delta H_R^{AB} + E_{A2} k_2 C_{Bs} \Delta H_R^{BC}}{R\vartheta_s^2 \rho C_P}$$

In practice, it may be necessary for one to know the concentration of the desired product B for other use, but the direct measure of the concentration by using traditional chemical approaches is usually expensive. An alternative yet non-expensive approach is to use signal processing approaches to estimate the concentration. In this example, only the measurements of the reactor temperature ϑ are used to estimate the concentration of the desired product B. To enhance the reliability of the estimation system against sensor failures and improve estimation performance, two sensors are deployed to monitor the reactor temperature, and one has $C_{p(1)} = C_{p(2)} = [0\ 0\ 1]$, $D_{p(1)} = D_{p(2)} = 1$, $L_p = [0\ 1\ 0]$. The sensors measure the reactor temperature with a time-varying sampling period $h_k \in \{\mathrm{T}_0, 2\mathrm{T}_0\}$, where $\mathrm{T}_0 = 1$ min. At each sampling instant, each sensor broadcasts its measurement and local estimate to the other sensors and meanwhile collects measurements and local estimates from the other sensors to generate its fused estimate. Random packet losses may happen during the data transmission, and the PAPs are $\theta_{12} = \theta_{21} = 0.9$. Discretizing system (4.37) with period T_0, one obtains

$$A_0 = \begin{bmatrix} 0.3872 & 0.0222 & 0.01823 \\ 0.2444 & 0.3897 & 0.0007102 \\ -0.06849 & 0.9711 & 0.4008 \end{bmatrix}$$

$$B_0 = \begin{bmatrix} 0.009496 \\ 0.6474 \\ 0.6779 \end{bmatrix}$$

By applying the modeling method in Sect. 4.2, the filtering system can be described as a stochastic switched system with two subsystems S_1 and S_2 since the sampling period h_k takes two values. Specifically, when h_k takes T_0 and $2\mathrm{T}_0$, the filtering

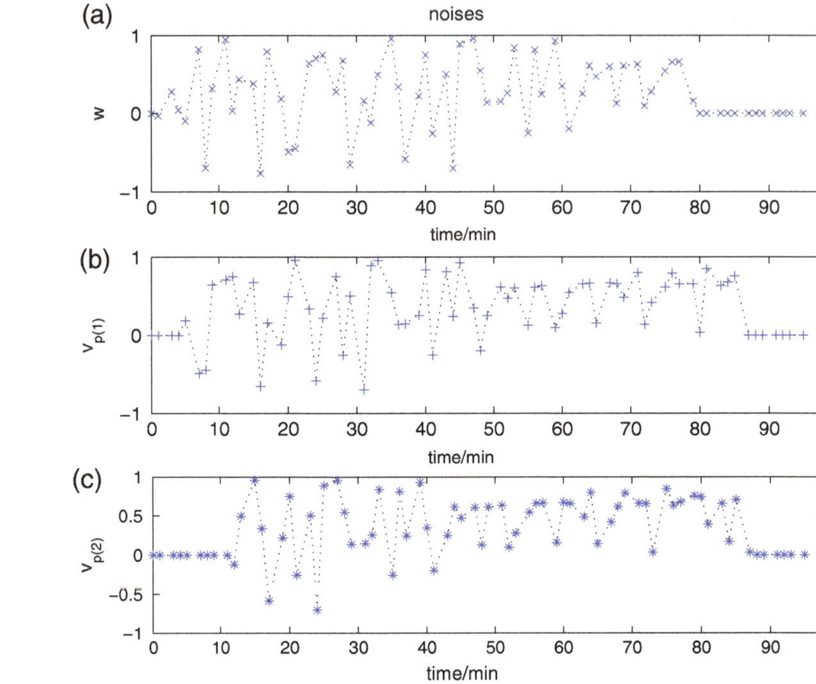

Fig. 4.2 The noises

system resides in the subsystem S_1 and S_2, respectively. Moreover, one has $A_i = A_0^i$, $B_i = B_0^i$, $i = 1, 2$.

Choose $\lambda_1 = 0.85$, $\lambda_2 = 0.90$, and $\mu = 1.05$ such that the LMIs in (4.32) have a feasible solution. Suppose that $\tau_a = 1.5$. Then, choose $\lambda = 0.94$ such that both the conditions $\tau_a > \tau_a^* = 0.7885$ and $\lambda > \bar{\lambda} = 0.90$ are satisfied. Then, by solving the minimization problem in (4.33), one obtains an optimal value $\kappa^* = 0.9617$ and all the corresponding filter gain matrices. Thus, the filtering errors in the two sensors satisfy an average H_∞ noise attenuation level $\bar{\gamma}^* = \sqrt{\dfrac{\kappa^*(1-\underline{\lambda})}{1-\bar{\lambda}/\lambda}} = 1.8412$.

In the simulation, the noises are chosen as those shown in Fig. 4.2. The simulations are shown in Figs. 4.3 and 4.4, where Fig. 4.3 shows the concentration and its estimates in the two sensors, while Fig. 4.4 depicts the estimation errors. It can be seen from the simulations that the designed filters perform well. Specifically, we obtain from the results in Figs. 4.2 and 4.4 that

$$\gamma = \frac{\sum_{r=1}^{2} \|e_{(r)}\|_2}{\sum_{r=1}^{2} \|\vartheta_{(r)}\|_2} = 0.7571 < \bar{\gamma}^* = 1.8412$$

Moreover, all the filtering errors finally converge to zero after the noises are eliminated. The exponential stability of the filtering error system is shown in Fig. 4.5,

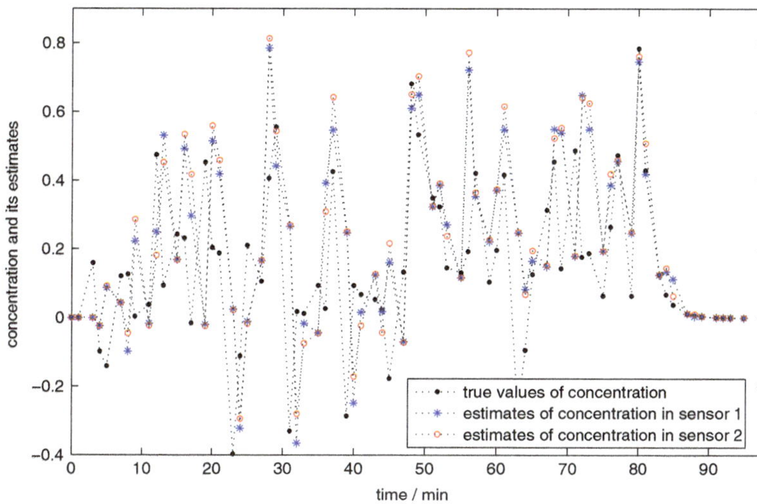

Fig. 4.3 The concentration and its estimates

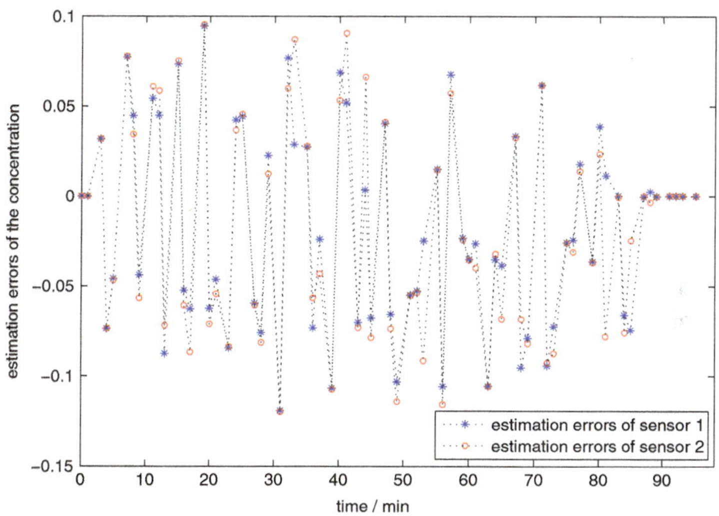

Fig. 4.4 Estimation errors

where the curve without star shows the trajectory of $g(t_k) = \sqrt{\dfrac{\beta_2}{\beta_1}\varepsilon^k \|\xi(t_0)\|^2} = 6.0328 \times 0.9298^k$ and the curve with stars shows the trajectory of $\|\xi(t_k)\|^2$. It can be seen from Fig. 4.5 that $\|\xi(t_k)\|^2 < g(t_k)$, then, according to Definition 4.2, the filtering error system is exponentially stable with decay rate 0.9298. The simulations demonstrate the effectiveness of the designed H_∞ filters.

Fig. 4.5 $\|\xi(t_k)\|^2$ and $g(t_k) = 6.0328 \times 0.9298^k$

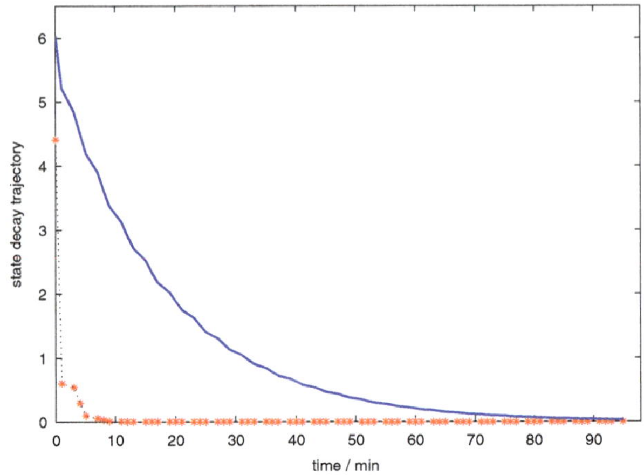

Table 4.2 Comparison of the H_∞ filters with uniform sampling period and nonuniform ones

	$\bar{\gamma}^*$	γ
F_n with h_k given by Fig. 4.3	1.8412	0.7571
F_u with $h_k = 1.5T_0$	1.7155	0.6810

The performance of the H_∞ filters with nonuniform sampling periods and uniform one are compared in Table 4.2, where F_n and F_u represents, respectively, the filters with nonuniform sampling periods and those with uniform one, and $\bar{\gamma}^*$ and γ represents, respectively, the calculated value and the simulation result of the average H_∞ noise attenuation level. It can be seen from Table 4.2 that both F_n and F_u consume the same amount of energy, and F_u performs slightly better than F_n. However, the main advantage of the proposed F_n lies in its flexibility of adjusting the sampling periods according to its energy status and being able to make a trade-off between the energy consumption and estimation performance.

4.6 Conclusions

Distributed sampled-data H_∞ filters have been developed in this chapter for sensor networks with nonuniform sampling periods and random packet losses. A discrete-time switched system with multiple stochastic parameters has been proposed to model the filtering system. It has been shown that the existence condition of the filters depends on both the lengths and variation rate of the sampling periods and the packet loss probabilities. The designed filters guarantee that all the filtering errors in the sensor network satisfy an average H_∞ noise attenuation level.

References

1. Shi P, de Souza CE, Xie LH (1993) Robust H_∞ filtering for uncertain systems with sampled-data measurements. In: Proceedings of the 32nd IEEE conferences on decision and control, San Antonlo, pp 793–798
2. Shi P (1998) Filtering on sampled-data systems with parametric uncertainty. IEEE Trans Autom Control 43(7):1022–1027
3. Mirkin L, Palmor ZJ (1999) On the sampled-data H_∞ filtering problem. Automatica 35(5):895–905
4. Nguang SK, Shi P (2000) Nonlinear H_∞ filtering of sampled-data systems. Automatica 36(2):303–310
5. Wang ZD, Huang B, Huo PJ (2001) Sampled-data filtering with error ovariance assignment. IEEE Trans Signal Process 49(3):666–670
6. Xu SY, Chen TW (2003) Robust H_∞ filtering for uncertain impulsive stochastic systems under sampled measurements. Automatica 39(3):509–516
7. Teixeira BOS, Santillo MA, Erwin RS, Bernstein DS (2008) Sapcecraft tracking using sampled-data Kalman filters. IEEE Control Syst Mag 28(4):78–94
8. Sun WQ, Nagpal KM, Khargonekar PP (1993) H_∞ control and filtering for sampled-data systems. IEEE Trans Autom Control 38(8):1162–1175
9. Li WH, Shah SL, Xiao DY (2008) Kalman filters in non-uniformly sampled multirate systems: for FDI and beyond. Automatica 44(1):199–208
10. Suplin V, Fridman E, Shaked U (2007) Sampled-data H_∞ control and filtering: nonuniform uncertain sampling. Automatica 43(6):1072–1083
11. Wu JL, Chen XM, Gao HJ (2010) H_∞ filtering with stochastic sampling. Signal Process 90(4):1131–1145
12. Shen B, Wang ZD, Liu XH (2011) A stochastic sampled-data approach to distributed H_∞ filtering in sensor networks. IEEE Trans Circuits Syst-I Regul Pap 58(9):2237–2246
13. Shi P, Luan XL, Liu F (2012) H_∞ filtering for discrete-time systems with stochastic incomplete measurement and mixed delays. IEEE Trans Ind Electron 59(6):2732–2739
14. Sinopoli B, Schenato L, Franceschetti M, Poolla K, Jordan MI, Sastry SS (2004) Kalman filtering with intermittent observations. IEEE Trans Autom Control 49(9):1453–1464
15. Wang ZD, Ho DWC, Liu XH (2003) Variance-constrained filtering for uncertain stochastic systems with missing measurements. IEEE Trans Autom Control 48(7):1254–1258
16. Sun SL, Xie LH, Xiao WD, Soh YC (2008) Optimal linear estimation for systems with multiple packet dropouts. Automatica 44(7):1333–1342
17. Fridman E, Seuret A, Richard JP (2004) Robust sampled-data stabilization of linear systems: an input delay approach. Automatica 40(8):1441–1446
18. Fujioka H (2009) Stability analysis of systems with aperiodic sample-and-hold devices. Automatica 45(3):771–775
19. Oishi H, Fujioka H (2010) Stability and stabilization of aperiodic sampled-data control systems using robust linear matrix inequalities. Automatica 46(8):1327–1333
20. Shen B, Wang ZD, Hung YS (2010) Distributed H_∞-consensus filtering in sensor networks with multiple missing measurements: the finite-horizon case. Automatica 46(10):1682–1688
21. Zhang WA, Yu L (2007) Output feedback stabilization of networked control systems with packet dropouts. IEEE Trans Autom Control 52(9):1705–1710
22. de Oliveira, MC, Bernussou J, Geromel JC (1999) A new discrete-time robust stability condition. Syst Control Lett 37(4):261–265
23. Klatt KU, Engell S (1998) Gain-scheduling trajectory control of a continuous stired tank reactor. Comput Chem Eng 22(4/5):491–502

Chapter 5
Fusion Estimation for WSNs Using Dimension-Reduction Method

5.1 Introduction

In Chaps. 2, 3, and 4, energy-efficient fusion estimation methods are presented by slowing down the transmission rates of measurements/local estimates and the estimation rate. In this chapter, a dimension-reduction method will be introduced for energy-efficient fusion estimation. To satisfy finite communication bandwidth and save energies consumed in communication, different dimensionality reduction approaches have been proposed in [1–7] to solve the fusion estimation problem, and the main idea of these approaches is that all the components of a vector signal are weighted and added to realize the objective of dimension reduction. Note that one should resort to the feedback information from a fusion center to obtain the compression matrices [3]. Different from the existing methods, this chapter presents the idea of directly choosing a part of components of local estimates to reduce the dimension of the local estimates to be transmitted to a fusion center. Specifically, when a local estimate is available at each sensor, only a part of the elements of the local estimate is selected and transmitted to the fusion center to save energy and meet the network bandwidth constraint. After the fusion center receives the local estimate with reduced dimension, a compensation strategy is proposed to reconstruct the local estimate and design the local unbiased estimator and improve the fusion estimation precision. Based on the optimal fusion estimation algorithm weighted by matrices, a recursive distributed fusion estimator is designed in the linear minimum variance sense. The gain matrix of the designed fusion estimator can be computed off-line as it does not need to know whether each component is sent or not at a particular time. Since the performance of the fusion estimator is dependent on the local estimate components selecting probabilities, some sufficient conditions, which are related to the selecting probabilities and system parameters, are derived such that the mean square error (MSE) of the fusion estimator is bounded. For linear time-invariant systems, some sufficient conditions are presented for the convergence of the fusion estimators.

W.-A. Zhang et al., *Distributed Fusion Estimation for Sensor Networks with Communication Constraints*, DOI 10.1007/978-981-10-0795-8_5

5.2 Problem Statement

5.2.1 System Models

Consider the following linear discrete-time stochastic system

$$x(t+1) = A(t)x(t) + \Gamma(t)w(t) \tag{5.1}$$

$$y_i(t) = C_i(t)x(t) + v_i(t),\ 1 \le i \le L \tag{5.2}$$

where $x(t) \in \Re^n$ represents the state of the process and $y_i(t) \in \Re^{q_i}$ is the measured output from sensor i. $A(t) \in \Re^{n\times n}$, $\Gamma(t) \in \Re^{n\times m}$, and $C_i(t) \in \Re^{q_i\times n}$ are time-varying matrices. $w(t) \in \Re^m$ and $v_i(t) \in \Re^{q_i}$ are uncorrelated zero-mean Gaussian white noises satisfying

$$\mathbf{E}\left\{[w^{\mathrm{T}}(t)\ v_i^{\mathrm{T}}(t)]^{\mathrm{T}}[w^{\mathrm{T}}(t_1)\ v_j^{\mathrm{T}}(t_1)]\right\} = \delta_{tt_1}\mathrm{diag}\{Q_w(t), \delta_{ij}Q_{v_i}(t)\} \tag{5.3}$$

where $\delta_{tt_1} = 0$ if $t \neq t_1$ and $\delta_{tt_1} = 1$ otherwise. A group of sensors are deployed to monitor the outputs of the process. Each sensor acts also as an estimator and has enough processing capabilities to generate local state estimates of $x(t)$. Based on the statistical properties (5.3) and the measurements $\{y_i(1), y_i(2), \ldots, y_i(t)\}$, the local optimal (in the linear minimum variance sense) estimate $\hat{x}_i(t)$ is recursively computed by the standard Kalman filter [8]:

$$\begin{cases} \hat{x}_i(t) = [I_n - \mathrm{K}_i(t)C_i(t)]A(t-1)\hat{x}_i(t-1) + \mathrm{K}_i(t)y_i(t) \\ \mathrm{K}_i(t) = P_{ii}^-(t)C_i^{\mathrm{T}}(t)[C_i(t)P_{ii}^-(t)C_i^{\mathrm{T}}(t) + Q_{v_i}(t)]^{-1} \end{cases} \tag{5.4}$$

and the optimal estimation error covariance matrix $P_{ii}(t)$ is defined by

$$P_{ii}(t) \triangleq \mathbf{E}\left\{[x(t) - \hat{x}_i(t)][x(t) - \hat{x}_i(t)]^{\mathrm{T}}\right\}$$

and is computed by

$$\begin{cases} P_{ii}(t) = [I_n - \mathrm{K}_i(t)C_i(t)]P_{ii}^-(t) \\ P_{ii}^-(t) = A(t-1)P_{ii}(t-1)A^{\mathrm{T}}(t-1) + \hat{\Gamma}(t-1) \end{cases} \tag{5.5}$$

where $P_{ii}^-(t)$ denotes the one-step prediction error covariance matrix and

$$\hat{\Gamma}(t-1) \triangleq \Gamma(t-1)Q_w(t-1)\Gamma^{\mathrm{T}}(t-1) \tag{5.6}$$

Define

$$\begin{cases} \tilde{x}_a^{\mathrm{T}}(t) \triangleq \left[(x(t)-\hat{x}_1(t))^{\mathrm{T}} \ \cdots \ (x(t)-\hat{x}_L(t))^{\mathrm{T}}\right] \\ I_0 \triangleq [I_n \ \cdots \ I_n]^{\mathrm{T}} \in \Re^{nL\times n} \\ \hat{P}(t) \triangleq \mathbf{E}\left\{\tilde{x}_a(t)\tilde{x}_a^{\mathrm{T}}(t)\right\} = (P_{ij}(t)) \in \Re^{nL\times nL} \end{cases} \tag{5.7}$$

Then it follows from (5.3) and (5.4) that the optimal estimation error cross-covariance matrix $P_{ij}(t)$ defined by

$$P_{ij}(t) \triangleq \mathbf{E}\left\{(x(t)-\hat{x}_i(t))(x(t)-\hat{x}_j(t))^{\mathrm{T}}\right\}$$

is computed by [9]

$$\begin{aligned} P_{ij}(t) = {} & [I_n - \mathrm{K}_i(t)C_i(t)][A_i(t-1)P_{ij}(t-1) \\ & \times A_i^{\mathrm{T}}(t-1) + \hat{\Gamma}(t-1)][I_n - \mathrm{K}_j(t)C_j(t)]^{\mathrm{T}},\ i \neq j \end{aligned} \tag{5.8}$$

Thus, the estimation error covariance matrix $\hat{P}(t)$ in (5.7) can be obtained from (5.5) and (5.8). After the fusion center receives all the local estimates $\hat{x}_i(t)$, $i = 1, 2, \ldots, L$, then it follows from Lemma 2.4 that the optimal fusion estimate $\hat{x}_o(t)$ is given by

$$\hat{x}_o(t) = \sum_{i=1}^{L} F_i(t)\hat{x}_i(t) \tag{5.9}$$

where $\hat{x}_i(t)$ is computed by (5.4) and the optimal matrix weights are determined by

$$[F_1(t), F_2(t), \ldots, F_L(t)] = \left(I_0^{\mathrm{T}}\hat{P}^{-1}(t)I_0\right)^{-1} I_0^{\mathrm{T}}\hat{P}^{-1}(t) \in \Re^{n\times nL} \tag{5.10}$$

and the fusion estimation error covariance matrix

$$P_o(t) \triangleq \mathbf{E}\left\{[x(t)-\hat{x}_o(t)][x(t)-\hat{x}_o(t)]^{\mathrm{T}}\right\}$$

is calculated by

$$P_o(t) = \left(I_0^{\mathrm{T}}\hat{P}^{-1}(t)I_0\right)^{-1} \tag{5.11}$$

Moreover, the relationship between the fusion estimation performance and the local estimation performance is

$$\mathrm{Tr}(P_o(t)) \leq \mathrm{Tr}(P_{ii}(t)),\ i = 1, 2, \ldots, L \tag{5.12}$$

Note that the covariance matrices (5.5) and (5.8) do not depend on the measurements and can thus be computed at the fusion center, which helps reduce communication consumptions.

As mentioned before, when each local estimate $\hat{x}_i(t)$ is transmitted to the fusion center through a WSN, the sensor energy and communication bandwidth constraints should be taken into account in designing the distributed fusion estimation algorithm. In this chapter, a dimensionality reduction method combined with a transmission rate reduction method is presented to solve this problem, and the detailed approach is described as follows: at a particular time t, since the communication channels are constrained by a limited bandwidth, it may not be able to allocate enough bits to send the local estimates. To satisfy finite communication bandwidth, only r_i $(1 \leq \mathrm{r}_i < n)$ components of the vector $\hat{x}_i(t)$ are allowed to be transmitted to the fusion center, and it is reasonable to consider that there are enough bits coding the r_i transmitted components such that the transmitted messages have no distortion. In this case, if the sensor i sends information to the fusion center at time t, the reorganized state estimate $\hat{x}_i^{\mathrm{r}}(t)$, which is received by the fusion center at time t, has Δ_i possible cases, and it follows from the alignment combination formula that

$$\Delta_i = C_n^{\mathrm{r}_i} = \frac{n(n-1)(n-2)\cdots(n-\mathrm{r}_i+1)}{\mathrm{r}_i(\mathrm{r}_i-1)(\mathrm{r}_i-2)\cdots 1} \tag{5.13}$$

and the reorganized state estimate $\hat{x}_i^{\mathrm{r}}(t)$ can only take one signal from the following finite set:

$$\chi_i(t) \triangleq \left\{H_1^i\hat{x}_i(t), \ldots, H_{h_i}^i\hat{x}_i(t), \ldots, H_{\Delta_i}^i\hat{x}_i(t)\right\} \tag{5.14}$$

where $H_{h_i}^i$, $h_i = 1, 2, \ldots, \Delta_i$ denote different diagonal matrices and $H_{h_i}^i$ contains r_i diagonal elements "1" and $n - \mathrm{r}_i$ diagonal elements "0". It is obvious that the set (5.14) contains all possible cases of the reorganized state estimate $\hat{x}_i^{\mathrm{r}}(t)$. On the other hand, when the bandwidth and energy constraints are taken into account simultaneously, the sensor may not send the local information to the fusion center at every fusion estimation instant. In the case that the local estimate is not chosen to be transmitted to the fusion center, the reorganized state estimate $\hat{x}_i^{\mathrm{r}}(t)$ is chosen from the set $\{0\}$.

To describe the reorganized state estimate $\hat{x}_i^{\mathrm{r}}(t)$ in a simple way, suppose that Δ_i elements of the set χ_i are indexed from 1 to Δ_i, then the following indication functions are introduced:

$$\sigma_{h_i}^i(t) = \begin{cases} 1 & \text{if } \hat{x}_i^{\mathrm{r}}(t) = H_{h_i}^i\hat{x}_i(t) \\ 0 & \text{if } \hat{x}_i^{\mathrm{r}}(t) \neq H_{h_i}^i\hat{x}_i(t) \end{cases}, \quad h_i = 1, 2, \ldots, \Delta_i \tag{5.15}$$

which means that if the h_ith element of the set (5.14) is chosen as $\hat{x}_i^{\mathrm{r}}(t)$, then $\sigma_{h_i}^i(t) = 1$. Otherwise, $\sigma_{h_i}^i(t) = 0$. When the sensor i does not send information to the fusion center at time t and the value of $\hat{x}_i^{\mathrm{r}}(t)$ is not in the set (5.14), then it follows from (5.15) that $\sigma_1^i(t) = \sigma_2^i(t) = \ldots = \sigma_{\Delta_i}^i(t) = 0$. In this case, the reorganized state estimate $\hat{x}_i^{\mathrm{r}}(t)$ can take at most one value from (5.14); thus, the introduced binary variables $\sigma_{h_i}^i(t)$, $h_i = 1, 2, \ldots, \Delta_i$ satisfy

$$\begin{cases} \sigma_{h_i}^i(t)\sigma_{h_i^o}^i(t) = 0, \ h_i \neq h_i^o \\ \left(\sum\limits_{h_i=1}^{\Delta_i} \sigma_{h_i}^i(t)\right) \in \{0, 1\}, \ i = 1, 2, \ldots, L \end{cases} \tag{5.16}$$

where $\sum_{h_i=1}^{\Delta_i} \sigma_{h_i}^i(t) = 0$ indicates that there is no communication between sensor i and the fusion center at time t. Therefore, it is derived from (5.15) and (5.16) that the reorganized state estimate $\hat{x}_i^{\mathrm{r}}(t)$ is

$$\hat{x}_i^{\mathrm{r}}(t) = H_i(t)\hat{x}_i(t) \tag{5.17}$$

where $H_i(t) \triangleq \sum_{h_i=1}^{\Delta_i} \sigma_{h_i}^i(t)H_{h_i}^i$. It follows from (5.15) and the definition of $H_{h_i}^i$ that $H_i(t)$ is a diagonal matrix, and the diagonal elements of $H_i(t)$ are 0 or 1. For presentation simplicity, the binary variables $\gamma_\ell^i(t) \in \{0, 1\}$ ($\ell = 1, 2, \ldots, n$) are introduced to denote the n diagonal elements of $H_i(t)$, i.e.,

$$H_i(t) = \mathrm{diag}\{\gamma_1^i(t), \ldots, \gamma_n^i(t)\} \tag{5.18}$$

It can be seen that each binary variable $\gamma_\ell^i(t)$, $\ell \in \{1, 2, \ldots, n\}$ is dependent on the choices of the values $\sigma_{\hbar_i}^i(t)$, $\hbar_i = 1, 2, \ldots, \Delta_i$. Moreover, it follows from (5.15) and (5.16) that

$$\left(\sum_{\ell=1}^{n} \gamma_\ell^i(t)\right) \in \{0, \mathrm{r}_i\}, \ i = 1, 2, \ldots, L \tag{5.19}$$

where r_i ($\mathrm{r}_i \in \mathrm{N}_+$ and $1 \leq \mathrm{r}_i \leq n$) denotes the finite bandwidth constraint. Particularly, it follows from (5.19) that if $\sum_{\ell=1}^{n} \gamma_\ell^i(t) = \mathrm{r}_i$ holds, then the partial sensor message satisfying the finite bandwidth will be sent to the fusion center at time t. Otherwise, $\sum_{\ell=1}^{n} \gamma_\ell^i(t) = 0$ means that there is no communication between sensor i and the fusion center and the energy of this sensor can be saved at time t.

For $\mathrm{r}_i = n$, it is derived from (5.20) that $\left(\sum\limits_{\ell=1}^{n} \gamma_\ell^i(t)\right) \in \{0, n\}$ and $\gamma_\ell^i(t) \in \{0, 1\}$; thus, $H_i(t)$ is only taken as I_n or 0 at time t. In this case, the model (5.17) only describes the energy constraint case. On the other hand, if the equation $\sum_{h_i=1}^{\Delta_i} \sigma_{h_i}^i(t) = 1$ always holds, then it follows from (5.15) and (5.16) that the sensors and fusion center communicate with each other at each time step, which means that the model (5.17) only describes the bandwidth constraint problem.

In what follows, when only the communication bandwidth constraints are considered, a simple example is given to explain how to obtain the reorganized state estimate $\hat{x}_i^{\mathrm{r}}(t)$ by using (5.17). For $n = 3$, $\mathrm{r}_1 = 2$, $\mathrm{r}_2 = 1$, and $L = 2$, it follows from (5.14) that

$$\begin{cases} \Delta_1 = 3, H_1^1 = \mathrm{diag}\{1, 1, 0\}, H_2^1 = \mathrm{diag}\{1, 0, 1\} \\ H_3^1 = \mathrm{diag}\{0, 1, 1\}; \Delta_2 = 3, H_1^2 = \mathrm{diag}\{1, 0, 0\} \\ H_2^2 = \mathrm{diag}\{0, 1, 0\}, H_3^2 = \mathrm{diag}\{0, 0, 1\} \end{cases} \tag{5.20}$$

Note that H_i^1 and H_i^2 in (5.20) represent different component transmission situations. For example, H_1^1 in (5.20) means that the first and second components of $\hat{x}_1(t)$ are transmitted to the fusion center, but the third component of $\hat{x}_1(t)$ is discarded at time t. On the other hand, it follows from (5.18) and (5.20) that

$$\begin{cases} H_1(t) = \mathrm{diag}\{\gamma_1^1(t), \gamma_2^1(t), \gamma_3^1(t)\} \\ \qquad\;\; = \mathrm{diag}\{1 - \sigma_3^1(t), 1 - \sigma_2^1(t), 1 - \sigma_1^1(t)\} \\ H_2(t) = \mathrm{diag}\{\gamma_1^2(t), \gamma_2^2(t), \gamma_3^2(t)\} \\ \qquad\;\; = \mathrm{diag}\{\sigma_1^2(t), \sigma_2^2(t), \sigma_3^2(t)\} \end{cases} \tag{5.21}$$

where

$$\sum_{\ell=1}^{3} \gamma_\ell^1(t) = 3 - \sum_{\ell=1}^{3} \sigma_\ell^1(t) = 2, \; \sum_{\ell=1}^{3} \gamma_\ell^2(t) = \sum_{\ell=1}^{3} \sigma_\ell^2(t) = 1$$

Therefore, the reorganized state estimate $\hat{x}_i^{\mathrm{r}}(t)$, $i = 1, 2$ is obtained by substituting (5.21) into (5.17). Obviously, for this example, (5.17) describes all possible cases of each reorganized state estimate.

5.2.2 *Problem of Interests*

According to the proposed communication strategy, it is considered that each component of the local estimate $\hat{x}_i(t)$ is randomly sent to the fusion center. In this case, $H_i(t)$ in (5.17) is a random matrix, and it is difficult to be known a priori, but it can be obtained from the identification process of reorganized state estimate $\hat{x}_i^{\mathrm{r}}(t)$. For each local estimate $\hat{x}_i(t)$, it is considered that if the order information of selected components is flagged before transmission, then the order information of the received components for each reorganized state estimate will be determined by their flags in the fusion center, and other untransmitted components are regarded as 0. It is noted that the required bandwidth for the added flags is negligible compared with that for the data packet transmission. Then, the diagonal element $\gamma_j^i(t) \in \{0, 1\}$ of the matrix $H_i(t)$ can be directly determined at time t by judging whether the flag of the jth component is included in the arrived data packet or not. A simple example is given to explain how to determine the matrix $H_i(t)$ at time t. For the ith local estimate $\hat{x}_i(t) = [1.2 \;\; 1.5 \;\; 0.8]^{\mathrm{T}}$, if the first and second components of $\hat{x}_i(t)$

are selected to send to the fusion center, the corresponding order information will be flagged before being transmitted. Once the transmitted components arrive at the fusion center, it follows from the flags of the data packet that $x_i^{\mathrm{r}}(t) = [1.2 \quad 1.5 \quad 0]^{\mathrm{T}}$, and only the flag of the third component is not included in this data packet; thus, one has $\gamma_3^i(t) = 0$ and $\gamma_j^i(t) = 1, j = 1, 2$, which means that $H_i(t) = \mathrm{diag}\{1, 1, 0\}$.

On the other hand, it follows from (5.15), (5.16), and (5.17) that the practical communication situation is determined by the binary variables $\sigma_{h_i}^i(t)$, $\hbar_i = 1, 2, \ldots, \Delta_i$; therefore, it is specified that each stochastic process $\{\sigma_{h_i}^i(t)\}$, $\hbar_i \in \{1, 2, \ldots, \Delta_i\}; i \in \{1, 2, \ldots, L\}$ is i.i.d (independent and identically distributed) and the random variables $w(t)$, $v_i(t)$, and $\sigma_{h_i}^i(t)$, $i = 1, 2, \ldots, L$ are mutually uncorrelated, i.e.,

$$\mathbf{E}\left\{\sigma_{h_i}^i(t) w^{\mathrm{T}}(t)\right\} = 0,\ \mathbf{E}\left\{\sigma_{h_i}^i(t) v_j^{\mathrm{T}}(t)\right\} = 0\ , \forall\ i, j \tag{5.22}$$

$$\mathbf{E}\left\{\sigma_{h_i}^i(t)\sigma_{h_j^o}^j(t_1)\right\} = \begin{cases} 0, & i = j, t = t_1, h_i \neq h_i^0 \\ \mathbf{E}\left\{\sigma_{h_i}^i(t)\right\}, & i = j, t = t_1, h_i = h_i^0 \\ \mathbf{E}\left\{\sigma_{h_i}^i(t)\right\} \mathbf{E}\left\{\sigma_{h_i^o}^i(t_1)\right\}, & i = j, t \neq t_1, \forall h_i, h_i^0 \\ \mathbf{E}\left\{\sigma_{h_i}^i(t)\right\} \mathbf{E}\left\{\sigma_{h_j^o}^j(t_1)\right\}, & i \neq j, \forall t, t_1, h_i, h_j^0 \end{cases} \tag{5.23}$$

Moreover, the occurrence probabilities of the cases $\sigma_{h_i}^i(t) = 1$ and $\sigma_{h_i}^i(t) = 0$ are given by

$$\mathrm{Prob}\{\sigma_{h_i}^i(t) = 1\} = \pi_{h_i}^i,\ \mathrm{Prob}\{\sigma_{h_i}^i(t) = 0\} = 1 - \pi_{h_i}^i \tag{5.24}$$

where $\pi_{h_i}^i$ is a given positive scalar satisfying

$$0 \leq \sum_{h_i=1}^{\Delta_i} \pi_{h_i}^i \leq 1 \tag{5.25}$$

Then it follows from (5.16) that the expected energy-saving rate η_i for the ith sensor is given by

$$\eta_i = \mathbf{E}\left\{1 - \sum_{h_i=1}^{\Delta_i} \sigma_{h_i}^i(t)\right\} = 1 - \sum_{h_i=1}^{\Delta_i} \pi_{h_i}^i \tag{5.26}$$

Additionally, it follows from the statistical properties (5.23) and the definition of $\gamma_\ell^i(t)$ that the binary variables $\gamma_\ell^i(t)$, $\ell = 1, 2, \ldots, n$ are independent Bernoulli distributed white sequences taking values of 1 or 0 with $\mathrm{Prob}\{\gamma_\ell^i(t) = 1\} \triangleq \gamma_\ell^i$ and $\mathrm{Prob}\{\gamma_\ell^i(t) = 0\} \triangleq 1 - \gamma_\ell^i$. Meanwhile, it follows from (5.16) and (5.19) that the condition $\sum_{\ell=1}^n \gamma_\ell^i(t) = \mathrm{r}_i$ is equivalent to $\sum_{h_i=1}^{\Delta_i} \sigma_{h_i}^i(t) = 1$; thus, it is derived from (5.24) and (5.26) that

$$\mathbf{E}\left\{\sum_{\ell=1}^{n}\gamma_{\ell}^{i}(t)\right\} = \mathrm{r}_i\sum_{h_i=1}^{\Delta_i}\pi_{h_i}^{i} = \mathrm{r}_i(1-\eta_i)\ , i=1,2,\ldots,L \tag{5.27}$$

Moreover, it is obtained from (5.22) that the random variables $\gamma_{\ell}^{i}(t)$, $w(t)$, and $v_i(t)$ are mutually uncorrelated, i.e.,

$$\begin{cases}\mathbf{E}\left\{\gamma_{\ell}^{i}(t)\gamma_{\ell_1}^{j}(t)\right\} = \gamma_{\ell}^{i}\gamma_{\ell_1}^{j},\ i\neq j\\ \mathbf{E}\left\{\gamma_{\ell}^{i}(t)w^{\mathrm{T}}(t)\right\} = 0, \mathbf{E}\left\{\gamma_{\ell}^{i}(t)v_j^{\mathrm{T}}(t)\right\} = 0,\ \forall i,j\end{cases} \tag{5.28}$$

Then, the problems to be solved in this chapter are described as follows: For a given arbitrary group of binary variables

$$\sigma_1^i(t),\ldots,\sigma_{h_i}^i(t),\ldots,\sigma_{\Delta_i}^i(t),\ i=1,2,\ldots,L$$

satisfying (5.22), (5.23), (5.24), and (5.25), design an optimal fusion estimate $\hat{x}(t)$ with bandwidth and energy constraints such that

$$\begin{cases}\hat{x}(t) &= \arg\min\limits_{\hat{x}_*(t)}\mathbf{E}\{(x(t)-\hat{x}_*(t))^{\mathrm{T}}(x(t)-\hat{x}_*(t))\}\\ \mathbf{E}\{\hat{x}(t)\} &= \mathbf{E}\{x(t)\}\end{cases} \tag{5.29}$$

where $\hat{x}_*(t)$ is an arbitrary linear combination of $\hat{x}_i^{\mathrm{c}}(t),\ i=1,2,\ldots,L$, and $\hat{x}_i^{\mathrm{c}}(t)$ denotes the ith compensation state estimate of $x(t)$ from the reorganized state estimate $\hat{x}_i^{\mathrm{r}}(t)$. Then, based on the fusion estimation algorithm, find a probability selecting criterion such that the MSE of the designed fusion estimate $\hat{x}(t)$ in (5.29) is bounded, i.e.,

$$\mathrm{Cov}\{x(t)-\hat{x}(t)\} = \mathrm{Tr}\{\mathbf{E}\{(x(t)-\hat{x}(t))(x(t)-\hat{x}(t))^{\mathrm{T}}\}\}\leq p_0 \tag{5.30}$$

holds for $t > N_0$, where p_0 denotes a positive scalar and N_0 represents a positive integer.

5.3 Design of Finite-Horizon Fusion Estimator

5.3.1 Compensating Strategy

According to the proposed communication strategy, each component of the local estimate $\hat{x}_i(t)$ is randomly sent to the fusion center at time t; thus, it is possible that the jth component of the reorganized state estimate $\hat{x}_i^{\mathrm{r}}(t)$ is zero at time t.

Particularly, when the energy and bandwidth constraints are taken into account simultaneously, the case that $\hat{x}_i^{\mathrm{r}}(t) = 0$ may occur when the ith sensor does not send information to the fusion center for reducing energy consumption. In this case, the jth component of the fusion estimate $\hat{x}(t)$ may be zero at time t; however, the real value of the state variable in the system (5.1) is not zero and may even be very large for unstable systems. In this sense, if the distributed fusion estimator is directly designed based on the local reorganized state estimates, then the overall fusion estimation performance may degrade seriously. Therefore, it is necessary to compensate each reorganized state estimate for improving its estimation precision. Let us define

$$\begin{cases} [e_1(t) \quad \cdots \quad e_L(t)] \triangleq [x(t) - \hat{x}_1^{\mathrm{c}}(t) \quad \cdots \quad x(t) - \hat{x}_L^{\mathrm{c}}(t)] \\ \Sigma(t) \triangleq \mathbf{E}\left\{[e_1^{\mathrm{T}}(t) \quad \cdots \quad e_L^{\mathrm{T}}(t)]^{\mathrm{T}}[e_1^{\mathrm{T}}(t) \quad \cdots \quad e_L^{\mathrm{T}}(t)]\right\} \end{cases} \tag{5.31}$$

When the local compensated state estimates are available, then it follows from (5.9) that the optimal fusion estimate $\hat{x}(t)$ with bandwidth and energy constraints is given by

$$\hat{x}(t) = \sum_{i=1}^{L} \Omega_i(t)\hat{x}_i^{\mathrm{c}}(t) \tag{5.32}$$

Then it follows from (5.10) and (5.11) that the optimal weighting matrices

$$\Omega_1(t), \Omega_2(t), \ldots, \Omega_L(t)$$

and the corresponding error covariance matrix

$$P(t) \triangleq \mathbf{E}\left\{(x(t) - \hat{x}(t))(x(t) - \hat{x}(t))^{\mathrm{T}}\right\}$$

are calculated by

$$\begin{cases} [\Omega_1(t), \ldots, \Omega_L(t)] = (I_0^{\mathrm{T}}\Sigma^{-1}(t)I_0)^{-1}I_0^{\mathrm{T}}\Sigma^{-1}(t) \\ P(t) = (I_0^{\mathrm{T}}\Sigma^{-1}(t)I_0)^{-1} \end{cases} \tag{5.33}$$

where I_0 is defined in (5.7) and one has

$$\sum_{i=1}^{L} \Omega_i(t) = I_n \tag{5.34}$$

Moreover, it follows from (5.32) and (5.34) that the optimal fusion estimate $\hat{x}(t)$ is unbiased only if each compensated state estimate $\hat{x}_i^{\mathrm{c}}(t), i \in \{1, 2, \ldots, L\}$ is unbiased, i.e.,

$$\mathbf{E}\{\hat{x}_i^{\mathrm{c}}(t)\} = \mathbf{E}\{x(t)\} \Rightarrow \mathbf{E}\{\hat{x}(t)\} = \mathbf{E}\{x(t)\} \tag{5.35}$$

Therefore, an appropriate compensating strategy will be presented in the following theorem such that the equations

$$\mathbf{E}\{\hat{x}_i^c(t)\} = \mathbf{E}\{\hat{x}(t)\} = \mathbf{E}\{x(t)\},\ i = 1, 2, \ldots, L$$

hold.

Theorem 5.1 *If the initial values of the optimal fusion estimate $\hat{x}(t)$ and the local estimates $\hat{x}_i(t), i = 1, 2, \ldots, L$ satisfy*

$$\mathbf{E}\{\hat{x}(0)\} = \mathbf{E}\{\hat{x}_i(0)\} = \mathbf{E}\{x(0)\},\ i = 1, 2, \ldots, L \tag{5.36}$$

then the ith *compensated state estimate $\hat{x}_i^c(t)$ is given by*

$$\hat{x}_i^c(t) = H_i(t)\hat{x}_i(t) + [I_n - H_i(t)]A(t-1)\hat{x}(t-1) \tag{5.37}$$

where $(I_n - H_i(t))A(t-1)\hat{x}(t-1)$ is used to compensate the diagonal elements "0" of $\hat{x}_i^r(t)$. Under this condition, the fusion estimate $\hat{x}(t)$ and the local compensated state estimate $\hat{x}_i^c(t)$ are unbiased estimates of $x(t)$, i.e.,

$$\mathbf{E}\{x(t)\} = \mathbf{E}\{\hat{x}(t)\} = \mathbf{E}\{\hat{x}_i^c(t)\} \tag{5.38}$$

Proof Each compensated state estimate $\hat{x}_i^c(t)$ designed in (5.37) means that when $n-\mathrm{r}_i$ components of the local estimate $\hat{x}_i(t)$ are not transmitted to the fusion center, they are replaced by one-step predictions of the fusion estimate $\hat{x}(t-1)$. In what follows, the unbiasedness of the designed compensated state estimate and the fusion estimate will be proved. First, it is well known that the local estimate $\hat{x}_i(t)$ is unbiased only if the initial value $\hat{x}_i(0)$ of the local estimate is the unbiased estimate of the initial value $x(0)$, i.e.,

$$\mathbf{E}\{\hat{x}_i(0)\} = \mathbf{E}\{x(0)\} \Rightarrow \mathbf{E}\{\hat{x}_i(t)\} = \mathbf{E}\{x(t)\} \tag{5.39}$$

It follows from (5.37) that

$$\hat{x}_i^c(1) = H_i(1)\hat{x}_i(1) + [I_n - H_i(1)]A(0)\hat{x}(0) \tag{5.40}$$

Taking (5.22), (5.39), and (5.40) into account yields

$$\mathbf{E}\{\hat{x}_i^c(1)\} = \mathbf{E}\{H_i(1)\}\mathbf{E}\{x(1)\} + \mathbf{E}\{[I_n - H_i(1)]\}A(0)\mathbf{E}\{\hat{x}(0)\} \tag{5.41}$$

Since $w(t)$ is a zero-mean white noise, it is verified from (5.1) and (5.22) that

$$\begin{aligned}\mathbf{E}\{x(1)\} &= \mathbf{E}\{H_i(1)\}\mathbf{E}\{x(1)\} + \mathbf{E}\{(I_n - H_i(1))\}\mathbf{E}\{x(1)\} \\ &= \mathbf{E}\{H_i(1)\}\mathbf{E}\{x(1)\} + \mathbf{E}\{(I_n - H_i(1))\}A(0)\mathbf{E}\{x(0)\}\end{aligned} \tag{5.42}$$

Then, it is derived from (5.41) and (5.42) that

$$\mathbf{E}\{\hat{x}(0)\} = \mathbf{E}\{x(0)\} \Rightarrow \mathbf{E}\{\hat{x}_i^c(1)\} = \mathbf{E}\{x(1)\} \tag{5.43}$$

Combining (5.35) and (5.43) yields

$$\mathbf{E}\{\hat{x}(1)\} = \mathbf{E}\{x(1)\} \tag{5.44}$$

Therefore, for $t > 1$, (5.38) can be obtained from the similar derivations of (5.44). The proof is completed.

The result in Theorem 5.1 implies that if the initial values of the system (5.1), the fusion estimate given in (5.32), and the compensated state estimates (5.36) are set to the same value, the fusion estimate $\hat{x}(t)$ is an unbiased estimate of $x(t)$, i.e., the second equation of (5.29) holds.

To guarantee the unbiasedness of the designed fusion estimator with bandwidth and energy constraints, the compensated state estimate of $x(t)$ can also be selected by

$$\hat{x}_i^{c*}(t) = H_i(t)\hat{x}_i(t) + [I_n - H_i(t)]A(t-1)\hat{x}_j^{c*}(t-1) \tag{5.45}$$

where $j \in \{1, 2, \ldots, L\}$. However, the estimation performance of (5.37) is better than that of (5.45).

5.3.2 *Design of Finite-Horizon Fusion Estimator*

In what follows, computations of the error covariance matrix $\Sigma(t)$, which are needed in the calculation of the weighting matrices $\Omega_i(t)$, $i = 1, 2, \ldots, L$, will be presented.

Two useful lemmas are given as follows before presenting the error covariance matrix $\Sigma(t)$.

Lemma 5.1 *For stochastic matrices M, B, and G, where*

$$M \triangleq \mathrm{diag}\{m_1, \ldots, m_n\}$$

$$B \triangleq \mathrm{diag}\{b_1, \ldots, b_n\}$$

$$G \triangleq \begin{bmatrix} g_{11} & \cdots & g_{1n} \\ \vdots & \ddots & \vdots \\ g_{n1} & \cdots & g_{nn} \end{bmatrix}$$

If each random variable g_{ij} in G is independent of any random variables of m_i and b_i, $i = 1, 2, \ldots, n$, then

$$\mathbf{E}\{MGB\} = \mathbf{E}\{M \odot B\} \otimes \mathbf{E}\{G\} \tag{5.46}$$

where "$\otimes$" is defined as $[G^1 \otimes G^2]_{ij} = G^1_{ij}G^2_{ij}$ (this product is called Hadamard product [10]) and the product "$\odot$" for the diagonal matrices M and B is defined by

$$M \odot B = \begin{bmatrix} m_1 b_1 & \cdots & m_1 b_n \\ \vdots & \ddots & \vdots \\ m_n b_1 & \cdots & m_n b_n \end{bmatrix} \tag{5.47}$$

Moreover, the product "$\odot$" has the following property

$$M \odot B = (B \odot M)^{\mathrm{T}} \tag{5.48}$$

Lemma 5.2 *Define*

$$\begin{cases} \Phi_i(t) \triangleq \mathbf{E}\{\tilde{x}(t-1)\tilde{x}_i^{\mathrm{T}}(t)\} \\ \hat{H}(t) \triangleq \mathrm{diag}\{H_1(t), \ldots, H_L(t)\} \\ \bar{H}(t) \triangleq [(I_n - H_1(t))^{\mathrm{T}}, \ldots, (I_n - H_L(t))^{\mathrm{T}}]^{\mathrm{T}} \end{cases} \tag{5.49}$$

where $\tilde{x}(t-1) = x(t-1) - \hat{x}(t-1)$ and $\tilde{x}_i(t) = x(t) - \hat{x}_i(t)$. Suppose that $P(t-1)$ and $\Sigma(t-1)$ have been obtained at time t, then $\Phi_i(t)$ is computed by the following recursive form

$$\begin{aligned} \Phi_i(t) = {} & \hat{\Sigma}(t-1)\bar{H}A(t-2)\Phi_i(t-1)\hat{A}^{\mathrm{T}}(t-1) \\ & +\hat{\Sigma}(t-1)\hat{H}\hat{P}_i(t-1)\hat{A}^{\mathrm{T}}(t-1) \\ & +\hat{\Sigma}(t-1)\bar{H}\hat{\Gamma}(t-2)[I_n - \mathrm{K}_i(t-1) \\ & \times C_i(t-1)]^{\mathrm{T}}\hat{A}^{\mathrm{T}}(t-1) \end{aligned} \tag{5.50}$$

where

$$\begin{cases} \hat{P}_i(t-1) = [P_{1i}^{\mathrm{T}}(t-1) \cdots P_{Li}^{\mathrm{T}}(t-1)]^{\mathrm{T}} \\ \hat{\Sigma}(t-1) = P(t-1)I_0^{\mathrm{T}}\Sigma^{-1}(t-1) \\ \hat{A}(t-1) = A(t-1) - \mathrm{K}_i(t)C_i(t)A(t-1) \\ \bar{H} = \mathbf{E}\left\{\bar{H}(t-1)\right\}, \hat{H} = \mathbf{E}\left\{\hat{H}(t-1)\right\} \end{cases} \tag{5.51}$$

and $\hat{\Gamma}(t-2)$ is defined in (5.6). Meanwhile, $\mathrm{K}_i(t)$ and $P_{ji}(t-1) = P_{ij}^{\mathrm{T}}(t-1)$ are computed by (5.4) and (5.8), respectively.

Proof It follows from (5.1) and (5.4) that

$$\tilde{x}_i(t) = A(t-1)\tilde{x}_i(t-1) + \Gamma(t-1)w(t-1) - \mathrm{K}_i(t)\varepsilon_i(t) \tag{5.52}$$

$$\varepsilon_i(t) = C_i(t)A(t-1)\tilde{x}_i(t-1) + C_i(t)\Gamma(t-1)w(t-1) + v_i(t) \tag{5.53}$$

Then, substituting (5.53) into (5.52) yields

$$\begin{aligned}\tilde{x}_i(t) = &(A(t-1) - \mathrm{K}_i(t)C_i(t)A(t-1))\tilde{x}_i(t-1)\\ &+(\Gamma(t-1) - \mathrm{K}_i(t)C_i(t)\Gamma(t-1))\\ &\times w(t-1) - \mathrm{K}_i(t)v_i(t)\end{aligned} \tag{5.54}$$

Following the facts $\tilde{x}_i(t-1)\perp w(t-1)$ and $\mathbf{E}\left\{v_i(t)w^{\mathrm{T}}(t-1)\right\} = 0$, it is derived from (5.54) that

$$\mathbf{E}\left\{\tilde{x}_i(t)w^{\mathrm{T}}(t-1)\right\} = (I_n - \mathrm{K}_i(t)C_i(t))\Gamma(t-1)Q_w(t-1) \tag{5.55}$$

Define $\varsigma_i(t) \triangleq \left[\sigma_1^i(t), \sigma_2^i(t), \ldots, \sigma_{\Delta_i}^i(t)\right]$, then one has by (5.32) and (5.37) that

$$\begin{aligned}\tilde{x}(t-1) \in \mathrm{Span}\{&w(0), w(1), \ldots, w(t-2),\\ &\underbrace{v_i(0), \ldots, v_i(t-1), \varsigma_i(1), \ldots, \varsigma_i(t-1)}_{i=1,2,\ldots,L}\}\end{aligned} \tag{5.56}$$

Thus, it follows from (5.22), (5.23), and (5.56) that

$$w(t-1)\perp\tilde{x}(t-1) \quad \text{and} \quad v_i(t)\perp\tilde{x}(t-1) \tag{5.57}$$

Then, it is derived from (5.55) and (5.57) that

$$\begin{aligned}\Phi_i(t) &= \mathbf{E}\{\tilde{x}(t-1)(\tilde{x}_i^{\mathrm{T}}(t-1)[A(t-1) - \mathrm{K}_i(t)\\ &\quad\times C_i(t)A(t-1)]^{\mathrm{T}} + w^{\mathrm{T}}(t-1)[\Gamma(t-1) - \mathrm{K}_i(t)\\ &\quad\times C_i(t)\Gamma(t-1)]^{\mathrm{T}} - v_i^{\mathrm{T}}(t)\mathrm{K}_i^{\mathrm{T}}(t))\}\\ &= \Psi_i(t-1)\hat{A}^{\mathrm{T}}(t-1)\end{aligned} \tag{5.58}$$

where

$$\Psi_i(t-1) \triangleq \mathbf{E}\left\{\tilde{x}(t-1)\tilde{x}_i^{\mathrm{T}}(t-1)\right\}$$

and $\hat{A}^{\mathrm{T}}(t-1)$ is defined in (5.51). Subsequently, it follows from (5.1) that

$$I_0x(t) = \hat{H}(t)I_0x(t) + \bar{H}(t)A(t-1)x(t-1) + \bar{H}(t)\Gamma(t-1)w(t-1) \tag{5.59}$$

where $\hat{H}(t)$ and $\bar{H}(t)$ are defined in (5.49). Define

$$\hat{x}^{c}(t) \triangleq \left[(\hat{x}_1^{c}(t))^{\mathrm{T}} \quad \cdots \quad (\hat{x}_L^{c}(t))^{\mathrm{T}}\right]^{\mathrm{T}}$$

Then, it is derived from the first equation of (5.33) and (5.59) that

$$\begin{aligned}\tilde{x}(t-1) = {} & \left(I_0^{\mathrm{T}}\Sigma^{-1}(t-1)I_0\right)^{-1}I_0^{\mathrm{T}}\Sigma^{-1}(t-1) \\ & \times(I_0x(t-1)-\hat{x}^{c}(t-1)) = \hat{\Sigma}(t-1)\hat{H}(t-1) \\ & \times\tilde{x}_a(t-1)+\hat{\Sigma}(t-1)\bar{H}(t-1)A(t-2)\tilde{x}(t-2) \\ & +\hat{\Sigma}(t-1)\bar{H}(t-1)\Gamma(t-2)w(t-2)\end{aligned} \tag{5.60}$$

where $\tilde{x}_a(t-1)$ and $\hat{\Sigma}(t-1)$ are defined in (5.7) and (5.51), respectively. Next, it follows from (5.55) and (5.60) that

$$\begin{aligned}\Psi_i(t-1) = {} & \hat{\Sigma}(t-1)\mathbf{E}\left\{\hat{H}(t-1)\right\}\hat{P}_i(t-1) \\ & +\hat{\Sigma}(t-1)\mathbf{E}\left\{\bar{H}(t-1)\right\}A(t-2)\Phi_i(t-1) \\ & +\hat{\Sigma}(t-1)\mathbf{E}\left\{\bar{H}(t-1)\right\}\Gamma(t-2)Q_w(t-2) \\ & \times\Gamma^{\mathrm{T}}(t-2)(I_n-\mathrm{K}_i(t-1)C_i(t-1))^{\mathrm{T}}\end{aligned} \tag{5.61}$$

where $\hat{P}_i(t-1)$ is defined in (5.51). Therefore, (5.50) is obtained by substituting (5.61) into (5.58). This completes the proof.

The intermediate variable $\Phi_i(t)$ is presented in (5.50) by a recursive form, and it follows from (5.51) that $\Phi_i(t)$ is dependent on $P(t-1)$ and $\Sigma(t-1)$; thus, if the initial values of $P(t)$ and $\Sigma(t)$ are given, then $\Phi_i(t)$ will be obtained. Notice that $\Phi_i(t)$ given by (5.50) will be used to derive the recursive form of $\Sigma(t)$.

Theorem 5.2 *Define*

$$\begin{aligned}\Lambda_{ij} &\triangleq \mathbf{E}\{H_i(t)\odot H_j(t)\} \\ \mathrm{W}_{ij} &\triangleq \mathbf{E}\{(I_n-H_i(t))\odot(I_n-H_j(t))\} \\ \mathrm{V}_{ij} &\triangleq \mathbf{E}\{H_i(t)\odot(I_n-H_j(t))\}\end{aligned}$$

then the estimation error covariance matrix $\Sigma_{ij}(t) \triangleq \mathbf{E}\left\{e_i(t)e_j^{\mathrm{T}}(t)\right\}$, $i,j \in \{1,2,\ldots,L\}$ *is computed by*

$$\begin{aligned}\Sigma_{ij}(t) = {} & \Lambda_{ij}\otimes P_{ij}(t)+\mathrm{V}_{ij}\otimes[\Phi_i^{\mathrm{T}}(t)A^{\mathrm{T}}(t-1)+(I_n \\ & -\mathrm{K}_i(t)C_i(t))\hat{\Gamma}(t-1)] + \mathrm{V}_{ji}^{\mathrm{T}}\otimes[A(t-1)\Phi_j(t)\end{aligned}$$

$$+\hat{\Gamma}(t-1)[(I_n - \mathrm{K}_j(t)C_j(t))^{\mathrm{T}}] + \mathrm{W}_{ij} \otimes [A(t-1)$$
$$\times P(t-1)A^{\mathrm{T}}(t-1) + \hat{\Gamma}(t-1)] \tag{5.62}$$

where $P_{ij}(t)(i = j)$ is computed by (5.5), $P_{ij}(t|t)(i \neq j)$ is calculated by (5.8), and $\hat{\Gamma}(t-1)$ is defined by (5.6). Moreover, the optimal fusion estimation error covariance matrix $P(t)$ in (5.33) is given by the following recursive form

$$P(t) = f(P(t-1), \underbrace{P_{ii}(t), P_{ij}(t), \mathrm{V}_{ij}, \Lambda_{ij}, \mathrm{W}_{ij}}_{i=1,2,\ldots,L;j=i,i+1,\ldots,L}) \tag{5.63}$$

Note that each local estimation error covariance matrix

$$\Sigma_{ii}(t) \triangleq \mathbf{E}\{e_i(t)e_i^{\mathrm{T}}(t)\}$$

can be obtained by (5.62) for $i = j$ and the relationship between the optimal fusion estimation performance and each local compensated state estimation performance given in (5.37) is

$$\mathrm{Tr}(P(t)) \leq \mathrm{Tr}(\Sigma_{ii}(t)), \; i = 1, 2, \ldots, L \tag{5.64}$$

Proof It follows from (5.48) and Lemma 5.2 that

$$\mathrm{V}_{ji}^{\mathrm{T}} = \mathbf{E}\{(I_n - H_i(t)) \odot H_j(t))\} \tag{5.65}$$

$$\mathbf{E}\left\{\tilde{x}_i(t)\tilde{x}^{\mathrm{T}}(t-1)\right\} = \Phi_i^{\mathrm{T}}(t), \mathbf{E}\left\{\tilde{x}(t-1)\tilde{x}_j^{\mathrm{T}}(t)\right\} = \Phi_j(t) \tag{5.66}$$

Meanwhile, it is derived from (5.1) and (5.37) that

$$e_i(t) = H_i(t)\tilde{x}_i(t) + (I_n - H_i(t))A(t-1)\tilde{x}(t-1)$$
$$+(I_n - H_i(t))\Gamma(t-1)w(t-1) \tag{5.67}$$

Since $H_i(t)$ and $I_n - H_i(t)$, $i = 1, 2, \ldots, L$ are all diagonal matrices, then it follows from (5.67) and Lemma 5.1 that

$$\Sigma_{ij}(t) = \Lambda_{ij} \otimes P_{ij}(t) + \mathrm{V}_{ij} \otimes \left[\mathbf{E}\{\tilde{x}_i(t)\tilde{x}^{\mathrm{T}}(t-1)\}\right.$$
$$\left.\times A^{\mathrm{T}}(t-1)\right] + \mathrm{V}_{ij} \otimes \left[\mathbf{E}\{\tilde{x}_i(t)w^{\mathrm{T}}(t-1)\}\Gamma^{\mathrm{T}}(t-1)\right]$$
$$+\mathbf{E}\{[I_n - H_i(t)] \odot H_j(t)\} \otimes [A(t-1)$$
$$\times \mathbf{E}\{\tilde{x}(t-1)\tilde{x}_j^{\mathrm{T}}(t)\}] + \mathbf{E}\{[I_n - H_i(t)] \odot H_j(t)\}$$
$$\otimes \left[\Gamma(t-1)\mathbf{E}\{w(t-1)\tilde{x}_j^{\mathrm{T}}(t)\}\right] + \mathrm{W}_{ij} \otimes [A(t-1)$$
$$\left.\times P(t-1)A^{\mathrm{T}}(t-1) + \hat{\Gamma}(t-1)\right] \tag{5.68}$$

Therefore, (5.62) is obtained by substituting (5.55), (5.57), (5.65), and (5.66) into (5.68). Under this condition, the recursive form of $P(t)$ is given by (5.63). Moreover, (5.64) is obtained from (5.12). This completes the proof.

From the definition of $\Sigma(t)$, a procedure for the determination of $\Sigma(t)$ is given by (5.62) in Theorem 5.2; thus, the weighting matrices $\Omega_i(t)$, $i = 1, 2, \ldots, L$ are computed by the first equation in (5.33). In this case, the optimal fusion estimate $\hat{x}(t)$ is computed by substituting the weighting matrices and (5.37) into (5.32). Moreover, for a given group of the probabilities $\pi_1^i, \ldots, \pi_{\Delta_i}^i$, $i = 1, 2, \ldots, L$ satisfying (5.25), according to Theorems 5.1 and 5.2, the computation procedures for the finite-horizon fusion estimate with bandwidth and energy constraints can be summarized as follows:

Algorithm 5.1

Step 1: Initialize $\{P_{ii}(0), \hat{x}_i(0), \Phi_i(0)\}_{i=1}^{L}$, $\{P_{ij}(0)\}_{j=i}^{L}$, $P(0)$, and $\hat{x}(0)$.
Step 2: Calculate each local estimate and estimation error covariance matrices:
For $i = 1 : L$
Calculate $\hat{x}_i(t)$ by using (5.4)
Calculate $P_{ii}(t)$ by using (5.5)
For $j = i + 1 : L$
Calculate $P_{ij}(t)$ by using (5.8)
End
End

Step 3: Calculate each local compensated state estimate and L intermediate variables:
For $i = 1 : L$
Calculate $\hat{x}_i^c(t)$ by using (5.37)
Calculate $\Phi_i(t)$ by using (5.50)
End
Step 4: Calculate the local estimation error covariance matrices of the compensate state estimates
For $i = 1 : L$
Calculate $\Sigma_{ii}(t)$ by using (5.62) with $i = j$
For $j = i + 1 : L$
Calculate $\Sigma_{ij}(t)$ by using (5.62) with $i \neq j$
End
End
Step 5: Calculate the fusion estimation error covariance matrix $P(t)$ and the weighting matrices $\Omega_1(t), \ldots, \Omega_L(t)$ by using (5.33).
Step 6: Calculate the finite-horizon fusion estimate $\hat{x}(t)$ by using (5.32).
Step 7: Return to Step 2 and implement Steps 2–6 for obtaining $\hat{x}(t+1)$.

It follows from Theorem 5.2 that the computation procedures for the error covariance matrix $\Sigma(t)$ are only dependent on the probabilities of the introduced binary variables. Therefore, it follows from (5.32) and (5.33) that the updating of the weighting matrices $\Omega_i(t)$, $i = 1, 2, \ldots, L$ does not need to know the transmitting situation of each component at time t. When the selecting probabilities $\pi_\ell^i(\ell = 1, 2, \ldots, \Delta_i; i = 1, 2, \ldots, L)$ are known a priori, the weighting matrices can be computed off-line, which helps reduce the computation burden of the fusion center. Under this condition, it is concluded from (5.37) that if the selected components of each local estimate $\hat{x}_i(t)$ are transmitted to the fusion center, then Algorithm 5.1 will be easily implemented in practical applications, where each random matrix $H_i(t)$ in (5.37) is obtained from the identification process of reorganized state estimate $\hat{x}_i^{\mathrm{r}}(t)$.

5.4 Boundness Analysis of the Fusion Estimator

In this section, we will discuss the performance of the designed fusion estimator. First, define $\varsigma_i \triangleq [\pi_1^i, \ldots, \pi_{\Delta_i}^i]^{\mathrm{T}}$, and then it follows from (5.18) that there exists a constant matrix $U_\ell^i \in \mathrm{R}^{1\times\Delta_i}$ such that

$$\gamma_\ell^i = U_\ell^i \varsigma_i, \ \ell = 1, 2, \ldots, n; \ i = 1, 2, \ldots, L \tag{5.69}$$

where an arbitrary element of U_ℓ^i is 1 or 0. In what follows, a probability selecting criterion will be given in Theorem 5.3 such that the MSE of the designed fusion estimator is bounded.

Theorem 5.3 *Consider optimal fusion estimator associated with systems (5.1) and (5.2) under the bandwidth and energy constraints.*

(C1). The system (5.1) is uniformly completely controllable, i.e., there exists an integer $N > 0$ and positive scalars ρ_1, ρ_2, such that the following inequality holds for $t \geq N$

$$\rho_1 I_n \leq \sum_{j=t-N+1}^{t} \Psi(t,j)\Gamma(j)Q_w(j)\Gamma^{\mathrm{T}}(j)\Psi^{\mathrm{T}}(t,j) \leq \rho_2 I_n \tag{5.70}$$

where $\Psi(t,j)$ is the state-transition matrix satisfying

$$\begin{cases} \Psi(t,j) = \prod_{\ell=1}^{t-j} A(t-\ell), \ t > j, \ \Psi(j,j) = I_n \\ \Psi(j,t) = \Psi^{-1}(t,j), \ t < j \end{cases} \tag{5.71}$$

(C2). *There exists at least one measurement equation $y_i(t)$ in (5.2) such that the* ith *subsystem (which is described by (5.1) and $y_i(t)$) is uniformly completely observable, i.e., there exist an integer $N > 0$ and positive scalars ρ_3, ρ_4, such that the following inequality holds for $t \geq N$*

$$\rho_3 I_n \leq \sum_{j=t-N+1}^{t} \Psi^{\mathrm{T}}(j,t) C_i^{\mathrm{T}}(j) Q_{v_i}^{-1}(j) C_i(j) \Psi(j,t) \leq \rho_4 I_n \tag{5.72}$$

(C3). *At each time t, there exists at least a set of selecting probabilities satisfying*

$$\mathrm{Tr}\{M_i \otimes [A(t-1)P(t-1)A^{\mathrm{T}}(t-1)]\} < \mathrm{Tr}\{P(t-1)\} \tag{5.73}$$

where $M_i = \mathrm{diag}\{1 - U_1^i \varsigma_i, \ldots, 1 - U_n^i \varsigma_i\}$ and U_ℓ^i can be obtained by (5.69).

It can be concluded that if the conditions C1, C2, and C3 hold, then the MSE of the designed fusion estimate $\hat{x}(t)$ will be bounded, i.e., there exists a scalar p_0 such that

$$\lim_{t \to \infty} \mathrm{Tr}\{P(t)\} \leq p_0 \tag{5.74}$$

Proof For the ith subsystem, it follows from Theorem 7.4 in [8] that the optimal local estimate given by (5.4), (5.5), and (5.6) is uniformly asymptotically stable when the conditions C1 and C2 hold. In this case, it follows from Lemma 7.1 in [8] that if $P_{ii}(0) \geq 0$, then $P_{ii}(t)$ is uniformly bounded for all $t \geq N$, i.e., there exists a scalar $\alpha_i > 0$ such that $P_{ii}(t) \leq \alpha_i I_n$, $t \geq N$, which implies that

$$\mathrm{Tr}(P_{ii}(t)) \leq n\alpha_i, \ t \geq N \tag{5.75}$$

Moreover, it follows from (5.70) that $\hat{\Gamma}(t)$ is bounded, i.e., there exists a scalar $\beta > 0$ such that

$$\mathrm{Tr}\{\hat{\Gamma}(t)\} \leq \beta \tag{5.76}$$

Define $\hat{\mathrm{W}}_i(t) \triangleq \Lambda_{ii} \otimes P_{ii}(t) + \mathrm{W}_{ii} \otimes \hat{\Gamma}(t-1)$, then it follows from (5.75) and (5.76) that there exist a scalar $\hat{m}_i > 0$ such that

$$\mathrm{Tr}\{\hat{\mathrm{W}}_i(t)\} \leq \hat{m}_i, \ t \geq N \tag{5.77}$$

On the other hand, it is derived from the definition of $\mathrm{V}_{ij}(t)$ in Theorem 5.2 and (5.47) that

$$\mathrm{V}_{ii} = \begin{bmatrix} 0 & \mathbf{E}\{\gamma_1(t)(1-\gamma_2(t)\} & \cdots & \mathbf{E}\{\gamma_1(t)(1-\gamma_n(t)\} \\ \mathbf{E}\{\gamma_2(t)(1-\gamma_1(t)\} & 0 & \cdots & \mathbf{E}\{\gamma_2(t)(1-\gamma_n(t)\} \\ \vdots & \vdots & \ddots & \vdots \\ \mathbf{E}\{\gamma_n(t)(1-\gamma_1(t)\} & \mathbf{E}\{\gamma_n(t)(1-\gamma_2(t)\} & \cdots & 0 \end{bmatrix} \tag{5.78}$$

Then, taking the property of the operator $\mathrm{Tr}(\cdot)$ into account, one has

$$\begin{cases} \mathrm{Tr}\{\mathrm{V}_{ii} \otimes [\Phi_i^{\mathrm{T}}(t)A^{\mathrm{T}}(t-1) + (I_n - \mathrm{K}_i(t)C_i(t))\hat{\Gamma}(t-1)]\} = 0 \\ \mathrm{Tr}\{\mathrm{V}_{ii}^{\mathrm{T}} \otimes [A(t-1)\Phi_i(t) + \hat{\Gamma}(t-1)(I_n - \mathrm{K}_i(t)C_i(t))^{\mathrm{T}}]\} = 0 \end{cases} \tag{5.79}$$

$$\begin{aligned} &\mathrm{Tr}\{\mathrm{W}_{ii} \otimes [A(t-1)P(t-1)A^{\mathrm{T}}(t-1)]\} \\ &= \mathrm{Tr}\{M_i \otimes [A(t-1)P(t-1)A^{\mathrm{T}}(t-1)]\} \end{aligned} \tag{5.80}$$

where M_i is defined in C3. Subsequently, it is derived from (5.80) that if the condition (5.73) holds, there exists a scalar $d_p(t-1)$ such that

$$\begin{aligned} &\mathrm{Tr}\{\mathrm{W}_{ii} \otimes [A(t-1)P(t-1)A^{\mathrm{T}}(t-1)\} \\ &= d_p(t-1)\mathrm{Tr}\{P(t-1)\},\ 0 < d_p(t-1) < 1 \end{aligned} \tag{5.81}$$

Meanwhile, it follows from (5.64) that there exists a scalar $d_{\Sigma_{ii}}(t)$ such that

$$\mathrm{Tr}\{P(t)\} = d_{\Sigma_{ii}}(t)\mathrm{Tr}\{\Sigma_{ii}(t)\}\ (0 < d_{\Sigma_{ii}}(t) \le 1) \tag{5.82}$$

Then, according to (5.62), (5.79), (5.81), and (5.82), $\mathrm{Tr}(\Sigma_{ii}(t))$ is rewritten as

$$\begin{aligned} \mathrm{Tr}(\Sigma_{ii}(t)) &= \mathrm{Tr}\{\hat{\mathrm{W}}_i(t)\} + d_p(t)\mathrm{Tr}\{P(t-1)\} \\ &= \mathrm{Tr}\{\hat{\mathrm{W}}_i(t)\} + \sum_{\ell=1}^{t-N}\left\{\left\{\prod_{\tau=1}^{\ell} d_p(t-\tau)d_{\Sigma_{ii}}(t-\tau)\right\}\right. \\ &\quad \times\mathrm{Tr}\{\hat{\mathrm{W}}_i(t-\ell)\}\} + d_p(t-N-1) \\ &\quad \times\left\{\prod_{\ell=1}^{t-N} d_p(t-\ell)d_{\Sigma_{ii}}(t-\ell)\right\}\mathrm{Tr}\{P(t-N+1)\} \end{aligned} \tag{5.83}$$

It is noted from (5.81) and (5.82) that there exists a scalar $d_{p\Sigma}$, $0 \leq d_{p\Sigma} < 1$ such that

$$d_p(t-\tau)d_{\Sigma_{ii}}(t-\tau) \leq d_{p\Sigma}, \quad t \geq N \text{ and } \forall \tau \tag{5.84}$$

Therefore, it follows from (5.77), (5.83), and (5.84) that the following inequality

$$\begin{aligned} \mathrm{Tr}\{\Sigma_{ii}(t)\} \leq \hat{m}_i + \left\{\sum_{\ell=1}^{t-N} d_{p\Sigma}^{\ell}\right\} \hat{m}_i + d_p(t-N-1) \\ \times \left\{\prod_{\ell=1}^{t-N} d_p(t-\ell)d_{\Sigma_{ii}}(t-\ell)\right\} \mathrm{Tr}\{P(t-N+1)\} \end{aligned} \tag{5.85}$$

holds for $t \geq N$. Moreover, it is derived from (5.77), (5.83), and (5.85) that

$$\begin{cases} \lim\limits_{t\to\infty} \left\{d_p(t-N-1)\left\{\prod\limits_{\ell=1}^{t-N} d_p(t-\ell)d_{\Sigma_{ii}}(t-\ell)\right\}\right\} = 0 \\ \lim\limits_{t\to\infty} \left\{\sum\limits_{\ell=1}^{t-N} d_{p\Sigma}^{\ell}\right\} = \dfrac{d_{p\Sigma}}{1-d_{p\Sigma}} \end{cases} \tag{5.86}$$

Then, taking limit on both sides of (5.85) yields

$$\lim_{t\to\infty} \mathrm{Tr}(\Sigma_{ii}(t)) \leq \hat{m}_i + \frac{d_{p\Sigma}}{1-d_{p\Sigma}}\hat{m}_i$$

which implies that there exists an integer $N_0 > N > 0$ such that

$$\mathrm{Tr}(\Sigma_{ii}(t)) \leq p_0, \ t \geq N_0 \tag{5.87}$$

where $p_0 = \hat{m}_i + \dfrac{d_{p\Sigma}}{1-d_{p\Sigma}}\hat{m}_i$. Therefore, (5.74) is obtained from (5.64) and (5.87). The proof is thus completed.

Generally, it is considered that the following optimal selecting probabilities

$$\{\varsigma_1^*, \varsigma_2^*, \ldots, \varsigma_L^*\}$$

in the finite time interval $[1, \mathrm{T}]$ can be obtained by solving the following optimization problem:

$$\begin{aligned} &\min_{\{\varsigma_1,\varsigma_2,\ldots,\varsigma_L\}} \frac{1}{\mathrm{T}} \sum_{t=1}^{\mathrm{T}} \mathrm{Tr}\{P(t)\} \\ &\text{s.t. (5.25) and } 0 \leq \pi_{h_i}^i \leq 1, \ i = 1, 2, \ldots, L \end{aligned} \tag{5.88}$$

where the optimal estimation error covariance matrix $P(t)$ is computed by the second equation in (5.33). For this optimization problem, an explicit optimal solution is far from clear at the present stage. However, the objective function and constraint conditions in (5.88) are independent of the sequence of the measurements, and thus, this problem can be solved off-line. In this case, it is reasonable that this optimization problem may be solved by using the exhaustive search algorithm. On the other hand, it can be seen from Theorem 5.3 that if the systems (5.1) and (5.2) satisfy C1 and C2, while the selecting probabilities are determined by C3, then the MSE of the designed fusion estimator will not diverge, which implies that the fusion estimation performance will not degrade seriously under the bandwidth and energy constraints.

For the systems (5.1) and (5.2) with constant system matrices, i.e., the systems (5.1) and (5.2) reduce to the following form:

$$x(t+1) = Ax(t) + \Gamma w(t) \tag{5.89}$$

$$y_i(t) = C_i x(t) + v_i(t),\ i = 1, 2, \ldots, L \tag{5.90}$$

where $w(t)$ and $v_i(t)$ are zero-mean white noises with stationary covariances $Q_w(t) \equiv Q_w$ and $Q_{v_i}(t) \equiv Q_{v_i}$, respectively. Then, one has the following theorem for the convergence of the MSE of the fusion estimator:

Theorem 5.4 *Consider the optimal fusion estimator for the systems (5.89) and (5.90) under the bandwidth and energy constraints.*

(C5) The linear stochastic system (5.89) is completely controllable, that is,

$$\mathrm{rank}([\Gamma, A\Gamma, \ldots, A^{n-1}\Gamma]) = n \tag{5.91}$$

Meanwhile, for the L measurement equations (5.90), there exists at least one observation matrix C_i satisfying

$$\mathrm{rank}([C_i^{\mathrm{T}}\ (C_iA)^{\mathrm{T}}\ \cdots\ (C_iA^{n-1})^{\mathrm{T}}]^{\mathrm{T}}) = n \tag{5.92}$$

where the condition (5.92) implies that the ith *subsystem is completely observable.*

(C6) At each time t, there exists at least a set of selecting probabilities satisfying

$$\mu_i(\varsigma_i) \triangleq \lambda_{\max}\{A^{\mathrm{T}}M_iA\} < 1 \tag{5.93}$$

or

$$\begin{cases} \mu_i(\varsigma_i) \triangleq \lambda_{\max}\{A^{\mathrm{T}}M_iA\} = 1 \\ \lambda_{\max}\{A^{\mathrm{T}}M_iA\} \neq \lambda_{\min}\{A^{\mathrm{T}}M_iA\} \end{cases} \tag{5.94}$$

where $M_i = \mathrm{diag}\{1 - U_1^i\varsigma_i, \ldots, 1 - U_n^i\varsigma_i\}$ and U_ℓ^i can be obtained by (5.69).

It can be seen that if the systems (5.89) and (5.90) satisfy C5, and the selecting probabilities satisfy C6, then the limit of the MSE exists, i.e.,

$$\lim_{t\to\infty} \mathrm{Tr}(P(t)) = p \tag{5.95}$$

Proof For the ith subsystem, it is well known that if the conditions (5.91) and (5.92) hold, the optimal local estimation error variance matrix $P_{ii}(t)$ will be convergent, i.e., $\lim_{t\to\infty} P_{ii}(t) = P_{ii}$. This implies that there exists an integer $N > 0$ such that

$$P_{ii}(t) = P_{ii} \ (t \geq N) \tag{5.96}$$

On the other hand, it follows from the property of the operator $\otimes$ that

$$\begin{aligned} \mathrm{Tr}\{M_i \otimes [AP(t-1)A^{\mathrm{T}}]\} &= \mathrm{Tr}\left\{M_i^{\frac{1}{2}} AP(t-1)A^{\mathrm{T}}\left(M_i^{\frac{1}{2}}\right)^{\mathrm{T}}\right\} \\ &= \mathrm{Tr}\left\{A^{\mathrm{T}} M_i A P(t-1)\right\} \end{aligned} \tag{5.97}$$

Since $A^{\mathrm{T}}M_iA$ is a symmetric matrix and $P(t-1)$ is a positive-definite matrix, it follows from the results in [11] that

$$\mathrm{Tr}\{A^{\mathrm{T}}M_iAP(t-1)\} \leq \lambda_{\max}\{A^{\mathrm{T}}M_iA\}\mathrm{Tr}\{P(t-1)\} \tag{5.98}$$

Consequently, if (5.93) holds, it is derived from (5.97) and (5.98) that

$$\begin{aligned} &\mathrm{Tr}\{M_i \otimes [AP(t-1)A^{\mathrm{T}}]\} - \mathrm{Tr}\{P(t-1)\} \\ &\leq \mathrm{Tr}\{A^{\mathrm{T}}M_iA\}\mathrm{Tr}\{P(t-1)\} - \mathrm{Tr}\{P(t-1)\} < 0 \end{aligned}$$

which implies that

$$\mathrm{Tr}\{M_i \otimes [AP(t-1)A^{\mathrm{T}}]\} < \mathrm{Tr}\{P(t-1)\} \tag{5.99}$$

Moreover, it is concluded from the proof of Lemma 1 in [11] that the symmetric matrix $A^{\mathrm{T}}M_iA$ is decomposed as

$$D = U^{\mathrm{T}}\left(A^{\mathrm{T}}M_iA\right)U \tag{5.100}$$

where D is a diagonal matrix formed by the eigenvalues of $A^{\mathrm{T}}M_iA$ and U is an orthogonal matrix whose columns are normalized eigenvectors. Then, it is derived from (5.100) that

$$\mathrm{Tr}\{A^{\mathrm{T}}M_iAP(t-1)\} = \mathrm{Tr}\{U^{\mathrm{T}}P(t-1)UD\} \tag{5.101}$$

According to the property of the matrix trace and the matrix structure of D, it is concluded from (5.101) that the equation

$$\mathrm{Tr}\left\{U^{\mathrm{T}}P(t-1)UD\right\} = \lambda_{\max}(D)\mathrm{Tr}\left\{U^{\mathrm{T}}P(t-1)U\right\} = \lambda_{\max}(D)\mathrm{Tr}\{P(t-1)\}$$

holds if and only if all the eigenvalues of $A^{\mathrm{T}}M_iA$ are the same. This means that if (5.94) holds, then (5.99) can also be obtained.

In what follows, based on the result (5.99), it will be proved that the MSE of the fusion estimator converges to a steady-state value.

From Theorem 5.3, one can obtain from (5.96) and (5.99) that there exists a positive scalar $\bar{p}_0$ such that

$$\mathrm{Tr}\{\Sigma_{ii}(t)\} \leq \bar{p}_0 \tag{5.102}$$

Define

$$\hat{M}_i(t) \triangleq \Lambda_{ii} \otimes P_{ii}(t) + \mathrm{W}_{ii} \otimes \left(\Gamma Q_w \Gamma^{\mathrm{T}}\right)$$

then it follows from (5.102) that

$$\hat{M}_i \triangleq \lim_{t\to\infty} \hat{M}_i(t) = \Lambda_{ii} \otimes P_{ii} + \mathrm{W}_{ii} \otimes (\Gamma Q_w \Gamma^{\mathrm{T}})$$

In this case, it is derived from (5.83) and (5.99) that for $t \geq N$

$$\begin{aligned}\mathrm{Tr}\{\Sigma_{ii}(t)\} &= \chi(t) + d_p(t-N-1) \\ &\quad \times \left\{\prod_{\ell=1}^{t-N} d_p(t-\ell)d_{\Sigma_{ii}}(t-\ell)\right\} \mathrm{Tr}\{P(t-N+1)\}\end{aligned} \tag{5.103}$$

where

$$\chi(t) = \mathrm{Tr}\{\hat{M}_i\} + \sum_{\ell=1}^{t-N}\left\{\left\{\prod_{\tau=1}^{\ell} d_p(t-\tau)d_{\Sigma_{ii}}(t-\tau)\right\} \mathrm{Tr}\{\hat{M}_i\}\right\}$$

Note that the sequence $\{\chi(t)|t = N_0, N_0+1, \ldots, \infty\}$ is monotonically increasing and the variable $\chi(t)$ is bounded from (5.102); hence, the limit of $\chi(t)$ exists, i.e.,

$$\lim_{t\to\infty} \chi(t) = \chi \tag{5.104}$$

Moreover, it follows from the first equation of (5.86) that there exists an integer $N_0 > N > 0$ such that

$$\begin{aligned} & d_p(t-N-1)\left\{\prod_{\ell=1}^{t-N} d_p(t-\ell) d_{\Sigma_{ii}}(t-\ell)\right\} \\ & \times \operatorname{Tr}\{P(t-N+1)\}=0,\ t \geq N_0 \end{aligned} \tag{5.105}$$

Therefore, it follows from (5.62), (5.79), (5.80), and (5.103), (5.104), and (5.105) that the limit of $\operatorname{Tr}\{\Sigma_{ii}(t)\}$ exists, i.e.,

$$\begin{aligned} \lim_{t\to\infty} \operatorname{Tr}\{\Sigma_{ii}(t)\} = & \lim_{t\to\infty} \{\operatorname{Tr}\{\Lambda_{ii} \otimes P_{ii}(t) \\ & + \mathrm{W}_{ii} \otimes [AP(t-1)A^{\mathrm{T}} + \Gamma Q_w \Gamma^{\mathrm{T}}]\}\} = \operatorname{Tr}\{\Sigma_{ii}\} \end{aligned} \tag{5.106}$$

Then, according to (5.106), in the structure of $\operatorname{Tr}\{\mathrm{W}_{ii} \otimes [AP(t-1)A^{\mathrm{T}} + \Gamma Q_w \Gamma^{\mathrm{T}}]\}$ and the recursive form of $P(t)$ in (5.63), one can obtain that $\lim_{t\to\infty} P(t) = P$ which implies that (5.95) holds. The proof is thus completed.

For the time-invariant systems (5.89) and (5.90) satisfying C5, it is concluded from Theorem 5.4 that if the selecting probabilities $\varsigma_1, \ldots, \varsigma_L$ satisfy C6, then the objective function in (5.88) will be convergent, that is,

$$\lim_{\mathrm{T}\to\infty} \frac{1}{\mathrm{T}} \sum_{t=1}^{\mathrm{T}} \operatorname{Tr}\{P(t)\} = p_{\{\varsigma_1,\varsigma_2,\ldots,\varsigma_L\}}$$

Under this condition, a group of suboptimal selecting probabilities $\varsigma_1^*, \varsigma_2^*, \ldots, \varsigma_L^*$ can be obtained by solving the following optimization problem:

$$\begin{aligned} & \min_{\{\varsigma_1,\varsigma_2,\ldots,\varsigma_L\}} \ p_{\{\varsigma_1,\varsigma_2,\ldots,\varsigma_L\}} \\ & \text{s.t.}: \begin{cases} \sum_{\ell=1}^{n} U_\ell^i \varsigma_i = \mathrm{r}_i(1-\eta_i)\ (i=1,2,\ldots,L) \\ 0 \leq U_\ell^i \varsigma_i \leq 1 (\ell = 1,2,\ldots,n) \\ \begin{cases} \lambda_{\max}\{A^{\mathrm{T}} M_i A\} < 1 \text{ or} \\ \begin{cases} \lambda_{\max}\{A^{\mathrm{T}} M_i A\} = 1 \\ \lambda_{\max}\{A^{\mathrm{T}} M_i A\} \neq \lambda_{\min}\{A^{\mathrm{T}} M_i A\} \end{cases} \end{cases} \end{cases} \end{aligned} \tag{5.107}$$

where

$$M_i = \operatorname{diag}\{1 - U_1^i \varsigma_i, \ldots, 1 - U_n^i \varsigma_i\}$$

and U_ℓ^i represents the relationship matrix between γ_ℓ^i and ς_i (see (5.69)); r_i, $i = 1,2,\ldots,L$ denote the finite-bandwidth constraints; and η_i, $i = 1,2,\ldots,L$ represent the expected energy-saving rates (ESRs) that can reflect the energy-saving efficiency. Compared with the original problem (5.88), the constraint conditions (5.93) and (5.94), which are added in (5.107), help decrease the searching range; thus, the time consumption of calculation may be shortened by using the same exhaustive search algorithm. Notice that if all the selecting probabilities ς_i, $i = 1, 2, \ldots, L$ satisfy C6, then the solution of the optimization problem (5.107) is globally optimal.

The controllability and observability conditions C1, C2, and C5 in Theorems 5.3 and 5.4, which are only dependent on the system parameters, can be easily satisfied in the practical applications. Particularly, it follows from the result in [8] that the conditions C1 and C2 are equivalent to C5 when the systems (5.1) and (5.2) reduce to (5.89) and (5.90). On the other hand, it can be seen from the proof of Theorem 5.4 that if the condition C5 and the inequality (5.99) (i.e., $\mathrm{Tr}\{M_i \otimes [AP(t-1)A^{\mathrm{T}}]\} < \mathrm{Tr}\{P(t-1)\}$) hold, then the MSE of the designed fusion estimator will converge to a steady-state value. Notice that the condition (5.99) is dependent on the variable $P(t)$, which implies that it is difficult to obtain an effective probability selecting range such that the MSE of the designed fusion estimator is convergent. In this sense, though the conditions (5.93) and (5.94) are given with certain conservatism, it is easily judged by (5.93) and (5.94) that whether a group of selecting probabilities can guarantee convergence of the MSE or not.

When the system matrix $A(t)$ in the time-varying system (5.1) is norm bounded, then there exists a scalar $\lambda_1 > 0$ such that $\lambda_{\max}(A^{\mathrm{T}}(t)A(t)) \leq \lambda_1$, $\forall t$. In this case, it follows from (5.97) and (5.98) that there exists a group of upper bounds $f_v^i(\varsigma_i, \lambda_1)$, $i = 1, 2, \ldots, L$, such that

$$\lambda_{\max}\left(A^{\mathrm{T}}(t-1)M_iA(t-1)\right) \leq f_v^i(\varsigma_i, \lambda_1), \ \forall t$$

Then, it is concluded from Theorem 5.3 that a straightforward judgment criterion for the time-varying systems (5.1) and (5.2) is given as follows: if there exists at least one upper-bound satisfying $f_v^i(\varsigma_i, \lambda_1) < 1$, and the conditions C1 and C2 hold, then the MSE of the fusion estimator is bounded.

When only energy constraint case is considered in some practical applications, based on Theorems 5.3 and 5.4, a simple judgment criterion, which is related to the expected ESR, will be given in Corollary 5.1 such that the MSE of the designed fusion estimator is bounded or convergent.

Corollary 5.1 *Consider the time-varying systems (5.1) and (5.2) satisfying C1 and C2, if there exists at least one expected ESR η_i satisfying*

$$\mathrm{Tr}\{\eta_i A^{\mathrm{T}}(t-1)A(t-1)P(t-1)]\} < \mathrm{Tr}\{P(t-1)\} \qquad (5.108)$$

for each time t, then the MSE of the corresponding fusion estimator will be bounded, i.e., there exists a scalar p_1 such that $\lim\limits_{t\to\infty} \mathrm{Tr}\{P(t)\} \leq p_1$. On the other hand, when the dynamic target and sensor measurements are described by (5.89) and (5.90), and if systems (5.89) and (5.90) satisfy C5, and there exists at least an expected

ESR η_i *satisfying*

$$u_i(\eta_i) \triangleq \lambda_{\max}\{\eta_i A^{\mathrm{T}} A\} < 1 \tag{5.109}$$

Then the limit of the MSE of the fusion estimator exists, i.e., $\lim_{t\to\infty} \mathrm{Tr}(P(t)) = p_2$.

5.5 Simulations

Consider a networked multisensor fusion system, where the maneuvering target is described by the following state-space model [3, 12]:

$$x(t+1) = Ax(t) + \Gamma w(t) \tag{5.110}$$

where

$$A = \begin{bmatrix} 1 & \mathrm{T}_0 \\ 0 & 1 \end{bmatrix}, \ \Gamma = \begin{bmatrix} 0.5\mathrm{T}_0^2 \\ \mathrm{T}_0 \end{bmatrix}$$

and T_0 is the sampling period and $w(t)$ is a zero-mean white noise with covariance Q_w. The state is $x(t) = [s(t)\ \dot{s}(t)]^{\mathrm{T}}$, where $s(t)$ and $\dot{s}(t)$ are the position and velocity of the moving target at time t, respectively. Suppose that this maneuvering target is monitored by two sensors, and the measurement equations are described by

$$y_i(t) = C_i x(t) + v_i(t),\ i = 1, 2 \tag{5.111}$$

where $C_1 = C_2 = I_2$. $v_1(t)$ and $v_2(t)$ are uncorrelated zero-mean white noises with covariances R_{v_1} and R_{v_2}, respectively, and they are also uncorrelated with $w(t)$. Since

$$\mathrm{rank}([\Gamma, A\Gamma]) = 2, \mathrm{rank}([C_i^{\mathrm{T}}, (C_i A)^{\mathrm{T}}]^{\mathrm{T}}) = 2 \tag{5.112}$$

the judgment condition C5 holds. For this example, it is assumed that each sensor has enough processing capabilities to compute local estimate. However, to satisfy the finite communication bandwidth and the limited energy of each sensor, at most one component of $\hat{x}_i(t)$ is allowed to be transmitted to the fusion center, i.e., $\mathrm{r}_1 = \mathrm{r}_2 = 1$. Under this condition, it follows from (5.14) that

$$H_1^1 = H_2^1 = \mathrm{diag}\{1, 0\},\ H_1^2 = H_2^2 = \mathrm{diag}\{0, 1\} \tag{5.113}$$

Then, it is derived from (5.113) and Theorem 5.1 that the compensated state estimates $x_i^c(t)(i = 1, 2)$ are given by

$$\begin{aligned}\hat{x}_i^c(t) &= \text{diag}\{\sigma_1^i(t), \sigma_2^i(t)\}\hat{x}_i(t) \\ &\quad + \text{diag}\{1 - \sigma_1^i(t), 1 - \sigma_2^i(t)\}A\hat{x}(t-1)\end{aligned} \tag{5.114}$$

where $\sigma_1^i(t)$ and $\sigma_2^i(t)$, $i = 1, 2$ are binary random variables satisfying

$$\text{Prob}\{\sigma_1^i(t) = 1\} = \pi_1^i, \ \text{Prob}\{\sigma_2^i(t) = 1\} = \pi_2^i$$

Then, it follows from (5.69) that $U_1^i = [1\ 0]$ and $U_2^i = [0\ 1]$, and thus, one has

$$M_1 = \text{diag}\left\{1 - \pi_1^1, 1 - \pi_2^1\right\}, \ M_2 = \text{diag}\left\{1 - \pi_1^2, 1 - \pi_2^2\right\}$$

In the simulation, choose

$$\text{T}_0 = 0.5\,\text{s}, \ Q_w = 0.3, \ \text{R}_{v_1} = \text{diag}\{0.5, 0.1\}, \ \text{R}_{v_2} = \text{diag}\{0.1, 0.3\}$$

and the initial values are taken as

$$\begin{aligned}\hat{x}(0) &= \hat{x}_1(0) = \hat{x}_2(0) = [0.15\ \ 0.25]^{\text{T}} \\ P(0) &= \text{diag}\{0.09, 0.21\} \\ \Phi_1(0) &= \begin{bmatrix} 0.02\ 0.03 \\ 0.02\ 0.01 \end{bmatrix} \\ \Phi_2(0) &= \begin{bmatrix} 0.05\ 0.01 \\ 0.03\ 0.02 \end{bmatrix}\end{aligned}$$

5.5.1 Bandwidth Constraint Case

To satisfy the constraints of the finite communication bandwidth, only one component of each local estimate $\hat{x}_i(t)$, $i \in \{1, 2\}$ is randomly transmitted to the fusion center at each time step. Therefore, the binary random variables $\sigma_1^i(t)$ and $\sigma_2^i(t)$ satisfy $\sum_{\ell=1}^{2} \sigma_\ell^i(t) = 1$, $i = 1, 2$, which means that $\pi_1^i = 1 - \pi_2^i$. First, consider the situation where $\pi_1^1 = 0$ and $\pi_1^2 = 1$, then it follows from C6 that

$$\mu_1(\varsigma_1) = 1.25, \mu_2(\varsigma_2) = 1 \tag{5.115}$$

$$\lambda_{\max}(A^{\text{T}}M_2A) \neq \lambda_{\min}(A^{\text{T}}M_2A) \tag{5.116}$$

By taking (5.112), (5.115), and (5.116) into account, it follows from Theorem 5.4 that the MSE of the fusion estimator $\hat{x}(t)$ will converge to a steady-state value.

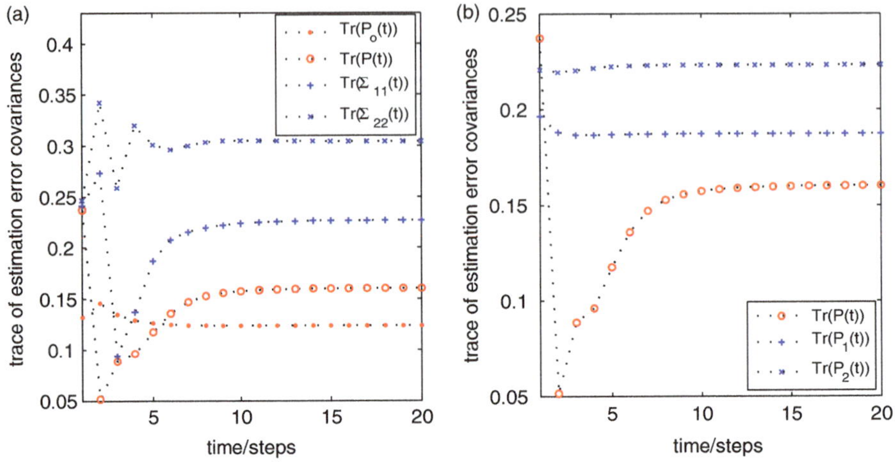

Fig. 5.1 (**a**) Comparison of the estimation performances for the fusion estimates $\hat{x}(t)$ and $\hat{x}_o(t)$ and local compensated state estimates $\hat{x}_i^c(t)$, $i = 1, 2$. (**b**) Comparison of the estimation performances for the fusion estimates $\hat{x}(t)$ and local estimates $\hat{x}_i(t)$

Then, applying Algorithm 5.1, the estimation performance (assessed by the trace of estimation error covariance matrix) of local compensated state estimates $\hat{x}_i^c(t)$, $i = 1, 2$; local estimates $\hat{x}_i(t)$, $i = 1, 2$; and fusion estimates $\hat{x}(t)$ and $\hat{x}_o(t)$ are shown in Fig. 5.1. It can be seen from Fig. 5.1a that the estimation performance of fusion estimate $\hat{x}(t)$ is better than that of each local compensated state estimate. However, the estimation performance of $\hat{x}(t)$ is worse than that of $\hat{x}_o(t)$, which implies that the bandwidth constraints degrade the estimation performance. On the other hand, Fig. 5.1b shows that though the estimate $\hat{x}(t)$ is obtained under the limited communication bandwidth, the estimation performance of the fusion estimate $\hat{x}(t)$ is still better than that of each local estimate.

For this networked fusion estimation system with communication bandwidth constraints, it can be obtained from the inequalities (5.93) and (5.94) that $0.25 \leq \pi_1^i \leq 1$. Then, it follows from Theorem 5.4 that when one chooses $0.25 \leq \pi_1^1 \leq 1, 0 \leq \pi_1^2 \leq 1$ or $0.25 \leq \pi_1^2 \leq 1, 0 \leq \pi_1^1 \leq 1$, the corresponding MSE of the fusion estimate $\hat{x}(t)$ will be convergent. In this sense, by solving the optimization problem (5.107), one obtains a group of suboptimal selecting probabilities $\pi_1^1 = 0$, $\pi_1^2 = 1$. To verify the above results, by taking different selecting probabilities, the corresponding estimation performances are depicted in Fig. 5.2. It can be seen from Fig. 5.2a that the MSE of the fusion estimate is minimal when the selecting probabilities are only taken as $\pi_1^1 = 0$ and $\pi_1^2 = 1$. Particularly, Fig. 5.2a also shows that all MSEs converge to some steady-state values for the selecting probabilities satisfying C6, which verifies the theoretical analysis results in Theorem 5.4. Moreover, define $\mu_i(\pi_1^i) \triangleq \mathrm{Tr}\{M_i \otimes [AP(t-1)A^{\mathrm{T}}]\} - \mathrm{Tr}\{P(t-1)\}$, then $\mu_i(\pi_1^i), i = 1, 2$ for different groups of selecting probabilities are depicted in Fig. 5.2b, which implies that the criterion C6 is effective.

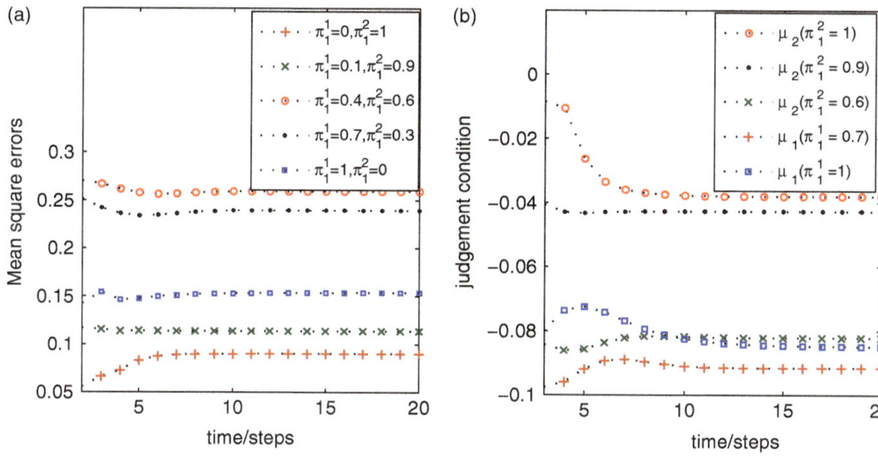

Fig. 5.2 (**a**) Comparison of the estimation performances with different selecting probabilities. (**b**) The trajectories of $\mu_i(\pi_1^i)$

5.5.2 *Energy Constraint Case*

In this subsection, only the energy constraint issue will be considered. According to the proposed communication strategy, each local estimate $\hat{x}_i(t),\ i \in \{1,2\}$ is intermittently transmitted to the fusion center for reducing the energy consumption, and each compensated state estimate $\hat{x}_i^c(t),\ i \in \{1,2\}$ is designed based on the one-step prediction of fusion estimate $\hat{x}(t-1)$, i.e., the local compensated state estimates are given by

$$\hat{x}_i^c(t) = \eta_i(t)\hat{x}_i(t) + (1-\eta_i(t))A\hat{x}(t-1),\ i = 1,2 \tag{5.117}$$

where the random binary variable $\eta_i(t)$ satisfies Prob$\{\eta_i(t) = 1\} = \mathbf{E}\{\eta_i(t)\} = 1 - \eta_i$ and η_i denotes the expected energy-saving rate. To specify the energy-saving efficiency, the practical energy-saving rate $\mathrm{c}_i(t)$ is defined as $\mathrm{c}_i(t) = 1 - \left(\sum_{\mathrm{T}=1}^{t} \eta_i(\mathrm{T})\right) \Big/ t$, which helps give a quantitative relationship between the expected and practical energy-saving rates.

Consider the situation where $\eta_1 = 0.2$ and $\eta_2 = 0.3$, then it follows from Corollary 5.1 that the MSE of the fusion estimates will converge to a steady value as time goes to infinity. Meanwhile, the expected energy-saving rates $\eta_i,\ i = 1,2$ and practical energy-saving rates $\mathrm{c}_i(t),\ i = 1,2$ are depicted in Fig. 5.3. It can be seen from Fig. 5.3 that the practical energy-saving rates approach the expected energy-saving rates as time increases, which implies that this energy-saving strategy performs well. On the other hand, the condition $\eta_1 = 0.1$ yields $u_1(\eta_1) < 1$, then it

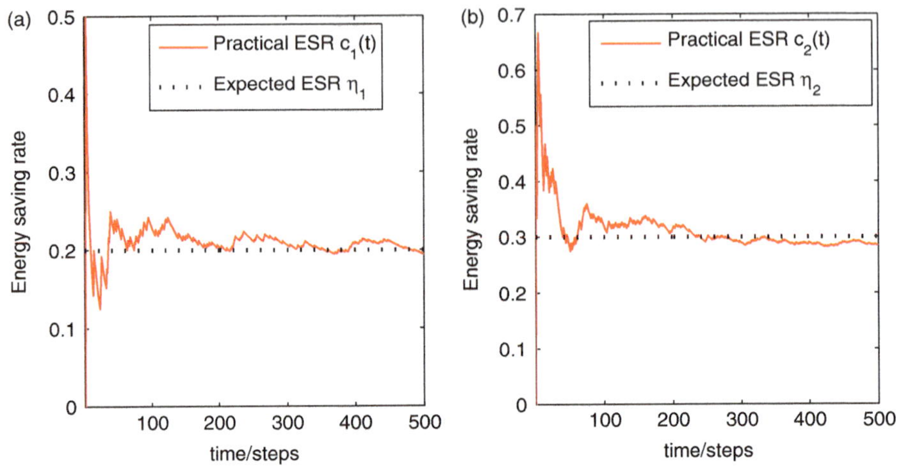

Fig. 5.3 Relationship between the practical energy-saving rate (ESR) $c_i(t)$ and the expected energy-saving rate η_i

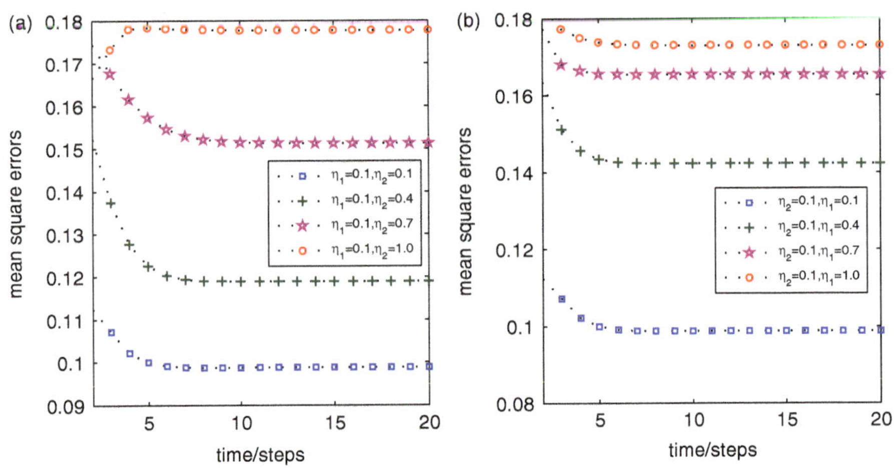

Fig. 5.4 Relationship between the expected energy-saving rates and fusion estimation performances

follows from Corollary 5.1 that the limit of MSE for the fusion estimator will always exist for choosing an arbitrary energy-saving rate η_2. The relationships between the expected energy-saving rates and the fusion estimation performance are depicted in Fig. 5.4. It is shown from Fig. 5.4 that the MSE of the fusion estimator converges to a steady-state value, which verifies the result of Corollary 5.1. Figure 5.4 also shows that the fusion estimation performance becomes better with the decrease of the expected energy-saving rates, which is as expected for this energy-saving strategy.

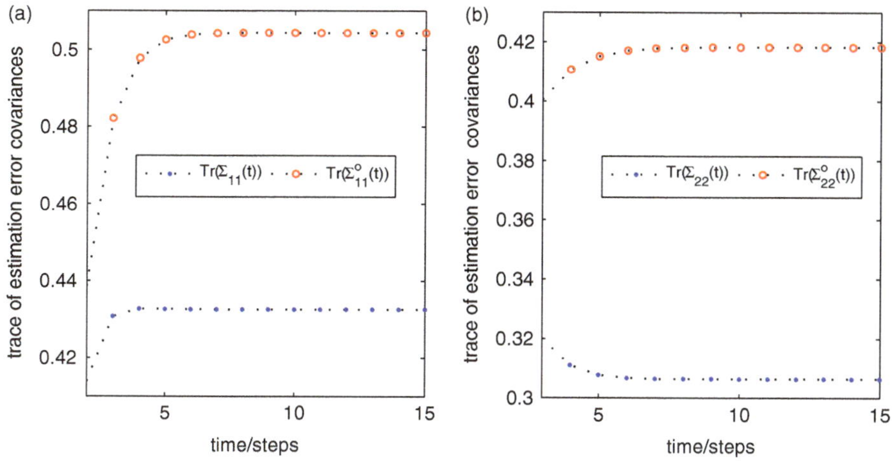

Fig. 5.5 Local estimation performances for different compensating strategies

To demonstrate the advantage of the proposed compensating strategy, it is compared with the compensating strategy of (5.45). Note that the idea of (5.45) has been used in [13] to solve the fusion estimation problem with limited communication rate. In this case, each compensated state estimate of $x(t)$ can be described by

$$\hat{x}_i^{c*}(t) = \eta_i(t)\hat{x}_i(t) + (1 - \eta_i(t))A\hat{x}_i^{c*}(t-1) \tag{5.118}$$

where the binary variable $\eta_i(t)$ has been defined in (5.117). Thus, it follows from the proof of Theorem 5.2 that the local estimation error covariance matrix $\Sigma_{ii}^{o}(t) \triangleq \mathbf{E}\{(x(t) - \hat{x}_i^{c*}(t))(x(t) - \hat{x}_i^{c*}(t))^{\mathrm{T}}\}$ is computed by

$$\Sigma_{ii}^{o}(t) = (1 - \eta_i)P_{ii}(t) + \eta_i(A\Sigma_{ii}^{o}(t-1)A^{\mathrm{T}} + \Gamma Q_w \Gamma^{\mathrm{T}}) \tag{5.119}$$

For $\eta_1 = 0.2$ and $\eta_2 = 0.3$, the relationship between $\mathrm{Tr}(\Sigma_{ii}(t))$ and $\mathrm{Tr}(\Sigma_{ii}^{0}(t))$ is depicted in Fig. 5.5, where the computation procedures for $\Sigma_{ii}(t)$ and $\Sigma_{ii}^{0}(t)$ have the same initial values. It can be seen from the simulations that the estimation performance of local compensated state estimate in (5.117) is better than that given by (5.118).

5.5.3 Bandwidth and Energy Constraints Case

When the bandwidth and energy constrains are taken into account simultaneously, it follows from the proposed communication strategy that at most one component of the local estimate $\hat{x}_i(t)$ is allowed to be transmitted to the fusion center at each time step. Under this condition, the local compensated state estimates are computed by (5.114), and the random variables $\sigma_1^i(t)$ and $\sigma_2^i(t)$ in (5.114) satisfy $\left\{\sum_{\ell=1}^{2} \sigma_\ell^i(t)\right\} \in \{0, 1\}$. Thus, it follows from (5.26) that the expected ESR η_i for the ith sensor is given by

$$\eta_i = 1 - \mathbf{E}\left\{\sum_{\ell=1}^{2} \sigma_\ell^i(t)\right\} = 1 - \sum_{\ell=1}^{2} \pi_\ell^i$$

which means that $\pi_1^i = 1 - \eta_i - \pi_2^i$. In this case, the expected and practical total energy-saving rates for all sensors are given by

$$\mathbf{E}_c = \frac{1}{2}\sum_{i=1}^{2} \text{Prob}\left\{\sum_{\ell=1}^{2} \sigma_\ell^i(t) = 0\right\} = 1 - \frac{1}{2}\sum_{i=1}^{2}\sum_{\ell=1}^{2} \pi_\ell^i \tag{5.120}$$

$$\text{c}(t) = \left(\sum_{\text{T}=1}^{t}\sum_{\ell=1}^{2} \sigma_\ell^1(\text{T}) + \sum_{\text{T}=1}^{t}\sum_{\ell=1}^{2} \sigma_\ell^2(\text{T})\right) \Big/ 2t \tag{5.121}$$

and the notation $\mu_i(\varsigma_i)$ in Theorem 5.4 is simplified as $\mu_i(\eta_i, \pi_1^i)$.

For this networked fusion estimation system, the power-efficient dimensionality reduction approach in [3] can also solve the problem of bandwidth and energy constraints by reducing the communication traffic at each time step. From Section II in [3], the sensor i should send the dimension-reduced signal $z_i(t) \triangleq \left(\hat{C}_i(t)[y_i(t) - \hat{y}_i(t|t-1)]\right) \in \Re$ to the fusion center, where $\hat{y}_i(t|t-1) = C_i(t)A(t-1)\hat{x}_i(t-1)$. When it is assumed that there is no noise in the fusion center, the compression matrices $\hat{C}_i(t)(i = 1, 2, \ldots, L)$ can be obtained by solving the similar problem (5.7) in [3]. Different from the proposed communication strategy, all sensors must send information to the fusion at each time step, and the fusion estimation algorithm in [3] is implemented under the centralized fusion framework. However, the experimental studies in [14] show that the communication tasks consume the largest portion of the total energy needed for the overall WSN. In this sense, if each dimension-reduced signal $z_i(t)$ is intermittently sent to the fusion center for the fusion estimation algorithm in [3], then the performance of the corresponding centralized fusion estimator may be worse than that of the proposed fusion estimator. This is because the centralized fusion method has weaker fault-tolerant abilities as compared with the distributed fusion method [9].

To illustrate the above result, it is considered that $z_i(t)$ is randomly sent to the fusion center at each time step, where the random variable $\eta_i(t) \in \{0, 1\}$ denotes whether the signal $z_i(t)$ is sent to the fusion center or not. Meanwhile, let $P_D(t)$ denote the centralized fusion estimation error covariance matrix based on the incomplete information $z_i(t)$. Then, for different expected energy-saving rates η_i, the trajectories of $\text{Tr}(P(t))$ and $\text{Tr}(P_D(t))$ are plotted in Fig. 5.6, where the initial values of $P(t)$ and $P_D(t)$ are different. It can be seen from (a) of Fig. 5.6 that the performance of the fusion estimator in [3] is better than that of the proposed fusion estimator when each sensor should send information to the fusion center at each time step. However, when each sensor intermittently sends information to the fusion center for reducing energy consumption, it can be seen from (b) to (c) of Fig. 5.6 that the trace of the error covariance matrix $P_D(t)$ becomes large as time increases,

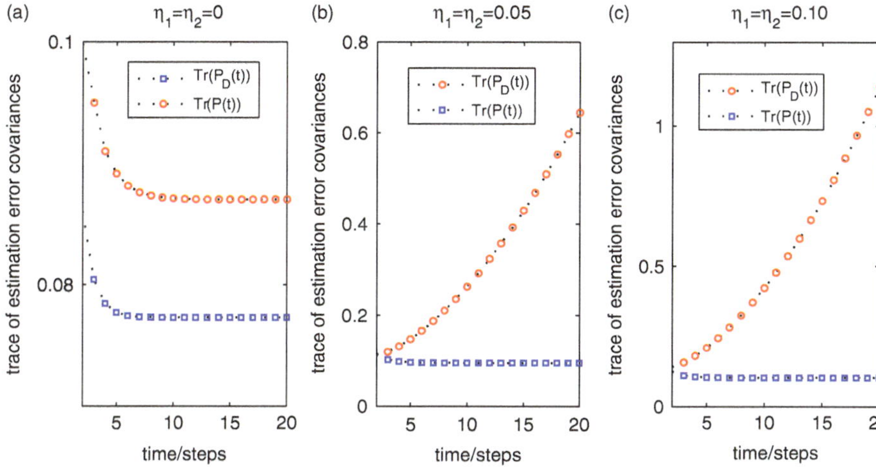

Fig. 5.6 Comparison of the estimation performance for the designed fusion estimator and the fusion estimator based on the power-efficient approach in [3]

but the trace of the error covariance matrix $P(t)$ converges to a steady-state value. Moreover, it can be seen from (b) to (c) of Fig. 5.6 that $\mathrm{Tr}(P_D(t)) > \mathrm{Tr}(P(t))(t > 3)$, which implies that the performance of the proposed fusion estimator is better than that of the centralized fusion estimator in [3] with intermittent transmissions.

In what follows, the situation for the proposed communication strategy will be considered, where $\eta_1 = 0.2$ and $\eta_2 = 0.4$. According to the condition C6 of Theorem 5.4, $\mu_2(\eta_2, \pi_1^2)$ is always larger than one, and there exists an approximate range $[0.38, 0.70]$ of π_1^1 such that $\mu_1(\eta_1, \pi_1^1) \leq 1$. Then, it can be seen from Theorem 5.4 that if $0.38 \leq \pi_1^1 \leq 0.70$ and $0 \leq \pi_1^2 \leq 0.60$, then the MSE of the designed fusion estimator will converge to a steady-state value. Therefore, choose $\pi_1^1 = 0.70$ and $\pi_1^2 = 0$, then the fusion estimator $\hat{x}(t)$ is obtained from Algorithm 5.1. The trajectories of $\hat{x}(t)$ and $x(t)$ are depicted in Fig. 5.7, which shows that the fusion estimator $\hat{x}(t)$ can track the maneuvering target well with bandwidth and energy constraints. Meanwhile, it can be seen from (a) of Fig. 5.8 that the trace of the covariance matrix $P(t)$ converges to a steady-state value and the performance of the fusion estimator is better than that of the local compensated state estimates. On the other hand, to compare the actual estimation precision between the fusion estimates and local compensated state estimates, the root-mean-square errors (RMSEs) for those estimators are computed with 100 Monte Carlo runs by using the RMSE formula in [15]. Then the trajectories of different RMSEs are plotted in (b) of Fig. 5.8, which shows that the estimation precision of the fusion estimator $\hat{x}(t)$ is higher than that of each local compensated state estimate. It can also be seen from Fig. 5.8 that the estimation precision of the fusion estimator $\hat{x}_0(t)$ is still higher than that of the $\hat{x}(t)$, which implies that the bandwidth and energy constraints may deteriorate the fusion estimation performance of the networked fusion systems. Moreover, Fig. 5.9 shows that the error between the practical and expected total

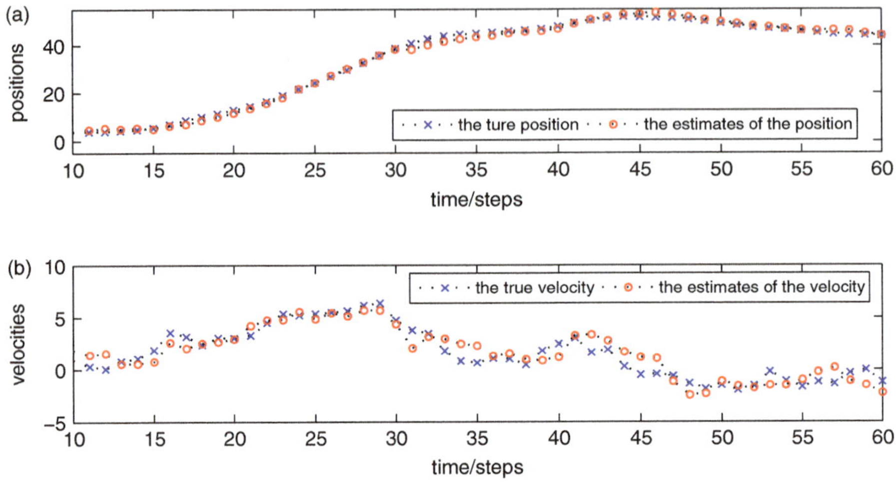

Fig. 5.7 Trajectories of $x(t)$ and the fusion estimator $\hat{x}(t)$ for $\pi_1^1 = 0.7$ and $\pi_1^2 = 0$

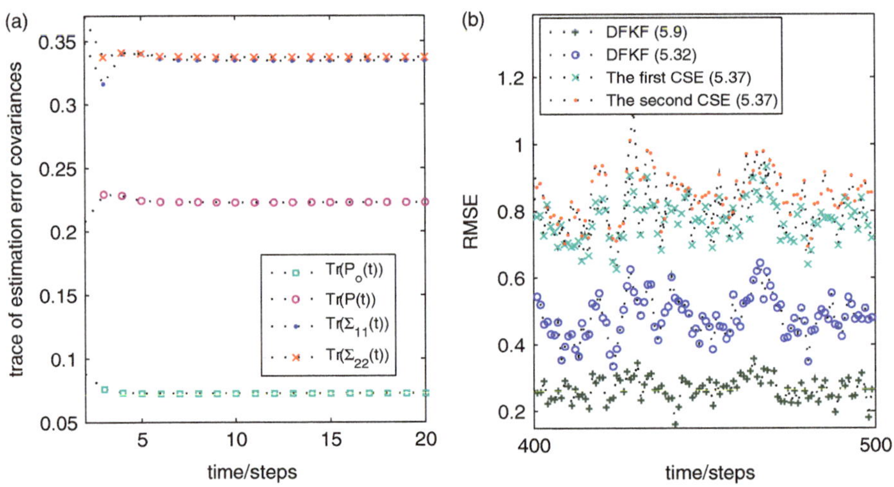

Fig. 5.8 (**a**) The traces of the estimation error variance matrix for the fusion estimates and local compensated state estimates. (**b**) The RMSEs for the fusion estimates and local compensated state estimates

energy-saving rates becomes smaller as time increases, which implies that the proposed energy-saving strategy is quite straightforward yet efficient. Therefore, it can be concluded from the above discussion that when the selecting probabilities are taken as $\pi_1^1 = 0.7$ and $\pi_1^2 = 0$ for this example, the designed fusion estimator not only satisfies the bandwidth constraint condition ($r_1 = r_2 = 1$) but also reduces about 30 % energy consumptions for all sensors. Particularly, the RMSE of the designed fusion estimator is bounded under the mixed constraint conditions.

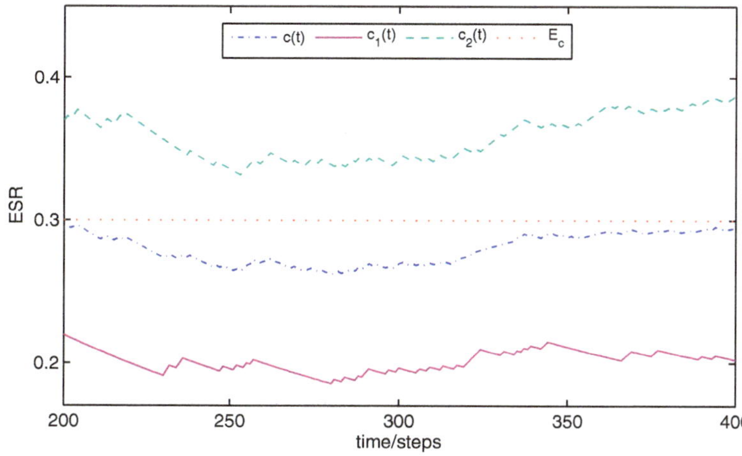

Fig. 5.9 The energy-saving effect of the proposed fusion estimation algorithm

5.6 Conclusions

In this chapter, the distributed finite-horizon fusion estimation problem was investigated for a class of networked multisensor fusion systems in a bandwidth- and energy-constrained WSN. Multiple binary random variables with known statistical properties were introduced to model the mixed constraints of bandwidth and energy. An optimal recursive fusion estimator was designed in the linear minimum variance sense by using the optimal fusion algorithm weighted by matrices. Moreover, some sufficient conditions, which were related to the selecting probabilities and system parameters, have been obtained such that the MSEs of the designed fusion estimator were bounded or convergent.

References

1. Xiao JJ, Cui S, Luo ZQ, Goldsmith AJ (2008) Linear coherent decentralized estimation. IEEE Trans Signal Process 56(2):757–770
2. Schizas ID, Giannakis GB, Luo ZQ (2007) Distributed estimation using reduced-dimensionality sensor observations. IEEE Trans Signal Process 55(8):4284–4299
3. Zhu H, Schizas ID, Giannakis GB (2009) Power-efficient dimensionality reduction for distributed channel aware Kalman tracking using WSNs. IEEE Trans Signal Process 57(8):3193–3207
4. Fang J, Li HB (2008) Distributed adaptive quantization for wireless sensor networks: from delta modulation to maximum likelihood. IEEE Trans Signal Process 56(10):5246–5257
5. Zhu Y, Song E, Zhou J, You Z (2005) Optimal dimensionality reduction of sensor data in multisensor estimation fusion. IEEE Trans Signal Process 53(3):1631–1639

6. Chen HM, Zhang KS, Li XR (2004) Optimal data compression for multisensor target tracking with communication constraints. In: Proceedings of the 43th IEEE conference on decision and control, Atlantis, pp 8179–8184
7. Behbahani AS, Eltawil AM, Jafarkhani H (2012) Linear decentralized estimation of correlated data for power-constrained wireless sensor networks. IEEE Trans Signal Process 60(11):6003–6016
8. Jazwioski AH (1970) Stochastic processes and filtering theory. Academic, New York
9. Sun SL, Deng ZL (2004) Multi-sensor optimal information fusion Kalman filter. Automatica 40(6):1017–1023
10. Horn RA, Johnson CR (1991) Topics in matrix analysis. Cambridge University Press, New York
11. Wang SD, Kuo TS, Hsu CF (1986) Trace bounds on the solution of the algebraic matrix riccati and lyapunov equation. IEEE Trans Autom Control 31(7):654–656
12. Bar-Shalom Y, Li XR, Kirubarajan T (2001) Estimation with applications to tracking and navigation. Wiley, New York
13. Battistelli G, Benavoli A, Chisci L (2012) State estimation with remote sensor and intermittent transmissions. Syst Control Lett 61:155–164
14. Shnayder V, Hempstead M, Chen B, Allen GW, Welsh M (2004) Simulating the power comsumption of large-scale sensor network applications. SenSys, Maryland, pp 188–200
15. Li XR, Zhu YM, Wang J, Han CZ (2003) Optimal linear estimation fusion-part I: unified fusion rules. IEEE Trans Inf Theory 49(9):2192–2208

Chapter 6
H_∞ Fusion Estimation for WSNs with Quantization

6.1 Introduction

By quantization, one is able to reduce the size of data packet containing the quantized signal and thus is able to satisfy the bandwidth constraint of the sensor network and reduce communication costs from the sensors to the fusion estimator. In this chapter, a design method for the H_∞ multisensor fusion estimator will be presented for sensor networks with quantized local estimates. The H_∞ estimator does not make any assumption on the statistics of the process and measurement noises; the only assumption is that the external disturbance has bounded energy [1, 2]. A group of finite-level logarithmic quantizers [3] are introduced to deal with the bandwidth constraints, and the corresponding fusion estimation error system model is established. By using the discrete-time bounded real lemma, a convex optimization problem on the choices of the optimal weighting matrices and quantization parameters is established in terms of linear matrix inequalities (LMIs). Moreover, it is proved that the performance of the designed fusion estimator is better than that of each local quantized estimator.

6.2 Problem Statement

Consider a dynamical stochastic process described by the following state-space model:

$$x(t+1) = Ax(t) + Bw(t) \tag{6.1}$$

W.-A. Zhang et al., *Distributed Fusion Estimation for Sensor Networks with Communication Constraints*, DOI 10.1007/978-981-10-0795-8_6

L sensors are deployed to monitor the outputs of the process, and the measurement equations are given by

$$y_i(t) = C_i x(t) + D_i w(t),\ i = 1, 2, \ldots, L \tag{6.2}$$

where $x(t) \in \Re^n$ is the state of the process, $y_i(t) \in \Re^{q_i}$ is the measured output from sensor i. A, B, C_i, and D_i are constant matrices with appropriate dimensions, where A is Schur stable. $w(t) \in l_2[0, \infty)$ is the noise signal. It is assumed that each sensor has the processing capabilities to compute the local estimate $\hat{x}_i(t)$ which is given by

$$\hat{x}_i(t+1) = A_{f_i}\hat{x}_i(t) + B_{f_i}y_i(t) \tag{6.3}$$

where $A_{f_i} \in \Re^{n\times n}$ and $B_{f_i} \in \Re^{n\times q_i}$ are filter gain matrices to be determined such that the corresponding estimation error system ensures an H_∞ performance level η_i. Note that the filter matrices A_{f_i} and B_{f_i} can be designed by using the result in [2]. Particularly, it is well known that the designed filter matrix A_{f_i} must be Schur stable if the system matrix A is Schur stable.

Remark 6.1 For ease of presenting the main idea, the process noise is considered to be the same as the measurement noise. When the process and measurement noises are different, the corresponding state-space model can be transformed to the form as in (6.1) and (6.2) by using the augmentation method.

When the local estimate generated by the sensor is transmitted to the fusion center through communication networks, it should be quantized before being transmitted. Due to the finite communication bandwidth, only finite-level quantized local estimates from the sensor are sent to the fusion center. Then, consider a logarithmic quantization strategy:

$$Q_i(\cdot) = \begin{bmatrix} q_{i1}(\cdot)\ q_{i2}(\cdot) \cdots q_{in}(\cdot) \end{bmatrix}^{\mathrm{T}} \in \Re^{n\times 1}$$

for the ith local estimate $\hat{x}_i(t)$, and $q_{ij}(\cdot) \in \Re$, $j \in \{1, 2, \ldots, n\}$ is called quantizer χ_{ij}, which is used to quantize the jth component of the vector signal $\hat{x}_i(t)$. The set of the quantization level of the quantizer χ_{ij} is represented by

$$\begin{gathered} \mathrm{U}_{ij} = \left\{\pm u_\hbar^{(ij)} : u_\hbar^{(ij)} = \rho_{ij}^\hbar u_0^{(ij)}, \hbar = 0, \pm 1, \pm 2, \ldots\right\} \bigcup \{0\} \\ 0 < \rho_{ij} < 1, u_0^{(ij)} > 0 \end{gathered}$$

where ρ_{ij} is the quantization density. Then the logarithmic quantizer $q_{ij}(\cdot)$ is defined as follows:

$$q_{ij}(v) = \begin{cases} u_\hbar^{(ij)}, & \frac{1}{1+\delta_{ij}}u_\hbar^{(ij)} < v \le \frac{1}{1-\delta_{ij}}u_\hbar^{(ij)} \\ 0, & v = 0 \\ -q_{ij}(-v), & v < 0 \end{cases} \tag{6.4}$$

where

$$\delta_{ij} \triangleq \frac{1-\rho_{ij}}{1+\rho_{ij}} \quad (0 < \delta_{ij} < 1) \tag{6.5}$$

It is known from [3] that $q_{ij}(v)$ can be expressed as $q_{ij}(v) = (1 + \tilde{\Delta}_{ij})v$ for certain $\tilde{\Delta}_{ij}$ satisfying $|\tilde{\Delta}_{ij}| \le \delta_{ij}$. Moreover, it is known that a larger δ_{ij} leads to a coarser χ_{ij}. This implies that the size of the transmitted data packet will be decreased as the value δ_{ij} increases. Therefore, it is reasonable to model the bandwidth constraints via δ_{ij} as follows:

$$\sum_{j=1}^{n} \delta_{ij} \ge \delta_i^0, \; i = 1, 2, \ldots, L \tag{6.6}$$

where δ_i^0, $i \in \{1, 2, \ldots, L\}$ is the minimum values satisfying the communication capacity of the channel i, and it is assumed that those lower bounds are known a priori. Notice that the quantization parameters δ_{ij}, $i = 1, 2, \ldots, L$, $j = 1, 2, \ldots, n$ can be adjusted to satisfy the constraint condition (6.6). However, the optimal quantization parameters are to be designed such that the fusion estimation performance is optimal.

Let $\hat{x}_i^r(t)$ denote the local quantized estimate, then it follows from (6.4) that

$$\hat{x}_i^r(t) = [q_{i1}(\hat{x}_{i1}(t)) \;\; q_{i2}(\hat{x}_{i2}(t)) \;\; \cdots \;\; q_{in}(\hat{x}_{in}(t))]^{\mathrm{T}} = (I + \tilde{\Delta}_i)\hat{x}_i(t) \tag{6.7}$$

where

$$\begin{cases} \tilde{\Delta}_i = \operatorname{diag}\{\tilde{\Delta}_{i1}, \tilde{\Delta}_{i2}, \ldots, \tilde{\Delta}_{in}\} \\ \tilde{\Delta}_{ij} \in [-\delta_{ij}, \delta_{ij}], \; j \in \{1, 2, \ldots, n\} \end{cases} \tag{6.8}$$

The distributed H_∞ fusion estimator $\hat{x}(t)$ is given by

$$\hat{x}(t) = \sum_{i=1}^{L} W_i \hat{x}_i^r(t) \tag{6.9}$$

where the weighting matrices $W_1, W_2, \ldots, W_L$ are to be designed. Then it is derived from (6.1), (6.7), and (6.9) that the fusion estimation error $e(t) \triangleq x(t) - \hat{x}(t)$ is given by

$$e(t) = x(t) - \sum_{i=1}^{L} \{W_i(I + \tilde{\Delta}_i)\hat{x}_i(t)\} \tag{6.10}$$

where $\tilde{\Delta}_i$ is defined by (6.8). Let

$$\mathrm{X}(t) = \left[\hat{x}_1^{\mathrm{T}}(t) \quad \cdots \quad \hat{x}_L^{\mathrm{T}}(t) \ \ x^{\mathrm{T}}(t)\right]^{\mathrm{T}}$$

then it is derived from (6.1), (6.2), (6.3) and (6.10) that

$$G : \begin{cases} \mathrm{X}(t+1) = \hat{A}\mathrm{X}(t) + \hat{B}w(t) \\ e(t) = \tilde{C}\mathrm{X}(t) \end{cases} \tag{6.11}$$

where

$$\hat{A} = \begin{bmatrix} A_{f_1} & 0 & \cdots & 0 & B_{f_1}C_1 \\ 0 & A_{f_2} & \cdots & 0 & B_{f_2}C_2 \\ \vdots & \vdots & \ddots & \vdots & \vdots \\ 0 & 0 & \cdots & A_{f_L} & B_{f_L}C_L \\ 0 & 0 & \cdots & 0 & A \end{bmatrix} \tag{6.12}$$

$$\hat{B} = \begin{bmatrix} B_{f_1}D_1 \\ \vdots \\ B_{f_L}D_L \\ B \end{bmatrix} \tag{6.13}$$

$$\tilde{C} = \left[-W_1 \ \cdots -W_L \ I\right] + \left[-W_1\tilde{\Delta}_1 \ \cdots -W_L\tilde{\Delta}_L \ 0\right] \tag{6.14}$$

Then it is known from (6.14) that $\hat{A}$ is a stable matrix. Moreover, it follows from [4] that the real rational transfer function matrix of the linear discrete-time systems (6.11) is given by

$$\mathrm{T}(z) = \tilde{C}\left[zI - \hat{A}\right]^{-1}\hat{B} \tag{6.15}$$

The objective of this chapter is to find a group of optimal weighting matrices $W_1, W_2, \ldots, W_L$ and the optimal quantization parameters $\delta_{i1}, \delta_{i2}, \ldots, \delta_{in}$, $i = 1, 2, \ldots, L$ such that, for the bandwidth constraint condition (6.6), the $H_\infty -$ norm bound of the system (6.11) is minimal, i.e.

$$\begin{aligned} \{W_i,\ \delta_{i1}, \delta_{i2}, \ldots, \delta_{in}(i = 1, 2, \ldots, L)\} &= \arg\min\ \gamma \\ \text{s.t.}\ \ ||\tilde{C}\left[zI - \hat{A}\right]^{-1}\hat{B}||_\infty &< \gamma \ \text{ and } \ (6.6) \end{aligned} \tag{6.16}$$

where $||\cdot||_\infty$ denotes the standard H_∞ norm, and γ represents the H_∞ disturbance attenuation level bound that is used as a fusion estimation performance index. As is well known, the $H_\infty-$ norm constraint in (6.16) is interpreted as the $\mathscr{L}_2-$ gain constraint and is represented as

$$\sum_{t=0}^{\infty} e^{\mathrm{T}}(t)e(t) < \gamma^2 \sum_{t=0}^{\infty} w^{\mathrm{T}}(t)w(t),\ w(t) \in \mathscr{L}_2[0,\infty)$$

under the zero initial condition.

Before giving the main results, the following lemma is introduced.

Lemma 6.1 ([5] (Schur complement lemma)) *For a given matrix*

$$S = \begin{bmatrix} S_{11} & S_{12} \\ S_{12}^{\mathrm{T}} & S_{22} \end{bmatrix}$$

with $S_{11} = S_{11}^{\mathrm{T}}$ *and* $S_{22} = S_{22}^{\mathrm{T}}$, *then the following statements are equivalent:*

(1) $S < 0$;
(2) $S_{22} < 0, S_{11} - S_{12}S_{22}^{-1}S_{12}^{\mathrm{T}} < 0$;
(3) $S_{11} < 0, S_{22} - S_{12}^{\mathrm{T}}S_{11}^{-1}S_{12} < 0$.

Lemma 6.2 ([1]) *Given appropriately dimensioned matrices* Σ_1, Σ_2, *and* Σ_3, *with* $\Sigma_1^{\mathrm{T}} = \Sigma_1$, *then the following inequality*

$$\Sigma_1 + \Sigma_3\Theta(t)\Sigma_2 + \Sigma_2^{\mathrm{T}}\Theta^{\mathrm{T}}(t)\Sigma_3^{\mathrm{T}} < 0$$

holds for all $\Theta(t)$ *satisfying* $\Theta^{\mathrm{T}}(t)\Theta(t) \le I$ *if and only if there exists a scalar* $\varepsilon > 0$ *such that the following inequality*

$$\Sigma_1 + \varepsilon^{-1}\Sigma_3\Sigma_3^{\mathrm{T}} + \varepsilon\Sigma_2^{\mathrm{T}}\Sigma_2 < 0$$

holds.

6.3 Distributed H_∞ Fusion Estimator Design

Theorem 6.1 *For given* $\gamma > 0$, $0 < \delta_{ij} < 1$, $i = 1, 2, \ldots, L$, $j = 1, 2, \ldots, n$, *the distributed* H_∞ *fusion estimate* $\hat{x}(t)$ *in the form of (6.9) can ensure an* H_∞ *disturbance attenuation level bound* γ *under the quantization effect, if and only if there exist* $P > 0$, $\varepsilon > 0$ *and the weighting matrices* W_i, $i = 1, 2, \ldots, L$ *such that the following linear matrix inequality holds*

$$\begin{bmatrix} -\varepsilon I & 0 & \varepsilon D & 0 & 0 & 0 \\ * & -P & P\hat{A} & P\hat{B} & 0 & 0 \\ * & * & -P & 0 & \hat{C}^{\mathrm{T}} & 0 \\ * & * & * & -\gamma^2 I & 0 & 0 \\ * & * & * & * & -I & E \\ * & * & * & * & * & -\varepsilon I \end{bmatrix} < 0 \tag{6.17}$$

where

$$\begin{cases} \Delta_i \triangleq \mathrm{diag}\{\delta_{i1}, \delta_{i2}, \cdots, \delta_{in}\} \\ D \triangleq \mathrm{diag}\{\Delta_1 \ \cdots \ \Delta_L \ 0\} \\ \hat{C} \triangleq [-W_1 \ \cdots \ -W_L \ I\,] \\ E \triangleq [-W_1 \ \cdots \ -W_L \ 0] \end{cases} \tag{6.18}$$

Proof when $\hat{A}$ is a stable matrix, it follows from the discrete-time bounded real lemma in [4] that the inequality $||\mathrm{T}(z)||_\infty < \gamma$ holds if and only if there exists $P > 0$ such that

$$\begin{cases} \hat{A}^{\mathrm{T}} P \hat{A} - P + \gamma^{-2} \hat{A}^{\mathrm{T}} P \hat{B} \left[I - \gamma^{-2} \hat{B}^{\mathrm{T}} P \hat{B} \right]^{-1} \hat{B}^{\mathrm{T}} P \hat{A} + \tilde{C}^{\mathrm{T}} \tilde{C} < 0 \\ \gamma^{-2} \hat{B}^{\mathrm{T}} P \hat{B} - I < 0 \end{cases} \tag{6.19}$$

According to Lemma 6.1, (6.19) is equivalent to

$$\begin{bmatrix} \hat{A}^{\mathrm{T}} P \hat{A} - P + \tilde{C}^{\mathrm{T}} \tilde{C} & \gamma^{-1} \hat{A}^{\mathrm{T}} P \hat{B} \\ * & \gamma^{-2} \hat{B}^{\mathrm{T}} P \hat{B} - I \end{bmatrix} < 0$$

which implies that

$$\begin{bmatrix} -P & P\hat{A} & P\hat{B} & 0 \\ * & -P & 0 & \tilde{C}^{\mathrm{T}} \\ * & * & -\gamma^2 I & 0 \\ * & * & * & -I \end{bmatrix} < 0 \tag{6.20}$$

On the other hand, it is known from (6.7) that

$$\tilde{\Delta}_i^{\mathrm{T}} W_i^{\mathrm{T}} = \Delta_i F_{\tilde{\Delta}_i} W_i^{\mathrm{T}} \tag{6.21}$$

where $F_{\tilde{\Delta}_i} \triangleq \mathrm{diag}\left\{ \frac{\tilde{\Delta}_{i1}}{\delta_{i1}}, \frac{\tilde{\Delta}_{i2}}{\delta_{i2}}, \ldots, \frac{\tilde{\Delta}_{in}}{\delta_{in}} \right\}$, and $F_{\tilde{\Delta}_i}$ satisfies

$$F_{\tilde{\Delta}_i} F_{\tilde{\Delta}_i}^{\mathrm{T}} \leq I \tag{6.22}$$

Define $\tilde{C}_{\tilde{\Delta}} \triangleq [-W_1 \tilde{\Delta}_1 \ \cdots -W_L \tilde{\Delta}_L \ 0]$, then it follows from (6.20), (6.21) and (6.22) that

$$\begin{bmatrix} 0\,0\,0 & 0 \\ 0\,0\,0 & \tilde{C}_{\tilde{\Delta}}^{\mathrm{T}} \\ 0\,0\,0 & 0 \\ 0\,0\,0 & 0 \end{bmatrix} = \begin{bmatrix} 0 \\ D \\ 0 \\ 0 \end{bmatrix} F_{\tilde{\Delta}} [0 \ \ 0 \ \ 0 \ \ E^{\mathrm{T}}] \tag{6.23}$$

where D and E are defined in (6.18), and

$$F_{\tilde{\Delta}} \triangleq \operatorname{diag}\left\{F_{\tilde{\Delta}_1}, F_{\tilde{\Delta}_2}, \ldots, F_{\tilde{\Delta}_L}, I\right\}$$

It is known from (6.22) that $F_{\tilde{\Delta}}F_{\tilde{\Delta}}^{\mathrm{T}} \leq I$, then according to (6.23), it can be concluded from Lemma 6.2 that the inequality (6.20) holds if and only if there exists a scalar $\varepsilon > 0$ such that

$$\begin{bmatrix} -P & P\hat{A} & P\hat{B} & 0 \\ * & -P & 0 & \hat{C}^{\mathrm{T}} \\ * & * & -\gamma^2 I & 0 \\ * & * & * & -I \end{bmatrix} + \varepsilon \begin{bmatrix} 0 \\ D \\ 0 \\ 0 \end{bmatrix}\begin{bmatrix} 0 \\ D \\ 0 \\ 0 \end{bmatrix}^{\mathrm{T}} + \varepsilon^{-1}\begin{bmatrix} 0 \\ 0 \\ 0 \\ E \end{bmatrix}\begin{bmatrix} 0 \\ 0 \\ 0 \\ E \end{bmatrix}^{\mathrm{T}} < 0$$

By using Lemma 6.1, the inequality (6.24) is equivalent to

$$\begin{bmatrix} -\varepsilon^{-1}I & 0 & D^{\mathrm{T}} & 0 & 0 & 0 \\ * & -P & P\hat{A} & P\hat{B} & 0 & 0 \\ * & * & -P & 0 & \hat{C}^{\mathrm{T}} & 0 \\ * & * & * & -\gamma^2 I & 0 & 0 \\ * & * & * & * & -I & E \\ * & * & * & * & * & -\varepsilon I \end{bmatrix} < 0 \tag{6.24}$$

Therefore, (6.17) is derived from pre- and post-multiplying (6.24) by the matrix $\operatorname{diag}\{\varepsilon I, I, I, I, I, I\}$. The proof is thus completed.

When the quantization parameters δ_{ij}, $i = 1, 2, \ldots, L; j = 1, 2, \ldots, n$ satisfying the condition (6.6) are given, a necessary and sufficient condition has been presented in Theorem 6.1 to judge whether there exists a group of weighting matrices or not such that the H_∞ – norm bound of the system (6.11) achieves a prescribed γ. However, the solutions of (6.16) cannot be obtained from Theorem 6.1 because the quantization parameters are required to be determined. In fact, to obtain the optimal weighting matrices and quantization parameters simultaneously, the quantization parameters δ_{ij}, $i = 1, 2, \ldots, L; j = 1, 2, \ldots, n$ will be considered as nL variables in (6.17). In this case, (6.17) is a nonlinear matrix inequality, which is difficult to be solved. Therefore, an equivalent linear matrix inequality representation for the inequality (6.17) is written as

$$\begin{bmatrix} -\varepsilon I & 0 & \hat{D} & 0 & 0 & 0 \\ * & -P & P\hat{A} & P\hat{B} & 0 & 0 \\ * & * & -P & 0 & \hat{C}^{\mathrm{T}} & 0 \\ * & * & * & -\hat{\gamma} I & 0 & 0 \\ * & * & * & * & -I & E \\ * & * & * & * & * & -\varepsilon I \end{bmatrix} < 0 \tag{6.25}$$

where

$$\hat{\gamma} \triangleq \gamma^2,\ \hat{D} \triangleq \mathrm{diag}\{\hat{\Delta}_1 \ \cdots \ \hat{\Delta}_L \ 0\}$$

For taking the constraint condition (6.6) into account, the variable $\hat{\Delta}_i$ is defined by

$$\hat{\Delta}_i \triangleq \mathrm{diag}\{\varepsilon\delta_{i1}, \varepsilon\delta_{i2}, \ldots, \varepsilon\delta_{in}\} \tag{6.26}$$

Moreover, according to the constraint condition (6.6), the variables $\hat{\Delta}_i$, $i = 1, 2, \ldots, L$ satisfy

$$0 < \hat{\Delta}_i \leq \varepsilon I \ \text{ and } \ \mathrm{Tr}(\hat{\Delta}_i) \geq \delta_i^0 \varepsilon \tag{6.27}$$

Based on the above analysis, the optimal weighting matrices W_i, $i = 1, 2, \ldots, L$ and the optimal quantization parameters Δ_i, $i = 1, 2, \ldots, L$ satisfying (6.6) can be obtained by implementing the following algorithm.

Algorithm 6.1

Step 1: Determine the optimal weighting matrices $W_1, \ldots, W_L$ and other optimal parameters $\hat{\gamma}$, ε, $\hat{\Delta}_i$, $i = 1, 2, \ldots, L$ by solving the following optimization problem:

$$\begin{aligned} &\min\ \hat{\gamma} \\ &\text{s.t. LMIs (6.25) and (6.27)} \end{aligned} \tag{6.28}$$

Step 2: Compute the optimal H_∞ disturbance attenuation level bound and quantization parameters by

$$\gamma = \sqrt{\hat{\gamma}},\ \Delta_i = \mathrm{diag}\{\underbrace{\varepsilon^{-1}, \ldots, \varepsilon^{-1}}_{n \text{ elements}}\}\hat{\Delta}_i (i = 1, 2, \ldots, L) \tag{6.29}$$

The optimization problem (6.28) can be directly solved by the function "*mincx*" of the MATLAB LMI Toolbox [5], and thus the solution of the optimization problem (6.16) can be easily obtained by implementing Algorithm 6.1.

Theorem 6.2 *For the local quantized estimate $\hat{x}_i^r(t)$ and the distributed H_∞ fusion estimate $\hat{x}(t)$, under the same bandwidth constraint condition (6.7), the performance of the distributed H_∞ fusion estimate is better than that of each local quantized estimate, i.e.,*

$$\gamma^* \leq \gamma_i^*,\ i = 1, 2, \ldots, L \tag{6.30}$$

where γ_i^* denotes the local optimal H_∞ disturbance attenuation level bound for the ith *local quantized estimate $\hat{x}_i^r(t)$, while γ^* represents the optimal H_∞ disturbance attenuation level bound for the fusion estimate $\hat{x}(t)$.*

Proof When the weighting matrices in (6.28) are taken as

$$W_i = I,\ W_j = \mathbf{0},\ j \neq i \tag{6.31}$$

then the local optimal disturbance attenuation level bound for the ith local quantized estimate can be obtained by solving the corresponding optimization problem (6.28). Moreover, when (6.31) holds, the fusion estimate in the form of (6.9) is reduced to the ith local quantized estimate, i.e., $\hat{x}(t) = \hat{x}_i^r(t)$. Note that the matrix weights in (6.9) include (6.31) as a special case. On the other hand, it is known from [5] that (6.28) is a convex optimization problem, and the solution of (6.27) is globally optimal. This implies that if the optimal weighting matrices determined by (6.28) are not equivalent to (6.31), then it must be $\gamma^* < \gamma_i^*$. Particularly, if the optimal weighting matrices are identical to (6.31), then $\gamma_i^* = \gamma^*$. This completes the proof.

6.4 Simulations

Consider a dynamic system which is monitored by two sensors, where the parameters of the systems (6.1) and (6.2) are given by

$$A = \begin{bmatrix} 0.5 & 1 \\ 0.3 & -0.6 \end{bmatrix},\ B = \begin{bmatrix} 1 \\ 0.5 \end{bmatrix}$$

$$C_1 = [1\ 0],\ C_2 = [0\ 1]$$

$$D_1 = 0.5,\ D_2 = 0.3$$

For $\eta_1 = 0.9553$ and $\eta_2 = 0.8169$, by using the result in [2], the filter matrices in (6.3) are obtained as

$$A_{f_1} = \begin{bmatrix} -0.0514 & 0.9999 \\ 0.0308 & -0.600 \end{bmatrix},\ B_{f_1} = \begin{bmatrix} 0.5514 \\ 0.2692 \end{bmatrix}$$

$$A_{f_2} = \begin{bmatrix} 0.5000 & -0.4695 \\ 0.3000 & -0.2817 \end{bmatrix},\ B_{f_2} = \begin{bmatrix} 1.4695 \\ -0.3183 \end{bmatrix}$$

In the simulation, the lower bounds δ_1^0 and δ_2^0 of the bandwidth constraint condition (6.6) are set as

$$\delta_1^* = 0.3, \delta_2^* = 0.5 \tag{6.32}$$

Then, by solving the optimization problem (6.28) using the MATLAB LMI Toolbox [5], it is obtained that the optimal distributed fusion H_∞ disturbance attenuation level bound is $\gamma^* = 1.7482$, and the optimal weighting matrices and quantization parameters are obtained as

$$\begin{aligned} W_1 &= \begin{bmatrix} 0.6178 & 0.5993 \\ 0.5934 & 0.9356 \end{bmatrix}, \quad \begin{cases} \delta_{11} = 0.0191 \\ \delta_{12} = 0.2809 \end{cases} \\ W_2 &= \begin{bmatrix} 0.4881 & -0.2249 \\ -0.5314 & 0.5778 \end{bmatrix}, \quad \begin{cases} \delta_{21} = 0.0094 \\ \delta_{22} = 0.4906 \end{cases} \end{aligned} \tag{6.33}$$

It can be seen from (6.33) that the inequalities $\delta_{11}+\delta_{12} \geq \delta_1^*$ and $\delta_{21}+\delta_{22} \geq \delta_2^*$ hold, which are in line with the constraint condition (6.6). Moreover, when the weighting matrices of (6.25) are taken as $W_1 = I, W_2 = \mathbf{0}$, or $W_1 = \mathbf{0}, W_2 = I$, then the corresponding optimization problem (6.28) can be solved, and thus the local optimal H_∞ disturbance attenuation level bounds are $\gamma_1^* = 2.0120$ and $\gamma_2^* = 1.9446$. Then it follows from the above results that

$$\gamma_1^* > \gamma^*, \gamma_2^* > \gamma^* \tag{6.34}$$

Then, the logarithmic quantizers $q_{ij}(\cdot)$, $i = 1, 2, j = 1, 2$ are determined by the parameters δ_{ij}, $i = 1, 2, j = 1, 2$ of (6.33), and the fusion estimate $\hat{x}(t)$ in the form of (6.9) is given by the weighting matrices of (6.33). Under this condition, the noise signal is chosen by

$$w(t) = (2 + 0.2\cos(1.7t))\exp\left(-\frac{t}{15}\right) \in l_2[0, \infty)$$

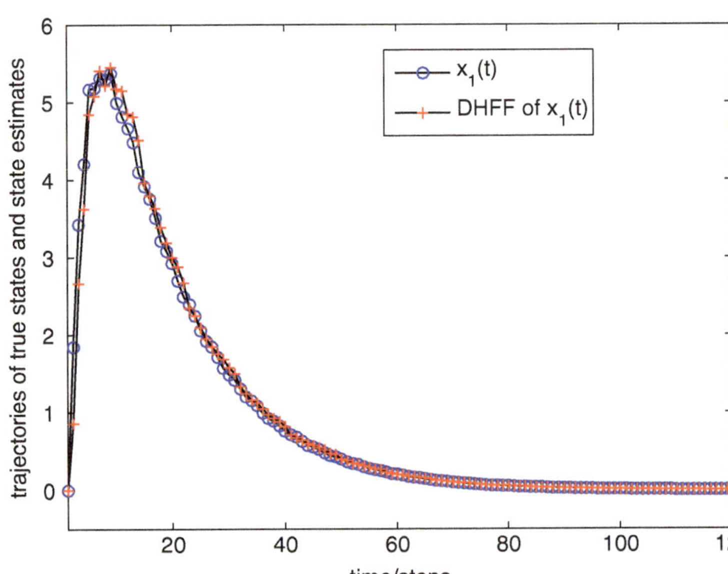

Fig. 6.1 Trajectories of $x_1(t)$ and the distributed H_∞ fusion estimate (DHFE) $\hat{x}_1(t)$

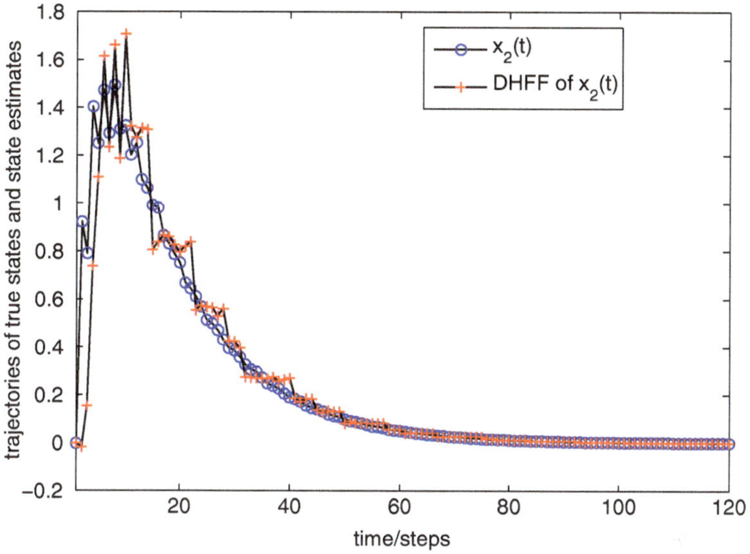

Fig. 6.2 Trajectories of $x_2(t)$ and the DHFE $\hat{x}_2(t)$

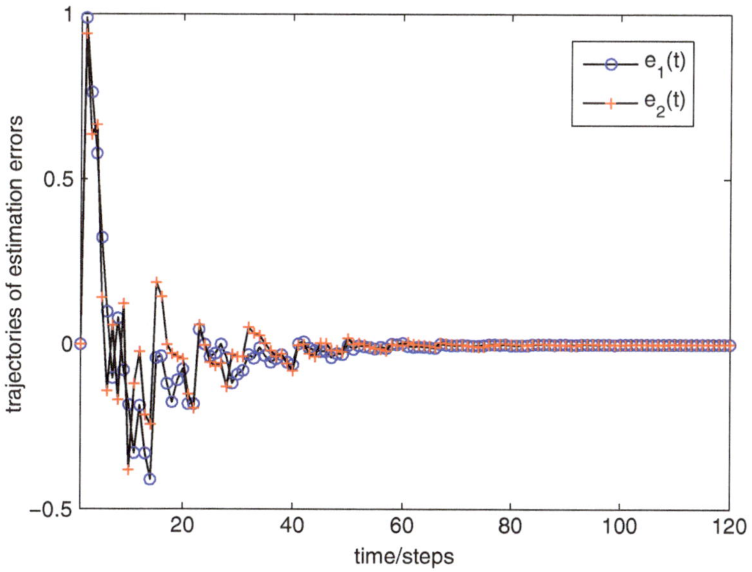

Fig. 6.3 Trajectories of $e(t)$

Then the trajectories of $x(t)$, $\hat{x}(t)$, and $e(t)$ are depicted in Figs. 6.1, 6.2 and 6.3, which shows that the fusion estimator performs well, and the estimation error converges to zero in the presence of disturbances and quantization effects. Moreover, one has by simple calculation that

$$\sqrt{\sum_{t=0}^{120} e^{\mathrm{T}}(t)e(t) \Big/ \sum_{t=0}^{120} w^{\mathrm{T}}(t)w(t)} = 0.4211$$

which verifies that $||\mathrm{T}(z)||_\infty < \gamma^*$, showing the effectiveness of the proposed distributed H_∞ fusion filter.

6.5 Conclusions

In this chapter, the distributed H_∞ fusion filtering problem was investigated for a class of networked multisensor fusion systems with communication bandwidth constraints, where the system model is subject to energy-bounded disturbance input. Based on the discrete-time bounded real lemma and LMI technique, the fusion estimation problem was converted into a convex optimization problem, which can be easily solved by using the MATLAB LMI Toolbox. It has been proved that the performance of the proposed fusion estimator is better than that of each local quantized estimator.

References

1. Gao HJ, Chen TW (2007) H_∞ estimation for uncertain systems with limited communication capacity. IEEE Trans Autom Control 52:2070–2084
2. He Y, Liu GP, Rees D, Wu M (2009) H_∞ filteirng for discrete-time systems with time-varying delay. Signal Process 89(3):275–282
3. Fu M, Xie L (2005) The sector bound approach to quantized feedback control. IEEE Trans Autom Control 50(11):1698–1711
4. de Souza CE, Xie L (1992) On the discrete-time bounded real lemma with application in the characterization of static state feedback H_∞ controllers. Syst Control Lett 18(1):61–71
5. Boyd SP, Ghaoui LE, Feron E, Balakrishnan V (1994) Linear matrix inequalities in system and control theory. SIAM, Philadelphia

Chapter 7
Hierarchical Asynchronous Fusion Estimation for WSNs

7.1 Introduction

Distributed fusion is a typical structure for multisensor fusion estimation in WSNs, where the sensors generate local estimates ahead and then send them to a fusion center (FC) for fusion estimation [1, 2]. When the number of sensors is large, it is wasteful to embed in each sensor an estimator, and the FC requires a large bandwidth to communicate with the various sensors in a short time, which is usually impossible since the WSN is limited in bandwidth. An improvement is to adopt a hierarchical structure for fusion estimation [3–6]. In a hierarchical fusion estimation system, the sensors are divided into several clusters, and the sensors within the same cluster are connected to a local estimator. Moreover, only the local estimators are linked to the FC, and the measurements from sensors in a cluster are pretreated by local estimators in advance. A structure of the hierarchical fusion system is shown in Fig. 7.1. There are mainly two deficiencies in the existing hierarchical fusion estimation. First, local estimations and the fusion estimation are assumed to be time synchronized, which is restrictive as the processing rates of different clusters may be different from each other. Second, during the estimation interval, each sensor communicates with the local estimator only once, which implies that only one measurement from a sensor can be used for local estimation.

In this chapter, a novel hierarchical fusion estimator design method will be presented, and the method provides two improvements to overcome the aforementioned deficiencies. First, local estimators are not required to be time synchronized and are allowed to be asynchronous with the FC. Second, in each cluster, the sensors transmit as many measurements as possible to the local estimator before an estimation instant begins. In the proposed estimator design method, a centralized optimal estimator is designed to aperiodically generate local estimates. Then, a covariance intersection (CI) fusion strategy is presented to design the fusion estimator by using the last fused estimate and the asynchronous local estimates,

W.-A. Zhang et al., *Distributed Fusion Estimation for Sensor Networks with Communication Constraints*, DOI 10.1007/978-981-10-0795-8_7

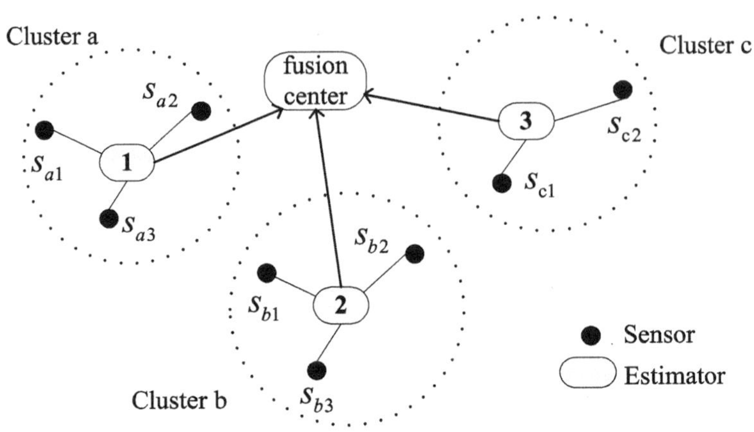

Fig. 7.1 Structure of a hierarchical fusion estimation system

without knowing the cross-covariances among local estimates and the last fusion estimate.

7.2 Centralized Aperiodic Optimal Local Estimation

In this section, a centralized multisensor estimation system in a cluster is considered. Suppose that there are n sensors in a cluster and the sensors connected to an estimator independently observe outputs of a linear continuous-time stochastic process described by the following state-space model:

$$\dot{x}(t) = Ax(t) + Bw(t) \tag{7.1}$$

where $x(t) \in \Re^p$ is the state, $w(t) \in \Re$ is a zero-mean white noise with covariance $Q_w \in \Re > 0$, and A and B are known matrices of appropriate dimensions. Denote by $\mathcal{T} = \{t_k : k = 1, 2, \ldots\}$ the set of estimation instants of the estimator. In view of the time effectiveness of the measurements and the energy consumption of the communications, two rules are set as follows:

Rule 1: At the estimation instant t_{k+1}, only those measurements produced during $(t_k, t_{k+1}]$ will be used for estimation.

Rule 2: In the estimator, the maximum time horizon of the sampled information is δ, i.e., the time horizon of the oldest measurement received by the estimator during $(t_k, t_{k+1}]$ should not be smaller than $t_{k+1} - \delta$.

Rule 1 is set to guarantee the timeliness of the estimation, i.e., only the measurements generated over the present estimation interval will be used to produce the estimate at the present estimation instant. Rule 2 is introduced to specify the allowable number of measurements during each estimation interval (note that more samplings and transmissions need larger energy consumption). Denote by Δ the minimum time interval of two consecutive samplings. To ensure that the estimator is able to use the latest several measurements, δ can be expressed as $\delta = a\Delta + \tilde{\delta}$, where $0 \leq \tilde{\delta} < \Delta$ and a is an integer. Then it follows from Rules 1 and 2 that the set of sampling instants of the sensors during the estimation interval $(t_k, t_{k+1}]$ can be specified as follows:

$$\mathcal{S}_k = \left\{t_{k,j} : t_{k,j} = t_{k+1} - (a_k - j)\Delta,\ j = 1, 2, \ldots, a_k\right\}$$

where $a_k = \min\left\{a, \left\lceil \frac{t_{k+1}-t_k}{\Delta} \right\rceil\right\}$ and $\lceil * \rceil$ denote the maximum integer that is no larger than $*$. Thus, the measurement equation of sensor i at time $t_{k,j}$ is given by

$$y_{k,j}^{(i)} = C^{(i)} x_{k,j} + D^{(i)} v_{k,j}^{(i)} \tag{7.2}$$

where $x_{k,j} = x(t_{k,j})$, $y_{k,j}^{(i)} \in \Re$ is the measurement from sensor i at time $t_{k,j}$, $v_{k,j}^{(i)} \in \Re$ is the measurement noise with zero mean and covariance $Q_v^{(i)} \in \Re > 0$, and $C^{(i)}$ and $D^{(i)}$ are known matrices of appropriate dimensions.

In view of sensor failures or communication link failures, the phenomenon of packet dropout is considered and described by a set of binary variables as follows: $\theta_{k,j}^{(i)} = 1$ if $y_{k,j}^{(i)}$ is successfully received by the estimator at time $t_{k,j}$ and $\theta_{k,j}^{(i)} = 0$ otherwise, where

$$\text{Prob}\left\{\theta_{k,j}^{(i)} = 1\right\} = \lambda_k^{(i)},\ \text{Prob}\left\{\theta_{k,j}^{(i)} = 0\right\} = 1 - \lambda_k^{(i)},\ 0 < \lambda_k^{(i)} \leq 1$$

$\theta_{k,j}^{(i)}$, $i = 1, 2, \ldots, L$, $j = 1, 2, \ldots, a_k$, are assumed to be independent of each other, i.e., the random packet loss procedures over the sensors are independent of each other. $1 - \lambda_k^{(i)}$ is the packet loss probability of sensor i over estimation interval $(t_k, t_{k+1}]$. During $(t_k, t_{k+1}]$, due to possible packet losses, the measurements available at the estimator from sensor i is given by

$$\tilde{y}_k^{(i)} = \left\{\theta_{k,1}^{(i)} y_{k,1}^{(i)}, \ldots, \theta_{k,a_k}^{(i)} y_{k,a_k}^{(i)}\right\}$$

Denote

$$\theta_k^{(i)} = \text{diag}\left\{\theta_{k,j}^{(i)}\right\}_{j=1}^{a_k},\ y_k^{(i)} = \text{vec}^{\text{T}}\left\{y_{k,j}^{(i)}\right\}_{j=1}^{a_k}$$

then, $\tilde{y}_k^{(i)}$ can be written in a vector form as $\tilde{y}_k^{(i)} = \theta_k^{(i)} y_k^{(i)}$.

Discretizing (7.1) at the sampling instants, then it follows from [7] that

$$x_{k,j} = \begin{cases} e^{A(t_{k,1}-t_k)} x_k + w_{k,0},\ j = 1 \\ e^{A\Delta} x_{k,j-1} + w_{k,j-1},\ j = 2, 3, \ldots, a_k \end{cases} \tag{7.3}$$

where

$$w_{k,j} = \begin{cases} \int_0^{t_{k,1}-t_k} e^{A\tau} B w(t_{k,1} - \tau) d\tau, & j = 0 \\ \int_0^{\Delta} e^{A\tau} B w(t_{k,j+1} - \tau) d\tau, & j = 1, 2, \ldots, a_k - 1 \end{cases}$$

It follows from (7.3) that

$$x_{k,j} = e^{A((j-1)\Delta + t_{k,1} - t_k)} x_k + \sum_{l=0}^{j-1} e^{(j-1-l)A\Delta} w_{k,l} \tag{7.4}$$

Thus, over the estimation interval $(t_k, t_{k+1}]$, the measurements available at the estimator from sensor i is given by

$$\theta_k^{(i)} y_k^{(i)} = \theta_k^{(i)} F_k^{(i)} x_k + \theta_k^{(i)} G_k^{(i)} w_k + \theta_k^{(i)} D_k^{(i)} v_k^{(i)} \tag{7.5}$$

where

$$F_k^{(i)} = \text{vec}^{\mathrm{T}} \left\{ \left(C^{(i)} e^{A(j\Delta + t_{k,1} - t_k)} \right)^{\mathrm{T}} \right\}_{j=0}^{a_k - 1}$$

$$G_k^{(i)} = \begin{bmatrix} C^{(i)} & O & \cdots & O \\ C^{(i)} e^{A\Delta} & C^{(i)} & \cdots & O \\ \vdots & \vdots & & \vdots \\ C^{(i)} e^{(a_k-1)A\Delta} & C^{(i)} e^{(a_k-2)A\Delta} & \cdots & C^{(i)} \end{bmatrix}$$

$$D_k^{(i)} = \text{diag} \left\{ \underbrace{D^{(i)}, \ldots, D^{(i)}}_{a_k} \right\}$$

$$w_k = \text{vec}^{\mathrm{T}} \{ w_{k,j} \}_{j=0}^{a_k - 1}$$

$$v_k^{(i)} = \text{vec}^{\mathrm{T}} \left\{ v_{k,j}^{(i)} \right\}_{j=1}^{a_k}$$

By using the local estimate $\hat{x}_k$ and the available measurements $\theta_k^{(i)} y_k^{(i)}$, $i = 1, 2, \ldots, n$, the following linear estimator will be designed to generate an estimate $\hat{x}_{k+1}$ at the estimation instant t_{k+1}

$$\hat{x}_{k+1} = e^{A(t_{k+1} - t_k)} \hat{x}_k + \sum_{i=1}^{n} H_k^{(i)} \left(\theta_k^{(i)} y_k^{(i)} - \tilde{\lambda}_k^{(i)} F_k^{(i)} \hat{x}_k \right) \tag{7.6}$$

where $\tilde{\lambda}_k^{(i)} = \text{diag} \left\{ \underbrace{\lambda_k^{(i)}, \ldots, \lambda_k^{(i)}}_{a_k} \right\}$ and $H_k^{(i)}$, $i = 1, 2, \ldots, n$, are the estimator gains to be determined.

Define the estimation error at t_k by $\varepsilon_k = x_k - \hat{x}_k$, then the estimation error covariance matrix at t_{k+1} is

$$P_{k+1} = \mathbf{E}\left\{\varepsilon_{k+1}\varepsilon_{k+1}^{\mathrm{T}}\right\} \tag{7.7}$$

Then, in what follows, a set of estimator gains $H_k^{(i)}$, $i = 1, 2, \ldots, n$, will be designed for the optimal estimator to generate an estimate $\hat{x}_{k+1}$ in the minimum variance sense, i.e.,

$$H_k^{(i)} = \arg \min_{H_k^{(i)},\, i=1,\ldots,n} \operatorname{tr}\{P_{k+1}\} \tag{7.8}$$

Before presenting the estimation algorithm, two useful propositions are first presented as follows.

Proposition 7.1 *It follows from the statistical characteristics of $w(t)$ that $w_{k,j}$, $j = 0, 1, \ldots, a_k$, are zero mean and*

$$\mathbf{E}\left\{w_{k,0}w_{k,0}^{\mathrm{T}}\right\} = \int_0^{t_{k,1}-t_k} \mathrm{e}^{A\tau}BQ_wB^{\mathrm{T}}\left(\mathrm{e}^{A\tau}\right)^{\mathrm{T}}\mathrm{d}\tau \triangleq W_{k,0} \tag{7.9}$$

$$\mathbf{E}\left\{w_{k,j}w_{k,j}^{\mathrm{T}}\right\} = \int_0^{\Delta} \mathrm{e}^{A\tau}BQ_wB^{\mathrm{T}}\left(\mathrm{e}^{A\tau}\right)^{\mathrm{T}}\mathrm{d}\tau \triangleq W \tag{7.10}$$

Moreover, $w_{k,l}$ is uncorrelated with $w_{k,q}$ for any $l \neq q$.

Proof Note that $\mathbf{E}\{w(t_{k,j}-\tau)w^{\mathrm{T}}(t_{k,j}-\sigma)\} = Q_w$ if $\tau = \sigma$ and $\mathbf{E}\{w(t_{k,j}-\tau)w^{\mathrm{T}}(t_{k,j}-\sigma)\} = 0$ if $\tau \neq \sigma$, then (7.9) and (7.10) hold.

Proposition 7.2 *For any positive semi-definite matrix $Q \geq 0$ with appropriate dimensions, one has*

$$\mathbf{E}\{\theta_k Q \theta_k\} = \lambda_k Q \lambda_k + Q \odot \left(\lambda_k - \lambda_k^2\right) \geq 0 \tag{7.11}$$

$$\mathbf{E}\{(\theta_k - \lambda_k) Q (\theta_k - \lambda_k)\} = Q \odot \left(\lambda_k - \lambda_k^2\right) \geq 0 \tag{7.12}$$

where $\theta_k = \operatorname{diag}\left\{\theta_k^{(i)}\right\}_{i=1}^n$ and $\lambda_k = \operatorname{diag}\left\{\tilde{\lambda}_k^{(i)}\right\}_{i=1}^n$, the symbol $\odot$ denotes the matrix dot product, namely, $\mathcal{A} \odot \mathcal{B} = [\alpha_{ij}\beta_{ij}]_{r_1\times r_2}$, where $\mathcal{A} = [\alpha_{ij}]_{r_1\times r_2}$ and $\mathcal{B} = [\beta_{ij}]_{r_1\times r_2}$. Moreover, $\mathbf{E}\{\theta_k Q \theta_k\}$ is positive definite if $Q > 0$.

Proof Note that $\mathbf{E}\left\{\theta_{k,j}^{(i)}\right\} = \lambda_k^{(i)}$, $\mathbf{E}\left\{\theta_{k,j}^{(i)}\theta_{k,j}^{(i)}\right\} = \lambda_k^{(i)}$, $\mathbf{E}\left\{\theta_{k,j}^{(i)}\theta_{k,l}^{(r)}\right\} = \lambda_k^{(i)}\lambda_k^{(r)}$ $(j \neq l)$, $\mathbf{E}\left\{\left(\theta_{k,j}^{(i)} - \lambda_k^{(i)}\right)\left(\theta_{k,j}^{(i)} - \lambda_k^{(i)}\right)\right\} = \lambda_k^{(i)}\left(1 - \lambda_k^{(i)}\right)$ and $\mathbf{E}\left\{\left(\theta_{k,j}^{(i)} - \lambda_k^{(i)}\right)\left(\theta_{k,l}^{(r)} - \lambda_k^{(r)}\right)\right\} = 0$ $(j \neq l)$, then (7.11) and (7.12) hold.

Denote

$$
\begin{aligned}
H_k &= \text{vec}\left\{H_k^{(i)}\right\}_{i=1}^{n} \\
F_k &= \text{vec}^{\mathrm{T}}\left\{\left(F_k^{(i)}\right)^{\mathrm{T}}\right\}_{i=1}^{n} \\
G_k &= \text{vec}^{\mathrm{T}}\left\{\left(G_k^{(i)}\right)^{\mathrm{T}}\right\}_{i=1}^{n} \\
D_k &= \text{diag}\left\{D_k^{(i)}\right\}_{i=1}^{n} \\
V_k &= \text{diag}\left\{Q_{v,k}^{(i)}\right\}_{i=1}^{n} \\
W_k &= \text{diag}\left\{W_{k,0}, \underbrace{W, \ldots, W}_{a_k-1}\right\} \\
Q_{v,k}^{(i)} &= \text{diag}\left\{\underbrace{Q_v^{(i)}, \ldots, Q_v^{(i)}}_{a_k}\right\} \\
y_k &= \text{vec}^{\mathrm{T}}\left\{\left(\theta_k^{(i)} y_k^{(i)}\right)^{\mathrm{T}}\right\}_{i=1}^{n} \\
v_k &= \text{vec}^{\mathrm{T}}\left\{\left(v_k^{(i)}\right)^{\mathrm{T}}\right\}_{i=1}^{n}
\end{aligned}
$$

The following theorem determines the estimator gains in the minimum variance sense and the estimation error covariance matrix at each estimation instant.

Theorem 7.1 *For system (7.1) and (7.2), the gains of the optimal estimator (7.6) is determined by*

$$
H_k = \Theta_k^{\mathrm{T}}\left(\sum_{i=1}^{4} \Gamma_k^{(i)}\right)^{-1} \tag{7.13}
$$

with the corresponding estimation error covariance matrix

$$
P_{k+1} = \varphi_k P_k \varphi_k^{\mathrm{T}} + \Omega_k W_k \Omega_k^{\mathrm{T}} - \Theta_k^{\mathrm{T}}\left(\sum_{i=1}^{4} \Gamma_k^{(i)}\right)^{-1} \Theta_k \tag{7.14}
$$

where

$$
\begin{aligned}
\varphi_k &= \mathrm{e}^{A(t_{k+1}-t_k)} \\
\Theta_k &= \lambda_k F_k P_k \varphi_k^{\mathrm{T}} + \lambda_k G_k W_k \Omega_k^{\mathrm{T}} \\
\Gamma_k^{(1)} &= \lambda_k F_k P_k F_k^{\mathrm{T}} \lambda_k^{\mathrm{T}} \\
\Gamma_k^{(2)} &= \left(F_k X_k F_k^{\mathrm{T}}\right) \odot \left(\lambda_k - \lambda_k^2\right) \\
\Gamma_k^{(3)} &= \lambda_k G_k W_k G_k^{\mathrm{T}\lambda_k} + \left(G_k W_k G_k^{\mathrm{T}}\right) \odot \left(\lambda_k - \lambda_k^2\right) \\
\Gamma_k^{(4)} &= \lambda_k D_k V_k D_k^{\mathrm{T}\lambda_k} + \left(D_k V_k D_k^{\mathrm{T}}\right) \odot \left(\lambda_k - \lambda_k^2\right) \\
\Omega_k &= \left[\, \mathrm{e}^{(a_k-1)A\Delta} \ \mathrm{e}^{(a_k-2)A\Delta} \ \cdots \ I \,\right] \\
X_{k+1} &= \mathbf{E}\left\{x_{k+1} x_{k+1}^{\mathrm{T}}\right\} = \varphi_k X_k \varphi_k^{\mathrm{T}} + \Omega_k W_k \Omega_k^{\mathrm{T}}
\end{aligned}
$$

Moreover, the local optimal estimates obtained by using (7.6) and (7.13) are unbiased.

Proof Note that

$$x_{k+1} = \mathrm{e}^{A(t_{k+1}-t_k)} x_k + \Omega_k w_k \tag{7.15}$$

$$\hat{x}_{k+1} = \mathrm{e}^{A(t_{k+1}-t_k)} \hat{x}_k + H_k \left(y_k - \lambda_k F_k \hat{x}_k\right) \tag{7.16}$$

$$y_k = \theta_k F_k x_k + \theta_k G_k w_k + \theta_k D_k v_k \tag{7.17}$$

By using Propositions 7.1 and 7.2, it follows from (7.7), (7.15), (7.16), and (7.17) that

$$
\begin{aligned}
P_{k+1} = {} & \varphi_k P_k \varphi_k^{\mathrm{T}} + \Omega_k W_k \Omega_k^{\mathrm{T}} - H_k \Theta_k \\
& - \Theta_k^{\mathrm{T}} H_k^{\mathrm{T}} + H_k \left(\sum_{i=1}^{4} \Gamma_k^{(i)}\right) H_k^{\mathrm{T}}
\end{aligned} \tag{7.18}
$$

Denote

$$
\begin{aligned}
\Theta_k &= \mathrm{vec}\left\{\Theta_k^{(i)}\right\}_{i=1}^{p} \\
H_k &= \mathrm{vec}^{\mathrm{T}}\left\{\left(h_k^{(i)}\right)^{\mathrm{T}}\right\}_{i=1}^{p} \\
\varphi_k &= \mathrm{vec}^{\mathrm{T}}\left\{\left(\varphi_k^{(i)}\right)^{\mathrm{T}}\right\}_{i=1}^{p} \\
\Omega_k &= \mathrm{vec}^{\mathrm{T}}\left\{\left(\Omega_k^{(i)}\right)^{\mathrm{T}}\right\}_{i=1}^{p}
\end{aligned}
$$

then one has $\mathrm{tr}\{P_{k+1}\} = \sum_{i=1}^{p} \pi_{k+1}^{(i)}$, where

$$\pi_{k+1}^{(i)} = \varphi_k^{(i)} P_k \left(\varphi_k^{(i)}\right)^{\mathrm{T}} + \Omega_k^{(i)} W_k \left(\Omega_k^{(i)}\right)^{\mathrm{T}} + h_k^{(i)} \left(\sum_{i=1}^{4} \Gamma_k^{(i)}\right) \left(h_k^{(i)}\right)^{\mathrm{T}}$$
$$-h_k^{(i)} \Theta_k^{(i)} - \left(\Theta_k^{(i)}\right)^{\mathrm{T}} \left(h_k^{(i)}\right)^{\mathrm{T}}$$

Note that $\pi_{k+1}^{(i)}$ depends only on $h_k^{(i)}$, and the trace of P_{k+1} is equivalent to the summation of $\pi_{k+1}^{(i)}$, $i = 1, 2, \ldots, n$. To minimize the trace of P_{k+1}, the condition $\partial \pi_{k+1}^{(i)} \Big/ \partial \left(h_k^{(i)}\right)^{\mathrm{T}} = 0$ should be satisfied, from which one has

$$h_k^{(i)} = \left(\Theta_k^{(i)}\right)^{\mathrm{T}} \left(\sum_{i=1}^{4} (\Gamma_k^{(i)})^{\mathrm{T}}\right)^{-1} \tag{7.19}$$

which implies that (7.13) holds. Substituting (7.13) into (7.19) yields (7.14). The proof is thus completed.

7.3 Hierarchical Asynchronous Fusion Estimation

This section is devoted to the hierarchical fusion estimation. A fusion strategy based on the asynchronous local estimates will be presented to generate the fused estimates. A clustered sensor network is deployed to measure outputs of the object (7.1) and is divided into L clusters. Denote by n_r the number of sensors in the rth cluster. The sensors within the same cluster are connected to a local estimator, and a FC is linked with the L local estimators.

Firstly, the local estimator r collects measurements from sensors in the rth cluster during each estimation interval and generates a local estimate at the estimation instant. Secondly, all local estimates are sent to the fusion center for generating the fused estimate. Denote by $\mathcal{T}_{fc} = \left\{t_k^{fc} : k = 1, 2, \ldots\right\}$ the set of the fusion instants of the fusion center and $\mathcal{T}_r = \{t_{r,k} : k = 1, 2, \ldots\}$ the set of the estimation instants of the local estimator r. The fusion instants and the local estimation instants are not necessarily synchronous. Denote by $\hat{x}_{r,k}$ and $P_{r,k}$ the local estimate and the local estimation error covariance matrix of the local estimator r generated by Theorem 7.1 at time $t_{r,k}$, respectively.

For each cluster, it is assumed that all the local estimates are sent to the fusion center in real time, and only the most recent local estimate received by FC during $\left(t_k^{fc}, t_{k+1}^{fc}\right]$ will be used for fusion at fusion instant t_{k+1}^{fc}. Denote by $\mathcal{U}_{r,k+1} =$

$\left\{t_{r,k} : t_k^{fc} < t_{r,k} \leq t_{k+1}^{fc},\ t_{r,k} \in \mathcal{T}_r\right\}$ the set of time instants when the local estimates are generated by the local estimator r during $\left(t_k^{fc}, t_{k+1}^{fc}\right]$. If $\bigcap_{r=1}^{L} \mathcal{U}_{r,k+1} = \varnothing$, then, it indicates that no local estimate is sent to the FC. If $\bigcap_{r=1}^{L} \mathcal{U}_{r,k+1} \neq \varnothing$, then the set of available local estimates at the FC during the fusion interval $\left(t_k^{fc}, t_{k+1}^{fc}\right]$ is denoted by

$$\mathcal{X}_{k+1} = \{\hat{x}_{r,k+1}^{e} = \hat{x}(t_{r,k+1}^{e}) : t_{r,k+1}^{e} = \max \mathcal{U}_{r,k+1},\ \mathcal{U}_{r,k+1} \neq \varnothing,\ r = 1, 2 \ldots, L\}$$

Then, the fusion rules are set as follows:

Case 1: If $\bigcap_{r=1}^{L} \mathcal{U}_{r,k+1} = \varnothing$, then $\hat{x}_{k+1}^{fc} = f_1\left(\hat{x}_k^{fc}\right) \in \mathcal{L}\left(\hat{x}_k^{fc}\right)$

Case 2: If $\bigcap_{r=1}^{L} \mathcal{U}_{r,s+1} \neq \varnothing$, then $\hat{x}_{k+1}^{fc} = f_2\left(\hat{x}_k^{fc}, \mathcal{X}_{k+1}\right) \in \mathcal{L}\left(\hat{x}_k^{fc}, \mathcal{X}_{k+1}\right)$,

where $\hat{x}_k^{fc}$ is the fused estimate at t_k^{fc} and $f_1(\cdot)$ and $f_2(\cdot)$ denote the fusion rules to be designed. For Case 1, the fusion rule is given by

$$f_1\left(\hat{x}_k^{fc}\right) = \mathrm{e}^{A\left(t_{k+1}^{fc} - t_k^{fc}\right)} \hat{x}_k^{fc} \tag{7.20}$$

For Case 2, the local estimates in $\mathcal{X}_{k+1}$ are first lifted to those at the fusion instant, i.e.,

$$\hat{x}_{r,k+1}^{fc} = \mathrm{e}^{A\left(t_{k+1}^{fc} - t_{r,k+1}^{e}\right)} \hat{x}_{r,k+1}^{e} \tag{7.21}$$

Then, by using the CI fusion method [8, 9], the fusion rule in Case 2 is given by

$$f_2\left(\hat{x}_k^{fc}, \mathcal{X}_{r,k+1}\right) = P_{k+1}^{fc} \sum_{r \in \mathcal{T}_{k+1}^{fc}} \alpha_{r,k+1} \left(P_{r,k+1}^{fc}\right)^{-1} \hat{x}_{r,k+1}^{fc} \tag{7.22}$$

where

$$\begin{aligned}
\hat{x}_{0,k+1}^{fc} &= \mathrm{e}^{A\left(t_{k+1}^{fc} - t_k^{fc}\right)} \hat{x}_k^{fc} \\
P_{0,k+1}^{fc} &= \mathrm{e}^{A\left(t_{k+1}^{fc} - t_k^{fc}\right)} P_k^{fc} \left(\mathrm{e}^{A\left(t_{k+1}^{fc} - t_k^{fc}\right)}\right)^{\mathrm{T}} + \tilde{W}_{0,k} \\
P_{r,k+1}^{fc} &= \mathrm{e}^{A\left(t_{k+1}^{fc} - t_{r,k+1}^{e}\right)} P_{r,k+1} \left(\mathrm{e}^{A\left(t_{k+1}^{fc} - t_{r,k+1}^{e}\right)}\right)^{\mathrm{T}} + \tilde{W}_{r,k} \\
\tilde{W}_{0,k} &= \int_0^{t_{k+1}^{fc} - t_k^{fc}} \mathrm{e}^{A\tau} B Q_w B^{\mathrm{T}} \left(\mathrm{e}^{A\tau}\right)^{\mathrm{T}} d\tau
\end{aligned}$$

$$\tilde{W}_{r,k} = \int_0^{t_{k+1}^{fc}-t_{r,k+1}} \mathrm{e}^{A\tau} B Q_w B^{\mathrm{T}} \left(\mathrm{e}^{A\tau}\right)^{\mathrm{T}} d\tau, r \in \mathcal{T}_{k+1}^{fc}/\{0\}$$

$$\left(P_{k+1}^{fc}\right)^{-1} = \sum_{r\in\mathcal{T}_{k+1}^{fc}} \alpha_{r,k+1}\left(P_{r,k+1}^{fc}\right)^{-1}$$

and $\mathcal{T}_{k+1}^{fc} = \{0\}\bigcup\{r : \mathcal{U}_{r,k+1} \neq \varnothing,\ r = 1, 2 \ldots, L\}$. The optimal weights $\alpha_{r,k+1}$ and $r \in \mathcal{T}_{k+1}^{fc}$ are determined by minimizing the trace of P_{k+1}^{fc}:

$$\begin{aligned} &\min\ \operatorname{tr}\left\{P_{k+1}^{fc}\right\} \\ &\text{s.t. } 0 \le \alpha_r \le 1 \text{ and } \sum_{r\in\mathrm{T}_{k+1}^{fc}} \alpha_{r,k+1} = 1 \end{aligned} \tag{7.23}$$

Different from the conventional CI fusion rule with only local estimates, past fused estimates are used for generating the fusion estimate at current fusion instant in both Cases 1 and 2.

Similar to the analysis in [9], for system (7.1) and (7.2), the actual fusion estimation error variance $\bar{P}_{k+1}^{fc}$ satisfies $\bar{P}_{k+1}^{fc} \le P_{k+1}^{fc}$. Moreover, the following accuracy relation

$$\operatorname{tr}\left(\bar{P}_{k+1}^{fc}\right) \le \operatorname{tr}\left(P_{k+1}^{fc}\right) \le \min_{r\in\mathcal{T}_{k+1}^{fc}} \left\{\operatorname{tr}\left(P_{r,k+1}^{fc}\right)\right\} \tag{7.24}$$

holds, which means that the actual fusion accuracy is higher than that of each local estimator and has an upper bound $\operatorname{tr}\left(P_{k+1}^{fc}\right)$.

7.4 Simulations

Consider a continuous-time linear stochastic system described by

$$\begin{cases} \dot{x}_1(t) = -0.3x_1(t) - 0.1x_2(t) + w(t) \\ \dot{x}_2(t) = -0.2x_2(t) - 0.15x_3(t) + 0.5w(t) \\ \dot{x}_3(t) = 0.1x_2(t) - 0.25x_3(t) + 0.75w(t) \end{cases} \tag{7.25}$$

where $x_i(t) \in \Re$, $i = 1, 2, 3$, are the states of the system, $w(t) \in \Re$ is the process noise with zero mean and covariance $Q_w = 1$. A clustered sensor network consisting of nine sensors is deployed to measure outputs of the system. The sensors are divided into three clusters, and the numbers of the sensors in each cluster are 2,

3, and 4. The measurement equations are given by (7.2) with

$$C_1^{(1)} = [1\ 0\ 0],\ C_1^{(2)} = [0\ 1\ 0]$$
$$C_2^{(1)} = [1\ 0\ 0],\ C_2^{(2)} = [0\ 1\ 0],\ C_2^{(3)} = [0\ 0\ 1]$$
$$C_3^{(1)} = [1\ 0\ 0],\ C_3^{(2)} = [0\ 1\ 0],\ C_3^{(3)} = [0\ 0\ 1],\ C_3^{(4)} = [1\ 0\ 1]$$
$$D_r^{(i)} = 0.1,\ r = 1, 2, 3,\ i = 1, 2 \ldots, n_r$$

The observation noises are zero mean with $Q_{v,r}^{(i)} = 1$. The minimum sampling period of the sensors is $\Delta = 1$ s, and the estimation periods of the clusters 1, 2, and 3 are 3 s, 4 s, and 5 s, respectively. The maximum time horizons of the allowable sampled information are $\delta_1 = 2$ s, $\delta_2 = 3$ s, and $\delta_3 = 4$ s. Given the initial local estimation error covariance matrices $P_{r,0} = \text{diag}\{5, 5, 5\}$, $r = 1, 2, 3$. The traces of the fusion estimation error covariance matrices under different packet dropout rates are depicted in Fig. 7.2, which shows that a smaller packet dropout rate results in a better fusion estimation performance. Figure 7.3 shows that the accuracy of the proposed fusion rule is higher than that of each local estimator. Compared with the centralized estimation, the performance loss due to the hierarchical network structure is also shown in Fig. 7.3. Figure 7.4 implies that the precisions of local estimators with multiple samplings are higher than that of single sampling ones.

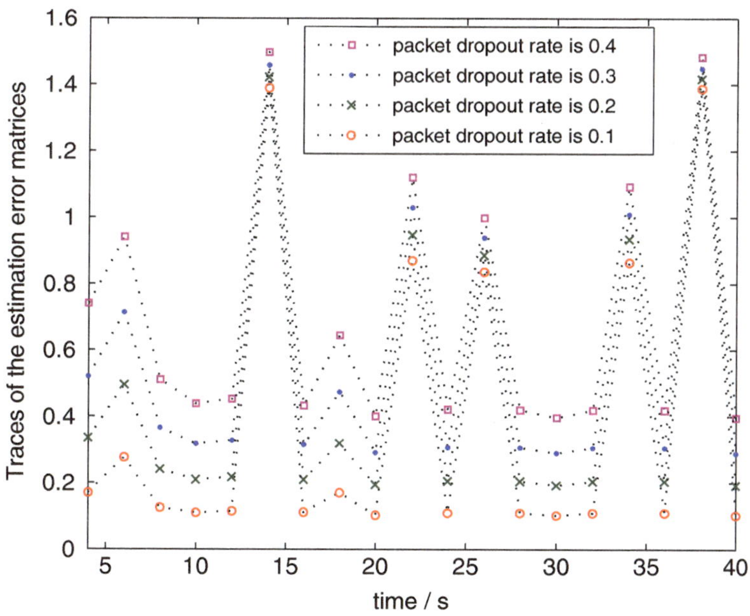

Fig. 7.2 Traces of the fusion estimation error covariance matrices under different packet dropout rates

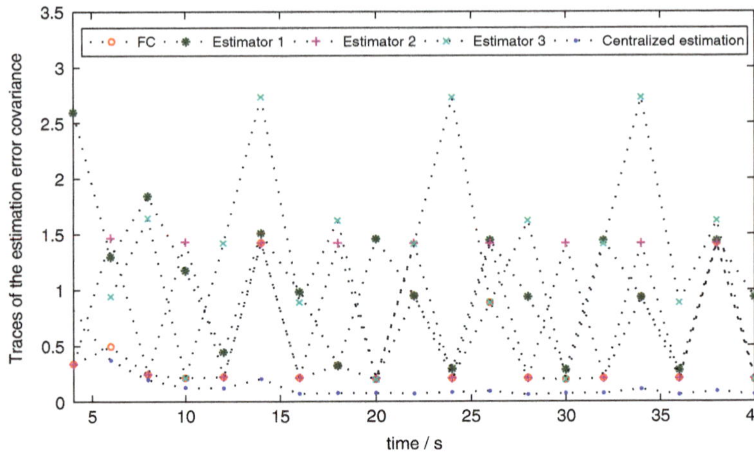

Fig. 7.3 Comparison of the traces of the estimation error covariance matrices

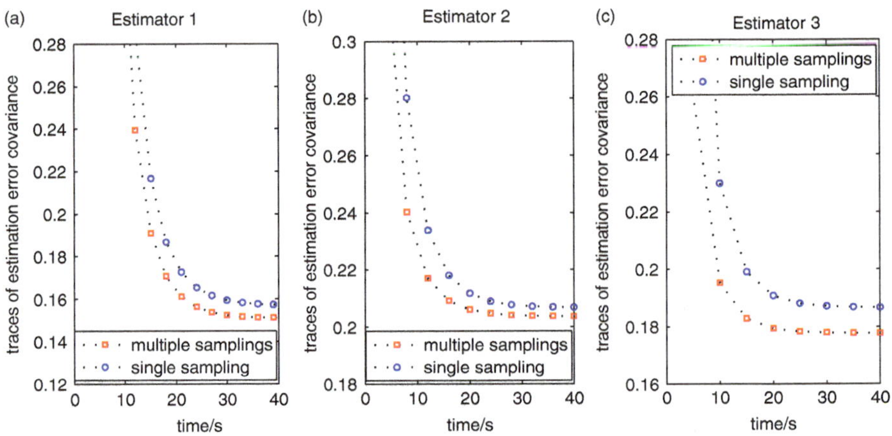

Fig. 7.4 Comparison of the traces of local estimation error covariance matrices with multiple samplings and single sampling

7.5 Conclusions

This chapter presents a hierarchical fusion estimator design method for clustered sensor networks, where local estimators and the fusion center are allowed to be asynchronous. Optimal local estimators were designed in the minimum variance sense, and a CI fusion strategy was presented to fuse both local estimates and past fused estimates.

References

1. Bar-Shalom Y, Li XR (1990) Multitarget-multisensor tracking: advanced applications, vol 1. Artech House, Norwood
2. Sun SL, Deng ZL (2004) Multi-sensor optimal information fusion Kalman filter. Automatica 40(6):1017–1023
3. Ahmad A, Gani M, Yang F (2008) Decentralized robust Kalman filtering for uncertain stochastic systems over heterogeneous sensor networks. Signal Process 88(8):1919–1928
4. Fang J, Li H (2009) Power constrained distributed estimation with cluster-based sensor collaboration. IEEE Trans Wirel Commun 8(7):3822–3832
5. Zhang P, Qi W, Deng Z (2015) Hierarchical fusion robust Kalman filter for clustering sensor network time-varying systems with uncertain noise variances. Int J Adapt Control Signal Process 29(1):99–122
6. Chaudhary MH, Vandendorpe L (2013) Performance of power-constrained estimation in hierarchical wireless wensor networks. IEEE Trans Signal Process 61(3):724–739
7. Chen CT (1999) Linear systems theory and design, 3rd edn. Oxford University Press, New York
8. Julier SJ, Uhlman JK (2009) General decentralized data fusion with covariance intersection. In: Liggins ME, Hall DL, Llinas J (eds) Handbook of multisensor data fusion. Theory and practice, 2nd edn. CRC Press, Boca Raton, pp 319–343
9. Deng ZL, Zhang P, Qi W, Liu J, Gao Y (2012) Sequential covariance intersection fusion Kalman filter. Inf Sci 189(4):293–309

Chapter 8
Fusion Estimation for WSNs with Delayed Measurements

8.1 Introduction

In this chapter, a state fusion estimator design method will be introduced for multisensor systems with measurement delays, which is usually inevitable in sensor networks. Due to delays in the measurements, it is difficult to construct an innovation sequence that is still white Gaussian as usually does in the standard Kalman filter. Therefore, many research works have been devoted to the design of optimal linear estimators for time-delay systems by using the innovation analysis approach and linear matrix inequality approach [1–7]. For the multisensor case, the information fusion problem has been investigated in [8, 9] for linear stochastic systems with time-delayed measurements, where the observation delays were assumed to be constant. Recently, based on the well-known federated filter, a practical architecture and some algorithms have been discussed in [10] for the networked data fusion systems with packet losses and variable delays, where one has to know the accurate time delay over each estimation interval. Most of the aforementioned results use the measurement augmentation method to deal with the delayed measurements, which increases the dimension of the measurement used in the state estimation and ultimately increases computation costs. On the other hand, the parameters of the system model may not be precisely known in practical applications due to a number of reasons such as model reduction and varying parameters. The parameter uncertainties in the system model degrade the performance of conventional information fusion estimators. Therefore, it is necessary to develop robust information fusion estimators. However, only a few results [11–14] were concerned with the robust information fusion problem for multisensor systems with parameter uncertainties. In [12, 13], the robust information fusion Kalman filtering problem was investigated for uncertain stochastic systems, where the deterministic parameter perturbations were considered in the system matrices. In view of the above consideration, a novel state fusion estimator will be designed in this chapter for multisensor systems with delayed measurements

W.-A. Zhang et al., *Distributed Fusion Estimation for Sensor Networks with Communication Constraints*, DOI 10.1007/978-981-10-0795-8_8

and parameter uncertainties without resorting to the measurement augmentation approach. The robust distributed estimator is derived by using the optimal fusion algorithm weighted by matrices in the linear minimum variance sense, and the dimension of the designed fusion estimator is the same as the system state, which helps reduce computation costs as compared with the augmentation method.

8.2 Problem Statement

Consider a discrete-time linear system with stochastic parameter perturbations described by the following state-space model:

$$x(t+1) = \left(A + \sum_{\vartheta=1}^{\hbar} A_{\vartheta} \alpha_{\vartheta}(t) \right) x(t) + \Gamma w(t) \tag{8.1}$$

where $x(t) \in \Re^{n}$ is the state; $A \in \Re^{n \times n}$ and $A_{\vartheta} \in \Re^{n \times n}$, $\vartheta = 1, 2, \ldots, \hbar$ are known matrices with appropriate dimensions; and $\Gamma \subset \Re^{n \times 1}$ is a constant matrix. The scalar $w(t)$ is a zero-mean white noise with covariance Q_w. The random sequences $\alpha_{\vartheta}(t)$, $\vartheta = 1, 2, \ldots, \hbar$ are introduced to describe the uncertainty of the system model; they are of zero mean and with variance θ_{ϑ} and are mutually uncorrelated.

Suppose that L sensors are deployed to monitor the outputs of system (8.1) and the measurement equations are given by

$$\tilde{y}_i(t) = H_i x(t), \; i = 1, 2, \ldots, L \tag{8.2}$$

where $H_i \in \Re^{m_i \times n}$ are constant matrices. The measurement $\tilde{y}_i(t)$ is transmitted to the local estimators via communication channels and may be delayed during transmission. Denote the random time delay in the ith channel as $\tau_i(t) = d_i(t)\mathrm{T}$, where T is the sampling period and $d_i(t)$ takes values from a finite set $\{0, 1, \ldots, d^i\}$. This means that the delay is assumed to be bounded, and the upper bound is d^i. Due to the random delays, several measurements from sensor i, $i \in 1, 2, \ldots, L$ may arrive at the estimator over an estimation interval. It is assumed that only the most recent measurement from sensor i, $i \in 1, 2, \ldots, L$, is adopted to generate a local state estimate $\hat{x}_i$ and the other measurements from sensor i will be discarded. Then, the measurement received by the estimator from sensor i is given by

$$y_i(t) = H_i x(t - d_i(t)) + D_i v_i(t) \tag{8.3}$$

where $v_i(t)$ is the noise from the communication channel and is assumed to be a zero-mean white noise with variance R_{v_i}.

The random delay $\{d_i(t)\}$ is assumed to be i.i.d. (independent and identically distributed) [15], and the occurrence probabilities of the delays are known a priori through statistical test, that is,

$$\text{Prob}\{d_i(t) = \ell\} = \pi_\ell^i,\ \ell = 0, 1, \ldots, d^i \tag{8.4}$$

Moreover, the following assumptions are needed in developing the main results.

Assumption 8.1 The random delays $d_i(t),\ i = 1, 2, \ldots, L$ are mutually independent and uncorrelated with $w(t)$, $v_i(t)$, and $\alpha_\vartheta(t)$.

Assumption 8.2 The random variables $v_i(t)$ are uncorrelated with $w(t)$ and $\alpha_\vartheta(t)$, and the random correlated variables $v_1(t), \ldots, v_L(t)$ satisfy

$$\mathbf{E}\{v_i(t)v_j^{\mathrm{T}}(t)\} = S_{ij}(i \neq j)$$

Assumption 8.3 Define $d = \max\{d^1, d^2, \ldots, d^L\}$, then the initial states $x(-t),\ t = 0, 1, \ldots, d-1$ are uncorrelated with $w(t)$, $v_i(t)$, $\alpha_\vartheta(t)$, and $d_i(t)$.

Since $d_i(t)$ takes only one value in $\{0, 1, \ldots, d^i\}$ randomly over an estimation interval, the following random binary-valued update function is introduced to describe the random delays in (8.3):

$$\sigma_{\{d_i(t)=\ell\}} = \begin{cases} 1, & d_i(t) = \ell \\ 0, & d_i(t) \neq \ell \end{cases} \quad \ell \in \{0, 1, \ldots, d\} \tag{8.5}$$

and $\sigma_{\{d_i(t)=\ell\}}$ satisfies the following property:

$$\sigma_{\{d_i(t)=\ell_1\}} \times \sigma_{\{d_i(t)=\ell_2\}} = 0,\ \ell_1 \neq \ell_2 \tag{8.6}$$

Then by (8.4) and (8.5), one has

$$\mathbf{E}\{\sigma_{\{d_i(t)=\ell\}} = 1\} = \text{Prob}\{d_i(t) = \ell\} = \pi_\ell^i \tag{8.7}$$

and the output equation (8.3) can be rewritten as

$$y_i(t) = H_i \sum_{\ell=0}^{d} \sigma_{\{d_i(t)=\ell\}} x(t-\ell) + D_i v_i(t) \tag{8.8}$$

It can be seen from (8.5) that $\sum_{\ell=0}^{d} \sigma_{\{d_i(t)=\ell\}} = 1$ if $d_i(t) \leq d$, which means that at least one measurement will be used by the estimator for generating a state estimate if the delay $d_i(t)$ is under the maximal bound d. In case that the delay $d_i(t)$ exceeds the maximal allowable upper bound d, that is, $d_i(t) > d$, then the packet containing the measurement will be considered to be lost, and only the noise $D_i v_i(t)$ will be used in generating the state estimates. In this case, one has by (8.5) that $\sum_{\ell=0}^{d} \sigma_{\{d_i(t)=\ell\}} = 0$

since $d_i(t) \neq l$. Therefore, one has

$$\sum_{\ell=0}^{d} \sigma_{\{d_i(t)=\ell\}} \in \{0, 1\}$$

Let

$$\text{Prob}\left\{\sum_{\ell=0}^{d} \sigma_{\{d_i(t)=\ell\}} = 1\right\} = \gamma_i, \text{ Prob}\left\{\sum_{\ell=0}^{d} \sigma_{\{d_i(t)=\ell\}} = 0\right\} = 1 - \gamma_i$$

Then, $1 - \gamma_i$ is defined as the packet loss rate.

Rewriting the state-space model (8.1) as the following compact form

$$x(t+1) = Ax(t) + \Omega(t) \tag{8.9}$$

where

$$\Omega(t) = \sum_{\vartheta=1}^{\hbar} A_\vartheta \alpha_\vartheta(t)x(t) + \Gamma w(t)$$

Then, it follows from Assumptions 8.1 and 8.2 that

$$\begin{aligned}
&\mathbf{E}\{\Omega(t)\} = 0, \mathbf{E}\{\Omega(t)v_i(t_1)\} = 0, \ \forall\ t, t_1 \\
&\mathbf{E}\{\Omega(t)\Omega^{\mathrm{T}}(t_1)\} = 0, \ \forall t \neq t_1 \\
&\mathbf{E}\{\Omega(t)\sigma_{\{d_i(t_1)=\ell\}}\} = 0, \ \forall t, t_1
\end{aligned} \tag{8.10}$$

which implies that $\Omega(t)$ is a zero-mean white noise and uncorrelated with other random variables. To calculate the covariance matrix of $\Omega(t)$, define

$$\Lambda(t, t) = \mathbf{E}\{x(t)x^{\mathrm{T}}(t)\}$$

Since $\alpha_\vartheta(t)$ and $w(t)$ are mutually uncorrelated white noises, $\Lambda(t, t)$ can be directly computed as follows:

$$\Lambda(t+1, t+1) = A\Lambda(t, t)A^{\mathrm{T}} + \Gamma Q_w \Gamma^{\mathrm{T}} + \sum_{\vartheta=1}^{\hbar} \theta_\vartheta A_\vartheta \Lambda(t, t)A_\vartheta^{\mathrm{T}} \tag{8.11}$$

Then the covariance matrix of $\Omega(t)$ is given by

$$\Sigma(t) = \mathbf{E}\{\Omega(t)\Omega^{\mathrm{T}}(t)\} = \sum_{\vartheta=1}^{\hbar} \theta_\vartheta A_\vartheta \Lambda(t, t)A_\vartheta^{\mathrm{T}} + \Gamma Q_w \Gamma^{\mathrm{T}} \tag{8.12}$$

In this chapter, the robust information fusion Kalman filtering problem for multisensor systems is described as follows: first, design a local optimal filter for system (8.1) based on $\{y_i(1),\ldots,y_i(t)\}$ such that

$$\min_{\hat{x}^i(t|t)}\{\mathbf{E}(\hat{x}^i(t|t)-x(t))^{\mathrm{T}}(\hat{x}^i(t|t)-x(t))\} \tag{8.13}$$

where $\hat{x}^i(t|t)$ is the local optimal state estimate. Second, design a fusion estimator with matrix weights in the form

$$\hat{x}(t|t)=\sum_{i=1}^{L}\bar{A}_i(t)\hat{x}^i(t|t) \tag{8.14}$$

where $\bar{A}_1(t),\bar{A}_2(t),\ldots,\bar{A}_L(t)$ are optimal weighting matrices to be designed such that the following function

$$\mathrm{Tr}(P(t|t))=\mathrm{Tr}(\mathbf{E}\{(x(t)-\hat{x}(t|t))(x(t)-\hat{x}(t|t))^{\mathrm{T}}) \tag{8.15}$$

is minimized, and $\mathbf{E}\{\hat{x}(t|t)\}=\mathbf{E}\{x(t)\}$.

Note that the random delay takes values in a finite set, the systems (8.1) and (8.3) can be transformed into a certain higher-order one by augmenting the measurements, and then the full-order fusion filter may be designed for the augmented system in a centralized framework by using the results of [11]. However, the centralized framework by using results of [11] may bring expensive computational cost and large memory space with the increase of communication delays and the number of sensors. Therefore, without resorting to the augmentation method, a recursive information fusion estimator will be designed in the following sections under the distributed state fusion framework of [16], and the dimension of the fusion filter is the same as the system state to be estimated.

8.3 Preliminary Results

In this section, some useful lemmas will be provided as follows before presenting the main results. Define the estimation error as $\tilde{x}^i(t_1|t)=x(t_1)-\hat{x}^i(t_1|t)$ and the innovation sequence as $\varepsilon^i(t)=y_i(t)-\hat{y}_i(t|t-1)$, then the following operators

$$\begin{aligned}\Phi_t^{i,j}(t_1,t_2)&=\mathbf{E}\{\tilde{x}^i(t_1|t)(\tilde{x}^j(t_2|t))^{\mathrm{T}}\}\\ G^{i,j}(t)&=\mathbf{E}\{\varepsilon^i(t)(\varepsilon^j(t))^{\mathrm{T}}\}\end{aligned}$$

are introduced, where $\hat{x}^i(t_1|t)$ is the ith linear minimum variance estimate of state $x(t_1)$ and $\hat{y}_i(t|t-1)$ is the ith linear minimum variance estimate of observation $y_i(t)$.

By the definition of the operator $\Phi_t^{i,j}(t_1,t_2)$, the local optimal prediction error covariance matrices are given by

$$P^i(t-\phi|t) \triangleq \Phi_t^{i,i}(t-\phi,t-\phi),\ \phi=-1,0,1,\dots,d-1$$

while the estimation error cross-covariance matrices between the ith and jth local estimates are given by

$$P^{i,j}(t-\phi|t) \triangleq \Phi_t^{i,j}(t-\phi,t-\phi),\ \phi=-1,0,1,\dots,d-1$$

Some useful notations are first given as follows.

$$\begin{aligned}
\Pi_\lambda^i(t) &\triangleq \mathbf{E}\{\varepsilon^i(t)(x(t-\lambda))^{\mathrm{T}}\}\\
\breve{\Pi}_\lambda(t) &\triangleq \mathbf{E}\{\varepsilon^i(t)(\tilde{x}^j(t-\lambda|t-1))^{\mathrm{T}}\}\\
\widehat{\Pi}_\lambda(t) &\triangleq \mathbf{E}\{\tilde{x}^i(t-\lambda|t-1)(\varepsilon^j(t))^{\mathrm{T}}\}\\
\mathrm{K}_\lambda^i(t) &\triangleq \mathbf{E}\{x(t-\lambda)(\varepsilon^i(t))^{\mathrm{T}}\}(G^{i,i}(t))^{-1}\\
\mathrm{N}_\lambda^i(t) &\triangleq \Phi_t^{i,i}(t,t-\lambda+1)\\
\breve{\mathrm{N}}_\lambda(t) &\triangleq \Phi_t^{i,j}(t-\lambda+1,t)\\
\widehat{\mathrm{N}}_\lambda(t) &\triangleq \Phi_t^{i,j}(t,t-\lambda+1)\\
\Theta_\tau^i(t,\ell) &\triangleq \Phi_t^{i,i}(t+1-\ell,t-\ell-\tau)\\
\widehat{\Theta}_\tau^{i,j}(t,\ell) &\triangleq \Phi_t^{i,j}(t+1-\ell,t-\ell-\tau)\\
\breve{\Theta}_\tau^{i,j}(t,\ell) &\triangleq \Phi_t^{i,j}(t-\ell-\tau,t+1-\ell)
\end{aligned}$$

Lemma 8.1 *Define*

$$\Lambda(t+1-\ell,t-\ell-\tau)=\mathbf{E}\{x(t+1-\ell)x^{\mathrm{T}}(t-\ell-\tau)\}$$

Then for $\ell=0,1,\dots,d-1$, $\Lambda(t+1-\ell,t-\ell-\tau)$ *satisfies*

$$\begin{aligned}
&\Lambda(t+1-\ell,t-\ell-\tau)=A^{\tau+1}\Lambda(t-\ell-\tau,t-\ell-\tau),\\
&\tau=0,1,\dots,d-\ell-1
\end{aligned}\tag{8.16}$$

where $\Lambda(t-\ell-\tau,t-\ell-\tau)$ *is computed by (8.11).*

Proof Equation (8.16) can be easily followed by the state equation (8.8) and Assumptions 8.1 and 8.2. The proof is thus completed.

Lemma 8.2 *For* $\lambda = 2, 3, \ldots d$, $\mathrm{N}^i_\lambda(t)$, $\breve{\mathrm{N}}^i_\lambda(t)$, $\widehat{\mathrm{N}}^i_\lambda(t)$ *can be computed by the following recursive equations:*

$$\mathrm{N}^i_\lambda(t) = A\mathrm{N}^i_{\lambda-1}(t-1) - \mathrm{K}^i(t)\Pi^i_{\lambda-1}(t) \tag{8.17}$$

$$\begin{aligned}\breve{\mathrm{N}}_\lambda(t) &= \breve{\mathrm{N}}_{\lambda-1}(t-1)A^{\mathrm{T}} + \mathrm{K}^i_{\lambda-1}(t)G^{i,j}(t)(\mathrm{K}^j(t))^{\mathrm{T}} \\ &\quad -\mathrm{K}^i_{\lambda-1}(t)\breve{\Pi}_0(t) - \widehat{\Pi}_{\lambda-1}(t)(\mathrm{K}^j(t))^{\mathrm{T}}\end{aligned} \tag{8.18}$$

$$\begin{aligned}\widehat{\mathrm{N}}_\lambda(t) &= A\widehat{\mathrm{N}}_{\lambda-1}(t-1) + \mathrm{K}^i(t)G^{i,j}(t)(\mathrm{K}^j_{\lambda-1}(t))^{\mathrm{T}} \\ &\quad -\mathrm{K}^i(t)\breve{\Pi}_{\lambda-1}(t) - \widehat{\Pi}_0(t)(\mathrm{K}^j_{\lambda-1}(t))^{\mathrm{T}}\end{aligned} \tag{8.19}$$

where $\mathrm{K}^i(t) = \mathbf{E}\{x(t)(\varepsilon^i(t))^{\mathrm{T}}\}(G^{i,i}(t))^{-1}$. *In particular, when* $\lambda = 1$, *one has*

$$\mathrm{N}^i_1(t) = P^i(t|t), \ \breve{\mathrm{N}}_1(t) = \widehat{\mathrm{N}}_1(t) = P^{i,j}(t|t). \tag{8.20}$$

Proof By the definitions of $\mathrm{N}_\lambda(t)$, $\breve{\mathrm{N}}_\lambda(t)$, and $\widehat{\mathrm{N}}_\lambda(t)$, one can easily obtain (8.20) for $\lambda = 1$. Moreover, the following recursive equations can be derived by using the projection theory [17]:

$$\hat{x}^i(t-\lambda+1|t) = \hat{x}^i(t-\lambda+1|t-1) + \mathrm{K}^i_{\lambda-1}(t)\varepsilon^i(t) \tag{8.21}$$

$$\mathrm{K}^i_{\lambda-1}(t) = \mathbf{E}\{x(t-\lambda+1)(\varepsilon^i(t))^{\mathrm{T}}\}(G^{i,i}(t))^{-1} \tag{8.22}$$

Therefore, it follows from (8.21) that

$$\begin{aligned}\Phi^{i,i}_t(t, t-\lambda+1) &= \Phi^{i,i}_{t-1}(t, t-\lambda+1) - \mathrm{K}^i(t)\mathbf{E}\{\varepsilon^i(t)(\tilde{x}^i(t-\lambda+1|t-1)^{\mathrm{T}})\} \\ &\quad -\mathbf{E}\{\tilde{x}^i(t|t-1)(\varepsilon^i(t))^{\mathrm{T}}\}(\mathrm{K}^i_{\lambda-1}(t))^{\mathrm{T}} \\ &\quad +\mathrm{K}^i(t)\mathbf{E}\{\varepsilon^i(t)(\varepsilon^i(t))^{\mathrm{T}}\}(\mathrm{K}^i_{\lambda-1}(t))^{\mathrm{T}}\end{aligned} \tag{8.23}$$

By considering

$$\Pi^i_{\lambda-1}(t) = \mathbf{E}\{\varepsilon^i(t)(x(t-\lambda+1))^{\mathrm{T}}\} = \mathbf{E}\{\varepsilon^i(t)(\tilde{x}(t-\lambda+1|t-1))^{\mathrm{T}}\}$$

and substituting (8.22) into (8.23), one obtains

$$\Phi^{i,i}_t(t, t-\lambda+1) = \Phi^{i,i}_{t-1}(t, t-\lambda+1) - \mathrm{K}^i(t)\Pi^i_{\lambda-1}(t) \tag{8.24}$$

By applying the projection theory [17], one can obtain the following recursive equations:

$$\hat{x}^i(t+1|t+1) = \hat{x}^i(t+1|t) + \mathrm{K}^i(t+1)\varepsilon^i(t+1) \tag{8.25}$$

$$\mathrm{K}^i(t+1) = \mathbf{E}\{x(t+1)(\varepsilon^i(t+1))^{\mathrm{T}}\}(G^{i,i}(t+1))^{-1} \tag{8.26}$$

Meanwhile, one can obtain the following equation by taking projection of both sides of (8.9):

$$\hat{x}^i(t+1|t) = A\hat{x}^i(t|t) \tag{8.27}$$

Combining (8.9) and (8.27) yields

$$\tilde{x}^i(t+1|t) = A\tilde{x}^i(t|t) + \Omega(t) \tag{8.28}$$

It follows from (8.28) that

$$\tilde{x}^i(t|t-1) = A\tilde{x}^i(t-1|t-1) + \Omega(t-1) \tag{8.29}$$

Then one has by the fact $\Omega(t-1)\perp\tilde{x}^i(t-\lambda+1|t-1)$ that

$$\Phi_{t-1}^{i,i}(t, t-\lambda+1) = A\Phi_{t-1}^{i,i}(t-1, t-\lambda+1) \tag{8.30}$$

By the definition of $\mathrm{N}_\lambda^i(t)$, (8.17) can be obtained by substituting (8.30) into (8.24).

On the other hand, it follows from (8.25) and (8.21) that

$$\begin{aligned}\Phi_t^{i,j}(t-\lambda+1, t) = {} & \Phi_{t-1}^{i,j}(t-\lambda+1, t) - \mathrm{K}_{\lambda-1}^i(t)\mathbf{E}\{\varepsilon^i(t)(\tilde{x}^j(t|t-1))^{\mathrm{T}}\} \\ & -\mathbf{E}\{\tilde{x}^i(t-\lambda+1|t-1)(\varepsilon^j(t))^{\mathrm{T}}\}(\mathrm{K}^j(t))^{\mathrm{T}} \\ & +\mathrm{K}_{\lambda-1}^i(t)\mathbf{E}\{\varepsilon^i(t)(\varepsilon^j(t))^{\mathrm{T}}\}(\mathrm{K}^j(t))^{\mathrm{T}}\end{aligned} \tag{8.31}$$

From the similar derivation process of (8.30), one obtains the following recursive equation:

$$\Phi_{t-1}^{i,j}(t-\lambda+1, t) = \Phi_{t-1}^{i,j}(t-\lambda+1, t-1)A^{\mathrm{T}} \tag{8.32}$$

By the definitions of $\breve{\mathrm{N}}_\lambda(t)$, $\breve{\Pi}_\lambda(t)$, and $\widehat{\Pi}_\lambda(t)$ and substituting (8.32) into (8.31) yields

$$\begin{aligned}\breve{\mathrm{N}}_\lambda(t) = {} & \breve{\mathrm{N}}_{\lambda-1}(t-1)A^{\mathrm{T}} - \mathrm{K}_{\lambda-1}^i(t)\breve{\Pi}_0(t) - \widehat{\Pi}_{\lambda-1}(t)(\mathrm{K}^j(t))^{\mathrm{T}} \\ & +\mathrm{K}_{\lambda-1}^i(t)G^{i,j}(t)(\mathrm{K}^j(t))^{\mathrm{T}}\end{aligned} \tag{8.33}$$

Moreover, (8.19) can be obtained by following the similar derivation procedures of (8.33). The proof is thus completed.

Lemma 8.3 *For $\ell = 2, 3, \ldots, d-1$, the following recursive equations hold*

$$\Theta_\tau^i(t,\ell) = \Theta_\tau^i(t-1,\ell-1) - \mathrm{K}_{\ell-1}^i(t)\Pi_{\ell+\tau}^i(t) \tag{8.34}$$

$$\begin{aligned}\breve{\Theta}_\tau^{i,j}(t,\ell) = {} & \breve{\Theta}_\tau^{i,j}(t-1,\ell-1) - \mathrm{K}_{\ell+\tau}^i(t)\breve{\Pi}_{\ell-1}(t) \\ & -\widehat{\Pi}_{\ell+\tau}(t)(\mathrm{K}_{\ell-1}^j(t))^{\mathrm{T}} + \mathrm{K}_{\ell+\tau}^i(t)G^{i,j}(t)(\mathrm{K}_{\ell-1}^j(t))^{\mathrm{T}}\end{aligned} \tag{8.35}$$

$$\begin{aligned}\widehat{\Theta}_\tau^{i,j}(t,\ell) = {} & \widehat{\Theta}_\tau^{i,j}(t-1,\ell-1) - \mathrm{K}_{\ell-1}^i(t)\breve{\Pi}_{\ell+\tau}(t) \\ & -\widehat{\Pi}_{\ell-1}(t)(\mathrm{K}_{\ell+\tau}^j(t))^{\mathrm{T}} + \mathrm{K}_{\ell-1}^i(t)G^{i,j}(t)(\mathrm{K}_{\ell+\tau}^j(t))^{\mathrm{T}}\end{aligned} \tag{8.36}$$

Meanwhile, one can obtain the following equations for $\ell = 0, 1$

$$\begin{cases} \Theta_\tau^i(t,0) = A\mathrm{N}_{\tau+1}^i(t), \ \Theta_\tau^i(t,1) = \mathrm{N}_{\tau+2}^i(t) \\ \breve{\Theta}_\tau(t,0) = A\breve{\mathrm{N}}_{\tau+1}(t), \breve{\Theta}_\tau(t,1) = \breve{\mathrm{N}}_{\tau+2}(t) \\ \widehat{\Theta}_\tau(t,0) = A\widehat{\mathrm{N}}_{\tau+1}(t), \ \widehat{\Theta}_\tau(t,1) = \widehat{\mathrm{N}}_{\tau+2}(t) \end{cases} \tag{8.37}$$

where $\tau = 0, 1, \ldots, d-\ell-1$, $\mathrm{N}_\lambda^i(t)$, $\breve{\mathrm{N}}_\lambda(t)$ and $\widehat{\mathrm{N}}_\lambda(t)$ are calculated by (8.17), (8.18), and (8.19), respectively.

Proof When $\ell = 0$ or $\ell = 1$, the results in (8.37) can be given from the definitions of $\Theta_\tau^i(t,\ell)$, $\widehat{\Theta}_\tau^{i,j}(t,\ell)$, and $\breve{\Theta}_\tau^{i,j}(t,\ell)$. On the other hand, it follows from the similar derivation process of (8.24) that

$$\Theta_\tau^i(t,\ell) = \Phi_{t-1}^{i,i}(t+1-\ell, t-\ell-\tau) - \mathrm{K}_{\ell-1}^i(t)\Pi_{\ell+\tau}^i(t) \tag{8.38}$$

Then by the definition of $\Theta_\tau^i(t,\ell)$, (8.34) can be obtained from (8.38).

The derivation processes for (8.35) and (8.36) are similar to the proof of (8.34), and they are thus omitted. This completes the proof.

Lemma 8.4 *For $\lambda = 2, 3, \ldots, d-1$, the following recursive equations*

$$\begin{aligned}\Phi_{t-1}^{i,i}(t-\ell, t-\lambda) = {} & (\mathrm{N}_{\ell+1-\lambda}^i(t-\lambda))^{\mathrm{T}} \\ & -\sum_{\varsigma=1}^{\lambda-1} \mathrm{K}_{\ell-\varsigma}^i(t-\varsigma)\Pi_{\lambda-\varsigma}^i(t-\varsigma)\end{aligned} \tag{8.39}$$

$$\Phi_{t-1}^{i,j}(t-\ell, t-\lambda) = \breve{\mathrm{N}}_{\ell+1-\lambda}(t-\lambda) - \sum_{\varsigma=1}^{\lambda-1} \{\mathrm{K}_{\ell-\varsigma}^i(t-\varsigma)\breve{\Pi}_{\lambda-\varsigma}(t-\varsigma)\}$$

$$+\sum_{\varsigma=1}^{\lambda-1} \mathrm{K}^i_{\ell-\varsigma}(t-\varsigma)G^{i,j}(t-\varsigma)(\mathrm{K}^j_{\lambda-\varsigma}(t-\varsigma))^{\mathrm{T}}$$

$$-\sum_{\varsigma=1}^{\lambda-1} \{\widehat{\Pi}_{\ell-\varsigma}(t-1)(\mathrm{K}^j_{\lambda-\varsigma}(t-\varsigma))^{\mathrm{T}}\} \tag{8.40}$$

$$\Phi^{i,j}_{t-1}(t-\lambda, t-\ell) = \widehat{\mathrm{N}}_{\ell+1-\lambda}(t-\lambda) - \sum_{\varsigma=1}^{\lambda-1} \{\mathrm{K}^i_{\lambda-\varsigma}(t-\varsigma)\breve{\Pi}_{\ell-\varsigma}(t-\varsigma)\}$$

$$+\sum_{\varsigma=1}^{\lambda-1} \mathrm{K}^i_{\lambda-\varsigma}(t-\varsigma)G^{i,j}(t-\varsigma)(\mathrm{K}^j_{\ell-\varsigma}(t-\varsigma))^{\mathrm{T}}$$

$$-\sum_{\varsigma=1}^{\lambda-1} \{\widehat{\Pi}_{\lambda-\varsigma}(t-1)(\mathrm{K}^j_{\ell-\varsigma}(t-\varsigma))^{\mathrm{T}}\} \tag{8.41}$$

hold, and for $\lambda = 1$, *the following equations*

$$\begin{cases} \Phi^{i,i}_{t-1}(t-\ell, t-1) = (\mathrm{N}^i_\ell(t-1))^{\mathrm{T}} \\ \Phi^{i,j}_{t-1}(t-\ell, t-1) = \breve{\mathrm{N}}_\ell(t-1) \\ \Phi^{i,j}_{t-1}(t-1, t-\ell) = \widehat{\mathrm{N}}_\ell(t-1) \end{cases} \tag{8.42}$$

are true, where $\ell = \lambda+1, \ldots, d$, $\mathrm{N}^i_{\ell+1-\lambda}(t-\lambda)$, $\breve{\mathrm{N}}_{\ell+1-\lambda}(t-\lambda)$, *and* $\widehat{\mathrm{N}}_{\ell+1-\lambda}(t-\lambda)$ *are computed by (8.17), (8.18), and (8.19), respectively.*

Proof For $\lambda = 1$, (8.42) can be easily obtained from the definitions of $\mathrm{N}^i_\lambda(t)$, $\breve{\mathrm{N}}_\lambda(t)$ and $\widehat{\mathrm{N}}_\lambda(t)$. For the other cases, the following recursive equations can be derived by using the similar derivation processes of (8.24) and (8.31):

$$\Phi^{i,i}_{t-\varsigma}(t-\ell, t-\lambda) = \Phi^{i,i}_{t-\varsigma-1}(t-\ell, t-\lambda) - \mathrm{K}^i_{\ell-\varsigma}(t-\varsigma)\Pi^i_{\lambda-\varsigma}(t-\varsigma) \tag{8.43}$$

$$\begin{aligned}\Phi^{i,j}_{t-\varsigma}(t-\ell, t-\lambda) = {} & \Phi^{i,j}_{t-\varsigma-1}(t-\ell, t-\lambda) - \mathrm{K}^i_{\ell-\varsigma}(t-\varsigma)\breve{\Pi}_{\lambda-\varsigma}(t-\varsigma) \\ & -\widehat{\Pi}_{\ell-\varsigma}(t-1)(\mathrm{K}^j_{\lambda-\varsigma}(t-\varsigma))^{\mathrm{T}} \\ & +\mathrm{K}^i_{\ell-\varsigma}(t-\varsigma)G^{i,j}(t-\varsigma)(\mathrm{K}^j_{\lambda-\varsigma}(t-\varsigma))^{\mathrm{T}}\end{aligned} \tag{8.44}$$

$$\begin{aligned}\Phi^{i,j}_{t-\varsigma}(t-\lambda, t-\ell) = {} & \Phi^{i,j}_{t-\varsigma-1}(t-\lambda, t-\ell) - \mathrm{K}^i_{\lambda-\varsigma}(t-\varsigma)\breve{\Pi}_{\ell-\varsigma}(t-\varsigma) \\ & -\widehat{\Pi}_{\lambda-\varsigma}(t-1)(\mathrm{K}^j_{\ell-\varsigma}(t-\varsigma))^{\mathrm{T}} \\ & +\mathrm{K}^i_{\lambda-\varsigma}(t-\varsigma)G^{i,j}(t-\varsigma)(\mathrm{K}^j_{\ell-\varsigma}(t-\varsigma))^{\mathrm{T}}\end{aligned} \tag{8.45}$$

On the other hand, it follows from the definitions of $\mathrm{N}_\lambda^i(t)$, $\breve{\mathrm{N}}_\lambda(t)$, and $\widehat{\mathrm{N}}_\lambda(t)$ that

$$\begin{cases} \Phi_{t-\lambda}^{i,i}(t-\ell, t-\lambda) = (\mathrm{N}_{\ell+1-\lambda}^i(t-\lambda))^{\mathrm{T}} \\ \Phi_{t-\lambda}^{i,j}(t-\ell, t-\lambda) = \breve{\mathrm{N}}_{\ell+1-\lambda}(t-\lambda) \\ \Phi_{t-\lambda}^{i,j}(t-\lambda, t-\ell) = \widehat{\mathrm{N}}_{\ell+1-\lambda}(t-\lambda) \end{cases} \tag{8.46}$$

Then, (8.39), (8.40), and (8.41) can be derived from (8.43), (8.44), and (8.45). The proof is thus completed.

8.4 Robust Information Fusion Kalman Estimator

Based on Lemmas 8.1, 8.2, 8.3, and 8.4, the optimal local estimator is given in the following theorem:

Theorem 8.1 *For systems (8.1) and (8.3) with Assumptions 8.1, 8.2, and 8.3 and given parameters $0 \le \pi_\ell^i \le 1$, $\ell = 0, 1, \ldots, d$ satisfying $\sum_{\ell=1}^d \pi_\ell^i \le 1$, $i = 1, 2, \ldots, L$, the* i*th optimal local recursive linear estimator is given by*

$$\hat{x}^i(t+1|t+1) = A\hat{x}^i(t|t) + \mathrm{K}^i(t+1)\{y_i(t+1) - \pi_0^i H_i A\hat{x}^i(t|t) \\ - \sum_{\ell=1}^{d} \pi_\ell^i H_i \hat{x}^i(t+1-\ell|t)\} \tag{8.47}$$

$$\begin{cases} \mathrm{K}^i(t+1) = \Big\{\pi_0^i P^i(t+1|t)H_i^{\mathrm{T}} \\ \qquad + \sum_{\ell=1}^{d} \pi_\ell^i A \mathrm{N}_\ell^i(t) H_i^{\mathrm{T}}\Big\} (G^{i,i}(t+1))^{-1} \\ P^i(t+1|t+1) = P^i(t+1|t) - \mathrm{K}^i(t+1) \\ \qquad \times \Big\{\pi_0^i P^i(t+1|t)H_i^{\mathrm{T}} + \sum_{\ell=1}^{d} \pi_\ell^i A\mathrm{N}_\ell^i(t)H_i^{\mathrm{T}}\Big\}^{\mathrm{T}} \\ P^i(t+1|t) = AP^i(t|t)A^{\mathrm{T}} + \Sigma(t) \end{cases} \tag{8.48}$$

$$\begin{cases} G^{i,i}(t+1) = \sum_{\ell=0}^{d} \{(\pi_\ell^i)^2 H_i P^i(t+1-\ell|t) H_i^{\mathrm{T}}\} \\ \qquad + \sum_{\ell=0}^{d} \{\pi_\ell^i (1-\pi_\ell^i) H_i \Lambda(t+1-\ell, t+1-\ell) H_i^{\mathrm{T}}\} \\ \qquad + \sum_{\ell=0}^{d-1} \{\mathrm{M}_\ell^i(t+1) + (\mathrm{M}_\ell^i(t+1))^{\mathrm{T}}\} + D_i R_{v_i} D_i^{\mathrm{T}} \\ \mathrm{M}_\ell^i(t+1) = \pi_\ell^i H_i \sum_{\tau=0}^{d-1-\ell} \pi_{\ell+\tau+1}^i \Theta_\tau^i(t,\ell) H_i^{\mathrm{T}} \\ \qquad - \pi_\ell^i H_i \sum_{\tau=0}^{d-1-\ell} \pi_{\ell+\tau+1}^i \Lambda(t+1-\ell, t-\ell-\tau) H_i^{\mathrm{T}} \end{cases} \tag{8.49}$$

$$\begin{cases} \hat{x}^i(t-\lambda|t) = \hat{x}^i(t-\lambda|t-\lambda) + \sum\limits_{\varsigma=0}^{\lambda-1} \mathrm{K}^i_{\lambda-\varsigma}(t-\varsigma)\varepsilon^i(t-\varsigma) \\ P^i(t-\lambda|t) = P^i(t-\lambda|t-\lambda) - \sum\limits_{\varsigma=0}^{\lambda-1} \mathrm{K}^i_{\lambda-\varsigma}(t-\varsigma)\Pi^i_{\lambda-\varsigma}(t-\varsigma) \\ \lambda = 1, 2, \ldots, d-1 \end{cases} \tag{8.50}$$

$$\mathrm{K}^i_{\lambda-\varsigma}(t-\varsigma) = (\Pi^i_{\lambda-\varsigma}(t-\varsigma))^{\mathrm{T}}(G^{i,i}(t-\varsigma))^{-1} \tag{8.51}$$

$$\begin{aligned} \Pi^i_{\lambda_1}(t) = &\left\{\sum_{\ell=0}^{\lambda_1-1} \pi^i_\ell H_i \Theta^i_{\lambda-(\ell+1)}(t-1,\ell)\right\} + \pi^i_{\lambda_1} H_i P^i(t-\lambda_1|t-1) \\ &+ \left\{\sum_{\ell=\lambda_1+1}^{d} \pi^i_\ell H_i \Phi^i_{t-1}(t-\ell, t-\lambda_1)\right\}, \ \lambda_1 = 1, 2, \ldots, d-1 \end{aligned} \tag{8.52}$$

where $\mathrm{N}^i_\ell(t)$, $\Theta^i_\tau(t,\ell)$ *and* $\Phi^{i,i}_{t-1}(t-\ell, t-\lambda)$ *are computed by (8.17), (8.34), and (8.39), respectively.* $\Sigma(t)$ *and* $\Lambda(t+1-\ell, t-\ell-\tau)$ *are calculated by (8.11) and (8.16), respectively.*

Proof The third equation in (8.48) can be derived from the fact $\Omega(t) \perp \tilde{x}^i(t|t)$ that

$$P^i(t+1|t) = AP^i(t|t)A^{\mathrm{T}} + \Sigma(t) \tag{8.53}$$

Taking projection of both sides of the output equation (8.3) yields

$$\hat{y}_i(t+1|t) = \pi^i_0 H_i \hat{x}^i(t+1|t) + \sum_{\ell=1}^{d} \pi^i_\ell H_i \hat{x}^i(t+1-\ell|t) \tag{8.54}$$

Therefore, (8.47) can be obtained by substituting (8.27) and (8.54) into (8.25).

The innovation sequence $\varepsilon^i(t+1)$ can be rewritten in the form

$$\begin{aligned} \varepsilon^i(t+1) = H_i &\sum_{\ell=0}^{d} (\sigma_{\{d_i(t+1)=\ell\}} - \pi^i_\ell) x(t+1-\ell) \\ &+ \pi^i_0 H_i \tilde{x}^i(t+1|t) + H_i \sum_{\ell=1}^{d} \pi^i_\ell \tilde{x}^i(t+1-\ell|t) \\ &+ D_i v_i(t+1) \end{aligned} \tag{8.55}$$

By Assumptions 8.1, 8.2, and 8.3, one has

$$\mathbf{E}\{(\sigma_{\{d_i(t)=\ell_1\}} - \pi^i_{\ell_1})(\sigma_{\{d_i(t)=\ell_2\}} - \pi^i_{\ell_2})\} = \begin{cases} \pi^i_{\ell_1}(1-\pi^i_{\ell_1}), & \ell_1 = \ell_2 \\ -\pi^i_{\ell_1}\pi^i_{\ell_2}, & \ell_1 \neq \ell_2 \end{cases} \tag{8.56}$$

It follows from the facts $\hat{x}^i(t+1|t) \perp \tilde{x}^i(t+1-\ell|t)$, $v_i(t+1) \perp \tilde{x}^i(t+1|t)$, $v_i(t+1) \perp \tilde{x}^i(t+1|t)$ that

$$\mathbf{E}\{x(t+1)(\varepsilon^i(t+1))^{\mathrm{T}}\} = \sum_{\ell=1}^{d} \pi_\ell^i \Phi_t^{i,i}(t+1, t+1-\ell) H_i^{\mathrm{T}} + \pi_0^i P^i(t+1|t) H_i^{\mathrm{T}} \tag{8.57}$$

and it can be derived from (8.28) and the fact $\Omega(t) \perp \tilde{x}^i(t+1-\ell|t)$ that

$$\Phi_t^{i,i}(t+1, t+1-\ell) = A\Phi_t^{i,i}(t, t+1-\ell) \tag{8.58}$$

Then substituting (8.58) into (8.57) leads to

$$\mathbf{E}\left\{x(t+1)(\varepsilon^i(t+1))^{\mathrm{T}}\right\} = \sum_{\ell=1}^{d} \pi_\ell^i A\Phi_t^{i,i}(t, t+1-\ell) H_i^{\mathrm{T}} + \pi_0^i P^i(t+1|t) H_i^{\mathrm{T}} \tag{8.59}$$

By the definition of $\mathrm{N}_\lambda^i(t)$, the first equation in (8.48) can be derived by substituting (8.59) into (8.26). Subsequently, the second equation of (8.48) can be easily obtained from (8.47) and the first equation of (8.48).

Moreover, it follows from (8.55) and (8.56) that

$$\begin{aligned} G^{i,i}(t+1) = & \sum_{\ell=0}^{d} \{(\pi_\ell^i)^2 H_i P^i(t+1-\ell|t) H_i^{\mathrm{T}}\} \\ & + \sum_{\ell=0}^{d} \{\pi_\ell^i (1-\pi_\ell^i) H_i \Lambda(t+1-\ell, t+1-\ell) H_i^{\mathrm{T}}\} \\ & + \sum_{\ell=0}^{d-1} \{\mathrm{M}_\ell^i(t+1) + (\mathrm{M}_\ell^i(t+1))^{\mathrm{T}}\} + D_i R_{v_i} D_i^{\mathrm{T}} \end{aligned} \tag{8.60}$$

where

$$\begin{aligned} \mathrm{M}_\ell^i(t+1) = & \pi_\ell^i H_i \sum_{\tau=0}^{d-1-\ell} \pi_{\ell+\tau+1}^i \Phi_t^{i,i}(t+1-\ell, t-\ell-\tau) H_i^{\mathrm{T}} - \pi_\ell^i H_i \\ & \times \sum_{\tau=0}^{d-1-\ell} \pi_{\ell+\tau+1}^i \mathrm{E}\{x(t+1-\ell) x^{\mathrm{T}}(t-\ell-\tau)\} H_i^{\mathrm{T}} \end{aligned} \tag{8.61}$$

Then, by the definitions of $\Theta_\tau^i(t,\ell)$ and $\Lambda(t+1-\ell,t-\ell-\tau)$, (8.49) can be obtained from (8.60) and (8.61).

Derivation procedures for $\hat{x}^i(t-\lambda|t)$ and $P^i(t-\lambda|t)$ are presented as follows. By using projection theory, one has

$$\hat{x}^i(t-\lambda|t-\varsigma) = \hat{x}^i(t-\lambda|t-\varsigma-1) + \mathrm{K}_{\lambda-\varsigma}^i(t-\varsigma)\varepsilon^i(t-\varsigma) \tag{8.62}$$

which leads to

$$P^i(t-\lambda|t-\varsigma) = P^i(t-\lambda|t-\varsigma-1) - \mathrm{K}_{\lambda-\varsigma}^i(t-\varsigma)\Pi_{\lambda-\varsigma}^i(t-\varsigma) \tag{8.63}$$

where

$$\mathrm{K}_{\lambda-\varsigma}^i(t-\varsigma) = \mathbf{E}\{(x(t-\lambda+\varsigma)(\varepsilon^i(t-\varsigma))^{\mathrm{T}}\}G^{i,i}(t-\varsigma) \tag{8.64}$$

then by the definition of $\Pi_\lambda^i(t)$, (8.51) can be obtained from (8.64).

Note that $\hat{x}^i(t-\lambda|t-\varsigma-1)$ and $P^i(t-\lambda|t-\varsigma-1)$ are, respectively, the estimate and estimation error covariance at instant one step before $\hat{x}^i(t-\lambda+1|t-\varsigma)$ and $P^i(t-\lambda+1|t-\varsigma)$. Then, one can obtain (8.50) from (8.62) and (8.63).

Since the set $\{\Pi_{\lambda_1}^i(t),\ \lambda_1 = 1,2,\ldots,d-1\}$ is the same as the set $\{\Pi_{\lambda-\varsigma}^i(t-\varsigma),\ \varsigma = 0,1,\ldots,\lambda-1\}$, then from the definition of $\Pi_{\lambda_1}^i(t)$, one has

$$\begin{aligned}
\Pi_{\lambda_1}^i(t) &= \sum_{\ell=0}^{d} \pi_\ell^i H_i \Phi_{t-1}^{i,i}(t-\ell,t-\lambda_1) \\
&= \left\{\sum_{\ell=0}^{\lambda_1-1} \pi_\ell^i H_i \Phi_{t-1}^{i,i}(t-\ell,t-\lambda_1)\right\} \\
&\quad + \pi_{\lambda_1}^i H_i P^i(t-\lambda_1|t-1) \\
&\quad + \left\{\sum_{\ell=\lambda_1+1}^{d} \pi_\ell^i H_i \Phi_{t-1}^{i,i}(t-\ell,t-\lambda_1)\right\}
\end{aligned} \tag{8.65}$$

For $0 \le \ell \le \lambda_1 - 1$, it follows from the definition of $\Theta_\tau^i(t,\ell)$ that

$$\Phi_{t-1}^{i,i}(t-\ell,t-\lambda_1) = \Theta_{\lambda_1-(\ell+1)}^i(t-1,\ell)$$

Then, substituting the above equation into (8.65) yields (8.51). The proof is thus completed.

The computation procedures of the local optimal estimator by using Theorem 8.1 is summarized as follows:

Algorithm 8.1 Given the initial values $P^i(-d+1|0),\ldots,P^i(0|0)$, $x(-d+1),\ldots,x(0)$, $\hat{x}^i(-d+1|0),\ldots,\hat{x}^i(0|0)$, $\Pi_1^i(0),\ldots,\Pi_{d-1}^i(0)$, and $\mathrm{N}_1^i(0),\ldots,\mathrm{N}_d^i(0)$.

Step 1. From $\lambda=d-1$ to $\lambda=1$, $\Phi_{t-1}^{i,i}(t-\ell,t-d+1),\ \ldots,\ \Phi_{t-1}^{i,i}(t-\ell,t-1)$, $\ell=\lambda+1,\ldots,d$ are computed by (8.39).
Step 2. Compute $\Pi_\lambda^i(t)$ by substituting (8.39) into (8.52), then $\mathrm{K}_\lambda^i(t)$, $\lambda=1,2,\ldots,d-1$ is calculated by substituting (8.52) into (8.51).
Step 3. Compute $\mathrm{N}_\ell^i(t)$, $\ell=1,2,\ldots,d$ by substituting (8.51) and (8.52) into (8.17), while $\hat{x}^i(t-\lambda|t)$ and $P^i(t-\lambda|t)$, $\lambda=1,2,\ldots,d-1$ are calculated by substituting (8.51) and (8.52) into (8.50).
Step 4. Compute $\Theta_\tau^i(t,0)$ and $\Theta_\tau^i(t,1)$ by substituting (8.12) into the first equation of (8.37), then based on the obtained $\Theta_\tau^i(t,0)$ and $\Theta_\tau^i(t,1)$, $\Theta_\tau^i(t,\ell)$, $\ell=1,2,\ldots,d-1$ are calculated by substituting (8.51) and (8.52) into (8.34).
Step 5. Compute $\mathrm{M}_\ell^i(t+1)$, $\ell=1,2,\ldots,d-1$ by substituting (8.16) and (8.34) into the second equation of (8.49), then $G^{i,i}(t+1)$ is calculated by substituting the second equation of (8.50) and $\mathrm{M}_\ell^i(t+1)$ into the first equation of (8.49).
Step 6. Compute $\mathrm{K}^i(t+1)$ by substituting (8.17) and the first equation of (8.49) into the first equation of (8.48), while $P^i(t+1|t)$ is calculated by the third equation of (8.48). Then $P^i(t+1|t+1)$ is computed by substituting $\mathrm{K}^i(t+1)$, $P^i(t+1|t)$, and (8.17) into the second equation of (8.48).
Step 7. Compute the local optimal state estimate $\hat{x}^i(t+1|t+1)$ by substituting $\mathrm{K}^i(t+1)$ and $\hat{x}^i(t-\lambda|t)$ into (8.47).

Based on the local estimates obtained by Theorem 8.1, the optimal state fusion estimator with matrix weights will be presented in the following theorem. The proof is similar to that given in [16] and is omitted for brevity:

Theorem 8.2 *For systems (8.1) and (8.3), the robust distributed state fusion estimator is given by*

$$\hat{x}(t|t)=\sum_{i=1}^{L}\bar{A}_i(t)\hat{x}^i(t|t) \tag{8.66}$$

$$\bar{A}(t)=\Psi^{-1}(t)I_0(I_0^{\mathrm{T}}\Psi^{-1}(t)I_0)^{-1} \tag{8.67}$$

where

$$\bar{A}(t)=[\bar{A}_1(t),\ldots,\bar{A}_L(t)]^{\mathrm{T}}\in\Re^{nL\times n}$$
$$I_0=[I_n,\ldots,I_n]^{\mathrm{T}}\in\Re^{nL\times n}$$
$$\Psi(t)=\begin{bmatrix}P^{1,1}(t|t) & P^{1,2}(t|t) & \cdots & P^{1,L}(t|t)\\ P^{2,1}(t|t) & P^{2,2}(t|t) & \cdots & P^{2,L}(t|t)\\ \vdots & \vdots & \ddots & \vdots\\ P^{L,1}(t|t) & P^{L,2}(t|t) & \cdots & P^{L,L}(t|t)\end{bmatrix}\in\Re^{nL\times nL}$$

Moreover, the corresponding error covariance matrix of the fusion estimator is given by $P(t|t) = (I_0^{\mathrm{T}}\Psi^{-1}(t)I_0)^{-1}$ *which satisfies*

$$P(t|t) \leq P^i(t|t),\ i = 1, 2, \ldots, L$$

It can be seen from Theorem 8.2 that one has to compute the estimation error cross-covariance $P^{i,j}$, $i, j \in \{1, 2, \ldots, L\}$ in the design of the fusion estimators, and the computation procedures are given in the following theorem.

Theorem 8.3 *For given parameters* $0 \leq \pi_\ell^i \leq 1$, $\ell = 0, 1, \ldots, d$, $i = 1, 2, \cdots, L$ *satisfying* $\sum_{\ell=1}^{d} \pi_\ell^i \leq 1$, *the estimation error cross-covariance matrix between the* ith *and the* jth *sensor subsystems at time instant* $t+1$ *is computed recursively by*

$$\begin{cases} P^{i,j}(t+1|t+1) = P^{i,j}(t+1|t) - \mathrm{K}^i(t+1) \\ \quad \times \left\{ \pi_0^i H_i P^{i,j}(t+1|t) + \sum\limits_{\ell=1}^{d} \pi_\ell^i H_i \breve{\mathrm{N}}_\ell(t) A^{\mathrm{T}} \right\} \\ \quad - \left\{ \pi_0^j P^{i,j}(t+1|t) H_j^{\mathrm{T}} + \sum\limits_{\ell=1}^{d} \pi_\ell^j A \widehat{\mathrm{N}}_\ell(t) H_j^{\mathrm{T}} \right\} \\ \quad \times (\mathrm{K}^j(t+1))^{\mathrm{T}} + \mathrm{K}^i(t+1) G^{i,j}(t+1) (\mathrm{K}^j(t+1))^{\mathrm{T}} \\ P^{i,j}(t+1|t) = A P^{i,j}(t|t) A^{\mathrm{T}} + \Sigma(t) \end{cases} \tag{8.68}$$

$$\begin{aligned} G^{i,j}(t+1) = & \sum_{\ell=0}^{d} \{\pi_\ell^i \pi_\ell^j H_i P^{i,j}(t-\ell+1|t) H_j^{\mathrm{T}}\} \\ & + \sum_{\ell=0}^{d-1} \left\{ \pi_\ell^i H_i \sum_{\tau=0}^{d-\ell-1} \pi_{\ell+\tau+1}^j \widehat{\Theta}_\tau^{i,j}(t,\ell) H_j^{\mathrm{T}} \right. \\ & \left. + \pi_\ell^j \sum_{\tau=0}^{d-\ell-1} \pi_{\ell+\tau+1}^i H_i \breve{\Theta}_\tau^{i,j}(t,\ell) H_j^{\mathrm{T}} \right\} + D_i S_{ij} D_j^{\mathrm{T}} \end{aligned} \tag{8.69}$$

$$\begin{aligned} P^{i,j}(t-\lambda, t) = & P^{i,j}(t-\lambda|t-\lambda) - \sum_{\varsigma=0}^{\lambda-1} \left\{ \mathrm{K}_{\lambda-\varsigma}^i(t-\varsigma) \breve{\Pi}_{\lambda-\varsigma}(t-\varsigma) \right. \\ & - \mathrm{K}_{\lambda-\varsigma}^i(t-\varsigma) G^{i,j}(t-\varsigma) (\mathrm{K}_{\lambda-\varsigma}^j(t-\varsigma))^{\mathrm{T}} \\ & \left. + \widehat{\Pi}_{\lambda-\varsigma}(t-\varsigma) (\mathrm{K}_{\lambda-\varsigma}^j(t-\varsigma))^{\mathrm{T}} \right\}, \lambda = 1, 2, \ldots, d-1 \end{aligned} \tag{8.70}$$

$$
\begin{cases}
\breve{\Pi}_{\lambda_1}(t) = \left\{ \sum\limits_{\ell=0}^{\lambda_1-1} \pi_\ell^i H_i \widehat{\Theta}_{\lambda_1-(\ell+1)}(t-1,\ell) \right\} \\
\quad + \pi_{\lambda_1}^i H_i P^{i,j}(t-\lambda_1|t-1) \\
\quad + \left\{ \sum\limits_{\ell=\lambda_1+1}^{d} \pi_\ell^i H_i \Phi_{t-1}^{i,j}(t-\ell, t-\lambda_1) \right\} \\
\widehat{\Pi}_{\lambda_1}(t) = \left\{ \sum\limits_{\ell=0}^{\lambda_1-1} \pi_\ell^j \breve{\Theta}_{\lambda_1-(\ell+1)}(t-1,\ell) H_j^{\mathrm{T}} \right\} \\
\quad + \pi_{\lambda_1}^j P^{i,j}(t-\lambda_1|t-1) H_j^{\mathrm{T}} \\
\quad + \left\{ \sum\limits_{\ell=\lambda_1+1}^{d} \pi_\ell^j \Phi_{t-1}^{i,j}(t-\lambda_1, t-\ell) H_j^{\mathrm{T}} \right\} \\
\quad \lambda_1 = 1, 2, \ldots, d-1
\end{cases}
\tag{8.71}
$$

where $\mathrm{K}^i(t+1)$ *and* $\mathrm{K}^i_{\lambda-\varsigma}(t-\varsigma)$ *are computed by (8.48) and (8.51), respectively, while* $\breve{\mathrm{N}}_\lambda(t)$, $\widehat{\mathrm{N}}_\lambda(t)$, $\breve{\Theta}_\tau(t,\ell)$, $\widehat{\Theta}_\tau(t,\ell)$, $\Phi_{t-1}^{i,j}(t-\ell,t-\lambda)$ *and* $\Phi_{t-1}^{i,j}(t-\lambda,t-\ell)$ *are computed by (8.18), (8.19), (8.35), (8.36), (8.40), and (8.41), respectively.*

Proof Equations (8.70) and (8.71) can be obtained by following the similar derivation procedures in (8.50) and (8.52), respectively. On the other hand, it follows from (8.53) that

$$
\begin{aligned}
P^{i,j}(t+1|t+1) = P^{i,j}(t+1|t) &- \mathrm{K}^i(t+1)\mathbf{E}\{\varepsilon^i(t+1)(\tilde{x}^j(t+1|t))^{\mathrm{T}}\} \\
&- \mathbf{E}\{\tilde{x}^i(t+1|t)(\varepsilon^j(t+1))^{\mathrm{T}}\}(\mathrm{K}^j(t+1))^{\mathrm{T}} \\
&+ \mathrm{K}^i(t+1)\mathbf{E}\{\varepsilon^i(t+1)(\varepsilon^j(t+1))^{\mathrm{T}}\}(\mathrm{K}^j(t+1))^{\mathrm{T}}
\end{aligned}
\tag{8.72}
$$

By Assumptions 8.1, 8.2, and 8.3, it follows from the similar derivation procedures in (8.59) that

$$
\begin{cases}
\breve{\Pi}_0(t+1) = \mathbf{E}\{\varepsilon^i(t+1)(\tilde{x}^j(t+1|t))^{\mathrm{T}}\} \\
\qquad = \pi_0^i H_i P^{i,j}(t+1|t) + \sum\limits_{\ell=1}^{d} \pi_\ell^i H_i \Phi_t^{i,j}(t-\ell+1,t) A^{\mathrm{T}} \\
\widehat{\Pi}_0(t+1) = \mathbf{E}\{\tilde{x}^i(t+1|t)(\varepsilon^j(t+1))^{\mathrm{T}} \\
\qquad = \pi_0^j P^{i,j}(t+1|t) H_j^{\mathrm{T}} + \sum\limits_{\ell=1}^{d} \pi_\ell^j A \Phi_t^{i,j}(t,t-\ell+1) H_j^{\mathrm{T}}
\end{cases}
\tag{8.73}
$$

Hence, by the definitions of $\breve{\mathrm{N}}_\ell(t)$ and $\widehat{\mathrm{N}}_\ell(t)$, the first equation in (8.68) can be obtained by substituting (8.73) into (8.72). Meanwhile, the second equation in (8.68) can be derived from (8.28) and the facts $\Omega(t) \perp \tilde{x}^i(t|t)$ and $\Omega(t) \perp \tilde{x}^j(t|t)$.

For $i \neq j$, it is easy to verify from Assumptions 8.1 and 8.2 that

$$\begin{cases} \mathbf{E}\{(\sigma_{\{d_i(t)=\ell_1\}} - \pi^i_{\ell_1})(\sigma_{\{d_j(t)=\ell_2\}} - \pi^j_{\ell_2})\} = 0 \\ \mathbf{E}\{v_i v_j\} = S_{ij} \end{cases} \tag{8.74}$$

Then, the following equation can be obtained from (8.55) and (8.74):

$$\begin{aligned} G^{i,j}(t+1) = & \sum_{\ell=0}^{d} \pi^i_\ell \pi^j_\ell H_i P^{i,j}(t-\ell+1|t) H_j^{\mathrm{T}} \\ & + D_i S_{ij} D_j^{\mathrm{T}} + \sum_{\ell=0}^{d-1} \{\widehat{\mathrm{M}}_\ell(t+1) + \breve{\mathrm{M}}_\ell(t+1)\} \end{aligned} \tag{8.75}$$

where

$$\widehat{\mathrm{M}}_\ell(t+1) = \pi^i_\ell H_i \sum_{\tau-0}^{d-\ell-1} \pi^j_{\ell+\tau+1} \widehat{\Theta}^{i,j}_\tau(t,\ell) H_j^{\mathrm{T}}$$

$$\breve{\mathrm{M}}_\ell(t+1) = \pi^j_\ell \left\{ \sum_{\tau=0}^{d-\ell-1} \pi^i_{\ell+\tau+1} H_i \breve{\Theta}^{i,j}_\tau(t,\ell) \right\} H_j^{\mathrm{T}}$$

Then, substituting the above equations into (8.75) leads to (8.71). The proof is completed.

The computation procedures for the estimation error cross-covariance matrix by using Theorem 8.3 are similar to Algorithm 8.1, and thus the detailed steps are omitted here.

To discuss the computational complexities of the proposed estimator design method, it is the number of multiplications and divisions that is used as the operation count. Let CK denote the number of multiplications and divisions. Note that the algorithm by Theorem 8.2 can be summarized as follows:

(i) Compute the local optimal estimates $\hat{x}^i(t|t)$, $i = 1, 2, \ldots, L$ using Theorem 8.1;
(ii) Compute the error cross-covariance matrices $P^{i,j}(t|t)$, $i = 1, 2, \ldots, L, j = i, i+1, \ldots, L$ by applying Theorem 8.3;
(iii) Compute the optimal state fusion estimate $\hat{x}(t|t)$ by applying Theorem 8.2.

It is easy to know the total CK number of obtaining $\hat{x}(t|t)$, for one step, denoted by CK_r, is given by

$$\begin{aligned} CK_r = & \sum_{i=1}^{L} \{nm^i(1+m^i)d^2 + ((n^3+1)m^i + 7n^2 m^i \\ & + (2(m^i)^2 - m^i)n)d + (m^i+2)n^3 + (1+2m^i)n^2 + m^i n\} \end{aligned}$$

$$+\sum_{i=1}^{L(L-1)/2}\{(n^2m^i+nm^i+3n^3)d^2+(n^2m^i$$
$$+3(m^i)^2n+2m^in-3n^3)d+4n^3+m^in(1+n)\}$$
$$+\{2n^3L^3+3n^3L^2+Ln^2\} \tag{8.76}$$

For the computational complexity function CK_r, the highest power of d is 2, which implies that the computational cost has been largely increased because of the time delay when the number of sensors is fixed. Meanwhile, denote CK_a as the computational complexity function for the augmentation approach, then the CK_a is of magnitude $O(d^3)$. Therefore, when the upper bound of the delay d is sufficiently large, it is easy to know that $CK_a > CK_r$. On the other hand, it follows from (8.76) that CK_r is of magnitude $O(L^3)$, which implies that as the number of the sensors increases, the computation cost will increase rapidly.

The distributed state fusion estimator $\hat{x}(t|t)$ obtained from Theorem 8.2 is computed off-line as it only depends on the upper bounds and the occurrence probabilities of delays at each step.

8.5 Simulations

In this section, two examples are presented to illustrate the effectiveness and applicability of the proposed fusion estimator. Throughout this section, the trace of estimation error covariance matrix is selected to specify the estimation performance.

Example 8.1 Consider the following state-space model with stochastic parameter perturbations [11]:

$$x(t+1)=(A+A_1\alpha_1(t))x(t)+\Gamma w(t) \tag{8.77}$$

where

$$A=\begin{bmatrix}0.3 & 0.7\\ 0.2 & 0.6\end{bmatrix}, A_1=\begin{bmatrix}0.1 & 0.05\\ 0.2 & 0.1\end{bmatrix}, \Gamma=\begin{bmatrix}1\\ 0.5\end{bmatrix}$$

and $w(t)$ and $\alpha_1(t)$ are zero-mean white noises with covariances Q_w and θ_1, respectively. Two sensors are deployed to measure the outputs of system (8.77), and the observations received by the fusion center are given by

$$\begin{cases} y_1(t)=H_1x(t-d_1(t))+D_1v_1(t)\\ y_2(t)=H_2x(t-d_2(t))+D_2v_2(t)\end{cases} \tag{8.78}$$

where

$$H_1 = [0.5\ 1], H_2 = [1\ 1], D_1 = 0.5, D_2 = 0.2$$

and $v_1(t)$ and $v_2(t)$ are correlated Gaussian white noises satisfying

$$\mathbf{E}\left\{\begin{bmatrix} v_1(t) \\ v_2(t) \end{bmatrix} \begin{bmatrix} v_1(t) & v_2(t) \end{bmatrix}\right\} = \begin{bmatrix} R_{v_1} & S_{12} \\ S_{12} & R_{v_2} \end{bmatrix}$$

Suppose that $d_1(t) \in \{0, 1, 2\}$ and $d_2(t) \in \{0, 1, 2\}$, i.e., $d = 2$, then (8.78) is rewritten in the form

$$\begin{cases} y_1(t) = H_1 \sum_{\ell=0}^{2} \sigma_{\{d_1(t)=\ell\}} x(t-\ell) + D_1 v_1(t) \\ y_2(t) = H_2 \sum_{\ell=0}^{2} \sigma_{\{d_2(t)=\ell\}} x(t-\ell) + D_2 v_2(t) \end{cases} \tag{8.79}$$

where

$$\sum_{\ell=0}^{2} \{\sigma_{\{d_i(t)=\ell\}}\} \in \{1, 0\},\ \text{Prob}\{\sigma_{\{d_i(t)=\ell\}} = 1\} = \pi_\ell^i$$

Then, the measurement receiving probability γ_i is given by $\gamma_i = \sum_{\ell=0}^{2} \pi_\ell^i$, and the measurement loss rate is $1 - \gamma_i$. Define the average measurement receiving probability of all the sensors as follows:

$$\gamma^0 = \frac{1}{L} \sum_{i=1}^{L} \gamma_i \tag{8.80}$$

Choose $Q_w = 0.1$, $R_{v_1} = R_{v_2} = 0.3$, $S_{12} = 0$, $\theta_1 = 0.1$. Suppose that the occurrence probabilities of the delays are $\pi_0^1 = 0.70$, $\pi_1^1 = 0.15$, $\pi_2^1 = 0.10$, $\pi_0^2 = 0.65$, $\pi_1^2 = 0.15$, and $\pi_2^2 = 0.05$. Then, one has $\gamma_1 = 0.95$ and $\gamma_2 = 0.85$.

To verify the effectiveness of the proposed estimator design method, the robust information fusion estimator $\hat{x}(t|t)$ for systems (8.77) and (8.78) are shown in Fig. 8.1, while the estimation performance is depicted in Fig. 8.2. It can be seen from Figs. 8.1 and 8.2 that the estimator provides satisfactory performance and the precision of the fusion estimator is higher than that of the local optimal estimators.

To demonstrate the advantage of the proposed estimator, its estimation performance is compared with that of the robust estimator in [11], where the communication delays were not considered. Using the approach in [11], the measurements will be regarded to be lost if they are not collected on time. Therefore, all the delayed measurements are considered to be missed, and the measurement receiving rate γ_i equals π_0^i, i.e., $\gamma_1 = 0.70$ and $\gamma_2 = 0.65$. Denote the estimation error covariance

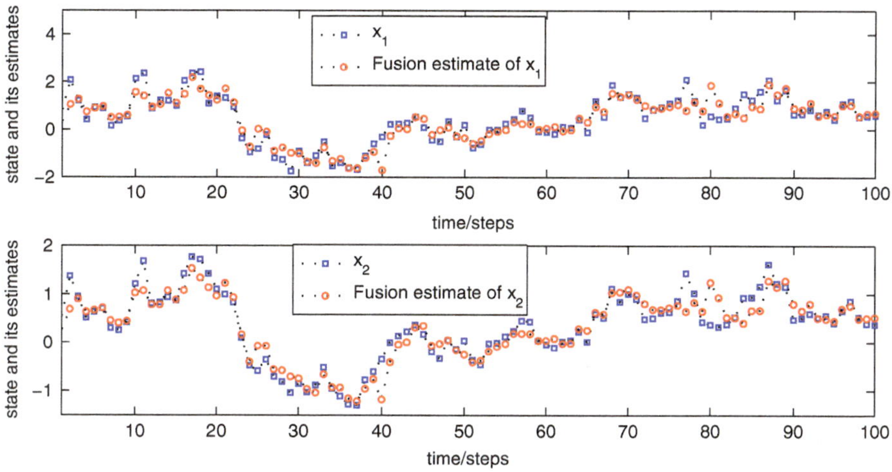

Fig. 8.1 The state $x(t)$ and its fusion estimate $\hat{x}(t|t)$

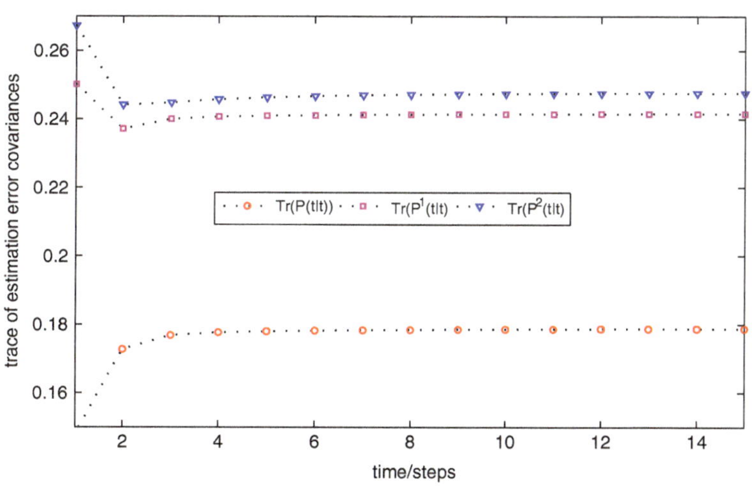

Fig. 8.2 The estimation performance of local optimal estimators and fusion estimator

matrix of [11] by $P^0(t|t)$, then by using Theorem 1 of [11] and Theorem 8.3, respectively, the relationship between $\mathrm{Tr}(P(t|t))$ and $\mathrm{Tr}(P^0(t|t))$ is depicted in Fig. 8.3. It can be seen from Fig. 8.3 that the performance of the proposed estimator is better than that of the centralized estimator in [11].

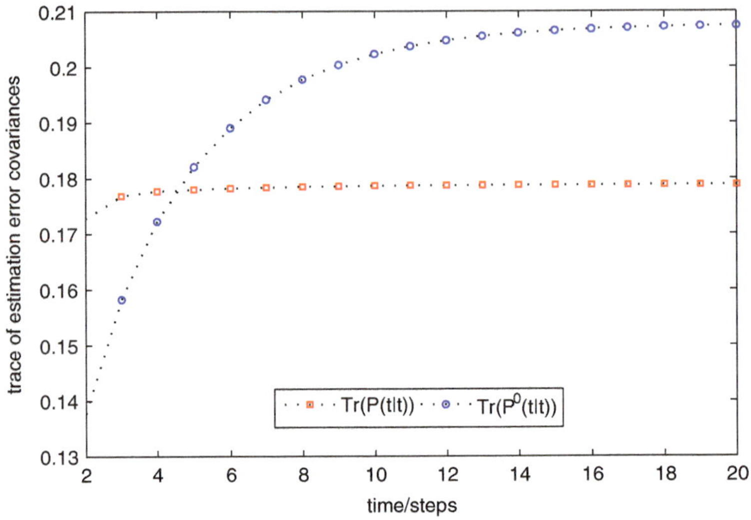

Fig. 8.3 The estimation performance of the proposed estimator and the centralized estimator in [11]

Table 8.1 The relationship between the steady-state values of Tr($P(t|t)$) and the average measurements receiving rate γ^0

γ^0	0.90	0.85	0.80	0.75	0.70
$S-$Tr(P)	0.2283	0.2670	0.2704	0.3030	0.3336

In what follows, the relationships between the average measurements receiving rate and the information fusion estimation performance will be presented by simulations. By applying Theorem 8.3, one obtains the information fusion estimation performance with respect to different average measurements receiving rate γ^0 as shown in Table 8.1, where $S-$Tr(P) denotes the steady-state values of Tr($P(t|t)$). It can be seen from Table 8.1 that the estimation performance becomes better with the increase of the average measurements receiving rate, which indicates that large measurement delays degrade the estimation performance.

Example 8.2 Consider a radar tracking system with two sensors

$$x(t+1) = \left\{ \begin{bmatrix} 1 & \mathrm{T_0} \\ 0 & 1 \end{bmatrix} + \begin{bmatrix} -0.1 & 0.1 \\ 0.1 & 0.1 \end{bmatrix} \alpha_1(t) \right\} x(t) + \begin{bmatrix} 0.5\mathrm{T_0^2} \\ \mathrm{T_0} \end{bmatrix} w(t) \quad (8.81)$$

$$y_i(t) = \gamma_i(t) H_i x(t - d_i(t)) + v_i(t),\ i = 1, 2 \quad (8.82)$$

where

$$H_1 = [1\ 0],\ H_2 = [0\ 1]$$

T^0 is the sampling period. The state consists of the position $s(t)$ and the velocity $\dot{s}(t)$ of the moving target as follows:

$$x(t) = \begin{bmatrix} s(t) \\ \dot{s}(t) \end{bmatrix}$$

$\alpha_1(t)$ and $w(t)$ are zero-mean white scalar noises with covariances 0.1 and 0.3, respectively. $v_1(t)$ and $v_2(t)$ are zero-mean white noises with covariances 0.2 and 0.3, respectively. Suppose that $d_1(t) \in \{0, 1, 2, 3\}$ and $d_2(t) \in \{0, 1, 2\}$, then $d = 3$. For $i = 1, 2$, (8.82) can be rewritten as

$$\begin{aligned} y_i(t) = {} & H_i\{\sigma_{\{d_i(t)=0\}}x(t) + \sigma_{\{d_i(t)=1\}}x(t-1) \\ & +\sigma_{\{d_i(t)=2\}}x(t-2) + \sigma_{\{d_i(t)=3\}}x(t-3)\} + v_i(t) \end{aligned}$$

where $\sigma_{\{d_i(t)=0\}}$, $\sigma_{\{d_i(t)=1\}}$, $\sigma_{\{d_i(t)=2\}}$, and$\sigma_{\{d_i(t)=3\}}$ are binary random variables satisfying

$$\begin{aligned} &\text{Prob}\{\sigma_{\{d_1(t)=0\}}= 1\} = 0.5, \text{Prob}\{\sigma_{\{d_1(t)=1\}}= 1\} = 0.2 \\ &\text{Prob}\{\sigma_{\{d_1(t)=2\}}= 1\} = 0.1, \text{Prob}\{\sigma_{\{d_1(t)=3\}}= 1\} = 0.1 \\ &\text{Prob}\{\sigma_{\{d_2(t)=0\}}= 1\} = 0.4, \text{Prob}\{\sigma_{\{d_2(t)=1\}}= 1\} = 0.2 \\ &\text{Prob}\{\sigma_{\{d_2(t)=2\}}= 1\} = 0.2, \text{Prob}\{\sigma_{\{d_2(t)=3\}}= 1\} = 0 \end{aligned}$$

then

$$\begin{aligned} \gamma_1 &= \text{Prob}\{\gamma_1(t) = 1\} = 0.9 \\ \gamma_2 &= \text{Prob}\{\gamma_2(t) = 1\} = 0.8 \end{aligned}$$

The objective is to estimate the position and velocity of the moving target system (8.81) when $T_0 = 0.04$.

The local optimal estimates $\hat{x}^1(t|t)$ and $\hat{x}^2(t|t)$ are computed by applying Theorem 8.1, while the fusion estimate $\hat{x}(t|t)$ is computed recursively by applying Theorems 8.2 and 8.3. The state $x(t)$ and its estimate $\hat{x}(t|t)$ are depicted in Fig. 8.4. It can be seen from Fig. 8.4 that the estimate $\hat{x}(t|t)$ is close to the state $x(t)$, which indicates that the proposed estimator provides satisfactory estimation performance. The estimation performance is shown in Fig. 8.5, and the estimation precision of the fusion estimator is higher than that of the local optimal estimator.

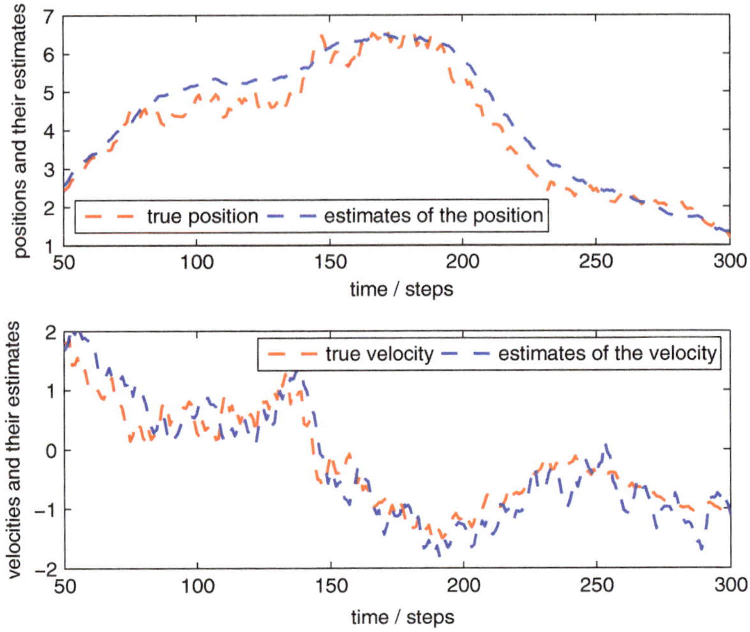

Fig. 8.4 The position and velocity of a moving target and their estimates

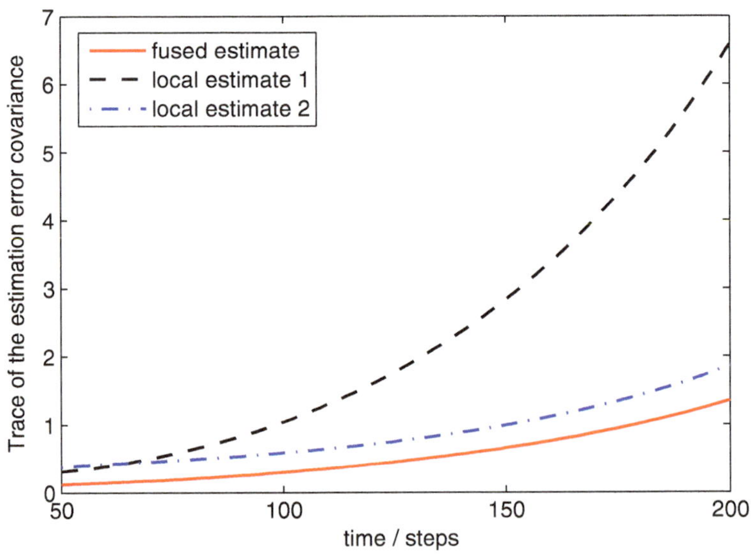

Fig. 8.5 The estimation precision of local estimators and the fusion estimator

8.6 Conclusions

In this chapter, the robust state fusion estimation problem was investigated for multisensor systems with randomly delayed measurements and stochastic parameter uncertainties. Multiple binary random variables with known statistical properties were introduced to model the delayed measurements. Both robust local estimators and state fusion estimators were designed without resorting to the measurement augmentation method.

References

1. Zhang H, Xie L, Zhang D, Soh YC (2004) A reorganized innovation approach to linear estimation. IEEE Trans Autom Control 49(10):1810–1814
2. Chen B, Yu L, Zhang WA (2011) Robust Kalman filtering for uncertain state delay systems with random observation delays and missing measurements. IET Control Theory Appl 5(17):1945–1954
3. Dong H, Wang Z, Gao H (2010) Robust H_∞ filtering for a class of nonlinear networked systems with multiple stochastic communication delays and packet dropouts. IEEE Trans Signal Process 58(4):1957–1966
4. Zhang H, Feng G, Han C (2011) Linear estimation for random delay systems. Syst Control Lett 60(7):450–459
5. Zhang H, Feng G, Duan G, Lu X (2006) H_∞ filtering for multiple-time-delay measurements. IEEE Trans Signal Process 54(5):1681–1688
6. Ma L, Da F, Zhang KJ (2011) Exponential H_∞ filter design for discrete time-delay stochastic systems with markovian jump parameters and missing measurements. IEEE Trans Circuits Syst-I Regul Pap 58(5):994–1007
7. Yang F, Wang Z, Feng G, Liu X (2009) Robust filtering with randomly varying sensor delay: the finite-horizon case. IEEE Trans Circuits Syst-I Regul Pap 56(3):664–672
8. Sun XJ, Deng ZL (2009) Information fusion wiener filter for the multisensor multichannel ARMA signals with time-delayed measurements. IET Signal Process 3(5):403–415
9. Lv N, Sun SL (2009) Scalar-weighted fusion estimators for systems with multiple sensors and multiple delayed measurements. In: Proceedings of IEEE conference on decision and control, Shanghai, Dec 2009, pp 7599–7602
10. Xia Y, Shang J, Chen J, Liu GP (2009) Networked data fusion with packet losses and variable delays. IEEE Trans Syst Man Cybern B Cybern 39(5):1107–1120
11. Hounkpevi FO, Yaz EE (2007) Robust minimum variance linear state estimators for multiple sensors with different failure rates. Automatica 43(7):1274–1280
12. Ahmad A, Gani M, Yang F (2008) Decentralized robust Kalman filtering for uncertain stochastic systems over heterogeneous sensor networks. Signal Process 88(8):1919–1928
13. Wang Z, Zhen Z, Zhang H, Chen Z (2009) Robust information fusion filtering method for discrete-time linear uncertain system. In: IEEE international conference on control and automation, Christchurch, Dec 2009, pp 1734–1738
14. Feng J, Wang Z, Zeng M (2013) Distributed weighted robust Kalman filter fusion for uncertain systems with autocorrelated and cross-correlated noises. Inf Fusion 14(1):78–86
15. Gao H, Meng X, Chen T (2008) Stabilization of networked control systems with a new delay characterization. IEEE Trans Autom Control 53(9):2142–2148
16. Sun SL, Deng ZL (2004) Multi-sensor optimal information fusion Kalman filter. Automatica 40(6):1017–1023
17. Kailath T, Syayed AH, Hassibi B (2000) Linear estimation. Prentice Hall, Upper Saddle River

Chapter 9
Fusion Estimation for WSNs with Delays and Packet Losses

9.1 Introduction

Communication delays and packet losses are usually unavoidable in sensor networks and should be taken into consideration in the estimator design. Both centralized and distributed fusion estimation methods have been presented in [1–3] for multisensor fusion estimation systems with delays or packet losses. To deal with the delays and packet losses simultaneously, the centralized fusion estimators have been designed in [4, 5] by using Kalman filtering and linear matrix inequality approaches, and the distributed fusion estimation algorithm was developed in [6] based on the well-known federated Kalman filtering approach. In [5, 6], the time-varying delay was identified by using the time-stamp method over each estimation interval, and exact values of the time delays should be known to update the estimator gain matrices online. Different from the delay models in [4–6], the distributed fusion Kalman filtering problem was investigated in [7] by assuming that the occurrence probabilities of delays were known a priori, and the filter gains can be computed off-line.

In this chapter, a distributed state fusion estimator is designed for sensor networks with random time delays and packet losses. First, a local optimal estimator is designed by taking missing measurements into consideration. Then, a distributed state fusion estimator is designed by fusion local estimates which may be delayed and lost during transmission from the local estimators to the fusion center. Some sufficient conditions are derived such that the MSE of the designed distributed state fusion estimator is bounded or convergent, and it is proved that the designed fusion estimator does not depend on the choice of the initial values. Moreover, a design method for the steady-state fusion estimator is also presented.

Throughout this chapter, it will be considered that $\prod_{\tau=\tau_1}^{\tau_2} F(\tau) = I_m$ and $\sum_{\tau=\tau_1}^{\tau_2} G(\tau) = 0$ if $\tau_1 > \tau_2$, where $F(\tau)$ and $G(\tau)$ represent different matrix functions with respect to the variable τ.

W.-A. Zhang et al., *Distributed Fusion Estimation for Sensor Networks with Communication Constraints*, DOI 10.1007/978-981-10-0795-8_9

9.2 Problem Statement

The distributed fusion estimation problem for a class of multisensor systems is shown in Fig. 9.1, where all the sensors are synchronized and have the same measurement sampling rates. The dynamics of the system to be monitored and the measurement equations of the L sensors are given by

$$x(t+1) = A(t)x(t) + \Gamma(t)w(t) \tag{9.1}$$

$$y_i(t) = \gamma_i(t)C_i(t)x_i(t) + v_i(t),\ i = 1, 2, \ldots, L \tag{9.2}$$

where $x(t) \in \Re^n$ is the state of the system and $y_i(t) \in \Re^{q_i}$ is the measured output from sensor i. $w(t) \in \Re^p$ and $v_i(t) \in \Re^{q_i}$ are zero-mean white noises with covariances $Q_w(t) > 0$ and $Q_{v_i}(t) > 0$, respectively, and are mutually uncorrelated. $A(t) \in \Re^{n\times n}$, $\Gamma(t) \in \Re^{n\times p}$, and $C_i(t) \in \Re^{q_i\times n}$ are time-varying matrices. The binary stochastic variable $\gamma_i(t)$, which is used to describe the missing phenomenon of the sensor measurement, is a Bernoulli distributed white sequence taking values of 1 and 0 with $\text{Prob}\{\gamma_i(t) = 1\} = \gamma_i$ and $\text{Prob}\{\gamma_i(t) = 0\} = 1 - \gamma_i$ [8], where $1 - \gamma_i$ is called the measurement missing rate. It is assumed that each sensor has enough processing capabilities to compute the optimal local state estimate of $x(t)$ based on the measurements $\{y_i(1), \ldots, y_i(t)\}$. For the ith subsystem (which is described by (9.1) and $y_i(t)$), the local Kalman filter is given by (Corollary 1 in [7]):

$$\begin{cases} \hat{x}_i(t|t) = (I_n - \gamma_i \mathrm{K}_i(t)C_i(t))A(t-1)\hat{x}_i(t-1|t-1) + \mathrm{K}_i(t)y_i(t) \\ \mathrm{K}_i(t) = \gamma_i P_{ii}^{-}(t)C_i^{\mathrm{T}}(t)\{\gamma_i C_i(t)[\gamma_i P_{ii}^{-}(t) \\ \qquad +(1-\gamma_i)\Lambda(t)]C_i^{\mathrm{T}}(t) + Q_{v_i}(t)\}^{-1} \\ P_{ii}(t|t) = [I_n - \gamma_i \mathrm{K}_i(t)C_i(t)]P_{ii}^{-}(t) \\ P_{ii}^{-}(t) = A(t-1)P_{ii}(t-1|t-1)A^{\mathrm{T}}(t-1) + \hat{\Gamma}(t-1) \end{cases} \tag{9.3}$$

where

$$\hat{\Gamma}(t-1) \triangleq \Gamma(t-1)Q_w(t-1)\Gamma^{\mathrm{T}}(t-1)$$

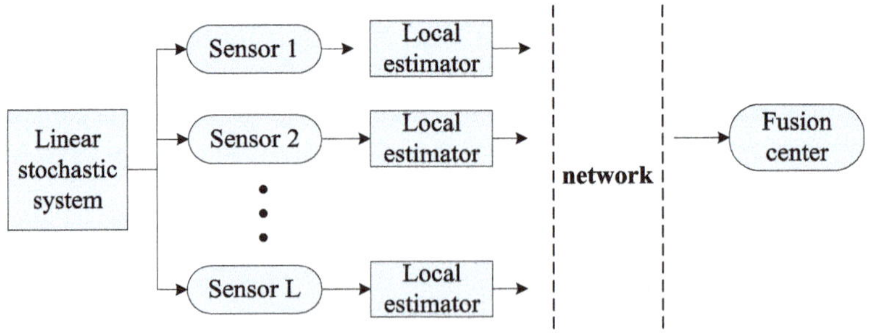

Fig. 9.1 A distributed fusion estimation system with delays and packet losses

and $\Lambda(t) \triangleq \mathbf{E}\{x(t)x^{\mathrm{T}}(t)\}$ is computed by

$$\Lambda(t) = A(t-1)\Lambda(t-1)A^{\mathrm{T}}(t-1) + \hat{\Gamma}(t-1) \tag{9.4}$$

The estimation error cross-covariance matrix $P_{ij}(t|t)$ is defined by

$$P_{ij}(t|t) \triangleq \mathbf{E}\left\{(x(t)-\hat{x}_i(t|t))(x(t)-\hat{x}_j(t|t))^{\mathrm{T}}\right\}$$

and it is calculated by:

$$\begin{aligned} P_{ij}(t|t) = {} & [I_n - \gamma_i \mathrm{K}_i(t)C_i(t)][A(t-1)P_{ij}(t-1|t-1) \\ & \times A^{\mathrm{T}}(t-1) + \hat{\Gamma}(t-1)][I_n - \gamma_j \mathrm{K}_j(t)C_j(t)]^{\mathrm{T}} \end{aligned} \tag{9.5}$$

When the local estimates $\hat{x}_i(t|t)$ are available, they are then transmitted to the fusion center through communication networks for generating a fusion estimate, where delay and packet loss may happen during transmissions. Denote the random delay in the ith local estimate as $d_i(t)$, and the random delay is assumed to be upper bounded and take values in a finite set as follows

$$d_i(t) \in \left\{d_i(t|t) \triangleq 0, d_i(t+1|t) \triangleq 1, \ldots, d_i(t+d_i|t) \triangleq d_i\right\} \tag{9.6}$$

where $d_i(t+\ell|t)(\ell \in \{0, 1, \cdots, d_i\})$ denotes that the local estimate $\hat{x}_i(t|t)$ is delayed by ℓ sampling periods and d_i represents the upper bound of the random delay. Moreover, the stochastic process $\{d_i(t)\}$ is assumed to be i.i.d. (independent and identically distributed), and the occurrence probabilities of the delays are known a priori through statistical test, that is,

$$\mathrm{Prob}\{d_i(t) = \ell\} = \pi_\ell^i,\ \ell = 0, 1, \ldots, d_i \tag{9.7}$$

where π_ℓ^i is a positive scalar and $\sum_{\ell=0}^{d_i} \pi_\ell^i = 1$. In the fusion center, there are L different buffers that store the corresponding local estimates. Due to the random transmission delays, multiple local estimates from a same sensor may arrive at the fusion center over an fusion estimation interval. Therefore, it is assumed that the local estimates $\hat{x}_i(t|t),\ i = 1, 2, \ldots, L$ are time stamped before being transmitted, and then similar to the signal storing mechanism in [9], each buffer stores the most recent local estimate from a sensor and discards the others according to the time stamps. Therefore, if multiple local estimates from a same sensor arrive at the fusion center over an estimation interval, then the fusion center selects only one local from the following set:

$$S_i(t) \triangleq \{\hat{x}_i(t|t), \hat{x}_i(t-1|t-1), \ldots, \hat{x}_i(t-d_i|t-d_i)\} \tag{9.8}$$

Let $\hat{x}_i^r(t|t)$ denote the local reorganized state estimate that is adopted by the fusion center, then $\hat{x}_i^r(t|t)$ can be computed by

$$\hat{x}_i^r(t|t) = \left(\prod_{\tau=1}^{\ell} A(t-\tau)\right)\hat{x}_i(t-\ell|t-\ell)$$

if the adopted local estimate at time t is $\hat{x}_i(t-\ell|t-\ell),\ \ell \in \{1,2,\ldots,d_i\}$. On the other hand, if no local estimate arrives at the fusion center over the fusion estimation interval, then the local reorganized state estimate $\hat{x}_i^r(t|t)$ will be compensated by one-step prediction as $\hat{x}_i^r(t-1|t-1)$.

Introducing the following indicator functions to describe the random delays

$$\sigma_{\{d_i(t+\ell|t)=\ell\}} = \begin{cases} 1 & \text{if } d_i(t) = \ell \\ 0 & \text{if } d_i(t) \neq \ell \end{cases}, \ \ell = 0,1,\ldots,d_i \tag{9.9}$$

where $\sigma_{\{d_i(t+\ell|t)=\ell\}},\ \ell = 0,1,\ldots,d_i$ satisfy

$$\begin{cases} \sum_{\ell=0}^{d_i} \sigma_{\{d_i(t+\ell|t)=\ell\}} = 1 \\ \sigma_{\{d_i(t+\ell_1|t)=\ell_1\}} \times \sigma_{\{d_i(t+\ell_2|t)=\ell_2\}} = 0,\ \ell_1 \neq \ell_2 \end{cases} \tag{9.10}$$

Therefore, it follows from (9.8), (9.9), and (9.10) that the local reorganized estimate $\hat{x}_i^r(t|t)$ is given by

$$\begin{aligned}\hat{x}_i^r(t|t) = &\sum_{\ell=0}^{d_i}\left\{\alpha_\ell^i(t)\left(\prod_{\tau=1}^{\ell} A(t-\tau)\right)\hat{x}_i(t-\ell|t-\ell)\right\} \\ &+\beta_i(t)A(t-1)\hat{x}_i^r(t-1|t-1)\end{aligned} \tag{9.11}$$

where the binary random variables $\alpha_\ell^i(t) \in \{0,1\}$ and $\beta_i(t) \in \{0,1\}$ are defined by

$$\begin{cases} \alpha_\ell^i(t) \triangleq \left\{\prod_{\tau_1=0}^{\ell-1}(1-\sigma_{\{d_i(t|t-\tau_1)=\tau_1\}})\right\}\sigma_{\{d_i(t|t-\ell)=\ell\}} \\ \beta_i(t) \triangleq \left\{\prod_{\tau_2=0}^{d_i}(1-\sigma_{\{d_i(t|t-\tau_2)=\tau_2\}})\right\} \end{cases} \tag{9.12}$$

where $\alpha_\ell^i(t) = 1$ means that the local estimate selected by the fusion center is $\hat{x}_i(t-\ell|t-\ell)$ at time t. Then it is derived from (9.10) that

$$\alpha_\ell^i(t) \times \beta_i(t) = 0,\ \sum_{\ell=0}^{d_i}\{\alpha_\ell^i(t)\} + \beta_i(t) = 1 \tag{9.13}$$

On the other hand, it follows from (9.6) and (9.7) that

$$\mathrm{Prob}\{d_i(t+\ell|t)=\ell\}=\pi_\ell^i$$

then one has by the statistical property of $d_i(t)$ and (9.12) that

$$\begin{cases} \mathbf{E}\{\alpha_\ell^i(t)\} \triangleq \alpha_\ell^i = \left\{\prod_{\tau_1=0}^{\ell-1}(1-\pi_{\tau_1}^i)\right\}\pi_\ell^i \\ \mathbf{E}\{\beta_i(t)\} \triangleq \beta_i = \prod_{\tau_2=0}^{d_i}(1-\pi_{\tau_2}^i) \end{cases} \tag{9.14}$$

Note that $\beta_i(t)=1$ means that no local estimates from sensor i arrive at the fusion center at time t; thus, the packet loss rate of the ith channel is given by β_i. Moreover, it follows from the well-known arithmetic-geometric average inequality that $\beta_i \le \left(\frac{d_i}{d_i+1}\right)^{d_i+1}$.

Assumption 9.1 The random variables $\gamma_i(t)$ and $d_i(t)$, $i=1,2,\ldots,L$ are mutually independent and uncorrelated with $w(t)$ and $v_i(t)$.

Then, the problem to be solved in this chapter is described as follows:

(1) Find a group of optimal weighting matrices $\Omega_1(t), \ldots, \Omega_L(t)$ such that the MSE of the fusion estimator $\hat{x}(t)=\sum_{i=1}^{L}\Omega_i(t)\hat{x}_i^r(t|t)$ is optimal, that is,

$$\begin{aligned} &\{\hat{x}(t),\Omega_1(t),\ldots,\Omega_L(t)\} = \arg\min \mathbf{E}\{(x(t)-\hat{x}_*(t))^{\mathrm{T}}(x(t)-\hat{x}_*(t))\} \\ &\text{s.t. } \hat{x}_*(t)=\sum_{i=1}^{L}\Omega_i^*(t)\hat{x}_i^r(t|t),\ \ \sum_{i=1}^{L}\Omega_i^*(t)=I_n \end{aligned} \tag{9.15}$$

(2) Find some sufficient conditions for the MSE of the fusion estimator in (9.15) to be bounded or convergent.

9.3 Design of Finite-Horizon Fusion Estimator

Define $e_i(t) \triangleq x(t)-\hat{x}_i^r(t|t)$; then, it follows from Lemma 2.4 that the distributed fusion estimation performance is optimal if and only if the matrix weights $\Omega_1(t),\ldots,\Omega_L(t)$ for (9.15) are determined by

$$[\Omega_1(t),\Omega_2(t),\ldots,\Omega_L(t)] = (I_0^{\mathrm{T}}\Sigma^{-1}(t)I_0)^{-1}I_0^{\mathrm{T}}\Sigma^{-1}(t) \tag{9.16}$$

where

$$I_0 \triangleq [I_n \cdots I_n]^{\mathrm{T}} \in \Re^{nL\times n}$$

$$\Sigma(t) \triangleq \mathbf{E}\{[e_1^{\mathrm{T}}(t) \ \cdots \ e_L^{\mathrm{T}}(t)]^{\mathrm{T}}[e_1^{\mathrm{T}}(t) \ \cdots \ e_L^{\mathrm{T}}(t)]\}$$

and $\sum_{i=1}^{L} \Omega_i(t) = I_n$. Thus, the designed fusion estimator is unbiased when $\mathbf{E}\{\hat{x}_i^r(t|t)\} = \mathbf{E}\{x(t)\}$, $i = 1, 2, \ldots, L$. The fusion estimation error covariance matrix $P(t) \triangleq \mathbf{E}\{(x(t) - \hat{x}(t))(x(t) - \hat{x}(t))^{\mathrm{T}}\}$ is calculated by

$$P(t) = (I_0^{\mathrm{T}} \Sigma^{-1}(t) I_0)^{-1} \tag{9.17}$$

In what follows, the recursive form of $\Sigma(t)$ will be given to obtain the optimal weighting matrices. Before presenting the main results, three useful lemmas are given as follows.

Lemma 9.1 *The binary random variables $\alpha_\ell^i(t)$, $\ell = 0, 1, \ldots, d_i$ and $\beta_i(t)$, $i = 1, 2, \ldots, L$ satisfy*:

$$\alpha_{\kappa_1}^i(t)\alpha_{\kappa_2}^i(t - t_1) = 0, \ d_i \geq \kappa_1 > \kappa_2, t_1 = 0, 1, \ldots, \kappa_1 - 1 \tag{9.18}$$

$$\prod_{\tau=0}^{d_i} \beta_i(t-\tau) = 0, \ \left(\prod_{\tau=0}^{d_i-1} \beta_i(t-\tau)\right) \alpha_\ell^i(t - d_i) = 0 \tag{9.19}$$

$$\begin{cases} \mathbf{E}\left\{\alpha_{\ell_1}^i(t)\alpha_{\ell_2}^j(t-t_1)\right\} = \begin{cases} \alpha_{\ell_1}^i \alpha_{\ell_2}^i & \text{if } i = j, \ t_1 \geq \ell_1 + 1 \\ \alpha_{\ell_1}^i \alpha_{\ell_2}^j & \text{if } i \neq j, \ \forall t_1 \end{cases} \\ \mathbf{E}\left\{\beta_i(t)\alpha_{\ell_2}^j(t-t_1)\right\} = \begin{cases} \beta_i \alpha_{\ell_2}^i & \text{if } i = j, t_1 \geq d_i + 1 \\ \beta_i \alpha_{\ell_2}^j & \text{if } i \neq j, \forall t_1 \end{cases} \\ \ell_1 \in \{0, 1, \ldots, d_i\}, \ \ell_2 \in \{0, 1, \ldots, d_j\} \end{cases} \tag{9.20}$$

where α_ℓ^i and β_i are computed by (9.14).

Proof Equations (9.18) and (9.19) can be directly obtained from (9.10) and (9.12). For $\ell_1^i \in \{0, 1, \ldots, d_i\}$ and $\ell_2^j \in \{0, 1, \ldots, d_j\}$, it follows from (9.6), (9.9), Assumption 9.1, and the statistical property of $d_i(t)$ that

$$\mathbf{E}\left\{\sigma_{\{d_i(t+\ell_1^i|t)=\ell_1^i\}}\sigma_{\{d_j(t_1+\ell_2^j|t_1)=\ell_2^j\}}\right\} = \mathbf{E}\left\{\sigma_{\{d_i(t+\ell_1^i|t)=\ell_1^i\}}\right\}\mathbf{E}\left\{\sigma_{\{d_i(t_1+\ell_2^j|t_1)=\ell_2^j\}}\right\}$$
$$\{i = j, t \neq t_1\} \text{ or } \{i \neq j, \forall t, t_1\}$$

Then, (9.20) is obtained from the above result, (9.12) and (9.13).

Lemma 9.2 *For the random variables $\Theta_\ell^{x_i}(t)$ and $\Theta_\ell^{w_i}(t)$ with the following forms*

$$\Theta_\ell^{x_i}(t) \triangleq \begin{cases} \sum_{\tau_0=0}^{\ell} \Upsilon_\ell^i(\tau_0),\ 0 \le \ell \le d_i \\ \sum_{\tau_2=0}^{2d_i-1-\ell} \Upsilon_\ell^i(\tau_2),\ d_i+1 \le \ell \le 2d_i-1 \end{cases} \tag{9.21}$$

$$\Theta_\ell^{w_i}(t) \triangleq \begin{cases} \sum_{k_0=\ell}^{d_i} \alpha_{k_0}^i(t) + \sum_{\varsigma_0=1}^{\ell-1} \hat{\Upsilon}_\ell^i(\varsigma_0) + \prod_{\varsigma_2=0}^{\ell-1} \beta_i(t-\varsigma_2),\ 1 \le \ell \le d_i \\ \sum_{\varsigma_3=0}^{2d_i-\ell-1} \hat{\Upsilon}_\ell^i(\varsigma_3),\ d_i+1 \le \ell \le 2d_i-1 \end{cases} \tag{9.22}$$

where $\Upsilon_\ell^i(\tau)$ and $\hat{\Upsilon}_\ell^i(\varsigma)$ are defined by

$$\Upsilon_\ell^i(\tau) \triangleq \begin{cases} \alpha_\tau^i(t-\ell+\tau) \prod_{\tau_1=0}^{\ell-\tau-1} \beta_i(t-\tau_1),\ 0 \le \ell \le d_i \\ \alpha_{d-\tau}^i(t-\ell-\tau+d_i) \prod_{\tau_3=0}^{\ell-d_i+\tau-1} \beta_i(t-\tau_3), \\ d_i+1 \le \ell \le 2d_i-1 \end{cases} \tag{9.23}$$

$$\hat{\Upsilon}_\ell^i(\varsigma) \triangleq \begin{cases} \left(\sum_{k_1=\varsigma}^{d} \alpha_{k_1}^i(t-\ell+\varsigma)\right) \prod_{\varsigma_1=0}^{\ell-\varsigma-1} \beta_i(t-\varsigma_1),\ 0 \le \ell \le d_i \\ \left(\sum_{k_2=d_i-\varsigma}^{d} \alpha_{k_2}^i(t-\ell-\varsigma+d_i)\right) \prod_{\varsigma_4=0}^{\ell+\varsigma-d_i-1} \beta_i(t-\varsigma_4), \\ d_i+1 \le \ell \le 2d_i-1 \end{cases} \tag{9.24}$$

The statistical correlations between the random variables $\Theta_\ell^{\chi_i}(t)$, $\ell = 0, 1, \ldots, 2d_i-1$, $\chi \in \{x, w\}$ satisfy

$$\begin{cases} \Theta_{ii}^{\chi\chi}(\ell_1,\ell_2) \triangleq \mathbf{E}\left\{\Theta_{\ell_1}^{\chi_i}(t)\Theta_{\ell_2}^{\chi_i}(t)\right\} = \mathbf{E}\left\{\Theta_{\ell_1}^{\chi_i}(t)\right\},\ \ell_1 = \ell_2 \\ \Theta_{ii}^{\chi\chi}(\ell_1,\ell_2) \triangleq \mathbf{E}\left\{\Theta_{\ell_1}^{\chi_i}(t)\Theta_{\ell_2}^{\chi_i}(t)\right\} = 0,\ \ell_1 \ne \ell_2 \\ \Theta_{ii}^{xw}(\ell_1,\ell_2) \triangleq \mathbf{E}\left\{\Theta_{\ell_1}^{x_i}(t)\Theta_{\ell_2}^{w_i}(t)\right\} = 0,\ \ell_2 > \ell_1 \end{cases} \tag{9.25}$$

$$\begin{cases} \Theta_{ij}^{xx}(\ell_1,\ell_2) \triangleq \mathbf{E}\left\{\Theta_{\ell_1}^{x_i}(t)\Theta_{\ell_2}^{x_j}(t)\right\} = \Theta_{ii}^{xx}(\ell_1,\ell_1)\Theta_{jj}^{xx}(\ell_2,\ell_2) \\ \Theta_{ij}^{xw}(\ell_1,\ell_2) \triangleq \mathbf{E}\left\{\Theta_{\ell_1}^{x_i}(t)\Theta_{\ell_2}^{w_j}(t)\right\} = \Theta_{ii}^{xx}(\ell_1,\ell_1)\Theta_{jj}^{ww}(\ell_2,\ell_2) \end{cases} \tag{9.26}$$

where $\mathbf{E}\{\Theta_{\ell_1}^{\chi_i}(t)\}$, $\chi \in \{x, w\}$ can be determined by (9.13) and (9.20).

Proof It can be obtained from (9.13) and (9.18) that

$$\begin{cases} \Upsilon^i_{\ell_1}(\tau^1)\Upsilon^i_{\ell_2}(\tau^2) = 0, \ [\ell_1 = \ell_2, \tau^1 \neq \tau^2] \text{ or } [\ell_1 \neq \ell_2, \forall \tau^1, \tau^2] \\ \hat{\Upsilon}^i_{\ell_1}(\varsigma^1)\hat{\Upsilon}^i_{\ell_2}(\varsigma^2) = 0, \ [\ell_1 = \ell_2, \varsigma^1 \neq \varsigma^2] \text{ or } [\ell_1 \neq \ell_2, \forall \varsigma^1, \varsigma^2] \end{cases} \tag{9.27}$$

$$\begin{cases} \Upsilon^i_{\ell_1}(\tau^1)\hat{\Upsilon}^i_{\ell_2}(\varsigma^1) = 0, \left(\sum_{k_0=\ell_2}^{d_i} \alpha^i_{k_0}(t)\right) \prod_{\varsigma_2=0}^{\ell_2-1} \beta_i(t-\varsigma_2) = 0 \\ \Upsilon^i_{\ell_1}(\tau^1)\left(\sum_{k_0=\ell_2}^{d_i} \alpha^i_{k_0}(t)\right) = 0, \Upsilon^i_{\ell_1}(\tau^1) \prod_{\varsigma_2=0}^{\ell_2-1} \beta_i(t-\varsigma_2) = 0 \\ \ell_2 > \ell_1, \forall \tau^1, \varsigma^1 \end{cases} \tag{9.28}$$

Then, it follows from (9.27) and (9.28) that

$$\begin{cases} \Theta^{\chi_i}_{\ell_1}(t)\Theta^{\chi_i}_{\ell_2}(t) = \Theta^{\chi_i}_{\ell_1}(t), \ \ell_1 = \ell_2, \chi \in \{x, w\} \\ \Theta^{\chi_i}_{\ell_1}(t)\Theta^{\chi_i}_{\ell_2}(t) = 0, \ \ell_1 \neq \ell_2, \chi \in \{x, w\} \\ \Theta^{x_i}_{\ell_1}(t)\Theta^{w_i}_{\ell_2}(t) = 0, \ \ell_2 > \ell_1 \end{cases} \tag{9.29}$$

Therefore, (9.25) is obtained from (9.29). Meanwhile, (9.26) can be derived from (9.20), (9.21), and (9.22).

Lemma 9.3 *Define*

$$\Psi_{ij}(t_1, t_2) \triangleq \mathbf{E}\left\{\tilde{x}_i(t_1|t_1)\tilde{x}_j^{\mathrm{T}}(t_2|t_2)\right\}$$

$$\Phi_i(t_1, t_2) \triangleq \mathbf{E}\left\{\tilde{x}_i(t_1|t_2)w^{\mathrm{T}}(t_2)\right\}$$

then one has

$$\Psi_{ij}(t_1, t_2) = \left(\prod_{\ell=0}^{t_1-t_2-1} [\Upsilon_i(t_1, \ell)A(t_1 - \ell - 1)]\right) P_{ij}(t_2|t_2), \ t_1 \geq t_2 \tag{9.30}$$

$$\begin{aligned} \Phi_i(t_1, t_2) = & \left(\prod_{\ell=0}^{t_1-t_2-2} [\Upsilon_i(t_1, \ell)A(t_1 - \ell_1 - 1)]\right) \Upsilon_i(t_1, t_1 - t_2) \\ & \times \Gamma(t_2)Q_w(t_2), \ t_1 > t_2 \end{aligned} \tag{9.31}$$

where $\Upsilon_i(t_1, \ell) = I_n - \gamma_i \mathrm{K}_i(t_1 - \ell)C_i(t_1 - \ell)$.

Proof For $t_1 \geq t_2$, it follows from (9.1) and (9.3) that the local estimation error $\tilde{x}_i(t_1|t_1) \triangleq x(t_1) - \hat{x}_i(t_1|t_1)$ is calculated by

$$\tilde{x}_i(t_1|t_1) = \left(\prod_{\ell=0}^{t_1-t_2-1} [\Upsilon_i(t_1, \ell)A(t_1 - \ell - 1)]\right) \tilde{x}_i(t_2|t_2)$$

$$
\begin{aligned}
&+\sum_{\hbar_1=1}^{t_1-t_2}\left\{\left(\prod_{\ell_1=0}^{\hbar_1-2}[\Upsilon_i(t_1,\ell_1)A(t_1-\ell_1-1)]\right)\right.\\
&\times\Upsilon_i(t_1,\hbar_1-1)\Gamma(t_1-\hbar_1)w(t_1-\hbar_1)\}\\
&-\sum_{\hbar_2=0}^{t_1-t_2-1}\{\left(\prod_{\ell_2=0}^{\hbar_2-1}\Upsilon_i(t_1,\ell_2)\right)[(\gamma_i(t-\hbar_2)-\gamma_i)C_i(t-\hbar_2)\\
&\times x(t-\hbar_2)+\mathrm{K}_i(t_1-\hbar_2)v_i(t_1-\hbar_2)]\}
\end{aligned}
\tag{9.32}
$$

By taking the facts $\tilde{x}_i(t|t)\perp w(t^1)$ $(t^1\geq t)$, $\tilde{x}_i(t|t)\perp v_i(t^2)$ $(t^2>t)$, and Assumption 9.1 into account, (9.30) and (9.31) follow from (9.32).

Theorem 9.1 *For given parameters γ_i, $i=1,2,\ldots,L$, and $0\leq\pi_\ell^i\leq 1$ satisfying $\sum_{\ell=0}^{d_i}\pi_\ell^i=1$, the local estimation error covariance matrix $\Sigma_{ii}(t)\triangleq\mathbf{E}\{e_i(t)e_i^{\mathrm{T}}(t)\}$ is calculated by*

$$
\begin{aligned}
\Sigma_{ii}(t)=&\sum_{\ell=0}^{2d_i-1}\left\{\Theta_{ii}^{xx}(\ell,\ell)\left(\prod_{\tau=1}^{\ell}A(t-\tau)\right)P_{ii}(t-\ell|t-\ell)\right.\\
&\left.\times\left(\prod_{\tau=1}^{\ell}A(t-\tau)\right)^{\mathrm{T}}\right\}+\sum_{\ell=1}^{2d_i-1}\left\{\Theta_{ii}^{ww}(\ell,\ell)\left(\prod_{\tau=1}^{\ell-1}A(t-\tau)\right)\right.\\
&\left.\times\hat{\Gamma}(t-\ell)\left(\prod_{\tau=1}^{\ell-1}A(t-\tau)\right)^{\mathrm{T}}\right\}
\end{aligned}
\tag{9.33}
$$

where $\Theta_{ii}^{xx}(\ell,\ell)$ and $\Theta_{ii}^{ww}(\ell,\ell)$ are computed by (9.25), $P_{ii}(t-\ell|t-\ell)$ are calculated by (9.3), and $\hat{\Gamma}(t-\ell)$ is defined in (9.3). Moreover, the estimation error cross-covariance matrix $\Sigma_{ij}(t)\triangleq\mathbf{E}\{e_i(t)e_j^{\mathrm{T}}(t)\}$ is given by

$$
\begin{aligned}
\Sigma_{ij}(t)=&\sum_{\ell=0}^{2d-1}\left\{\Theta_{ij}^{xx}(\ell,\ell)\left(\prod_{\tau=1}^{\ell}A(t-\tau)\right)P_{ij}(t-\ell|t-\ell)\right.\\
&\left.\times\left(\prod_{\tau=1}^{\ell}A(t-\tau)\right)^{\mathrm{T}}\right\}+\sum_{\ell=1}^{2d-1}\left\{\Theta_{ij}^{ww}(\ell,\ell)\left(\prod_{\tau=1}^{\ell-1}A(t-\tau)\right)\right.\\
&\left.\times\hat{\Gamma}(t-\ell)\left(\prod_{\tau=1}^{\ell-1}A(t-\tau)\right)^{\mathrm{T}}\right\}+\sum_{\ell=0}^{2d-2}\left\{\left(\prod_{\tau=1}^{\ell}A(t-\tau)\right)\right.\\
&\left.\times\,\Xi_\ell^{ij}(t)+\hat{\Xi}_\ell^{ji}(t)\left(\prod_{\tau=1}^{\ell}A(t-\tau)\right)^{\mathrm{T}}\right\}
\end{aligned}
\tag{9.34}
$$

where $d = \max\{d_i, d_j\}$, $\Theta^{x_i}_{\ell_i}(t) = 0$, $\Theta^{w_i}_{\ell_i}(t) = 0$ $(\ell_i > 2d_i - 1)$ *and* $\Theta^{x_j}_{\ell_j}(t) = 0$, $\Theta^{w_j}_{\ell_j}(t) = 0$ $(\ell_j > 2d_j - 1)$, $P_{ij}(t|t)$ *is calculated by (9.5), while* $\Xi^{ij}_{\ell}(t)$ *and* $\hat{\Xi}^{ji}_{\ell}(t)$ *are computed by*

$$
\begin{aligned}
\Xi^{ij}_{\ell}(t) = \sum_{\hbar=0}^{2d-2-\ell} \Bigg\{ & \Theta^{xx}_{ij}(\ell, \ell-\hbar-1)\Psi_{ij}(t-\ell, t-\ell-\hbar-1) \\
& \times\left(\prod_{\tau_1=1}^{\ell+\hbar+1} A(t-\tau_1)\right)^{\mathrm{T}} + \Theta^{xw}_{ij}(\ell, \ell-\hbar-1)\Phi_i(t-\ell, t \\
& -\ell-\hbar-1)\Gamma^{\mathrm{T}}(t-\ell-1)\left(\prod_{\tau_1=1}^{\ell+\hbar} A(t-\tau_1)\right)^{\mathrm{T}}\Bigg\}
\end{aligned} \tag{9.35}
$$

$$
\begin{aligned}
\hat{\Xi}^{ji}_{\ell}(t) = \sum_{\hbar=0}^{2d-2-\ell} \Bigg\{ & \Theta^{xx}_{ij}(\ell-\hbar-1, \ell)\left(\prod_{\tau_1=1}^{\ell+\hbar+1} A(t-\tau_1)\right) \\
& \times\Psi^{\mathrm{T}}_{ji}(t-\ell, t-\ell-\hbar-1) + \Theta^{xw}_{ij}(\ell-\hbar-1, \ell) \\
& \times\left(\prod_{\tau_1=1}^{\ell+\hbar} A(t-\tau_1)\right)\Gamma(t-\ell-1)\Phi^{\mathrm{T}}_{j}(t-\ell-\hbar-1, t-\ell)\Bigg\}
\end{aligned} \tag{9.36}
$$

where $\Psi_{ij}(t-\ell, t-\ell-\hbar-1)$ *and* $\Phi_i(t-\ell, t-\ell-\hbar-1)$ *are computed by (9.30) and (9.31), while* $\Theta^{xx}_{ij}(\ell_1, \ell_2)$ *and* $\Theta^{xw}_{ij}(\ell_1, \ell_2)$ *are determined by (9.26). Moreover, the relationship between the optimal fusion estimator* $\hat{x}(t)$ *and local reorganized estimate* $\hat{x}^r_i(t|t)$ *is given by*

$$
\mathrm{Tr}\{P(t)\} \le \mathrm{Tr}\{\Sigma_{ii}(t)\} \tag{9.37}
$$

Proof It follows from (9.1), (9.11), and (9.13) that

$$
\begin{aligned}
e_i(t) = & \sum_{\ell=0}^{d_i}\left\{\alpha^i_{\ell}(t)\left[x(t) - \left(\prod_{\tau=1}^{\ell} A(t-\tau)\right)\hat{x}_i(t-\ell|t-\ell)\right]\right\} \\
& +\beta_i(t)[x(t) - A(t-1)\hat{x}^r_i(t-1|t-1)]
\end{aligned} \tag{9.38}
$$

Then, it follows from (9.19) that (9.38) is equivalent to

$$e_i(t) = \sum_{\ell=0}^{2d_i-1} \left\{ \Theta_\ell^{x_i}(t) \left(\prod_{\tau=1}^{\ell} A(t-\tau) \right) \tilde{x}_i(t-\ell|t-\ell) \right\} + \sum_{\ell=1}^{2d_i-1} \left\{ \Theta_\ell^{w_i}(t) \left(\prod_{\tau_1=1}^{\ell-1} A(t-\tau_1) \right) \Gamma(t-\ell)w(t-\ell) \right\} \tag{9.39}$$

where $\Theta_\ell^{x_i}(t)$ and $\Theta_\ell^{w_i}(t)$ are defined by (9.21) and (9.22), respectively. Meanwhile, it follows from Assumption 9.1 that

$$\begin{aligned} &\mathbf{E}\{\Theta_{\ell_1}^{x_i}(t)\tilde{x}_i(t-\ell_1|t-\ell_1)\tilde{x}_j^{\mathrm{T}}(t-\ell_2,t-\ell_2)\Theta_{\ell_2}^{x_j}(t)\} \\ &= \Theta_{ij}^{xx}(\ell_1,\ell_2)\Psi_{ij}(t-\ell_1,t-\ell_2) \end{aligned} \tag{9.40}$$

where $\Theta_{ij}^{xx}(\ell_1,\ell_2)$, $\forall i,j$ is obtained from Lemma 9.2 and $\Psi_{ij}(t-\ell_1,t-\ell_2)(\ell_1 \le \ell_2)$ is computed by using (9.30). Note that it follows from (9.30) that

$$\Psi_{ij}(t-\ell_1,t-\ell_2) = \Psi_{ji}^{\mathrm{T}}(t-\ell_2,t-\ell_1),\ \ell_1 > \ell_2$$

By taking the fact $\tilde{x}_i(t-\ell_1,t-\ell_1) \perp w(t-\ell_2)$, $\ell_1 \ge \ell_2$, $i \in \{1,2,\ldots,L\}$ into account, (9.33) is obtained from (9.25), (9.39), and (9.40), while (9.34) is derived from (9.26), (9.39), and (9.40). Moreover, at time t, the fusion estimation error covariance matrix for $\hat{x}(t)$ is computed by (9.17), and the local estimation error covariance matrix for $\hat{x}_i^r(t|t)$ is calculated by (9.33), and then (9.37) is obtained from the result of [10]. This completes the proof.

Based on Theorem 9.1, the computation procedures for the fusion estimate $\hat{x}(t)$ are summarized as follows:

Algorithm 9.1 For given γ_i, $i = 1,2,\ldots,L$ and $0 \le \pi_\ell^i \le 1$ satisfying $\sum_{\ell=0}^{d_i} \pi_\ell^i = 1$, one can determine the parameters $\Theta_{ii}^{\chi\chi}(\ell_1,\ell_2)(\chi \in \{x,w\})$, $\Theta_{ii}^{xw}(\ell_1,\ell_2)$, $i = 1,2,\ldots,L$, $\Theta_{ij}^{xx}(\ell_1,\ell_2)$, and $\Theta_{ij}^{xw}(\ell_1,\ell_2)$, $j = i, i+1,\ldots,L$ by using Lemma 9.2.

Step 1. Calculate the local estimates $\hat{x}_i(t|t)$, the error variance matrices $P_{ii}(t|t)$, and $P_{ij}(t|t)(i \ne j)$ by using (9.3) and (9.5).
Step 2. Calculate the local reorganized estimates $\hat{x}_i^r(t|t)$ by substituting $\hat{x}_i(t-\ell|t-\ell)$, $\ell = 0,1,\ldots,d_i$ into (9.11).
Step 3. Calculate $\Psi_{ij}(t_1,t_2)$ and $\Phi_i(t_1,t_2)$ by (9.30) and (9.31).
Step 4. Calculate $\Sigma_{ij}(t)$ by substituting $P_{ij}(t|t)$, $\Psi_{ij}(t_1,t_2)$ and $\Phi_i(t_1,t_2)$ into (9.33) and (9.34).
Step 5. Calculate $\Omega_1(t),\ldots,\Omega_L(t)$ by substituting $\Sigma_{ij}(t)$ into (9.16).
Step 6. Calculate the optimal fusion estimate $\hat{x}(t)$ by substituting $\Omega_1(t),\ldots,$ $\Omega_L(t)$, and $\hat{x}_i^r(t|t)$ into $\hat{x}(t) = \sum_{i=1}^{L} \Omega_i(t)\hat{x}_i^r(t|t)$.

In [4–6], the estimator gain matrices should be computed online as they need to know the delay exactly at each step. Different from these results, it is known from (9.16) and Theorem 9.1 that the optimal matrix weights $\Omega_i(t),\ i = 1, 2, \ldots, L$ are independent of the sequences of the measurements and the local reorganized estimates. Therefore, the optimal matrix weights can be computed off-line or at the fusion center, which helps reduce the computational complexity of the fusion center and the communication traffic between the sensors and the fusion center.

9.4 Stability Analysis for the Fusion Estimator

First, it is considered that the stochastic system (9.1) is uniformly completely controllable, i.e., there exist an integer $N > 0$ and positive scalars ρ_1 and ρ_2, such that the following inequality

$$\rho_1 I_n \leq \sum_{j=t-N+1}^{k} A_c(t,j)\Gamma(j)Q_w(i)\Gamma^{\mathrm{T}}(j)A_c^{\mathrm{T}}(t,j) \leq \rho_2 I_n \tag{9.41}$$

holds for $t \geq N$, where $A_c(t,j)$ satisfies

$$A_c(t,j) = \prod_{\ell=1}^{t-j} A(t-\ell)(t > j), A_c(j,j) = I_n \tag{9.42}$$

$$A_c(t,j) = A_c^{-1}(j,t),\ t < j \tag{9.43}$$

Theorem 9.2 *Consider the optimal fusion estimator for systems (9.1) and (9.2), where the system (9.1) is uniformly completely controllable. If*

(C2.1) For $0 < \gamma_i < 1$, there exist an integer $N_0 > 0$ and a positive matrix Λ_0 such that $\Lambda(t) \leq \Lambda_0\ (t \geq N_0)$.
(C2.2) There exist an integer $N_1 > N_0 > 0$ and positive scalars ρ_3 and ρ_4 such that the following inequality

$$\rho_3 I_n \leq \mathrm{M}_i(t-N+1,t) \leq \rho_4 I_n,\ i = 1, 2, \ldots, L \tag{9.44}$$

holds for $t \geq N_1$, where the stochastic observability matrix $\mathrm{M}_i(t-N_1+1,t)$ is computed by

$$\begin{aligned}\mathrm{M}_i(t-N_1+1,t) = \gamma_i^2 \sum_{j=t-N_1+1}^{t} \{A_c^{\mathrm{T}}(j,t)C_i^{\mathrm{T}}(j)[\gamma_i \\ \times(1-\gamma_i)C_i(j)\Lambda_0 C_i^{\mathrm{T}}(j) + Q_{v_i}(j)]^{-1}C_i(j)A_c(j,t)\}\end{aligned} \tag{9.45}$$

where $A_c(t, j)$ is given by (9.43). Then, the MSE of the designed fusion estimate $\hat{x}(t)$ is bounded, i.e., there exist a scalar $p_0 > 0$ such that

$$\mathrm{Tr}\{P(t)\} \le p_0 \tag{9.46}$$

Moreover, the following equation

$$\lim_{t\to\infty} P_1(t) = \lim_{t\to\infty} P_2(t) \tag{9.47}$$

always holds, where $P_1(t)$ and $P_2(t)$ are any fusion estimation error covariance matrices with different initial conditions.

Proof The measurement equation (9.2) can be rewritten as

$$y_i(t) = \gamma_i C_i(t)x_i(t) + \hat{v}_i(t) \tag{9.48}$$

where $\hat{v}_i(t) = (\gamma_i(t) - \gamma_i)C_i(t)x(t) + v_i(t)$. Then, it follows from the statistical characteristics of $\gamma_i(t)$ and $v_i(t)$ that $\hat{v}_i(t)$ is a zero-mean white noise with covariance $Q_{\hat{v}_i}(t) = \gamma_i(1 - \gamma_i)C_i(t)\Lambda(t)C_i(t) + Q_{v_i}(t)$. Moreover, the stochastic observation matrix $\hat{\mathrm{M}}_i^{\gamma_i}(t - N + 1, t)$ of the systems (9.1) and (9.48) is given by

$$\hat{\mathrm{M}}_i^{\gamma_i}(t - N + 1, t) = \gamma_i^2 \sum_{j=t-N+1}^{t} \left\{A_c^{\mathrm{T}}(j, t)C_i^{\mathrm{T}}(j)Q_{\hat{v}_i}^{-1}(j)C_i(j)A_c(j, t)\right\} \tag{9.49}$$

Then, it is concluded from (9.49) and C2.2 that

$$\rho_3 I_n \le \hat{\mathrm{M}}_i^{\gamma_i}(t - N_1 + 1, t) \le \rho_4^1 I_n,\ t > N_1 \tag{9.50}$$

Under the conditions (9.41) and (9.50), it follows from Theorem 7.4 in [11] that the local estimate $\hat{x}_i(t|t)$ is uniformly asymptotically stable and the local optimal estimation error covariance matrix $P_{ii}(t|t)$ is independent of the initial value $P_{ii}(0|0) > 0$ as t goes to ∞. Moreover, it follows from Lemma 7.1 in [11] that if (9.41) and (9.50) hold, the covariance matrix $P_{ii}(t|t)$ will be bounded. Then, (9.46) is obtained from (9.37).

On the other hand, the local estimation error $\tilde{x}_i(t|t) \triangleq x(t) - \hat{x}_i(t|t)$ is equivalent to

$$\begin{aligned}\tilde{x}_i(t|t) &= \mathrm{X}_i(t, t-1)\tilde{x}_i(t-1|t-1) + \mathrm{X}_i(t, t-1)\\ &\quad \times A^*(t-1)\Gamma(t-1)w(t-1) - \mathrm{K}_i(t)v_i(t)\end{aligned} \tag{9.51}$$

where $A^*(t)$ satisfies $A(t)A^*(t) = I_n$ and

$$\mathrm{X}_i(t, t-1) \triangleq [I_n - \gamma_i \mathrm{K}_i(t)C_i(t)]A(t-1)$$

is the state-transition matrix of the estimator. Then, the estimation error cross-covariance matrix (9.5) is rewritten as

$$\begin{aligned}P_{ij}(t|t) = {} & \mathrm{X}_i(t,t-1)[P_{ij}(t-1|t-1) \\ & +A^*(t-1)\hat{\Gamma}(t-1)[A^*(t-1)]^{\mathrm{T}}]\mathrm{X}_j^{\mathrm{T}}(t,t-1)\end{aligned} \tag{9.52}$$

Let $P_{ij}^1(t|t)$ and $P_{ij}^2(t|t)$ denote any covariance matrices with initial conditions $P_{ij}^1(0|0)$ and $P_{ij}^2(0|0)$, respectively; then, $\Delta P_{ij}(t) \triangleq P_{ij}^1(t|t) - P_{ij}^2(t|t)$ is computed by

$$\Delta P_{ij}(t) = \mathrm{X}_i(t,t-1)\Delta P_{ij}(t-1)\mathrm{X}_j^{\mathrm{T}}(t,t-1)$$

which yields

$$\Delta P_{ij}(t) = \mathrm{X}_i(t,t_k)\Delta P_{ij}(t_k)\mathrm{X}_j^{\mathrm{T}}(t,t_k)(t > t_k \geq 0) \tag{9.53}$$

For the state-transition matrices $\mathrm{X}_i(t,t_1)$ and $\mathrm{X}_j(t,t_2)$ of the local estimates, it can be derived from the results in [11] that there exist $c_1 > 0$ and $c_2 > 0$ such that

$$\begin{cases} ||\mathrm{X}_i(t,t_{k*})|| \leq c_1 \mathrm{e}^{-c_2(t-t_{k*})} \\ ||\mathrm{X}_j(t,t_{k*})|| \leq c_1 \mathrm{e}^{-c_2(t-t_{k*})} \end{cases} \tag{9.54}$$

holds for $t > t_{k*}$. Then, it follows from (9.53) and (9.54) that

$$\left\|\Delta P_{ij}(t)\right\| \leq \left\|\mathrm{X}_i(t,t_{k*})\right\| \left\|\Delta P_{ij}(t_{k*})\right\| \left\|\mathrm{X}_j^{\mathrm{T}}(t,t_{k*})\right\| = c_1^2 \mathrm{e}^{-2c_2(t-t_{k*})} \tag{9.55}$$

and thus $\left\|\Delta P_{ij}(t)\right\| \to 0$ as $t \to \infty$, which implies that the estimation error cross-covariance matrix (9.52) is independent of the initial conditions.

It can be concluded from the above analysis that the covariance matrices $P_{ii}(t|t)$ and $P_{ij}(t|t)$ are independent of the initial conditions. On the other hand, it follows from (9.17) that the fusion estimation error covariance matrix $P(t)$ is dependent on $P_{ii}(t|t)$, $i = 1,2,\ldots,L$ and $P_{ij}(t|t)$, $j = i+1,\ldots,L$. Thus, the covariance matrix $P(t)$ is independent of the initial conditions, which implies that (9.47) holds. This completes the proof.

For the systems (9.1) and (9.2) with constant system matrices, i.e., the systems (9.1) and (9.2) reduce to

$$\begin{cases} x(t+1) = Ax(t) + \Gamma w(t) \\ y_i(t) = \gamma_i C_i x(t) + \bar{v}_i(t),\ i = 1,2,\ldots,L \end{cases} \tag{9.56}$$

where $w(t)$ and $\bar{v}_i(t) \triangleq (\gamma_i(t) - \gamma_i)C_i x(t) + v_i(t)$ are zero-mean white noises with covariances Q_w and $Q_{\bar{v}_i}(t) = \gamma_i(1-\gamma_i)C_i\Lambda(t)C_i^{\mathrm{T}} + Q_{v_i}$, respectively. Then, (9.41) is equivalent to

$$\operatorname{rank}([\Gamma, A\Gamma, \ldots, A^{n-1}\Gamma]) = n \tag{9.57}$$

which implies that system (9.56) is completely controllable.

Theorem 9.3 *Consider the optimal fusion estimator for systems (9.56) with (9.57). If each observation matrix C_i, measurement missing rate $1-\gamma_i$, and the system matrix A satisfy*

$$-1 < \lambda_{\max}(A) < 1,\ 0 < \gamma_i < 1 \tag{9.58}$$

$$\operatorname{rank}(\gamma_i[\,C_i^{\mathrm{T}}\ (C_iA)^{\mathrm{T}} \cdots (C_iA^{n-1})^{\mathrm{T}}\,]^{\mathrm{T}}) = n \tag{9.59}$$

then for any initial values $P_{ii}(0|0) > 0$, $i = 1, 2, \ldots, L$ and $P_{ij}(0|0)$, $j = i+1, \ldots, L$, the fusion estimation error covariance matrix $P(t)$ converges to a unique positive-definite matrix, i.e., $\lim_{t\to\infty} P(t) = P$. Under this condition, the steady-state fusion estimator for systems (9.56) is given by

$$\begin{cases} \hat{x}_s(t) = \sum\limits_{i=1}^{L} \Omega_i \hat{x}_i^s(t|t),\ \Omega_i = \lim\limits_{t\to\infty} \Omega_i(t) \\ \hat{x}_i^s(t|t) = (I_n - \mathrm{K}_iC_i)A\hat{x}_i^s(t-1|t-1) + \mathrm{K}_i y_i(t) \\ \mathrm{K}_i = \lim\limits_{t\to\infty} \mathrm{K}_i(t) \end{cases} \tag{9.60}$$

Proof For the system (9.56), it follows from (9.4) that

$$\Lambda(t) = A^t\Lambda(0)(A^t)^{\mathrm{T}} + \sum_{\kappa=0}^{t-1} A^\kappa \Gamma Q_w \Gamma^{\mathrm{T}} (A^\kappa)^{\mathrm{T}} \tag{9.61}$$

Then, one has by (9.58) and (9.61) that $\lim_{t\to\infty} \Lambda(t) = \Lambda$. Let $\Lambda_1(t)$ and $\Lambda_2(t)$ denote any state covariance matrices with initial values $\Lambda_1(0)$ and $\Lambda_2(0)$, respectively, and then $\Delta\Lambda \triangleq \Lambda_1(t) - \Lambda_2(t)$ is computed by $\Delta\Lambda(t) = A^t\Delta\Lambda(0)(A^t)^{\mathrm{T}}$. Taking the above equation and (9.58) into account yields $\lim_{t\to\infty} \Delta\Lambda(t) = 0$, which means that the limit Λ is the unique solution of (9.4). Following this fact, one obtains

$$\lim_{t\to\infty} Q_{\bar{v}_i}(t) = Q_{\bar{v}_i} = \gamma_i(1-\gamma_i)C_i\Lambda C_i^{\mathrm{T}} + Q_{v_i}$$

This implies that there exist an integer $\mathrm{T}_0 > 0$ such that the equation $Q_{\bar{v}_i}(t) = Q_{\bar{v}_i}$ holds for all $t \geq \mathrm{T}_0$. Under this conditions, (9.59) is equivalent to C2.2 for $t \in [\mathrm{T}_0, \infty)$; then, it follows from Theorem 9.2 that the covariance matrices $P(t)$, $P_{ii}(t|t)$ and $P_{ij}(t|t)$ for the systems (9.56) are independent of any initial condition.

On the other hand, it is well known that if the conditions (9.57) and (9.59) hold for $t \geq \mathrm{T}_0$, then each local estimate $\hat{x}_i(t|t)$ for the systems (9.56) will be stable, and

$P_{ii} \triangleq \lim_{t\to\infty} P_{ii}(t)$ must be the unique steady-state value of the sequence $\{P_{ii}(t|t)\}$. Following the above facts, the gain matrix $\mathrm{K}_i(t)$ converges to a steady-state value, i.e., $\lim_{t\to\infty} \mathrm{K}_i(t) = \mathrm{K}_i$, and the limit K_i is also independent of any initial condition. Therefore, the state-transition matrix $\hat{\mathrm{X}}_i(t) \triangleq [I_n - \mathrm{K}_i(t)C_i]A$ of each local estimate for systems (9.56) converges to a unique steady-state value. Moreover, the limit $\hat{\mathrm{X}}_i \triangleq \lim_{t\to\infty} \hat{\mathrm{X}}_i(t)$ is a stable matrix, i.e.,

$$-1 < \lambda_{\max}(\hat{\mathrm{X}}_i) < 1,\ i = 1, 2, \ldots, L \tag{9.62}$$

Meanwhile, it follows from (9.52) that $P_{ij}(t|t)$ for (9.56) can be rewritten as

$$P_{ij}(t|t) = \hat{\mathrm{X}}_i(t)[P_{ij}(t-1|t-1) + A^* \Gamma Q_w \Gamma^{\mathrm{T}} (A^*)^{\mathrm{T}}]\hat{\mathrm{X}}_j^{\mathrm{T}}(t) \tag{9.63}$$

Following the similar derivations of Theorem 9.2, it is derived from (9.62) and (9.63) that $\lim_{t\to\infty} P_{ij}(t|t) = P_{ij}$. Therefore, it is concluded from the above analysis that the fusion estimation error covariance matrix $P(t)$ for systems (9.56) converges to a unique positive-definite matrix. Under this condition, the steady-state fusion estimate for the systems (9.56) can be given by (9.60). The proof is thus completed.

The optimal matrix weights of the steady-state fusion estimator (9.59) are not required to be calculated at each step; thus, the steady-state fusion estimator is easy to be implemented in practices. On the other hand, for the multisensor fusion estimation system without missing measurements, it can be seen from Theorems 9.2 and 9.3 that if the conditions (9.41), (9.44) (or (9.57), and (9.59)) hold, then the MSE of the designed fusion estimator will be bounded or convergent.

9.5 Simulations

Consider a networked multisensor fusion estimation system with two sensors, where the system parameters in (9.1) and (9.2) are given by [12]

$$A(t) \equiv \begin{bmatrix} 1 & \hat{\mathrm{T}} \\ 0 & 1 \end{bmatrix},\ \Gamma(t) \equiv \begin{bmatrix} 0.5\hat{\mathrm{T}}^2 \\ \hat{\mathrm{T}} \end{bmatrix}$$

$$C_1 = C_2 = I_2$$

$$Q_w(t) \equiv 0.5,\ Q_{v_1}(t) \equiv \begin{bmatrix} 0.5 & 0 \\ 0 & 0.2 \end{bmatrix},\ Q_{v_2}(t) \equiv \begin{bmatrix} 0.8 & 0 \\ 0 & 0.3 \end{bmatrix}$$

$$\gamma_1 = 0.90,\ \gamma_2 = 0.85$$

where $\hat{\mathrm{T}}$ is the sampling period. The state of system (9.1) is $x(t) = [s(t)\ \dot{s}(t)]^{\mathrm{T}}$, where $s(t)$ and $\dot{s}(t)$ are, respectively, the position and velocity of the moving target

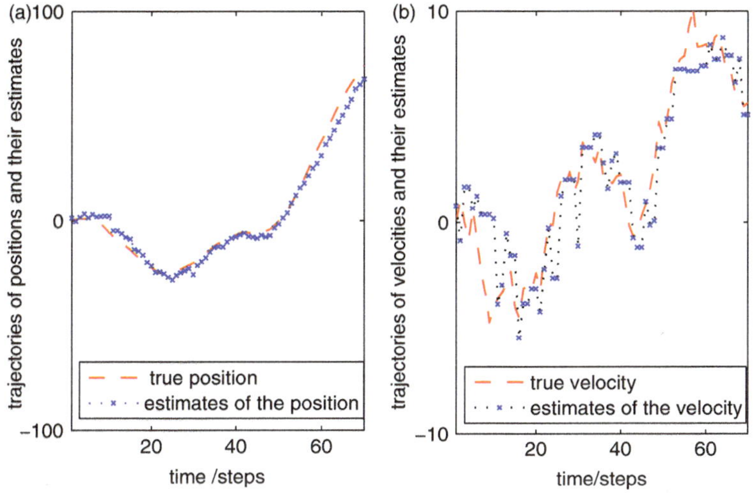

Fig. 9.2 Trajectories of the system state $x(t)$ and the fusion estimate $\hat{x}(t)$

at time t. For $\hat{\mathrm{T}} = 0.5$, it is assumed that $d_i(t) \in \{0, 1, 2\}$, $i = 1, 2$; then, the occurrence probabilities of delays are taken as $\pi_0^1 = 0.4, \pi_1^1 = 0.3$, $\pi_2^1 = 0.3$, $\pi_0^2 = 0.5$, $\pi_1^2 = 0.4$, $\pi_2^2 = 0.1$. Under this condition, the local reorganized state estimates $\hat{x}_i^r(t|t)$, $i = 1, 2$ are calculated by (9.11). To verify the effectiveness of the proposed fusion estimator in Algorithm 9.1, the trajectories of the state $x(t)$ and the fusion estimate $\hat{x}(t)$ are shown in Fig. 9.2a, b, which shows that the designed fusion estimator is able to track the maneuvering target well. Moreover, the estimation performance (assessed by the trace of the estimation error covariance matrix) of local reorganized state estimates $\hat{x}_i^r(t|t)$, $i = 1, 2$ and the fusion estimate $\hat{x}(t)$ is depicted in Fig. 9.3; then, it can be seen from these figures that the performance of the fusion estimator is better than that of the local estimators. Meanwhile, the relations between the fusion estimation performance and the measurement missing rates are plotted in Figs. 9.4 and 9.5, which shows that the estimation performance degrades as the measurement missing rate increases.

On the other hand, it can be verified that the conditions (9.57) and (9.59) hold for $\gamma_1 = \gamma_2 = 1$; then, by using Theorem 9.3, the fusion estimation error covariance matrix $P(t)$ converges to the unique positive matrix, and the steady-state fusion estimates $\hat{x}_s(t)$ exists for this estimation system without missing measurements. Moreover, one obtains the following parameters for the steady-state estimators by applying Algorithm 9.1:

$$
\begin{aligned}
\mathrm{K}_1 &= \begin{bmatrix} 0.2491 & 0.2211 \\ 0.0884 & 0.6263 \end{bmatrix}, \mathrm{K}_2 = \begin{bmatrix} 0.2414 & 0.2263 \\ 0.0848 & 0.5562 \end{bmatrix} \\
\Omega_1 &= \begin{bmatrix} 0.5961 & -0.0679 \\ 0.0611 & 0.3795 \end{bmatrix}, \Omega_2 = \begin{bmatrix} 0.4039 & 0.0679 \\ -0.0611 & 0.6205 \end{bmatrix}
\end{aligned}
\tag{9.64}
$$

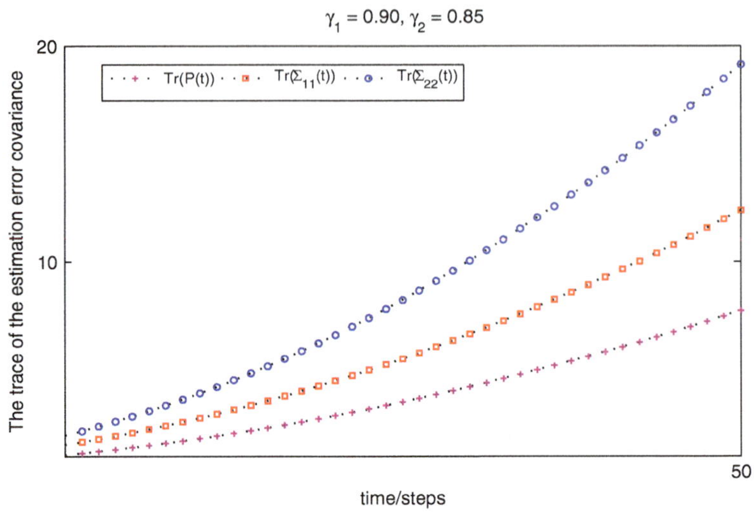

Fig. 9.3 The relationship between the local estimation performance and the fusion estimation performance

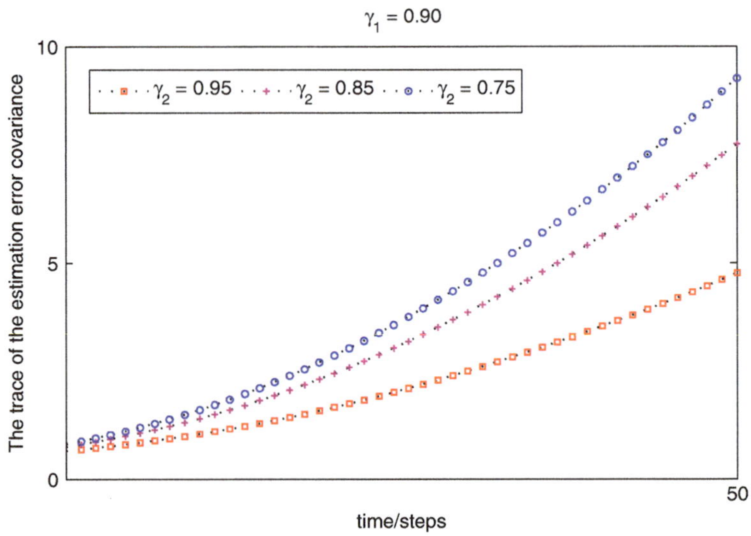

Fig. 9.4 The relationship between measurements loss rate and the performance of the fusion estimator ($\gamma_1 = 0.9$)

Then, the steady-state estimate $\hat{x}_s(t)$ is calculated by substituting (9.64) into (9.60). The trajectories of $x(t)$ and $\hat{x}_s(t)$ are depicted in Fig. 9.6a, b, which shows that the steady-state estimator also performs well. Moreover, the trajectories of $\mathrm{Tr}(P(t))$, $\mathrm{Tr}\{\Sigma_{11}(t)\}$, and $\mathrm{Tr}\{\Sigma_{22}(t)\}$ are plotted in Fig. 9.7a by applying Algorithm 9.1, and

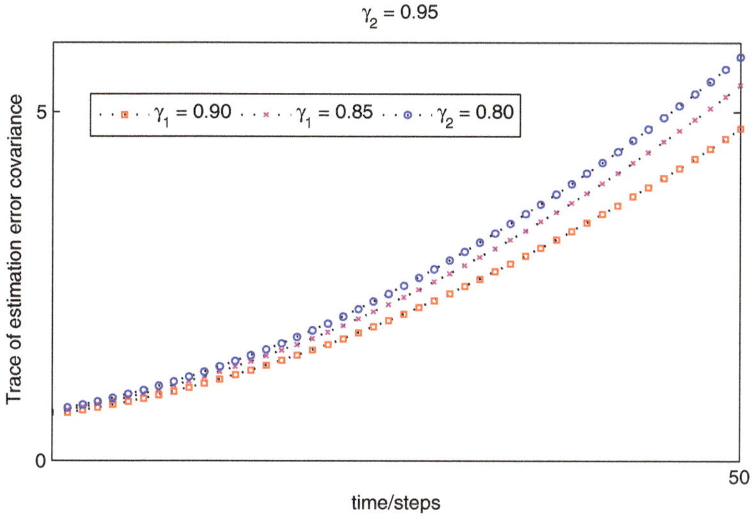

Fig. 9.5 The relationship between measurements loss rate and the performance of the fusion estimator ($\gamma_2 = 0.95$)

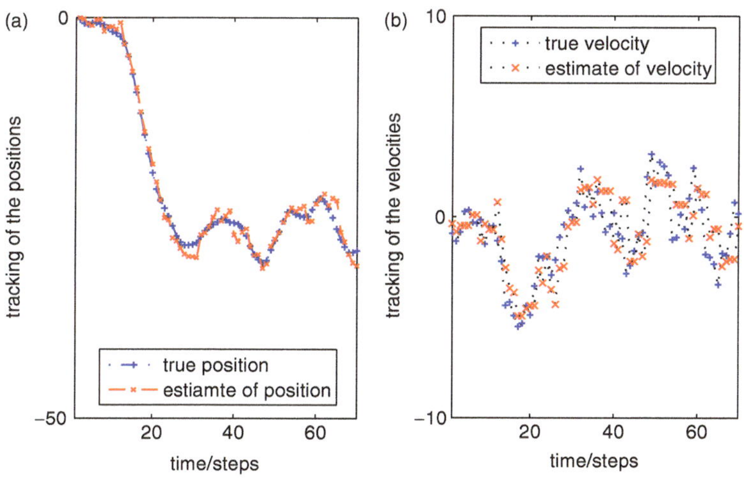

Fig. 9.6 The trajectories of $x(t)$ and steady-state fusion estimate $\hat{x}_s(t)$

then it can be seen from the figure that the MSE of the designed fusion estimator converges to a steady-state value very fast. To compare the estimation performance between the finite-horizon estimator and the steady-state estimator, the trajectories of $e^r(t) \triangleq \hat{x}(t) - \hat{x}_s(t)$ are depicted in Fig. 9.7b, which shows that the steady-state estimator provides a estimation precision that is very close to the finite-horizon estimator.

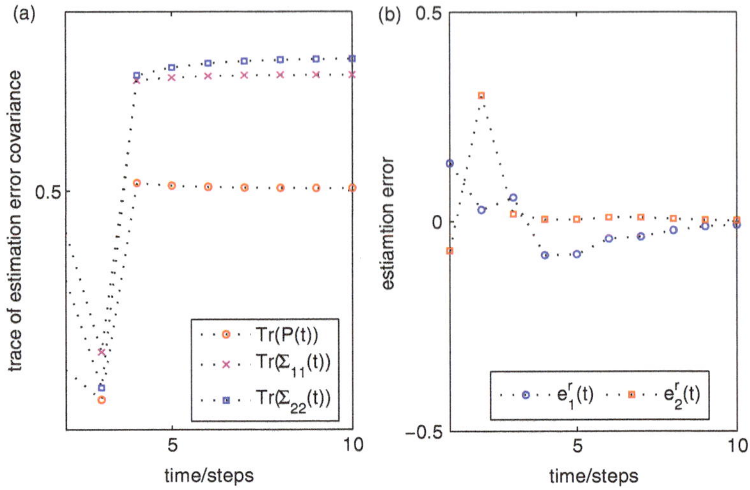

Fig. 9.7 (**a**): The relationship between the local estimation performance and the fusion estimation performance; (**b**): The errors between the finite-horizon fusion estimates $\hat{x}(t)$ and the steady-date fusion estimates $\hat{x}_s(t)$

9.6 Conclusions

In this chapter, the distributed fusion estimation problem has been investigated for a class of networked multisensor fusion systems with time delays and packet losses. By using the optimal fusion algorithm weighted by matrices, an optimal recursive state fusion estimator has been designed in the linear minimum variance sense. Moreover, some sufficient conditions were given such that the MSE of the designed fusion estimator is bounded or convergent.

References

1. Chiuso A, Schenato L (2011) Information fusion strategies and performance bounds in packet-drop networks. Automatica 47:1304–1316
2. Ma J, Sun S (2011) Information fusion estimators for systems with multiple sensors of different packet dropout rates. Inf Fusion 12(3):213–222
3. Hounkpevi FO, Yaz EE (2007) Robust minimum variance linear state estimators for multiple sensors with different failure rates. Automatica 43(7):1274–1280
4. Schenato L (2007) Optimal sensor fusion for distributed sensors subject to random delay and packet loss. In: Proceedings of the 46th IEEE conference on decision and control, New Orleans, pp 1547–1552
5. Penarrocha I, Sanchis R, Albertos P (2012) Estimation in multisensor networked systems with scarce measurements and time varying delays. Syst Control Lett 61:555–562
6. Xia Y, Shang J, Chen J, Liu GP (2009) Networked data fusion with packet losses and variable delays. IEEE Trans Syst Man Cybern B Cybern 39(5):1107–1120

7. Chen B, Yu L, Zhang WA, Liu AD (2013) Robust information fusion estimator for multiple delay-tolerant sensors with different failure rates. IEEE Trans Circuits Syst-I Regul Pap 60(2):401–414
8. Wang ZD, Ho DWC, Liu XH (2003) Variance-constrained filtering for uncertain stochastic systems with missing measurements. IEEE Trans Autom Control 48(7):1254–1258
9. Gao H, Meng X, Chen T (2008) Stabilization of networked control systems with a new delay characterization. IEEE Trans Autom Control 53(9):2142–2148
10. Sun SL, Deng ZL (2004) Multi-sensor optimal information fusion Kalman filter. Automatica 40(6):1017–1023
11. Jazwioski AH (1970) Stochastic processes and filtering theory. Academic, New York
12. Bar-Shalom Y, Li XR, Kirubarajan T (2001) Estimation with applications to tracking and navigation. Wiley, New York

Index

W.-A. Zhang et al., *Distributed Fusion Estimation for Sensor Networks with Communication Constraints*, DOI 10.1007/978-981-10-0795-8

FSC
www.fsc.org
MIX
Papier | Fördert gute Waldnutzung
FSC® C083411

Kolibri 360 GmbH
Ferdinand-Jühlke-Straße 7
99095 Erfurt, Deutschland
produktsicherheit@kolibri360.de